DEADLY BEAT DEADLY BEAT **DEADLY BEAT**

DEADLY BEAT

INSIDE THE ROYAL ULSTER CONSTABULARY

Richard Latham

MAINSTREAM
PUBLISHING

EDINBURGH AND LONDON

First published in Great Britain in 2001 by
MAINSTREAM PUBLISHING COMPANY (EDINBURGH) LTD
7 Albany Street
Edinburgh EH1 3UG

This edition 2001

ISBN 1 84018 512 0

A catalogue record for this book is available from the British Library

Typeset in Excelsior and Stone Print
Printed and bound in Great Britain by Cox & Wyman Ltd

CONTENTS

All names and home areas of the persons involved
with the RUC described in this account have
been amended to avoid identification.

PROLOGUE

It was a time of ceasefire, yet in 1995, as now, there were far too many guns in circulation in the city. The terrorists still had their weapons, although they were now being used in the escalating Belfast drugs war. At least for the time being they were not being turned on policemen. It made a pleasant change from my experience of the previous four years in the Royal Ulster Constabulary. The RUC was a force that throughout the terrorist campaign tried to be like any other UK police force. In reality it was a paramilitary organisation, and had to be, faced as it was with relentless threat from the most efficient terrorist killing machine in the world.

In 1995, to see the terrorists-turned-drug-dealers shooting each other was not a cause for much sadness. That year saw seven individuals shot dead in their jockeying for dominance in the exploding Northern Irish drugs scene. In 1996 the trend continued. Most were murdered by fellow republicans under the IRA cover organisation DAAD [Direct Action Against Drugs]. The DAAD name would prove to be a handy way for the IRA to continue removing individuals throughout all the ceasefires, and on into current times. Call yourself something else when you murder, and apparently the cessation of violence is still intact! At the time it appeared to be nothing more than a temporary badge of convenience.

At last, though, there was a sense of justice in the air. It was an interesting development to stop republican suspects and find them wearing body armour, running shit scared of their own. Killers now hunted by their fellow gangsters.

At that time one former member of INLA gave himself up to me in the city centre. He walked up to me and announced that he was wanted on a warrant for theft. He was a big lad. Many republican terrorists I had met were

9

physically unimpressive, but he was fit and muscular-looking. I had only met a handful of people in my life who combined a sense of evil with a lethal physical presence. The ones I had met had been special forces. This guy gave off that vibe.

As I searched the man before placing him in the police car, I realised that he must belong to a paramilitary organisation. Normal people do not wear body armour in the middle of the afternoon while doing their shopping. He admitted in a roundabout way that he was next on DAAD's hit list. When he identified himself, I recognised the name as someone responsible for the close-quarter shootings of at least two police officers. To walk up to a man in broad daylight and hold a gun to his head, blowing him away while you look into his face, requires a certain kind of ruthlessness. This individual had never been charged due to insufficient evidence. Now he was giving himself up to the police to save his own skin. It was ironic that he was looking to the RUC for protection: a man like that, a killer of policemen.

It is a measure of the force that such an individual can be arrested and treated with complete impartiality. We took him into the back of a Land-Rover. It would have been easy to manufacture a struggle which would have resulted in the man getting a beating. In many countries that would have happened as a matter of course, but it would just have put us on the same level. I had become resigned to the fact that no matter how well you treated suspects in Northern Ireland, allegations of abuse and mistreatment still came. One thing was for sure this time, though – I have never seen a man so delighted to come into police custody. His mood was almost elated as he was tucked away in a cell to await the day's court proceedings.

As well as the criminals on the loyalist and republican sides carrying guns, all police were still armed, both on and off duty. At that time the best place to tell who the off-duty policemen were was in the supermarket, because as they leaned forward to pull something from the shelves, the gun would always show itself against the clothing, tucked in to the back of the waistband.

Even during the height of the troubles, some policemen failed to carry a weapon at all times. A few had paid for that with their lives. Whenever I went out and was tempted to leave my revolver at home, I would visualise that moment of helpless terror when a killer walked across to where I sat in a pub, gun in hand, and I would be left scrabbling at my waistband for a weapon that was not there. It had happened to other off-duty policemen and was an image that kept me right. I still carried my personal protection weapon at all times, simply because, despite the so-called ceasefire, I did not want to be the first to regret running into a terrorist on the day the IRA decided to break it.

In addition to police, you had certain military lads carrying weapons off duty. Prison officers also still had personal protection weapons, even some territorial army members. Building contractors and businessmen who had done work for the security forces had been permitted to carry personal protection weapons. There were far too many guns around. Unfortunately, most of them were still very necessary to protect their owners. On any day in Belfast there were dozens of weapons floating about, and not all of them in the hands of the good guys!

———————

I was working out of Musgrave Street RUC station in the main response car. Although I had worked as a plain-clothes detective in England for several years, in the RUC the uniformed work was always the most interesting. I had been called to a robbery scene in the city centre with Steve, my partner for the day. Steve was a typical young Northern Irish peeler who had seen a huge chunk of life in his twenty-eight years. In eight years' service he had seen many murders and been involved directly in several shooting incidents. During service with the mobile support units in Belfast, he had learnt the level of hatred instilled in the republican communities towards the RUC.

Steve had no tolerance for aggression towards the police. He was handy to have around when it came to public disorder. Once I had come around the corner after an assistance call to find him and one other RUC man beating back a mob of a dozen or more with their batons. They had tried to give them a severe kicking after they had gone to a call at a particularly nasty city-centre pub. A common tactic was for yobs to try and lure police into pubs with the intention of giving them a beating. On this occasion, the afternoon crowd of drunken hooligans was sent scuttling back to their rat holes.

This tactic of luring police to pubs had been successfully countered for a while by sending the SSU [Special Support Unit] to calls suspected to be set-ups. The SSU were the SAS-trained police firearms team who backed up

Special Branch operations. They were an extremely fit and aggressive unit. Taking a break from their normal firearms duties, they would arrive at a pub ambush in place of the local unit, and would then give a nasty surprise to their would-be attackers. They carried defunct MP5 weapons with the working parts removed, which the assailants would try to steal in the fighting. None was ever stolen, but a few did come into intimate contact with the odd scumbag's head.

I was doing the tick-box thing on the crime sheets. A couple of men had walked into a shop and stuck a machine pistol up the manager's nose. He was quite blasé about the whole thing. It was his third robbery. He could have run a course in robbery stress management. They had only made off with a couple of hundred quid, but the bizarre gist of the description I was writing down was that the men involved were half pissed. They hadn't worn masks. It was beginning to sound like a 'loyalist job'. That had become a cliché to describe many loyalist paramilitary operations, but there was a certain truth in it. Time after time they would mess up, and if they did carry out a killing, it was generally the case that suspects were arrested before too long.

Steve was looking at a stereo. It was a sleek black monster of a thing with loads of silver buttons. He was about as good on the technical stuff as I was.

'What's this bit here?'

I glanced over. 'Graphic equaliser.'

He nodded knowingly. 'So it's got another graphic equaliser apart from this other bit that says "graphic equaliser"?'

I ignored him and carried on with my crime sheet.

'Would you do any police discount?' he casually asked the shop owner. The manager shook his head. He was well used to the question from passing town beat officers who saw every shift as a bargain-hunting foray. That was characteristic of police the world over. They loved a bargain.

'Stevie, I'll just put this new description out, okay? You just stay there and play with your new toy. Don't you worry about me!'

He nodded acknowledgement as he continued to prod at the buttons of the stereo.

'They'll be long gone,' he muttered, as he fiddled with what might have been the graphic equaliser. I tended to agree.

I updated the descriptions over the air: two men, early forties, ruddy complexions, smelling of drink, both thick set. One with a long black coat, carrying a machine pistol. The description could have fitted many men wandering around Belfast in more ways than one. The city was full of afternoon drinkers in badly fitting dark clothes.

The robbery was fifteen minutes old. You make the logical assumption that the offenders will have legged it pretty far in that time span; I would think at least a mile on foot or several miles by taxi or car. Belfast is a small city and you can cross it, or be well out of it, in minutes, if the traffic flow goes with you. Deep down, however, you also know from experience that you should never make assumptions based on logic. At least fifty per cent of criminals are dickheads, and this lot were to prove to be up there in the premier league of stupidity.

As we walked out of the shop, having taken all the details for the crime report, the city-centre crime team came over on the net. There was an urgency to the message that made our ears tune in immediately. The words 'weapon' and 'armed robbery suspects' probably helped.

The crime team worked in plain clothes to target street robberies and large-scale shoplifters in the city. They had started a 'follow' on three men, two of whom matched the description of the armed robbers. One officer thought he had glimpsed a barrel under a long dark coat. Strangely enough they were walking back to the shop, just around the corner from where Steve and I were about to clamber into the unmarked armoured police car. They were literally walking towards us. I felt a tightening of the stomach, excitement tinged with a little apprehension. Arrests for robbery did not normally come that easy.

'What do you reckon?' Steve said.

'Well, if it is them, they should be about to walk right past us.'

'What way do you want to deal with this?'

'Carefully,' he said, all thoughts of the shiny buttons on the graphic equaliser now gone from his head. Like me, he was scanning every pedestrian passing the junction.

'We'll check it out from the corner.' I nodded over to the near side of the street we were in. If they came into view now, they could bolt and be immediately out of view and away down one of the many alleyways that led off the main street. From the corner we would have a clear view if they ran.

I was annoyed that I had not taken out the MP5 carbine today, but it could be a hindrance in the city. I pushed down on the thumb break on my

13

revolver holster, making sure the button had popped. We both moved forward, listening to the commentary from the plain-clothes unit.

Steve showed absolutely no tension. I was never too sure if this was because he just had a mega-cool personality or if there was a bit missing from his head in that department. Whatever the case, he was a good, calming influence.

I too was now well used to situations involving the possible use of firearms. What would have seemed unusual years ago in England, when I was on the beat, was by now commonplace. Like most things, once you've been put in the situation a few times the initial instinct to flap goes, and you learn to focus on what needs done.

I was visualising drawing my revolver and pulling the trigger on a human target instead of a paper one. The thought of killing someone had never been a dilemma in my mind. Making the wrong decision and being crucified in the courts was. It was a moment that could change your life. Get it right, and you save your own life or your colleague's. The guy would be dead and, in the circumstances, justifiably. A wrong call and you were screwed. Rightly, too. It was all down to a split second. That was a big burden to carry, and if you thought about it too much you'd just chuck in your police uniform and go and be a salesman.

We let the communications man know where we were in relation to the team following the suspects. I moved my radio onto their back-to-back channel. I could now talk to them direct, although it was impossible to break into the commentary of the follow. Adrenaline was racing. Again, the barrel of what was believed to be the weapon had been glimpsed. Nothing was confirmed as yet. I was aware of my own mouth going dry as an inevitable confrontation unravelled.

The basic criteria of any spontaneous firearms incident are to identify, locate, contain and then neutralise armed suspects. That is a very nice little sequence in the firearms textbooks, but in reality, several of those elements can occur at once. Every incident is unique, so within the basic framework of textbook response, a little flexibility is often needed. This situation, with a moving containment on the suspects, in a street full of shoppers, was in dire need of imaginative thinking. There were a great many people's safety at stake. Mostly happy little shoppers, with not a clue what was going on around them.

14

We warily rounded the corner and took up a static position next to the hard cover of the corner wall to try and locate the suspects coming up the street. It was an extremely busy shopping day, not ideal for picking out individuals. Steve and I kept talking to each other, mouths moving but eyes on the throngs of people. Anyone looking at us would have put as down as two peelers talking about last night's game. I suddenly spotted one of the plain-clothes team thirty yards back on the other side of the road, then in the next split second I saw the three men they were following.

'Stevie. Our side of the street. Twenty yards. Middle of the pavement.'

'Got them.'

The men were much closer than we had anticipated. They had started to slow on seeing us, but were still only a few yards away. Their body language, as much as anything, made them stand out from the other shoppers brushing past, oblivious of the potential danger. Their flushed faces were apprehensive at the sight of uniformed police.

There was a sense of events moving down a gear. In the seconds that followed, a mass of thoughts bombarded my decision-making process. If I pulled my revolver I would be aiming at a target which had members of the public in front and behind. Bustling middle-aged ladies with kids in tow were pushing past the suspects, directly into my line of fire. If I had reason to shoot, I could well end up regretting it for the rest of my life. I didn't take the job to find myself in a dock explaining why I had shot a little old lady armed with a Spar bag.

I could not in that split second ID the man with the weapon. There were three targets. They were, by the sound of it, drunk, and therefore unpredictable. If I was fired at there were many shoppers behind me too, who would take rounds from the armed robber. I realised now that we were facing the same problem as the plain-clothes team: how and when to challenge in that environment. Unfortunately, at that stage you can't walk away. In every situation you reach a point of no return. We were there.

Steve later told me that the same thoughts, and the conclusion I reached in those brief seconds, also came to him. The suspects were not aware of being followed. As far as they were concerned, Steve and I were just on foot patrol. As we came closer we bluffed this, and they continued to walk in an attempt to bluff us. My right hand rested casually on the grip of my revolver as I walked, ready to push down and draw if absolutely necessary.

Five yards away I saw the weapon inside one of the men's jackets. It was slung over his shoulder with the barrel facing down. He was trying to conceal it by covering it with his arm, but his jacket kept flapping open. It was clear at that moment that he was not immediately going to raise the weapon. If he had tried to I would have had him. We were close now. The situation had to be gripped and a call made.

I decided to take a highly calculated risk. Events forced a decision and it became one of those 'you had to have been there' moments. I shouted 'Go!', to myself as much as to Steve or anyone else who was listening, and in that moment jumped forward, taking hold of the suspect's left arm from which the weapon hung.

The sequence of events had taken us so close to the suspects that good old-fashioned hand-to-hand stuff became the best option. Fortunately I was both bigger and stronger than he was. I was glad that I had spent a lot of time in the gym recently. His arm was definitely not moving in the grip I had on him. Steve had one of the other men down on the ground. The third was taken out by the plain-clothes lads.

Within a second of my grabbing the gunman, another of the crime team gripped the suspect's right arm and, with me, had him tight up against a fence. A third officer extracted his weapon. It was a 9mm machine pistol. As we cuffed and arrested the men, now face down on the Belfast pavement chewing at the litter, the lad who had taken possession of the weapon cleared it. The magazine was empty. There was no round in the chamber. Despite the excitement of the moment that registered in my head, and quietly I reflected that it was lucky I had not just shot the guy. That the weapon was unloaded was in itself rare in Ulster. Even stranger was that the arrest had been carried out without anybody even drawing a weapon. Virtually English police style! All those guns around, and not one of them came out the holster. So much for the RUC shoot-to-kill policy!

The suspects were on the fringes of loyalist paramilitary groups. They had 'borrowed' the weapon for the day. It hadn't helped that they had all gone down the pub before the job. That outing had contributed to the shambolic nature of the robbery. In the end, they were lucky not to be shot. Loaded or not, one wrong movement with the machine pistol and they would have been shot dead either by myself or one of my colleagues. It was an odd one, but in the potential for lethal violence, a fairly typical day in Belfast.

We went home and had a few beers. Talked over what we could or should have done. We reflected on how everyone not involved suddenly becomes an expert in firearms incidents after the event. As far as I was concerned, it's simply good when nobody is hurt.

One ex-squaddie who worked as a reserve constable, with the incisive judgement of someone who spends eight hours a day staring out of a box and opening and shutting a barrier, took me to one side and said, almost angrily, 'Why didn't you shoot the bastard? You won't get many chances like that.'

I know that others thought the same. It was amazing how brave and decisive some people could get when they imagined themselves in a situation, in retrospect. Fortunately I had never viewed my time in the RUC as one in which I had to grab at any chance of killing someone. I knew I was capable and willing to do so in the right circumstances; I had no moral problem with it at all. My thoughts were crystal clear. I had made the right choice – the location and circumstances made it the right choice. On another day, with fewer people around, more certainty, a slight movement with the weapon, the gunman would have been dead.

The divisional commander praised our 'good work' in his little monthly magazine. We should have had a commendation for the arrest, but the sergeant doing the file messed up the paperwork. The main thing was that another of those guns was off the street. What tragedy that may have averted in the future, we'll never know.

A LONG WAY FROM HOME

A year or so after leaving the police force, I was boring my mate Douglas about the RUC. We were visiting Buenos Aires in Argentina, me with work, him because I had acquired a cheap extra airline ticket. My wife could not accompany me, as she was five months pregnant. Douglas had kindly offered to come and drink South American beer with me for a week.

As we sat in a bar in the seedy San Telmo district, I kept referring to Northern Ireland as 'home'. 'But you don't fucking live there any more,' Douglas said as he pulled on a Marlboro. 'That place isn't out of your system. Finish the book.' I had been telling him how I had been put in contact with a literary agent, but now, with the book half done, I was going to give up. 'If you don't finish it, you could carry on boring the tits off me for ever.' He was right.

Douglas had served in Northern Ireland as a soldier: he was an ex-Grenadier Guardsman. Although he was now a copper on the mainland, his heart was still with the military. He appreciated how serving in Ulster left a permanent mark. I was thousands of miles from Europe, in one of the most interesting, vibrant cities in the world, yet for an hour I had talked about nothing else but the proposed changes to the RUC in Northern Ireland and the period I had served there as a policeman. Perhaps the best therapy was to put it down on paper. I shut up and sank another beer.

It had been a long, and at times sad, path that brought me to serve as a policeman in Belfast city. It was not the obvious choice for someone with parents from Cheshire, who had been brought up in the home counties. By the time I was twenty-four my marriage to the girl I had been with since a young teenager had broken up – lives going down different paths and all that. Like many, I had lost a lot of money in the housing crash of the late '80s. I was looking for somewhere different to start again.

Ulster had an increasing fascination for me. My interest in Northern Ireland had developed while working with the Special Branch in England. The more I thought about the alternatives, the more moving to the province made sense.

Serving in Ulster with the RUC became my choice. Some people, generally those who had never been to Northern Ireland, thought I was mad. 'Why don't you just go the whole way and join the foreign legion?' someone said.

I rarely came back to the mainland in the time I served in Ulster, but when I did, I found that the stress of being a constant terrorist target, stress which I was unaware of most of the time, bubbled to the surface. I was no different from any other policeman in the province. You go to work and you might be shot dead. You imagine being horribly maimed in a bomb blast. You come home and wonder if you'll be shot at the front door. You go to bed with a revolver on the bedside cabinet. At times, you wonder if this is really part of the UK. We were all a potential kill for the IRA. There are times when you cope with that stress well. Other times, it creeps up on you. That's when you have to take a severe grip on yourself.

Christmas time, 1992. Mum had insisted on shoving money for lagers into my hand. Despite the family's recent problems she still loved to give, so I took the £5 note as an excuse to come up for air. The incessant heat of that fucking house was stifling. It was like a centrally heated tomb, one of those houses that old people buy to decay in. A smog of tobacco smoke and despair hung in the air. The sound of the mantel clock marked the chipping away of two sad lives. The ticking seemed to pick at the fringes of my mind, until my thoughts had become wildly disorientated.

My parents had retired back to Cheshire in 1991, but unfortunately the move had not gone well for them. The place had moved on three decades since they had left in the late 1950s: the people they once knew were dead or had moved away. They were lonely, unwell and unhappy. In the despairing atmosphere my brain was slowly unravelling. I was glad to escape the 'festivities' for a while.

In the off-licence I handed over a £10 note, not realising it was an Ulster Bank note: legal tender, like Scottish notes, but sometimes just not worth the hassle of using in England. The old hag behind the counter looked at me as if I had two heads. 'We don't take Irish money,' she hissed.

'It's legal tender, you see it has the word 'sterling' on it. It's not like punts from the south of Ireland.' I jabbed angrily at the word 'sterling'.

I felt myself choking with an irrational anger that threatened to explode savagely, out of all proportion to the event. The kind of anger that brings up a mist and makes you start visualising violence in anticipation of it happening. A good sign that you're losing the plot.

The stupid witch cut me short. She wanted to be a friggin' dead woman. 'We don't take Irish money,' she repeated. A dumb, defiant expression spread across her flabby face. I just looked at her. My hands turned to claws and there was a beating in my head which started to cloud my sight. I wanted to rip her stupid fat face off. Pull out my Ruger revolver and push it up her hairy nostril before blowing her matted wig away. I do not consider myself an unnecessarily violent person, but if I'd had my gun I would've liked to have shot her. Luckily it was sitting in an armoury in a police station in Belfast.

I had become hyper-defensive of anything Northern Irish. I'd recently watched a young man die in a part of the United Kingdom – a part of the United Kingdom that any fool should know is known as Ulster, and yet this creature would not take money which had that word on it. Like it was carrying a disease.

It was an attitude I had resigned myself to when I was back in England. I would tell people I lived in Ireland and they'd say, 'Oh, how nice.' Clarify that I lived in Northern Ireland, and the top lip would curl. 'Don't you find that rather depressing?' was the next likely comment. I was sick of the general ignorance about the beautiful country I knew, a country ruined only by a minority of lethal extremists.

I had to turn wordlessly in order to prevent my anger from letting loose the violence I felt. Get control. Get things into perspective. I started to breathe evenly again. The only good thing about the incident was that it made me seriously worried about myself. If I had not been aware that my feelings were becoming irrational, then it would have been harder to control them.

I bought my lager elsewhere. Sat long into the night after my parents had shuffled off to their separate bedrooms. Smoked. (I smoked a lot then.) Drank six cans, but felt the same as before I began drinking. Why did I care about Northern Ireland so much when nobody on the mainland gave a damn, wouldn't even touch the 'dirty' money? Why did I feel so angry all the time?

I didn't crawl downstairs until 11 a.m. My mum was crying in the kitchen, a glass of screw-top Soave wine in her shaking hands. It was that time of the morning. Her drinking had been serious since my early twenties. I had been through all the crap you go through with an alcoholic parent, but by now I had reached the stage of ignoring it. Despite that, she still went through the little rituals: the glass 'hidden' in the top right of the kitchen cupboard, already wet from a couple of sips after breakfast; the bogus little tasks she set me, to have me out the house for half an hour so that she could slurp away. I played along now because the situation was insoluble – a bit of a parallel with Ulster at the time!

Dad told me I had changed: I had left two empty cans of lager on the coffee table, and Mum had had to clear them away. I had become 'selfish'. I thought of Alan's family. The empty space at the table. Murdering their son had been selfish of the IRA, all right. I felt disgusted with England in general, and twisted with hatred at the petty crap that people thought was important.

I left for the airport a day early, pretending I had been called back to work for operational reasons. As I flew into Belfast I was still thinking about Alan. A man I never really knew, except by sight. A man I had watched die. Our only bond, it seemed, being members of the RUC. I was beginning to realise how strong an attachment that was.

———

The year 1992 was not a great one. I had been in Northern Ireland for nearly two years, yet I was still the new boy. An English policeman in Ulster. You don't earn trust overnight in the province – like one's understanding of the place, it comes little by little. To many of my colleagues I was still the unknown quantity in the peeling, filthy briefing room. The foreigner in their world. I had learnt not to expect too much too quickly. After a few drinks, you may get slapped on the back and told 'You're all right for an Englishman,' a few may even call you an 'honorary Ulsterman', but deep down you know you're not quite one of the tribe.

I had already signed out my weapon: an H&K MP5. It sat between my feet, facing the rear wall like a faithful metal pet. I held the magazine containing the 9mm rounds in my left hand and my pen in the other. It would have been a bizarre-looking scene in any other police station in the UK, but this was the world of weapons and body armour. In the RUC, guns were just there. No big deal. Once out of the depot training, weapon handling was so laid back it was virtually in a coma. Magazines were loaded walking across the briefing rooms, MP5s cleared pointing into lockers or musty corners of the room. The loading and unloading bays outside each station grew weeds amongst the sandbags. They were used only by the military.

Even when we returned weapons and loaded magazines, the rounds were not accounted for. You simply signed in your own weapon and stuck the full magazine back on the rack. If you were wise, you counted the rounds out every time you received the firearm. Most did not. I sometimes felt it was an achievement to reach the end of a shift without being shot by one of my own workmates.

My bedraggled notebook, twisted from drying out after vehicle checkpoints in the incessant Fermanagh rain, sat on my lap. I prepared myself for the usual briefing ritual. Lists of suspects, 'out of bounds' areas known as OOBs, and vehicle checkpoints to be completed over the shift.

The briefings were usually formal, tedious affairs, conducted like briefings in the force had been for the past umpteen decades. A far cry from the briefings I would experience when I returned to the English police force years later. Those virtually started with a group hug and meditation period. This briefing, unfortunately, did not run the usual uneventful course, with lists of people trying to kill us and areas in which we were likely to be shot or blown up if we strayed into them.

Enniskillen RUC Station stands on an island on the narrow waterway between Upper and Lower Lough Erne. It is an imposing building, in the style of a large military barracks. It had previously been the RUC training depot, until the mortar attack in 1985 and other terrorist acts aimed at new recruits led to the moving of the training depot to a 'safe' area of Belfast.

It was a miracle that no officers were killed during the mortar attack. Mark 10 mortars had literally rained down on the main building, but fortunately, recruits who were housed in the part of the building which took the brunt of the attack were not in their rooms at the time. There were some nasty injuries, but on this occasion the terrorists' timing was a few minutes off.

Now the station was the base for the local police and a couple of mobile support units. Many of the areas of the complex were in terminal decay. Whereas in England budgets were spent on pot plants and pastel colours for station walls, in Northern Ireland weapons, body armour and hours and hours of overtime drained the divisional commander's cash resources.

As usual, the banter from the boys on my section flew around the room with pinpoint accuracy. Sharp Ulster wit in a Belfast twang, or with that sing-song Fermanagh lilt. I felt subdued. I don't know why I knew that tragedy was in the air, I just did. I often sense things; I think I get it from my grandmother. In 1941 she had dreamed of her son Jack, who was in the Royal Navy, floundering in water. The same night he was killed at Tobruk. In the morning, she had come down and sadly told my mother: 'Jack's drowned.' A month later she received the telegram. A few weeks after that, a parcel she had sent for Jack's twenty-first birthday was returned, unopened.

Uncle Jack's photograph in his Royal Navy uniform fascinated me as a child. Taken not long before he was killed, the fresh-faced twenty-year-old, in one of those classic picture-postcard poses, stared out at me from my grandmother's dressing table. She had lost a son, but I was certainly aware, even at the age of four or five, that I had a missing uncle. To me, he was a hero, someone who had died fighting the Nazis. I used to chat to the photograph as if Uncle Jack was in the room with me. Maybe he was. All I knew was that he would have been a great uncle.

Jack's brother, Frank, also in the Royal Navy, was a huge, quiet man who survived the war despite doing the dangerous convoy runs to Northern Russia. He too was a hero in my young eyes, although he would have been the last to consider himself such.

Frank and Jack's father, my grandfather, had been at the Battle of the Somme in 1916. He was injured and sent home to recover. That saved his life and was, I worked out quite early in life, the reason I existed. A lucky shell explosion had severely injured him, sent him home to Blighty and greatly improved his chances of survival. He survived the war. I still carry around the small cross he wore during the battle. My grandmother gave it to me to keep me safe. After the war he went into the building trade and many years later, in the 1950s, fell off a scaffold, broke his leg, and shortly after died due to a blood clot which formed as a result of the accident. Strange old business – imagine surviving some of the worst carnage in military history only to die of a broken leg a few decades later!

Like my grandmother, I believed in fate. That when your number's up, it is well and truly up. Like her, I have premonitions. At that moment, I knew something bad was about to happen.

I sat in my own world while the bubbling joviality washed over me and felt like I had a bag of coal on my shoulders. Someone said, 'Cheer up Rick, it might never happen.' I just curled my lip up in a half response. Policemen don't really share emotions. Especially ones as vague as mine at that moment. To me, the weight of apprehension was excruciating. It was five minutes before the twelve o' clock briefing was due to start.

Words were tumbling over in my introverted thoughts: 'Every waking moment, all they have to sit and think about is how to murder you. To use their own words, they only have to be lucky once. You have to be lucky all the time.' I remembered the words being spoken during a lecture from a Special Branch officer. He had come to the training centre at Garnerville, Belfast, to heighten our own personal security awareness.

We were given booklets advising us on our personal security measures. Keep changing your routes and times of departure. Make reservations in a false name. Never hang police shirts on the washing line. The list was endless. All common sense, yet to lapse in only one aspect could cost you or your family their lives.

Most of the lads in training didn't need that kind of reminder. Many had brushed pretty close to death already, having served with the RUC Reserve or the military. At that time, the death toll of policemen killed as a result of terrorism in Northern Ireland since 1969 was nearing 300 – in an area about the size of Sussex. My colleagues that day in the lecture hall had no illusions about the danger. For the size of the area and population, Northern Ireland was the most dangerous place in the world to be a policeman.

The words of that SB man were there in my head as Sergeant A loomed out of the blackness of the yard into the bright, animated briefing-room. The silence was immediate. Sergeant A was a huge man. A big, solid, straight-backed individual in his early forties. It was rumoured that, in Armagh, a man had once tried to steal his firearm. After arresting him, instead of calling for backup, the sergeant had kicked him all the way back to the police station gates. He had been suspended for a long time for that, and now kept himself right by imposing strict discipline on himself and those around him.

He looked like he would be incapable of feeling pain, yet as he stood in the doorway his face was as ashen as if his insides were being twisted in knots.

'There's been a shooting in Belcoo. One of the station party's been hit.' The sergeant said the words calmly, but with great sadness. It was the kind of news he had previously carried many times to briefing-rooms in his twenty years' service with the RUC. I had already met men who had seen a dozen close friends murdered over the course of a career. Many had lost brothers and fathers to the violence.

Bringing news of a death is always a heavy burden to carry. In Northern Ireland, it is usually yet another tragedy adding to the layers of previous unexpected loss. In the early '70s, murders of police and army occurred on a massive scale. Police training had turned out huge squads of men who in many respects, according to several men I know who served over that period, were regarded as cannon fodder. Now, with the equipment and training thoroughly modernised, and with terrorist tactics changed to take account of this, killings were less frequent. But that did not make it any easier to deal with when it was on your own doorstep.

Constable B, a local man with a quiet, thoughtful manner, was the first to speak and break the horrified silence.

'Do we know who it is, Sarge?' he asked.

'No,' he replied. 'It's only just come into comms. We should have an update by the end of the briefing.'

There were a few moments of quiet as the sergeant carried on a conversation with the section inspector in the corner of the shabby room. The inspector was a small man from the south of Ireland who walked with a limp, due to injuries received during the 1985 mortar attack on the depot. He was one of several men from the south who had chosen to join the RUC. For all of them to return home and be recognised would have been a death sentence. Like the Roman Catholics in the force, their chosen occupation excluded them from returning home except in complete secrecy.

A great friend of mine who originated from Londonderry had not been home for ten years. While I served with him, the IRA broke into his parents' home, where they had lived for fifty years in a nationalist area. They were looking for the addresses of the two sons who were in the RUC. They did not find what they wanted, and so burnt his parents out of their home. They were both in their seventies.

The inspector's and the sergeant's voices were barely audible, just a murmur above the tangible thoughts of the men, who visualised colleagues out at the border station of Belcoo and feared the worst. It was a collective blow. It's odd, but sometimes the only word that comes into your head at times like that is simply 'fuck', said under the breath with a biting of the lip. Shortly followed by 'fucking bastards', said with more venom, but still in a hoarse whisper from the back of the throat. Language is so inadequate. Maybe those words do hit the spot. In any case, they were the words I heard most in the next few minutes.

I saw the inspector glance over at me and nod. I thought of my own friend out in Belcoo, and of his wife and kids. It was a black moment of uncertainty. That terrible feeling of not knowing. At times like that, you actually start going over in your head what you will say to the man's widow. It is morbid, but perhaps it's the mind's way of preparing you for the worst.

The skipper walked over to me. He took me to one side. We had got on well since my arrival in Enniskillen. He seemed to have a respect for me and my way of doing things as an ex-English policeman. The respect was mutual.

Sergeant A was disliked by some because he was tight on the lads, a strict taskmaster. Hot on discipline and, worse still to an RUC man, hot on paperwork. I had been stunned when I first arrived in Enniskillen at how little paperwork there was compared to the police in England. The truth was that there was very little crime in County Fermanagh: the fight against terrorism was the staple diet of your policing day.

In contrast to the closed, hate-filled villages of South Armagh, Fermanagh had a veneer of normality. The place did not have the same permanent feel of impending attack. Security was less pervasive, which in turn made patrols more vulnerable to attack when the terrorists struck. The files we had, and they were mainly road traffic accident [RTA] reports, were meticulously scrutinised by Sergeant A. Nothing without the 'i's dotted and the 't's crossed sneaked past him. A pain in the hole at times, but it kept the boys right. Discipline in the small things bred good habits for when it did matter.

'Richard, you get up the hospital and meet the ambulance. Let me know when it arrives and I'll meet you up there.'

'Yes Sarge.' I signed my MP5 back into the armoury and had a quiet word with a couple of mates on the section. There was a shocked and bitter atmosphere in the parade-room. I knew that it was going to be one shit night.

Belcoo RUC station stood on the border with County Cavan, a concrete fortress with a station party made up of half a dozen policemen, supported by periodically changing army regiments who stayed in the station permanently.

Two sections of policemen worked the station in turn. In for several days, on duty twenty-four hours. A changeover would then occur, usually by helicopter, a Puma or Wessex bringing the human cargo. One station party would then take over the station from the other. This unusual method of working was brought about by the risk of terrorist attack in the local area.

The station was what was known in RUC terms as a 'concession' station. The 'concession' was the authorities allowing this method of working to prevent a massacre every time policemen went to work. It was a long way from the method of policing in Worthing, where I had started my police career seven years earlier, yet this was still part of the United Kingdom. At the age of twenty-one I had sauntered up and down a beat on Worthing seafront with an ice cream in my hand and not a care in the world. Now, every day I went to work I was not sure if I would live through the shift.

That was the big difference between working in Ulster and on the mainland. On the mainland, police officers were killed on duty when fate brought them into contact with a life-threatening situation and events went horribly wrong. In Ulster, every working day, there were people out there who were trying to kill you simply because you were a police officer. At play. At home. There was a permanent sense of being hunted, tracked by a merciless organisation that seemed unable to respond to reason or normal argument.

I signed out a radio as the subdued briefing commenced and drove up to the hospital in the soft-skin supervision car. We patrolled as a matter of course in armoured cars. Big, cumbersome Ford Sierras which, although equipped with that life-saving shell, had the disadvantage of being clearly a police vehicle as soon as they came into view. There were a few soft-skin cars for more discreet enquiries, or for use right out on the border where they were not so easily picked out by an IRA Active Service Unit [ASU].

It was a cold, black night. I positioned myself in the foyer of the Erne Hospital. My role was only to report back to the communications-room when the ambulance arrived and to be on hand for any other task that might arise. Staff waited at the door for the arrival with arms folded, as if steadying themselves for the work ahead. Tensely checking the access road for the ambulance. No words were said.

An aura of intense sadness pervaded the Accident and Emergency ward entrance. I wondered how many of the staff had taken in victims from the Enniskillen Remembrance Sunday bombing in 1987. The bomb had killed eleven people and injured sixty-three. In a town the size of Enniskillen, the atrocity touched a large proportion of the population. No one has ever been brought to court for the killings. That fact must be particularly galling.

The Belcoo station party of RUC men had been carrying out a routine vehicle check within the village area. It was routine, but also highly dangerous, because of the proximity to the border. A straight road passed the RUC station and within a couple of hundred yards crossed a small bridge which marked the border with the South. The border was the frustrating line that the terrorist could operate behind. It was a line the RUC men could not cross. As if in some bad US movie from the '60s, once the 'baddies' made it across that state line nothing could be done. But this was not a bad movie. It was all too real, and the impunity with which terrorists were able to operate from within the Republic of Ireland was a fucking disgrace.

Constable Alan Corbett had taken on the role of stopper that day. As a likely vehicle approached, it would be his task to step out from cover into the road, and, with a circling motion of the red-lensed torch, bring the car to a halt. In close proximity were a police colleague and military personnel. All well under cover. Eyes straining in the dark for tell-tale signs of danger. The glint of car lights off metal, the unnatural movement of undergrowth, a strange vehicle in the area which would suddenly make the hairs on your neck stand up.

Alan had the most dangerous task that day. It was a role that all operational RUC men perform daily as a matter of course. He would have been wearing his dark-green police uniform. Border issue dartex jacket over a NATO jumper. A thick leather belt for the holster containing the Ruger revolver personal protection weapon, pouches for ammunition and field dressings. Border men wore loose-fitting combat-style trousers which were gathered in above the boot by bungie cords. The RUC cap was worn during VCPs, but could be taken off during long-range cross-country patrols. Covering the torso was an immense body-armour shell. Far heavier than military body armour, it was a couple of stones in weight.

A colleague of mine once described to me what it was like being hit with a round while wearing body armour. It had happened to him a couple of years earlier, also in the Main Street in Belcoo. As he and his sergeant had come into view of the border bridge, they had quickened their pace to reach the cover of an alleyway. His sergeant had been struck in the arm by a sniper's round and, as he was flung around like a rag doll, my friend had been launched backwards into space as if 'knocked back by a cannon ball'. The round had cut through the flesh on the sergeant's arm, deflected off the bone and back out towards my colleague's chest. It still had the power to knock the man off his feet. Despite the thickness of the plate in the armour, the contact left a massive bruise and had him off work for a month.

Such escapes were rare, and over the next months increasingly so for policemen targeted by snipers on the border. Tragically for Alan, for the IRA killer who was lurking in the undergrowth on the south side of the Belcoo bridge the night was to go exactly as planned. On this occasion the body armour was to become irrelevant. The IRA were to achieve their piece of 'luck'.

The terrorist, later believed to be a local man, would have dug himself into the undergrowth several hours earlier. The man had allegedly been stopped in previous weeks on his motorcycle, wearing an unusually large number of layers of clothing under his bike leathers to keep him warm while lying in the open. Whether this was on practice runs or live operations where the opportunity of a kill had not presented itself could not be ascertained, but the local men were aware of the threat. However, knowing about it did not change the job. There was always a level of threat, and the men in the border stations were not ones to sit in and hide. A delicate balance had to be struck between facing the threat and assessing the risk on a day-to-day basis, or accepting a no-go environment created by killers.

The killer had trained for the moment in the isolated forest area across the border, where it was safe to practise his sniper skills in the under-policed 'freedom' of the Irish Republic. He had collected the sniper rifle from a hide in the south. Now he lay waiting for his opportunity.

In the chilly Fermanagh evening, Alan stepped out from an alleyway into the main road through Belcoo village. He would then have given a friendly casual greeting to the motorist he had stopped. It was the Fermanagh way. I had seen policemen there chat to IRA suspects at road stops as if they were old friends, then walk away with a page full of information ranging from the mileage on the clock to the sweet wrappers on the front seat. Fermanagh men could seem slow in manner, but were never stupid.

I knew Alan by sight only, to nod to as he passed with the Belcoo lads through the station in Enniskillen on his journeys to and from work. He was close friends with T, a good friend and drinking buddy of mine. Through T I knew Alan to be a really decent young bloke. A non-drinker who would look after the wilder men on nights out. He was friendly and unassuming, unbigoted and professional. The kind of policeman that Northern Ireland needs. You can't measure that sort of loss.

The terrorist's high velocity round struck Alan in the head as he stood signalling a car to stop. In the words of one of the men who were there: 'All hell broke loose. At first it appeared like an utter cluster fuck. Everyone trying to get on the radio at the same time. The military net going mad. Enniskillen trying to find out what was happening. Trying to let the Garda know. Then we just got on with it.'

As he fell to the ground, Alan's police colleague and covering soldiers ran to his aid, despite the risk of further shots being fired from the south. A frantic battle to save his life began. The round had entered the top part of the brain and exited towards the lower back of the head. As with all shootings, the exit wound was the worst. It was horrific.

The long wait by the hospital doors ended as the ambulance screeched up to the A&E unit. Belcoo was over half an hour from Enniskillen by road and the boys, working desperately to save Alan, had placed him in the station car and set off for Enniskillen to meet the ambulance halfway. An army medic had been with Alan from the moment he was shot. He did all he could. Once into the ambulance the furious effort to preserve his life continued.

In a surge of RUC and army greens and hospital white, Alan was carried past me into the A&E area. Even through the bloody dressings I could see that it was an extremely serious head wound. His face was as white as the doctor's coat. Eyes closed. Hopefully he was oblivious to the activity around him. I remember thinking, 'So this is terrorism. Are they happy now that a young lad's had his head shot away?'

The cowardly nature of the murder defied belief. I wished there was a TV crew there at that moment. Maybe then people on the mainland would have a clue about what was going on.

I stood by the door to prevent any members of the public walking into the room. The doctors and nursing staff worked rapidly, cutting off clothing. Setting up drips. Lads from the station party stood about. Hard young men, with tears in their eyes. Too shocked to speak. Knowing they had done all they could for Alan. By their prompt, immediate response, they had given him the best hope of survival. Now it was in the hands of the medical staff.

I had radioed in as soon as the ambulance had arrived. I was glad to see Sergeant A striding into the hospital.

'What's the situation, Richard?' he asked.

'They're working on him now, but to be honest it looks like a very serious injury,' I said in as low a voice as possible. It was hard not to be negative, but it would be disastrous to be overheard. If your best mate's there dying, the last thing you need to hear is that he hasn't got a hope.

There was a dark, fatigued appearance to the big sergeant's face, yet he remained the model of the practical efficiency which was his trademark. He said, 'Traffic Branch are bringing his parents over. They live a couple of hours away. Go and get yourself into a suit. I want you to do hospital guard with L. I want you to be as near to Alan as you can without intruding on the family.'

I was pleased. L was one of the best policewomen in Enniskillen, and I knew she would be very capable in this situation. I was glad to get out of the hospital environment for a few minutes, into the coolness of the night air. I drove back down to the station compound to put on a civilian suit and find L.

It was a tragic fact that all police officers who went into hospital, whatever the reason – even for an ingrowing toenail – had to have two other police officers there as a guard. The IRA always preferred to kill RUC officers when they were at their most vulnerable. Bitter experience had taught the force that no act was too despicable for certain terrorist minds. The hospital environment was dangerous ground.

I returned with L a quarter of an hour later and we made our way up to the intensive care unit where Alan was now on a life support machine. The family had now arrived and were by his side. He appeared to be slightly propped up in the bed, almost casual looking, except for the tubes and bandaging to his head. The whole scenario looked unreal. It was almost incomprehensible how so many lives could be changed in an instant.

A female doctor passed me in the corridor. 'Are you a policeman?' she asked. She was young, mid-twenties I guessed. She was English and appeared close to tears.

'Yes, I'm from Enniskillen RUC station.'

'Do you know Alan?'

'No, not really,' I said, feeling strangely guilty that I did not. 'He had worked out on the border since I arrived,' I added.

I could see that the young doctor had latched onto my London accent.

'It's so terrible here, isn't it? How do you work in an environment like this, where this can happen?' She gestured towards the ward. A tear was now clearly visible on her hot, blotchy cheek. 'One day it will be a great place to live,' I said. What I meant to say was that it was a great place to live except for the bastards who did things like this. I didn't feel like a debate, though.

The doctor composed herself as quickly as the tears had come into her stunned eyes. 'I must get back.' She turned and walked back into the ward. She looked like a small fragile girl in an oversized white coat. She was, it transpired, new to the hospital. New to Northern Ireland. At the start of that Northern Ireland learning curve, at the first stage of the hardening process.

It soon became clear that although on a life support system, Alan was now technically dead. The news was gently broken to his mother and father who dissolved in the grief of the moment with only each other's arms as support. Later, like a man searching for something unknown, his father walked around the ward. He paused as he walked close to where I stood. Words do not come easily in moments like that. I touched his arm and simply said, 'I'm so sorry.'

His eyes were glazed with incomprehension. He was hardly aware of me speaking to him. He circled the ward again, back towards the bed. I wished I could have said more, but in reality there was nothing that could be said. The words that would console them for the complete destruction of their world, their hopes and dreams for their son, did not exist.

The family were saying their goodbyes to Alan. The Sub-Divisional Commander of my station walked over to me. In the RUC, the 'authorities', as the officer ranks are known, are far more distant than within the English police. The RUC was still a world of standing to attention, saluting senior officers and only speaking when spoken to. There was even an officer's mess, separate from the canteen.

Even though I had met him on several occasions, the senior officer did not recognise me.

'Are you driving the ACC?' he barked.

I was momentarily taken aback, for a split second even angry that the man who ran the station did not recognise one of his own men. Then I took in his face. He, like everyone there, was in shock. I looked very different in a suit. Despite his gruff and distant manner, nobody could ever accuse the Superintendent of not caring about his men.

'No, Sir, I'm from Enniskillen. Sergeant A's section.' He looked at me blankly for a second and then it registered.

'Oh yes, the English policeman.'

He turned away without saying anything further.

I couldn't help but wonder what my parents would have made of the abrupt old bugger if it had been me lying in the hospital bed. Would he have known my name then? It didn't matter in any case. It wasn't me. In the scale of things within the RUC, it's your immediate colleagues who are of greatest

34

value. My expectations of the authorities were now low, to say the least.

I stood and watched as Alan's family were led away by the nursing staff. As always, they were superb. Experienced arms cradled the grieving parents. A religious minister had joined the group. The Northern Irish are good at death. They do not suffer the embarrassment that many English people have when consoling the bereaved. They are practised funeral goers, and seem to know exactly what to do in that situation, whereas an English person would be stumbling about in a confused daze. I often thought that if I was to die in Ulster at least I would have the consolation that the whole thing would be done right.

I watched as the medical devices were turned off and the curtains drawn around Alan's body. With the turn of a few switches, all hope for life was gone. He was dead. It was a sickening moment and moments like this had occurred nearly 3,000 times during the present conflict. Sometimes the death was in an instant out on an Ulster street, but often it happened like this, at a hospital bedside. The victims were from both communities, and all areas of Northern Irish life. It certainly didn't lessen the pain. A tragic loss through senseless murder was as dreadful in Northern Ireland as it would be in the English Shires.

An hour later, L and I were tasked to drive Alan's parents home. It was now in the early hours and Alan's mother and father appeared shrunken in the back seat of the car with the terrible emotions of that tragic day. Their composure in the face of their loss was humbling. It was a two-hour drive to the 'home place'. I was glad L was there. Although it was clear that Alan's bereaved parents did not wish to talk at first, when they did L's sensitive and easy manner was good to hear. Sergeant A had picked her for the right reasons.

A few days later I stood at the funeral, outside a large country church. The landscape was pure Ulster. Muddy fields and tight thorny hedges stretched away into the grey horizon. Alan's station party carried the casket with precise dignity. They had practised for the task from the day of the killing, hours of drill with a weighted casket in the gym at Enniskillen. In England, the lads would have been given hours of counselling and weeks off work. In

Northern Ireland they just get on with it. If you gave leave to everyone suffering trauma, half the force would be sitting in the police convalescent home that the RUC used on the mainland, lip diddling into a glass of vodka. The rain lashed down and the cold turned cheeks raw on the exposed hillside. It felt a long way from home. I later found out that the murder was given a brief mention in the English national press, but was then quickly forgotten. When I spoke to police friends in England, nobody could recall the killing. Surely a police officer's death was worth more than a few lines in the daily press? Happening as it did over in Northern Ireland, of course it wasn't.

I gazed around me. It was so isolated, this bleak place where the wind cut through the dark huddle of overcoated mourners. The force itself; part of the United Kingdom, yet in policing terms it could have been on the moon. Finally me. There were very few English eyes observing this funeral scene. However much you wanted to belong here, you would still always be a Brit 'blow-in'. A 'poll tax dodger'. I had lost count of the abusive terms aimed at my nationality I heard every week, and that was from my colleagues.

I left the funeral with some friends from Enniskillen station. On the way home, we stopped off in Fivemiletown and got seriously drunk. Sometimes that was the only sensible thing to do.

PC TO SB

The marching season in Northern Ireland in the run-up to the twelfth of July was, and still is, a time of confrontation and violence. To the observer on the mainland, it is at times baffling as to how such passion can be generated around a celebration of historical events which took place over 400 years ago. Perhaps only in Ulster could the defeat of the Catholic King James by the Protestant forces of King William at the Battle of the Boyne in 1690, continue to have such significance today. The battle was by no means an Irish affair. King William's mercenaries, battle hardened from the continental wars, consisted of English, Dutch, Danish, German, French Huguenot and Irish troops. Some early accounts even mention African participants. The Irish force was predominantly strengthened by French troops. This was a truly European confrontation, polarised since the Protestant victory into a yearly celebration by Northern Irish Protestants.

In July 2000 I was driving through Belfast early in the morning. No longer in the police, I was crossing the city at 6 a.m. to avoid the street demonstrations against the blocking of the Orange march at Drumcree. The violence over the last few days had been broadcast all around the world.

As usual, the extreme face of loyalism did itself no favours. While visitors from all over the globe who had come to Northern Ireland to observe the marching season watched, the violent, depraved behaviour of the Orangemen's supporters was in marked contrast to that of the Republicans, who absorbed the abuse and intimidation in peaceful protest. Republicans had long since learned the power of portraying a user-friendly international image. Punishment squads shooting off teenagers' kneecaps never made it to the front pages of US newspapers. Peaceful protest in the face of extreme loyalist provocation did.

At that time of the morning, I had taken a calculated risk that the violence would have calmed. However, no longer equipped with first-hand information as I would have been in the RUC, I had not counted on the deviousness of the Drumcree protesters that year. I turned into a road block in east Belfast. A crowd of a dozen or more were manning it to disrupt the commuters trying to avoid inevitable delays later on in the morning. Up to now the road blocks had started appearing just before 8 a.m., and then again in the late afternoon.

I was in a borrowed car as I was only visiting the province for a week to carry out some research. The last thing I wanted was to lose the car or for the protesters to catch on to my English accent. It was odd how these days I felt more uncomfortable driving through Protestant east Belfast than the odd time I drove through the west of the city.

It was a typical, hard Protestant Ulster scene. Every vantage point in the street was festooned with red, white and blue or orange regalia. The local UVF battalion had a huge paramilitary mural over the entire side of an end terrace. On nearby wasteground, the yearly bonfire was being put together. Anything combustible, from pallets to pieces of furniture, lay strewn about the place. There was an overpowering air of hate. The road was strewn with bottles and the splattered remnants of paint bombs from the previous night's disturbances.

Gangs of thugs were still out on the street, licking their wounds and comparing stories between drags on tightly held fag ends. I suppose it was one way of passing the morning. Now two of them were stepping off the pavement towards where I had stopped my car short of the group blocking the road, eyes full of malice.

At that point two RUC Land-rovers trundled around the corner behind me. I thanked fuck for my good luck and the RUC. I felt relief because although I knew I could have driven out of the road block, I simply did not need the hassle, and I didn't want to take my mate's car back covered in dents. With the men on the road block now watching the police, I reversed up the street. As I was moving away, out of the view of the loyalists, I saw the first bottle bounce off the roof of one of the police vehicles.

Those hate-filled expressions took me back almost ten years. In Enniskillen, the local loyalist bands generally behaved themselves. But occasionally we would have visiting bands from Belfast or Londonderry, intent on causing as much mayhem as possible before being poured back onto their coaches after an intense day of boozing and fighting.

It was a scenario played out in dozens of towns. The ludicrous pageant would begin with a planned and authorised parade through the town centre. One particular summer I was on foot patrol in the town, covering the parade. I watched the bands with increasing distaste as they stopped in turn outside the main Catholic pub in the High Street, playing 'The Sash' and shouting abuse at the punters inside.

After the parade, the bandsmen headed for the couple of pubs in town where they were sure of a welcome. They dispersed in small groups, their tight, military-style imitation uniforms by now completely dishevelled. Cans of beer seemed stuck to the palms of their hands. The bad marching now turned to a staggering, intoxicated stumble.

It was not long before the trouble started. We raced to the top of the town after receiving a report of fights breaking out. Thirty or more bandsmen were milling about, while two local lads lay bleeding in the middle of the street.

As soon as we arrived, the allegations started. Locals versus visiting bandsmen. All the same religion, all pissed out of their minds. My mate T was making an arrest for one of the assaults. There were six RUC men, and thirty bandsmen trying to take the prisoner back.

The situation was slowly escalating. Bottles came down on our heads from another group of loyalists. Fists started flying. Batons were drawn. I started to beat back the arms that were trying to pull T's prisoner away. Shouts of 'You black bastards', and 'SS RUC' flew with the fists. Despite the green uniform, 'black bastard' was still a common abusive term in Northern Ireland for police, originating from the darker uniform the police had once worn.

More RUC arrived in a Land-rover. The street was now full of policemen fighting with visiting Londonderry loyalists; locals in some cases helping local RUC; off-duty UDR men throwing themselves in, to help police or just because they fancied a fight; split, bleeding heads all over the scene.

We made a couple more arrests and slowly drove the visitors back to their coaches. Unlike Belfast, where fifty or more police could be at a violent confrontation within minutes, we could only count on thirty or so officers being at the disturbance, including the local mobile support unit, and that could take up to twenty minutes. The distance between stations caused a real and dangerous delay factor, and while the one MSU was in the town on public order duties, the other would be detailed out in a country area on anti-terrorist operations.

I had a drunken bandsman in my grasp at last. He had done a runner from the main group after I had seen him throw a bottle into a colleague's face. He started to punch me as I grabbed his collar, so I struck the back of his legs with the baton, making excellent contact. After two heavy blows he crumpled. I arrested him, and he slurred back: 'You're a fuckin' Brit, what the frig are you doin' here?' It was a question I often heard, and, for the likes of my prisoner, never answered. We lived in two different Ulsters.

────────────

I was drawn to being a police officer at an early age, nearly joining as a cadet when I was sixteen. It was always clear in my mind that I wanted to specialise, and when I finally joined up at twenty-one years of age, I had no intention of walking around wearing outdated pointy head-gear for thirty years. That suited some blokes, and a very good job they made of it, but I thrived on constant change, and in the police force there were many paths worth exploring. Variety, irregular hours and excitement were the main attractions of the job. At the time I was applying for the police force, the salary had reached a very reasonable level, and consequently it had become a desirable occupation. Competition for places, especially in the county forces, was fierce.

An added attraction was that everyone started at the same level. I knew that I would have to complete my two-year probationary period before progressing from that *Dixon of Dock Green* netherworld that the English police were emerging from in the early '80s.

As far as I was concerned, I was getting into uniform to be able to discard it for a more exciting world of detective work and undercover villain chasing. I was of the first-time-around *Sweeney* and *Professionals* generation. If it was going to be like *Z Cars*, I wasn't going to play. It was fortunate that my career path would take me out of uniform in less than two years, and eventually to the RUC. I need not have worried about lack of excitement. One thing you would not die of in the RUC was boredom.

I thought about the Met Police, but in the end opted for Sussex. Brighton, where I had spent my late teens, fascinated me. The coppers there seemed to be on a permanent adrenaline rush: one long blue light run between skirmishes on West Street, then Brighton's clubland heart, and unknown incidents on the fringes of town. Whitehawk and Moulsecomb were names I heard often, decaying council estates which provided the bread and butter garbage of a policeman's day. I felt drawn to where the blue lights went. I desperately wanted to be part of that world.

'Why do you wish to join the police service, Mr Latham?'

'So that I can get stuck into the mucky jobs at the end of those blue light runs.'

That would not have been, I guessed, what the stern, shiny faces on the interview board wanted to hear. Many policemen do have a fascination with the seedy side of life. I suppose in many respects I was the same.

Some people grow into a policeman's view of the world as the awareness of crime comes from experience, but from a very young age I had that perspective almost built in. When I looked at a park, I didn't think, 'What a nice park.' I would see it as a haven for rapists and perverts. By the age of twelve, I was spotting thieves at work in shops. I was, if you like, naturally tuned in to crime. In the interview I stuck to the usual line of 'service to the community' and 'working in a disciplined environment'. Those motivations were true in any case, although deep down I did have that love of the dark side. There was also nothing appealing in flogging myself nine to five in order to make somebody else wealthy.

I made the right noises. Ten minutes after the interview I was informed that I was being offered a position as a police constable.

In retrospect, I was without doubt destined for a life administering law and order. For my first eight years I did my growing up in a probation home in Kent. It was a probation home with a difference, in that it was a working farm which took the most unmanageable teenage yobs from South London and taught them to be farm labourers.

The regime was harsh in terms of the hours spent on the farm. The boys were turfed out of their dormitory beds at dawn and worked well into the evening. Relations with the staff were, however, excellent. My dad ran the farm. He treated the boys with respect, not as criminals but as regular employees, as he would have done when managing any farm. If they worked hard, he made life good for them. If they messed about he came down on them hard.

Dad was a fair man, and clearly respected. It helped that he was exceptionally strong, with shovel-like hands and huge forearms developed from a lifetime working on farms. He was able to lift huge weights on his back even into his early fifties, and no doubt would have remained a big, healthy, elderly man had not illness struck him down at the age of fifty-two.

Dad had started working on farms when he was thirteen, just before the end of the Second World War. Prior to that, he managed to go through the war years receiving no formal education whatsoever. His parents had lived out in the wilds of the country. The local school was closed and as a result my father simply slipped through the educational net. My mother finally taught Dad to read and write when he was in his thirties. He was later to become a lecturer in agriculture with a hard-earned teaching qualification. Like all who miss out on a decent education, he was to develop a thirst for knowledge which meant that by the time I was old enough to know him, he seemed to know everything about everything. At least, it seemed that way to me as a questioning young brat.

A cottage was provided for our family in the probation home grounds, but I was aware that we had less than other families. My father's salary was clearly low, and money, or the lack of it, was always an underlying source of tension. It never bothered me, since the probation home was a child's paradise. It had been a secretive training base and communications centre during the war. There were still the remnants of an old commando training course in the woods. Air raid shelters and mysterious underground bunkers, long forgotten in the adult world, lay covered by thick brambles, only capable of being penetrated by a determined six-year-old. I discovered an army helmet in one of the bunkers, proudly smuggled it into school and wore it during lunch break. A puzzled and somewhat worried teacher of the peace-and-love generation returned it to my parents at the end of the day. 'Richard does appear to have a fascination with war,' she said.

'Well, he's just a normal young boy then,' replied my mother, relieved.

The helmet was allowed to remain in my dressing-up box, which consisted entirely of military uniforms, on the condition that I did not launch an invasion of the school playground wearing my enormous metal headgear.

My mother was the ambitious one. She hated being poor. A lady who would have been entirely at home in a manor house was stuck in a poverty-ridden existence. Mum was fun-loving and generous, yet at times the pressure became too much and she was swept away by it into financial despair. I have an early memory of hearing a crashing and a shouting from upstairs. Like any six-year-old would, I toddled up to investigate. 'Richard, get your brother!' bellowed my father's voice.

He was wrestling with my mother across the bed. She was screaming. My brother, Andy, who was a large twelve-year-old, had by now run into the bedroom. He helped hold the squirming, diminutive figure of my mum while Dad scooped dozens of pills out of her hands. He had caught her in the middle of taking an overdose. She probably meant him to. She disappeared in an ambulance and was gone for a couple of weeks. When she came home, recovered from her 'illness', she was back to her normal happy self.

Ironically, as I have already mentioned, it was my father who was to become disabled by illness relatively early in life. He was a man who rarely drank alcohol, and never to excess, smoked a pipe occasionally, and generally was kept as fit as an ox by hard graft on the farm. Years later, in his early fifties, he noticed a tremor in his hand. It was the beginning of Parkinson's disease. The gradual destruction of mind and body that comes with the illness began.

When I was nine my parents moved to Uganda. My father was there to teach agriculture to the locals. We lived way out in the west of the country. The compound of the agricultural college was six miles from the local village. That consisted of two shops and a garage.

I lived a idyllic life for a boy of that age, roaming about in the company of Edward, our house boy. The sights and sounds of Africa made a strong impression on my young mind. In tune with the environment, for a while I literally ran wild. One day in the compound when they were cutting the grass I nearly trod on a black mamba which was curled up on a path. If it had struck at me I probably would have died, we were so far from a hospital.

I loved the country and the people. Hoped we would stay forever. Unfortunately, the move had been badly timed. President Idi Amin was in power, and after a couple of years he threw first the Asians and then the whites out of the country. My father was one of the last to leave. He told me later that on his final trip to the capital, Kampala, he had been held at gunpoint by young soldiers. A weapon had been put to his head while one of the boy soldiers had been 'reading' his passport, upside down. He was saved by a local Ugandan police inspector who appeared out of nowhere on a pedal bike and ordered his release. At that stage, the British-trained police still had some authority. It would not be long before military rule dominated the whole country, setting it on a path towards civil war, destruction and twenty years of chaos.

My brother was nearly seven years older than I was, and at that age a complete tearaway. He loved to tie me up on the family swing. He would push me back and forwards to within inches of his outstretched flick knife. Another of his pranks was to set up barricades on a road running behind the probation home grounds, set up a hide and then shoot at motorists with an airgun when they jumped out to clear the road.

Both my parents were very moral and law-abiding, and I developed a keen sense of right and wrong. As a child I dreamed of being a soldier. It could have happened, but instead it was my brother who went down that road. He made a good career out of it, transforming from young thug to the most responsible person I know. From his first leave home after joining the army, he spoiled me rotten. He reached the rank of sergeant, and only after his nine years were up did he leave, eventually becoming a policeman. On reflection, we probably each went down the correct path.

I also had a sister, Rachel, one year younger than my brother. They were later to come into serious conflict when my brother was serving in Northern Ireland, and she as an art student developed a relationship with a boy from the Falls Road in Belfast.

I recall one evening when my brother was back on leave. She was going on about how badly the army treated the poor Falls residents, who were all 'innocent'. On a visit to Belfast to meet her boyfriend's family she had been verbally abused by some young squaddies. She went on to say that she understood why the IRA were out shooting 'Brits'. Big mistake. Unfortunately for her, my brother had just completed a particularly nasty tour. There had been deaths and injuries to his army colleagues. As my sister reached a hysterical pitch in the argument, a recently poured cup of tea was thrown into her face.

It was a good lesson in the strength of feeling that Ulster generates. I was sixteen at the time and I already fully understood why my brother reacted in such a way. Although I loved my sister, I did not have her capacity for seeing another's point of view to the extent that the use of violence could be justified. It's funny how brothers and sisters can be so different.

My sister went through some tough times with relationships and then in her late thirties had a child. She brings up the kiddie on her own and has recently got into the church in a big way. She is feeling, she told me recently, a calling to be a priest, or whatever the equivalent is in the evangelical church which she attends. I wish her luck. In a role where tolerance and forgiveness are a necessity, she will do well.

On the day before I took the train up to the police training centre, Mum asked me anxiously, 'You're not going to stay a PC, are you?' It meant a lot to her to be able to show off her kids' achievements. Mum would have loved me to have become a vet or a doctor. I could see she was beginning to think that being a police constable was a little low in status. Deep down I enjoyed my mum's aspirations and would always try to give her something positive to latch on to.

I had just finished reading about the Special Branch in a history of the Met police. An idea flashed into my head. 'I'm going to join the Special Branch after my probation, then I'll be a detective,' I said.

'Can you do that?' she asked.

'Oh yes, I'll be straight off the beat in a couple of years and that will be me into major crime investigations.'

By good fortune that would come true, but at the time I knew if I said it Mum would be happier with my choice.

It did please her. She had no idea what the Special Branch was, but she liked the sound of it. It sounded pretty damn special. She told all our sceptical neighbours at the time that I had gone straight into Special Branch.

My mum, God bless her, was never able to keep a secret. Even when I joined the RUC and told her that under no circumstances was she to tell anyone what I did for a living, she would invariably blurt it out if I came up in conversation. I once visited her in hospital in England to be greeted by a nurse, who it turned out was from west Belfast, with the words, 'So, you're the son who's a peeler.' When we were told in police training school in Belfast that the biggest threat to our lives came from our mothers, they weren't kidding!

Having joined a namby-pamby southern police force, I should have trained in Ashford, in Kent. It was overbooked that year, so five of us from the thirty or so Sussex contingent of recruits were sent to do our training at the Midlands police training centre of Ryton-on-Dunsmore.

'Who the hell are you?' bellowed a West Mids sergeant as we five Sussex recruits walked into the hall to be processed by the course instructors. We had all miraculously managed to arrive an hour later than all the recruits from the Midlands forces. We were all in jeans. Everybody else was in suits. We looked a right fucking shower. Somehow our joining instructions had whole bits missed out. With the eyes of 200 potential policeman boring into us, we were processed. 'The odds and sods from Sussex,' muttered one skipper. Not a great start.

Police training centres in England had begun the transformation from military-based institutions with an emphasis on drill to the 'sit in a circle, let's hold hands and share the experience' places that they were to become in the 1990s. Ryton had not headed too far down that path at that stage. Although duvets had found their way onto the beds and there were single rooms rather than dormitories, discipline in class was still fairly tight. If asked a question you stood up. The sergeants were still allowed to shout at you, which they did regularly. It was obvious to anyone with half a brain that this was a good thing, because it prepared recruits for being abused far worse when out on the street.

Unbelievably, recruits who did not like being screamed at walked down the drive in the first two days. A large number of middle-class graduates were entering the police at this time and I don't think many had ever experienced any form of confrontation apart from with the bank manager when extending their student overdrafts.

We had two sergeants: an excellent young woman sergeant called Carol and a larger-than-life old sweat, Sergeant X from the West Midlands force.

46

He had been one of the first on the scene at the Birmingham pub bombings in the 1970s and was disgusted at the efforts to free the Birmingham Six. 'Birmingham Six,' he would say, 'don't ever let anyone fool you into thinking that shower of bastards are not guilty.'

He described the scene of carnage to us. Placing bits of bodies into bags. The smell of burnt flesh. Tears would come into his eyes as he relived the horrific moments as he scrambled through the rubble to help the maimed.

I had always had a passionate hatred of the republicans terrorists, perhaps fuelled by my own brother's many stories from his tours in Northern Ireland during the '70s and early '80s. I resolved to do my course project on the anti-terrorist legislation. The seeds of my interest and later hands-on involvement were sown.

It was during training that I met my first RUC officer. Conspicuous by his green uniform, he was on secondment from the RUC training depot, no doubt casting a sceptical eye over the liberal training methods of his English compatriots. On one occasion he was asked to take part in one of the training scenarios we had to play-act, to prove we could be little trainee policemen. He was the drunk. I was the officer sent to talk him into going home peacefully. He played the part to perfection with his broad Belfast accent. 'Listen here, wee lad, just be leaving me in peace to have a quiet drink.' He was very realistic. I was later to realise how much practice some RUC men had in being pissed, or 'blocked' as it was more commonly called.

He started to manhandle my lapels, to the grinning delight of the rest of the onlooking class. They sensed a ruck.

'Well, if you're not going home you're under arrest.'

'You and whose fucking army, you Brit bastard.' It was a phrase I was to hear often in the future.

Stupidly I tried a throw we had been taught in self-defence class. Naturally it was completely useless and my victim, who, it transpired, was a genuine black belt in judo, had no trouble hoisting my eleven-and-a-half stone weight skyward. Somehow I managed to hold on to his neck and as I hit the deck like a sack of shit he was brought down with me. It was still very clear from the state of my uniform and totally destroyed 'bulled' boots who had come out on top.

I had in my late teens attended kickboxing classes for three years, so I was used to the odd serious whack. The humiliation of being up-ended by this old sergeant (he was probably in his late thirties) took longer to repair. It was a good lesson – never underestimate an opponent, and if you are going to go for it, hit them hard and never use a technique taught in police self-defence classes. My first brush with the RUC was a sore one.

During my training I was appointed class captain and drill leader. Unusually there were no ex-military in my class, so I had to learn drill from scratch, to the standard which would allow me to march my own class around without too much chaos. We came out overall top class, and I passed out a fit-as-fuck probationer desperate to fight crime with my ancient-looking wooden truncheon and all those definitions of the law that had been drummed into us over the fourteen weeks of training.

There are a few differences between then, when I first joined the police, and now. One is that when you put on the uniform then you felt proud of it. I was recently talking to some policemen in Sussex who related how, during an open day at their police station to which certain members of the local ethnic community were invited, police in the station were banned from wearing uniform because it could be viewed as oppressive! It appears that the deranged politically correct ideals of the current generation of decision makers have now infected the upper ranks of the police service. I was proud of the uniform. That I looked smart in it. That my boots were immaculately bulled. I think that is how most decent people would like to see police officers.

On a similar tack, there are those who advocate taking away the discipline of drill in training. They really have missed the point of the whole thing. Of course drill has little to do with modern police work, but it does have a lot to do with self control under provocation. About bearing. It creates a sense of pride. It is that sense of pride which seems to be rapidly disappearing.

I eagerly opened my envelope to find out where I would be posted. I knew it would be Brighton. I gazed in horror at the sub-division listed on the paper. It was Worthing. Boring old Worthing on the Sussex coast. I could have cried with frustration. I could not imagine there being any crime in Worthing. I was, thankfully, wrong.

My time in the town was to prove relatively short, and I was to start on the rapid learning curve I craved almost immediately. Within four weeks, I had a murderer's confession in my pocket notebook and had instigated the arrest at the scene of a particularly brutal murder.

Thorn Road in Worthing was not a typical road in which to find a murder victim. A quiet street of terraced houses, it was gradually being transformed by yuppie flat conversions. Some of the residents were the original owners, the elderly who had lived there since the war, minding their own business. Seeing out their days with strolls along the adjacent promenade.

I was out walking in the freezing December early turn with my shadowing tutor constable, Tony, when the early-shift town car called up for some uniform assistance and CID to attend a ground-floor flat. The lads had noticed that the flat door was slightly ajar, and that a pane of glass in the door had been smashed.

Tony and I arrived at the scene shortly after the PCs first attending had made a gruesome discovery. Tony was a real star, an old-style copper who still lived in a police house on a council estate. He was an excellent tutor for a young PC, because he had worked the town beats in Worthing for all of his fourteen years' service. Even he took a step back at the sight we were greeted with.

The body of a woman in her late eighties was lying in a massive pool of blood on the kitchen floor. We were asked by the lads who discovered the body to go around the back into the rear yard of the flat to prevent any nearby residents seeing the body as they strolled past the kitchen window.

Tony and I stood at the open back door looking at the bloody mess that had once been a sweet old lady. You never enter a murder scene after the initial discovery. The phrase 'any contact leaves a trace' is drummed into you at training school. But it was not necessary to go in to see the full horror of the attack. We later discovered that the woman had been stabbed more than a dozen times with a large military bayonet. The chest area was completely shredded with the frenzy of the attack. Gore and flesh hung in chunks from the frail body, with further damage to the hands and arms. Tony, with his fourteen years' service, had seen it all before. 'First of many, Richard. You better get used to it.'

I had already dealt with a number of dead bodies, some in various states of decay, but this was the first time I had seen a murder victim. I stared for several minutes, taking in every detail. I thought I would feel more anger, but my overriding emotion was one of complete and utter sadness for the victim. To go through all those years. To now be alone in the world as a widow, her husband long since dead and no longer able to protect her. To see it all end in that bloody, despicable carnage. Was it robbery? A sexual attack? The motive was to be discovered a great deal faster than anyone anticipated.

CID arrived and swiftly commenced the scene investigation. Chubby men with bad haircuts and brown suits sauntered around looking self-important and I, as the dumb probationer, was given the job of standing by the rear door, looking like the dumb probationer at the rear door of a murder scene. I did not even get the job of standing at the front door, where I would have ended up being featured on the local TV news.

My task did have some interest in that I was able to watch the complete scene examination. Crime officers and a senior detective dressed in white paper suits painstakingly collated the injuries apparent to the body and all aspects of the murder scene. Even though I could have been relieved by another officer to have a break, I chose to stay at the rear of the house. It was bitingly cold, but the sight of real, worthwhile police work kept me fascinated for hours. The body was removed, together with the cut-away lino from the floor as well as numerous other unidentified items in brown paper bags.

Finally, after several hours, the scene was wound up and all that remained was me, by this time allowed to guard the front door, another probationer freezing his bollocks off at the rear, and a CID sergeant sitting as warm as a hot toddy in the nearby incident caravan. We learned a man was in custody for the murder and was being interviewed by the DI. 'Good,' I thought. 'They've got the bastard.'

With a bitter wind coming off the sea, I was lulling myself into a numb daydream when suddenly I nearly leaped out of my immaculate new uniform. A hand had landed on my shoulder from nowhere. At first I thought it was from the murder scene, which was worrying since I knew there was nobody in there. I then saw the owner of the hand, a very drunk Glaswegian from the flat above. The door to his flat was directly next to the entrance to the victim's home.

He looked at me, swaying from left to right, stinking of drink. 'Officer,' he slurred. 'Upstairs. I've got your man. It's my son. He did it.' My first thought was that it was a wind-up, it was some ignorant old drunk who'd become confused about the murder downstairs and had descended into alcoholic fantasy land. On the other hand, if this was the real thing everything had to be done just right for future evidential purposes.

I must have looked completely sceptical, as the man was becoming more urgent. 'Come upstairs. He's upstairs. 'Fumes from the drink were clinging to my nostrils.

I resisted the temptation to go upstairs alone, and called the detective sergeant who was basking in the heat of the incident room wall heater. 'Charlie 4 to Whiskey. Can I have a talk through with DS M in the incident van?'

'Go ahead Charlie 4.' The DS cut in. He was clearly bored enough to be listening to the PR.

'Please come out to the entrance to the flat.'

There was a puzzled silence. I could sense he was wondering what could not be passed over the air.

'Roger.'

He was by my side in a few seconds. His eyes flickered interest as I introduced the drunk Scot to him, who again said, 'I've got your man.' The DS was no doubt pissed off that he had not been included in the interview team who were now with the suspect. The wrong suspect, as it turned out.

Upstairs in a grotty two-bedroomed flat we were met by the drunk man's wife and their sixteen-year-old son George. The mother was as drunk as her husband. The son sat silently on the sofa. He was a pasty, ginger-haired creature. Hardly noticeable, even now that he was the centre of attention. I instinctively reached for my notebook and recorded the questions that the DS asked him.

'Have you got something to tell me?' he asked.

'I didn't do it,' said George, with the emphasis on the 'I'.

'What have you told your parents?' The DS was gentle with the lad, aware that the parents were pissed and not the most reliable of informants.

'That I didn't do it.'

'For God's sake, George, tell them,' cut in his father. The DS gave him a look that shut him up.

'Were you there?' the DS continued.

'Yes, I was.'

'What happened then?'

51

'I didn't want him to do it.'

The story slowly came out. Young, harmless George was a schizophrenic. A voice had told him to go and see the lady downstairs, who he had been previously friendly with. He had talked his way in and proceeded to rip her to bits with an army bayonet which he kept in his bedroom. It was as simple as that. The victim had been unlucky enough to live below this dysfunctional family, and by showing some kindness to little George, by giving him biscuits occasionally, had become a target in his twisted mind. He'd even had the presence of mind to break the glass pane in the door to create the illusion of a burglary.

He was a pathetic little excuse for a killer. Sixteen years old, and not even ten stone in weight. George was arrested and taken into a police car. At this point his mother came downstairs still out of her tree. I said, 'Your son's been arrested.'

She collapsed into my arms. When she came around, she told me how George had seen his brother decapitated in a road accident when he was younger. Since then the brother had been telling him to do bad things, an evil little voice in his head. The case never went to trial. George was found to be completely barking and has been detained at Her Majesty's pleasure in a high-security mental hospital.

I resumed normal duty with a couple of hours to run before my shift finished. I remember it was that night that I met my second RUC officer. Within minutes of leaving the murder scene, on my way back to write my statement, a fight started in one of the town discos. A bundle of fighting, gouging, kicking yobs fell down the club stairs onto the pavement. It was shit fighting shit, nobody wishing to make allegations despite a collection of black eyes and bleeding heads.

I yanked one of the yobs to one side to take his details. He gave me a broad grin and produced an RUC warrant card. 'They called me an IRA bastard,' he said indignantly. 'I couldn't be doing with that, could I?'

There were no complaints from the other parties involved. I let the guy go, bemused. 'Funny lot, these RUC,' I thought. Eight years later, I was to be one of those 'funny lot'.

It was 4 a.m. and I was lying next to my skipper, the big lad. For a big bloke he could keep very still. We had to because we were both horizontal under a bush at a certain border crossing point, waiting to kill the IRA ASU who we knew were going to come down the lane to try to kill us. We were with four soldiers of the regiment then serving in Belleek. The regiment I won't name, but they were all good northern lads.

We had been out since midnight, spread out on either side of the lane. Blackened-up faces and covered by foliage. Deep in the shadows, hardly daring to breathe. We had crept out of the rear wriggly tin gate and crawled like dogs to our position. Soldiers don't crawl like dogs, of course, they 'leopard crawl'. My leopard crawl was probably a bit suspect but it had done the job.

Once in position, you couldn't let the squaddies down. They were trained to lie motionless for hours while the cold wet of the ground soaked up into their balls and froze their limbs into lumps of soon senseless flesh. To policemen who liked their creature comforts, this was a novelty. To fuck it up would be potentially deadly to all there. We weren't there to catch a gang of burglars. It would be a heavily armed ASU of up to twelve dedicated terrorists who would come down that lane. So we lay as quietly and as patiently as the soldiers around us, knowing that any day now the IRA would trundle a mortar down that lane, and if we did not kill them in the process, our own lives and all those sleeping in the station could be lost.

That would be in the future. Back in Worthing, while I was still a uniformed constable, I had my first indication of how fucked up service in Northern Ireland can make a person when I had dealings with an ex-squaddie. The incident also taught me never to accept what is said to you at face value.

One day, while on my way to arrest a shoplifter, I was stopped by a shabby-looking bloke in his mid-twenties, who asked me for advice on drug addiction. He appeared agitated and tearful, but after a while I concluded he was just odd. Worthing was full of strange people. At times the town appeared to be one big care-in-the-community project. Aware that my shoplifter had been waiting a while, I brought the conversation with the weirdo to an end and gave him a telephone helpline number for drug problems.

Three hours later, I was back out on patrol when a call came through. A man had called the Samaritans and was sitting on the top of the town centre multi-storey car park threatening to throw himself off. When I reached the car park roof, sure enough it was the man I had spoken to earlier.

The guy from the Samaritans was already there keeping a distance, but he had developed a line of communication with the potential jumper, whose name was John. He was able to tell me that John was an ex-squaddie who had gone into a complete flashback of his last tour of Northern Ireland. He had seen a couple of his regiment killed in a bomb explosion. The terrible images still haunted him. He had left the army, and, gradually, over a couple of years, his life had fallen apart. It had come to a head the night before when he had beaten up his wife and walked out of the house. He had been walking the streets since then.

John did not have a drug problem. He simply wanted someone to talk to. I had been too busy to give him enough time to tell me his problem.

When he saw me on the roof, John told me as much. It had been the last straw, he said. Nobody cared. Gradually I talked him around to taking a cigarette off me. I apologised for not having time for him earlier. He was crying by now and again talking about Northern Ireland. He saw no point in going on. He never slept because of nightmares; he knew he would be violent towards his wife again. He felt like attacking people all the time. It was clear that this had become more than a cry for help.

John was sitting with both legs dangling over the edge. It was at least a hundred feet to the concrete below. As I gave him a cigarette, I took the chance to grab him. It was lucky that I had all my weight pulling him back from the edge, because at that point the stupid bastard actually tried to jump. The guy from the Samaritans rushed over and helped me pin him to the ground until I had some backup. John was detained under the Mental Health Act.

I resolved in future to look a little deeper the next time I was approached in the street by someone who appeared distressed.

Worthing may not have been the crime capital of the UK but it did at least break me into the sight of dead bodies. Due to the huge number of elderly in the town, not many early turns would go by without a call to a G5, as the

54

sudden deaths were known. The G5 was the form that relatives' details went on. We would sometimes deal with three before breakfast, generally the old and anonymous living in decaying bedsits around the town.

Eventually an indifferent neighbour would notice that the little old lady below hadn't been seen for two weeks. We would break in, and if we were lucky we got to the body before the flies had. If not, especially into the summer months, a brown, stinking mass of flesh and maggots would greet you as you crawled in via a window.

On one occasion my partner climbed into a flat while I waited on the other side of the front door in the communal hallway, which we had been unable to force open. I suddenly heard him swearing. 'Fucking hell, Rich, get me out of here!'

As he tried to clear the heap of rags obstructing the door, the bundle had started to wriggle and the chest cavity had caved in. It was a maggot fest. The missing old person. My partner came back out the window a lot quicker than he had squeezed in. We beat a noble retreat and called environmental health to mop up the mess.

Worthing nick in those days even had a separate card file from the criminal index we relied on. It was known as the TWR file (Typical Worthing Resident). When a call was received from someone suspected of being a local mad person, you could look up the entries and see what their usual form was. 'Mrs Hargreaves reports that MI5 have come and stolen her radiators'; 'Tom Kelly states the aliens living next door are sending radio beams through his walls trying to kill his cat'. There were hundreds of entries. We always attended the calls, but it was better to be pre-warned about them in case a real call came in. I often found myself chasing the pygmies from Miss Sullivan's bedroom in Goring during the early hours of the morning. It kept her happy, gave us a bit of variety, and in many ways it summed up what being a copper was about. When we had old ladies hearing voices from the plug-hole, one of us would become the officer in charge of drainage and chase the bad voice away. They were the good times. Keeping the vulnerable feeling secure, not scrabbling around the streets with yobs and druggies. Sometimes the insanity in the town was more tragic.

One incident always stuck in my mind. One day the DI spotted me in the back yard. 'Richard, I've got a good one here to go to. I want to check a suspicious death scene.' With ambitions towards non-uniform work burning brighter than ever as my probation ticked by, I could hardly look less than thrilled, even though I was about to go into the canteen for a large, greasy fried breakfast.

We arrived at a council house in the east of the town. The police had been notified by the local GP when one of his female patients had come in to say she was worried about her husband, who had not moved for a week and was now refusing food. Unfortunately, the reason he hadn't moved was that he had fallen and struck his head on the mantel a week earlier. He had died almost immediately from the head injury.

The man's wife had got him ready for bed, got him up in the mornings, dressed him in his day clothes and fed him three meals a day for six days. The stupid woman just wouldn't accept that he was dead!

When the DI had decided it was not a murder, he handed me a body bag. Bizarrely, instead of being the usual blue colour, this body bag was transparent. It took me a good twenty minutes to get the twisted, unfortunate but well-fed corpse into the see-through bag. By this time, most of the food his wife had stuck down his throat was erupting out over me and the insides of the zip-up body holder.

I still sometimes wake up from a disturbed dream seeing that guy's face pressed up against the plastic with old dinner smeared around his gawping mouth. Although not the worst thing I have seen by far, it is the one that stays with me.

I was just beginning to become seriously hacked off with the life of a uniformed copper when I heard of my next posting in the way that policemen have heard of their postings throughout the ages. It was from the station cleaner in the gents' toilets on the first floor of Worthing nick.

'I see you're on the sub-divisional drugs unit from Monday, young fella.'

'Am I?'

'Yes, mate' said the cleaner, chuffed that I did not know. 'Read it in a tray somewhere.'

He went off whistling.

Two days later it was confirmed. The DS in charge of the unit was the same DS from the Thorn Road murder. He had asked for me specifically, and to this day I am eternally grateful. My policing day changed overnight, from the unenthusiastic prosecution of motorists (I had no interest in traffic matters) and an incessant stream of shoplifters, to surveillance, informants and crashing doors in at dawn, warrant in hand.

Certain images stick in my mind from my time working with the drugs unit. The first is of doing a warrant on the flat of a guy we had in custody and finding his girlfriend on the bed, fucked out of her mind on heroin and cradling a bandaged stump where her hand had been. She had recently had the hand amputated because of infection from dirty needles. The stump was weeping through the bandages. Anyone else would have gone back to the hospital to have it seen to, but all she wanted to do was pump more shit into her body. She had once been extremely attractive, and had worked in the town's Boots store on the pharmacy counter. It was such a waste of a life.

The other is of doing a warrant one day and calling again the next to find the druggie dead from an overdose. You could get on quite well with the druggies once you got to know them, could actually feel a sense of friendship towards some. Many were highly intelligent. It made the sense of waste even more acute when you found them dead.

During my time with the drugs unit I became aware of the workings of the Special Branch. A strange bearded man could be seen around the station dressed in a combat jacket and baggy, well-worn canvas trousers. He looked like an overweight '60s dropout. He talked in whispers, usually to the intelligence collator or the older CID men. This man was the area Special Branch officer.

I finally met him when the front office staff had a call which did not fit with the normal run-of-the-mill calls at Worthing police station's front office. 'Richard, there's an African geezer here who thinks someone is going to assassinate him. He wants to speak to an anti-terrorist detective. You're in plain clothes and you read books, so you'll do.'

Despite the piss-taking I was glad to go in and have a chat. It had been a quiet day and I was just kicking my heels waiting to go home.

Worthing police station received its fair share of nuisance callers, but it soon became clear that this was not one of them. I took details from the young man, who was visiting from an African state. He was here on a conference visit being hosted at one of the town's seafront hotels. At some point he had been approached by what he believed to be government agents from his homeland, operating in the UK. Various threats had been made due to his own political leanings at home.

After taking down the basic details I called the SB man, who fell on the information with relish and took the caller away for a long, detailed chat, thanking me enthusiastically for taking the trouble to call him out. It pays at times to take the strangest stories seriously. My appetite for the secretive and diverse world of SB was by now thoroughly saturated.

The drugs unit were at times called on to deal with other more mundane matters, and it was at one of those times that I decided to apply to SB. For two weeks we had collated information on a gay traffic warden in the local area. The problem was not the fact he was gay, but that unfortunately he used his position as a traffic warden to have time away from his wife and kids visiting men's toilets for mutual masturbation and other vigorous activities, while dressed in his traffic warden uniform.

Since he did not know me, along with the fact that I was the most junior officer in the unit, I had the pleasure of installing myself in the cubicles before he arrived in the hope that he would blatantly offer up sex. This would give us evidence of misconduct on duty, as well as of the criminal offence.

The name of the game was to obtain enough evidence to make him resign when it was presented to him, avoiding a scandal. Unfortunately, through the intelligence we had, we knew he never made the first move. I was not allowed to, either; this would have been seen in court as entrapment. Consequently, he and I spent countless minutes staring at each other through peepholes between cubicles breathing heavily, but he never made the crucial offer. Perhaps he didn't like my eyes!

The allegations were eventually put to the traffic warden and he resigned, but I knew there was more to police life than standing in a stinking cubicle waiting for some deviant to pass a note under the door inviting me to suck his twelve-inch dick. I applied for Special Branch.

After my application went in, some old sweat, a wreck of a CID man, stopped me in the corridor. He too had applied for the branch. I had three years' police service at the time.

'SB? Maybe one day, son,' he said, with a sneer on his face.

To my great pleasure, he didn't even make the interview.

The Special Branch role is an ever-shifting area of police activity, with the responsibility of countering subversive actions aimed at the state. The days when the department spent hours monitoring domestic left-wing subversion were long gone. The Socialist Workers' Party was not the danger to the state that it was once perceived to be. Right-wing extremists were monitored but, at this period, had also declined in numbers and importance. In recent years neo-Nazi lunatics such as Combat 18 have again become a grave threat to stability, but in the late 1980s the vast majority of Special Branch work consisted of gathering intelligence to combat the terrorist groups on both sides of the spectrum in Northern Ireland.

In addition, Special Branch look at all potential threats from abroad with connections with the UK: the activities of major crime groups such as the Triads and the Yardies. Special Branch work closely with the security service and carry out arrests and search warrants with them, and on their behalf. The list is diverse and extensive.

I had ensured that by the time of my interview my knowledge of terrorism was as extensive as I could make it. I had an excellent police record to date, so the interview proved to be a relaxed affair once it became clear that I understood the responsibilities of SB and had a clear understanding of the nature of the work.

SB is in fact a submersion process into the world of 'need to know'. On arrival you are entrusted with little secrets, and as time goes on the secrets become bigger and better. All SB officers are positively vetted (known as PVd) by the security service. Until this process is complete, you remain on the fringes of each job that comes in. Gradually one is let into the bigger picture – but rarely the complete one. If you don't need to know, you don't get to know.

In view of my age and short service I started work with the Special Branch office based at Gatwick airport. On the first day the DI gave a talk to the new recruits, six of us in all.

'Not my neighbours, my friends or even my wife know what I do,' he began. 'From the moment you start this job you are of interest to the IRA. People talk, and that talk could bring serious or even fatal consequences to you or your family members.' He dramatically picked up one of the office bins. 'You will notice it is empty. Our bins are always empty. Any shred of paper generated in this office either goes in as a report to the relevant agency or is shredded.'

I could see that this was going to be a very different world.

On the first day we were put into two groups of three and taken around the airport. We were shown mirrors with rooms behind to which only we had access, from which we could monitor suspects. At the end of the day we arrived back in the office to find our photographs spread out on a desk. We had been followed and photographed by a couple of SB lads using a camera concealed in a bag. Despite it being a 'secret squirrel' world, it came across as very professional. I knew I was going to enjoy it.

I soon received a letter regarding my positive vetting. It read:

Dear Mr Latham

You will no doubt know that in the interests of security it is necessary for enquiries to be made about civil servants, police officers and others, who in the course of their current or future duties may have access to exceptionally secret information.

The procedure which is followed provides for certain particulars to be sought from them, and from other persons, so that it may be decided whether they are fit to be entrusted with such information. Any considered to be unfit, including members of the Communist Party or of a fascist organisation or those associated with such bodies in such a way as to raise legitimate doubts about their reliability, will be barred from posts which give them access to such information. The procedure also contains safeguards for persons removed from secret work on account of such associations, and they are transferred to other work wherever possible.

As you have been nominated as a person to whom the procedure should apply, and in order that any necessary enquiries can be made, I should be grateful if you would complete and return to me the enclosed questionnaire. At a later stage it will be necessary for an Investigating Officer from the Ministry of Defence to interview you and your nominated referees.

I was now lined up for the dreaded PV interview, in which the last ten years of my life would be trawled over with scrupulous detail. It was a necessary process if I wanted work of greater interest, but it was not pleasant to sit and be grilled for two and a half hours by the vetting officer.

'Have you ever had an affair? Have you ever had group sex? Have you ever had sex with a man?'

I was beginning to wonder if I had 'sex maniac' tattooed on my forehead, but it transpired that everyone was asked the same.

Towards the end of the interview, the officer asked me if I had attended any political rallies. I made the mistake of saying that I had – a CND rally in 1982, but only to see Madness play at it. He grilled me for a further twenty minutes on that one. I think he thought Madness was a politically subversive organisation. It took a while to convince him that it was only a pop group.

The majority of SB work at the airport is intelligence-led. Acting on the information that terrorists or criminals are travelling and taking appropriate action to curtail their activities. Occasionally we would just trawl for 'goodies', standing by the immigration officers, waiting for the feeling that someone was of particular interest. Sometimes it paid off.

On one occasion in 1989 I spotted a West Indian passing through the departures control. He appeared uneasy so I did a quick passport check, memorising his name and date of birth, and then allowing him to proceed without writing the details down. It was a good way to ensure that the subject wasn't entirely sure if he had been recorded. On this occasion the quick flick through his passport did not panic the guy, and he carried on through, down to the departures gate for a Kingston, Jamaica flight.

I did a quick check on the police national computer. In the previous hour he had been placed on the computer; he was wanted for murder. A stabbing in Bristol. We stopped him as he boarded the aircraft, and I said those great words, 'I am arresting you for murder.' You don't get to say those words too often in a police career. The next person I would arrest for that crime would be an IRA terrorist. In the meantime I was chuffed with my little catch. It made the hours of trawling on the immigration controls worthwhile.

On other occasions we would have to react to a name that the immigration officer had spotted from his blue book. These books contained the names of criminals or terrorists who were of interest when travelling through ports. Sometimes there would be a telephone number to ring, alerting some squad that their target was on the move. A number of times I found myself on trains to Victoria, tailing an individual who I would then have to point out to a hastily placed surveillance team ready to take the target from the platform. It was frustrating never to know the big picture, but very few in SB ever did. If I was not involved in a particular job a colleague was on, I would never have dreamed of asking for the details, and I was tasked to do things they were not aware of. We all lived in that odd world of secrets.

On a daily basis we pulled people in off the Belfast and Dublin flights who were the associates of terrorists, and every so often an active IRA or loyalist hood. We had the power to do so under the examination powers provided at ports by the Prevention of Terrorism Act. We were trained to know the political persuasion of every street by postcode. Dozens of photographs of terrorists were kept in the safe and could be studied in the hope that one day a face would click as it walked past. The information gleaned from these examinations was, of course, invaluable, but due to the sensitive and potentially life-threatening consequences of revealing it, at this time it cannot be spoken of.

One role we had at the airport was to introduce potential informants to the security service. A few holiday makers would be surprised, no doubt, that the intense huddle of three men from very different backgrounds, having a drink in the airport bar, was the first meeting between a disillusioned IRA member, a Special Branch introducer and an agent from MI5, or 'Box' as it was called.

———

'Today we are running a training exercise with MI6.'

I looked up at the skipper with interest. I had met many of the MI5 agents, but never any from the sister organisation which handles British intelligence needs overseas. Box was a mixed bag. Sometimes I felt that the operatives were a little naive; too many theorists and not enough practical experience. After seeing the MI6 operatives, even in a training exercise, it was clear they were of a different calibre.

The agents had spent a few weeks in Europe, constantly monitored by surveillance teams, with different tasks to perform en route. They were all on false passports with assumed identities, and to their knowledge their training operation had come to an end in a particular European capital. The flight home was, to them, purely incidental. My own role, given at a briefing with the security service trainers, was to pull one of the trainee agents at passport control, purporting to be a CID officer investigating passport fraud, and then find a fault in the man's passport. The purpose was to unsettle the other team members who would be travelling independently but had instructions to keep each other in sight at all times. The detained individual was to be arrested, but then questioned within a cell SB had within the terminal and monitored as to how he reacted under the unexpected circumstance of being pulled by civilian police. If at any time he revealed his participation in a government training exercise, of course his career would have come to an abrupt halt.

'Can I see your passport, Sir?' I stepped down from the immigration officer's box and took my target to one side. I flicked through the pages and then went back to the serial number.

'Is this your first passport?' I could see that the agent was not fazed at all. In appearance he was of a certain foreign nationality, so I tried a different approach.

'Were your parents British passport holders?' My questions became gradually more abrupt. I could feel his anger rising. 'I have a query about this serial number. I won't keep you a second.' I then disappeared into the office and watched the guy become increasingly irritated until the trainers asked me to go out and arrest him twenty minutes later.

The guy was kept in custody for another couple of hours. He always remained polite but indignant. When I touched on the race issue again, a look came into his eyes that told me he could be a very dangerous bloke. It was his only flash of temper. Afterwards I found out he was an ex-SAS officer. He could have ripped out my windpipe in a second. When I met the other men at the debriefing they were all equally impressive. It gave me faith in the security service overseas.

Between 1988 and 1991, violence and grief brought about by the terrorist campaign continued to infringe one of the main human rights of the majority of the decent people of the United Kingdom – the basic right to have political decisions determined by democratic means. Not by fear and intimidation. Attacks continued on the mainland and in Northern Ireland. In 1988, two corporals from the Royal Corps of Signals were brutally murdered by an animalistic mob in west Belfast at the funeral of one of the loyalist Michael Stone's victims.

The pictures on live TV captured the true nature of the republicans' hatred for the British, and the depravity of their blood lust. Republicans have tried to justify the killing by claiming that the two men, Derek Wood and David Howes, were undercover soldiers linked to 14 Int. I have chatted to several special forces operatives who have all maintained that they were just regular soldiers who were over-curious, and drove into the wrong place at the wrong time. An easy mistake to make in Ulster. The men died at the hands of the mob in the most brutal manner. They were beaten, stabbed and shot. Two of their murderers, convicted in 1998, have now been freed as part of the current government's policy of releasing terrorist killers.

A couple of months later, eight soldiers were killed by a car bomb as the coach in which they were being transported was blown up near Ballygawley. Throughout 1989 and 1990 policemen continued to be murdered. Constables Colin Gilmore, Clive Graham, John Warnock, John Larmour, Hugh McCrone and Stephen Montgomery all were brutally killed by the IRA. On the mainland I reflected how, if this had been a series of murders of policemen in London by one organisation, public pressure would have forced the government to wipe that organisation off the face of the earth.

The deaths of police officers in the province continued into 1991. Something was badly rotten with the government's security policy.

During my three years with SB, I made regular trips to Northern Ireland. Our counterpart SB officers there were a very different breed. Wary of us, quite rightly, since there was no way on earth we could appreciate the threat they were under in their daily lives. The regular RUC officers I met impressed me with their resilience and understated bravery in the face of continuing terrorist atrocities.

I was friendly with an officer in Omagh and visited Omagh and Enniskillen RUC stations. Colleagues even in the SB office thought it a little odd that I was taking my holidays in Northern Ireland.

It was only later that I would discover the great divide between SB in the province and the regular police. SB ran the RUC in terms of the ultimate decision making. Planned arrests, searches, arranging where an officer went during his working day, were all decided by the branch. Much has been made recently of the fact that CID will, under the Patten recommendations, take control of SB. Stories of SB collusion with paramilitaries and dirty tricks are now the staple diet of sensationalist documentaries. The reality is that the obsessive secrecy and control was probably unavoidable in the context of the time. One overheard conversation could mean death to an informant and in turn could stop information regarding the assassination of a police officer. Of course SB mixed with paramilitaries and had close relationships with some. If you work at the dirty end of a war, that is the company you keep. My impression was that as far as SB went in the province , it was a lonely, dangerous and thankless job. All the good work done, as with the rest of the force is now in danger of being eclipsed by republican propaganda, so readily repeated by the media.

Finally, I had to admit to myself that intelligence gathering and sneaking about in the SB world was not enough. My Northern Irish world was one of orange and green street maps. I wanted something more tangible. Even though I had at this stage passed my detective CID course and could have moved on to a full-time detective posting, there were stronger forces at work in my mind. If one really believed that Northern Ireland was a part of the United Kingdom, and that to murder for political gain was evil, then the right action to take was to go and live in the province and work as a police officer there. No more sneaking about in Italian designer suits or peering over the shoulders of immigration officers. I was determined to wear the green uniform. The plan fitted in with my wish to make a fresh start away from England. In the end, it was not a difficult decision.

I put in my application for the force I admired so much and undertook the rigorous RUC selection procedure. To help myself get fit, I cycled the fifteen miles to and from work each day for six months. I stared at maps of Ulster for hours, and built up a mental map of all the main area of Belfast. I read all I could regarding Northern Ireland.

The test day was hard and nerve-racking. I came away completely unsure as to whether it had gone well. The senior officers on the recruitment panel gave nothing away.

It was a long wait to see if I had been successful. Many apply to the force, and the huge numbers of applicants mean that the recruitment procedure can be both selective and unhurried. I was concerned that being English would go against me.

Months went by, and I began to wonder whether I should join the Met police and continue my Special Branch career there. After a while I even went as far as applying to the Met, and within a few weeks had passed the selection and had a date set for transfer.

It was not to be. Finally I heard from the RUC. The day I received the letter to say I had been successful in my application, I could have burst with pride. I said 'thanks but no thanks' to the Metropolitan Police. Purposely, I had kept it quiet up to that moment that I was applying for the force, so the news that I was going was a shock to many, including my parents. My point of view was that I was going regardless of what anyone said, so why give them additional time to worry about it? My dream of serving in Ulster had come true.

I went to a car boot sale with my good mate Doreen, a mad Scottish policewoman, and we both sold off most of our possessions. She was going away to travel abroad for a year. I think we made less than fifty quid between us! I tidied up bits of my life, and booked a ticket to Belfast. After working my month's notice with Sussex, I was off, with a suitcase and not much else. At the age of twenty-six, I was joining the Royal Ulster Constabulary.

TRAINING IN BELFAST, 1991

I flew into the harbour airport in Belfast on the kind of dark, briskly cold spring day that could only be produced by Ulster's overcast cloud-choked skies. The city I knew so well from maps in the SB office in England looked like a dulled version of the map images. It appeared small, regimental and cold. In my head, as the aircraft circled the small, turbulent city, I began filling in the orange and green shading below. Previously I had looked down on the scene as a tourist. I felt very different on this arrival.

As the wheels of the aircraft touched down, my stomach was churning with several emotions. I felt apprehension only in that I wanted to be good enough as a police officer to serve this community I had chosen to live in. I had read every book available on the RUC, for the little that was worth, and I was aware that I was joining a force which not only faced unique challenges, but was also one with a proud history. One book in particular, *The RUC: A Force Under Fire* by Chris Ryder, provided a fine overview of the sacrifice and dedication of the force in the long struggle against terrorism. Chris Ryder states in his book that 'Interpol figures showed that Northern Ireland was the most dangerous place in the world to be a policeman. The risk factor was twice as high as in El Salvador, the second most dangerous.'

I knew that those figures were worked out taking police officers in a ratio to the rest of the population. In a nutshell, the odds on being killed or injured on duty were high.

The RUC had come into being in June 1922. The current period of terrorist violence had begun in the serious disturbances of 1969. In fact, the early

1990s was the start of just another decade in the long war of Irish nationalists fighting against the British presence in Ireland. It was a war that ebbed and flowed according to numerous historical factors. The republican terrorists of the early 1990s clearly believed that their day had come, and as a result pressure on the security forces was unrelenting. From 1969 to 1991, 283 police officers had been killed and 6,789 injured as a result of terrorism or related public disorder.

The size of the force I was joining in 1991 was huge compared to comparable English forces. To police an area of a similar size to Sussex, with roughly the same population of 1.5 million, were 8,254 regular RUC officers and 4,533 members in the RUC reserve – 2,989 of the reserve force were employed full-time. This compared with a force of fewer than 3,000 officers policing the area I had left behind. In the force I had left, however, there were no extra men needed to guard every corner of police stations in concrete sangars. There was not huge public disorder on a basis so regular you could predict it on a calendar. It was not necessary in England to go out three or six in a patrol to lessen the odds of being murdered. It was a deadly kind of beat that I was going to be policing. Comparisons in population size and area covered were a little inadequate.

The night before I travelled across to Belfast, I slept in a police section house in England. I had been out with the boys on a big, big drinking session. I went to sleep with images of Ulster streets tumbling through my mind. Checkpoints, terrorists in dark clothing, helicopters overhead.

I was in a deep, disturbed dream world when the door of the room burst open. Two men in balaclavas, screaming with Northern Irish accents. In a fraction of a second I had taken in their wild eyes in the blackness of the masks. I jumped from my bed, and in a wild adrenaline rush kicked one of the 'terrorists' in the face. I thrashed out wildly with my fists, wondering why I was not dead yet. Why had they not fired? The 'terrorists' were now talking in English accents, standing back in the corridor pulling off their masks. I was standing there panting like a disorientated animal.

'Jesus, Richard, it's us, are you okay? You kicked me full in the gob.'

It was my mate Steve. He was later to join a territorial regiment of the SAS. Steve was now laughing as I stood shaking my head to stimulate my brain back into waking mode. My heart was going like an angry piston.

'You bastards.'

'That'll teach you to lock your door.'

He was right.

I was dropped off at the training centre in Garnerville, in north-east Belfast, by an RUC friend. He too was English, but was on the verge of heading back to the police in England for personal reasons. He had served in Ulster for ten years but had become homesick after his wife had left him. I hoped he would find happiness in the English police, but as I was later to find out for myself, going back can be a big mistake.

I stood with my case in hand, looking at a building which had previously been a catering college but appeared to have more in common with a South London 1970s comprehensive school. The only clue that this was not a school came on the drive up to the peeling blue panels and dirty glass of the prefabricated blocks. Reserve constables with Sterling sub-machine guns plodded towards the main building for another circuit of the grounds in a perpetual state of vigilance. They were older men who had done their time but were conscientious in guarding the new recruits.

The new recruits were mustered together in the gym. Not much was said, although a few lads who recognised each other from the initial interview stage whispered away. It soon became clear that there was the classroom world, and then there was everything that happened outside class. That was the land of the drill sergeants. They were big, booted creatures who stalked the depot grounds like rabid beasts looking for prey. All recruits initially fell into their hands.

We were told to stand by a reserve constable, and our group of thirty-two stood nervously in a row waiting for the arrival of the drill sergeant devils. It was Sunday evening. If we had expected to be shown politely to our accommodation, given a hearty supper and told to report in the morning for class, we would have been badly disappointed. Training started from the moment the two sergeants entered the hushed, anxious atmosphere of the gym hall.

'Right you lot, you ugly bunch of men . . . and ladies [there were just two women in the squad]. You have five minutes to find your rooms, deposit your cases and be back in here in your PT kit.'

The drill sergeant was an ex-guardsman and a man of legendary physical robustness within the ranks of the RUC. In his late forties, with a barrel chest and immaculate military bearing, he was the bellowing drill sergeant of your worst nightmares. It later became clear that he appeared to function solely on Ulster fries and Bushmills whiskey. It was said he could drink a bottle of Bush of an evening and still be up at dawn to beast recruits on a fifteen-mile run. He had a terrifying aura, yet as we were to learn, he was both decent and fair underneath the shouting, stamping exterior.

We grabbed snatches of conversation in the frantic minutes we had to be changed and back into the drill hall. The most common reaction to my accent was, 'So, you're an ex-squaddie?' There was a puzzled expression when the answer was 'No'.

I was the only Englishman on the course and as such became immediately very aware of my accent. I began to realise what it must have been like for the one Irish lad, from Cork, in the police station in Worthing. Not a day went by without some reference being made to his nationality. I could see it was going to be the same for me.

We were formed up in ranks of three according to size, and then, in our scruffy array of PT attire, the squad was beasted around the complex in quick time until the sweat ran in torrents down our backs and our lungs plucked at the inadequate air for reserves of oxygen. I had done drill in the English training environment, but that was second division stuff. This was the sadistic premier league.

By the twentieth circuit of the complex in quick time we looked like a bunch of floundering epileptics, arms and legs thrashing in all directions, out of time and held together only by the determination not to be the one who dropped. We did hundreds of press-ups and sit-ups, until our stomachs felt on the verge of ripping open. Faces from the senior squad in training grinned at us from the upper accommodation windows, careful not to be seen.

At last, after an hour and a half, the drill came to an end. As we staggered back into the gym I saw that several mats had been laid out on the floor. A pile of boxing gloves lay ominously at each end of the mats.

Another of the devils spoke to us. 'During your RUC service you will be involved in many one-to-one confrontations. You will have to be able to stand up for yourself and your colleagues. The following exercise is to test your ability to be aggressive when the need arises. You will mill continuously with an opponent for one minute. Milling is not boxing. It is not a skill, it is merely self-preservation. You will punch your opponent continuously until the whistle goes. If you don't mill, you will be off down the drive with your suitcase.'

Apprehension gave way to animal instinct as each bout took place. We all knew we were being judged on our aggression, and to look weak now would be a label carried throughout the course. Fists flew like demonic windmills. If you had boxed before it was of no value, since technique went out of the window. It was just one minute of scrapping, non-stop and relentless, until the whistle blew.

My opponent was Sid, who was shorter than me, but stockier. We smashed each other around the head with the small padded gloves, trading blow for blow. He was a hard little fucker. A typical all-drinking, hard-fighting ex-reserve constable. It was only weeks later over a pint that we both admitted we had hurt each other. We walked away from the milling with more than the end-of-bout whistle ringing in our burning ears.

'Good lads,' said the drill sergeant as we removed the gloves. We had passed a crucial test. The biggest cheer went up for the two girls on the course. They too had milled with each other with great enthusiasm. I would have been happy with either one of them beside me in a punch-up.

The next two hours was spent bulling boots. Hours of making little circles on your boot leather to bring up a mirrored surface. Myself and some of the ex-military lads gave advice on looking after kit to the boys who had never spent a night away from home. It was incredible, but some had reached their early twenties without even ironing a shirt. I later realised that this was due in part to the nature of Ulster mothers. They really fussed over their sons. Now the boys paid the price as they struggled over the next few weeks with the complexities of a steam iron or creating perfect creases down the arms of their uniform jacket.

The RUC tunic and trousers were made out of material which seemed to date from the First World War. Excessively thick and uncomfortable to wear, it looked very smart when it was heavily pressed for ceremonial occasions. Worn day to day, and subjected to the battering of a policeman's routine, it could quickly start looking like a bag of shit. We were only to discover that later, since every day in the depot was a ceremonial day as far as appearance went.

For the first couple of days we did not have uniforms, but we were told we would have to parade holding our gleaming bulled boots in the morning. Even with the effort put in, several of the pairs of boots were destined to be picked out and kicked across the drill square by the sergeants as 'not satisfactory'. Of course, they were no different from the other pairs. The sergeants were not testing the boots, but the man.

It was with weary steps that we made our way up to our rooms on the first night. In my room a couple of us lit up by the window and enjoyed the smoke seeping into our lungs, tortured by the healthy pursuits of the day. The bonds of training together were already forming.

We were joined by an ex-military lad. He closed the curtains in the room. 'Sniper,' he said. We must have looked at him with scepticism. 'Just because it hasn't happened before doesn't mean it won't happen.'

He was right. The IRA has a great imagination for killing. Thinking of the best way to kill you is all they have to do each and every day. The day you think you're safe is the day that they will have you. I determined that any advice I was given I would take on board religiously. Build good habits into my daily routine. That way, you didn't even have to think about them. They became part of your creed for staying alive. Check under the car each time you get in it. Go that bit further and check the wheel arches. Never answer the door without the Ruger revolver in the hand. Always vary your route. Never tell a stranger what you do for a living.

I had never had any difficulty in keeping confidential information to myself. I carried around many events in my head, especially from my time in SB, that I could not reveal to anyone, and still cannot talk about. Before you put your mouth in gear, it is always wise to think of the worst possible scenario which could occur if you talk about a sensitive event or policing operation.

At 3 a.m. the doors of each room were kicked open. We knew who it would be: the senior squad pretending to be staff members not yet introduced to us. It was a depot tradition, but one that had become an open secret. We played along for a while, but when they tried to get us all down to the gym for PT they were told to fuck off. My squad was too long in the tooth for that. Far too cynical even to play along with the seniors' bit of fun. It almost ended in a punch-up in the corridor. To them our squad was immediately labelled 'a bunch of cheeky wankers'. We were indifferent, and generally ignored them. There were bigger things to worry about.

The squad was a motley selection of all shapes and sizes. The ages went from nineteen to thirty-six, all thrown together for the four months of training in law, firearms and operational tactics which would prepare us for serving Ulster.

It soon became clear that my classmates had various motivations for joining the force. Perhaps the main difference from the mainland environment I was used to was the high status of policemen within the mainstream majority community in Northern Ireland. This status was what the majority of new recruits craved. Parents loved to have a son or two in the RUC. Many an Ulster father could be found leaning up against a golf club bar, talking in hushed tones about his son's or daughter's new posting, or relating the latest piece of RUC gossip that had been passed on to the family.

Many businesses and shops gave huge discounts to RUC officers. Along with status came money. Loads of it. In a country where salaries dragged behind the rest of the UK, a constable with a lot of overtime, before the 1994 ceasefire, could earn over £35,000 per annum. That kind of money went a long way in the province, where houses were at least a third less in price than the mainland, and the cost of going out socially was as low as parts of the north of England.

Unfortunately, along with increased salaries came opportunities for easy credit. Companies fell over themselves to lend money to RUC men. Debts were a big danger area for new recruits. One lad in a course prior to our intake could hardly wait to use his new-found credit facility. During class in his first week, he fabricated the story of a family funeral in order to slip out and arrange the car finance on a brand new turbo XR boy racer machine to flaunt his wealth-to-be. By the time he arrived back at the depot in the afternoon in his red striped acquisition, his class sergeant had already made a few phone calls and had established that the funeral story was complete bollocks. The recruit was sacked on the spot and drove off tearfully into the sunset with £12,000 of debt and no income.

Status, money, certainly a wish to serve, but in very few cases when I looked around me was there an individual who simply and solely had a burning desire to fight the IRA. The recruiting system seemed to have successfully weeded out all the 'death wish' avenging angels, and what was left was a selection of very sound individuals wanting to be policemen, and taking the fight against terrorism, and the risk of being murdered, as part and parcel of that.

During the introduction period in the class, when we all had to provide a potted history of our backgrounds, a tall young fella, Robert, from the country, stood up.

'I'm a Christian,' he said. 'I love my family, my mother and father, my brothers and sisters. They fully support me in being a policeman because it is the right thing to do.'

He talked frankly about his Christian beliefs. I was sure that this would have been rare in English police training schools. There was an openness about him that I had to admire.

Robert and I were to become good friends, and it transpired that his Christian upbringing did not stop him going out and enjoying himself at weekends. He was a very good rugby player, so much of his social life centred around a local rugby club. He did have a brilliant family, who made me very welcome whenever I visited them in their small country town. If he and I were nursing sore heads in the morning there were no harsh words or judgmental looks, just large mugs of tea and enormous amounts of fried food.

I was a bit of an oddity at the depot since I had no home to go to at weekends. I had arrived in Northern Ireland literally with my one suitcase, and until I knew where I was to be posted there was little point in buying or renting somewhere. My colleagues soon adopted a 'take an Englishman home for the weekend' policy. The hospitality of the Northern Irish is legendary and throughout my time there, it was a constant source of amazement how a land of such friendly and welcoming people could be torn apart by such violence. Over the months of training close friendships developed.

Ironically, many of the lads were amazed at the way English policemen walked about on the beat alone and unarmed. They were horrified at the amount of paperwork the job generated over the water. The lads were even fascinated by what it was like to drive a panda car! By now, ten years later, in the wake of the changes brought about by the political manoeuvering after the Patten report, I'm sure many of them are having a taste of all those things. Whatever happens in the long term with the terrorist situation, the RUC will become increasingly like the English police services.

My best mate, Rob, was a wiry ex-full-time reserve constable who had previously served in border stations. Reserve men in the RUC were on three-year contracts which were automatically renewed, but otherwise they did the same job as full-time officers. He became my mentor and guide to Northern Irish ways. He was also a dedicated policeman and was later to join Special Branch.

Rob had been one of the first at the scene of the Ballygawley coach bombing in 1988. He had been driving to work at the time. The eight soldiers of the Light Infantry Regiment killed in the bomb attack were aged between eighteen and twenty-one. Nineteen other soldiers were injured. Rob had held one of the dying soldiers in his arms at the roadside. 'He was just a wee boy,' he would say. 'Dying in a ditch in a strange country, only an hour or so after he got here. Not even knowing why he was there.'

I was later to work with one of the soldiers who was a survivor of the bomb. He was a very effective army intelligence officer down in Belleek. Like Rob, the sight at first hand of the carnage that the terrorists bring had focused his mind.

Another friend was Tim, an energetic little racing snake of a fella from east Belfast. He too had been a full-time reserve man in a hard area. Tim had been subjected to numerous bomb and sniper attacks while at his previous station. He was also a vodka drinker of the highest order. His cry of 'More vodka!' at the end of huge drinking sessions still rings in my ears.

At the time, he had a steady girlfriend who, to my surprise, always treated me with great hostility. I later discovered that this was because I was used as an excuse every time he went drinking with the boys. Apparently, I was going through some permanent crisis and kept forcing him to come drinking! She knew me as 'horrible'. Fortunately, he at last made the break from her and I was spared the puzzling icy stares I had to endure every time I visited the house. Only then did the little vodka monster admit I had been his alibi.

As well as ex-reserve men, we had a couple of super-fit ex-Royal Marines, one of them, Bill, an ardent Christian of the more extreme variety, the other, Jim, the drinking buddy of the vodka monster. I once went home for the weekend with the Christian ex-Marine. It was a big mistake. His parents were Plymouth Brethren. The Saturday night had been my birthday, so a few bevvies were taken. Bill could not even let on to his parents that we had gone out to a pub, although where they thought we were going at 8 p.m. on a Saturday night I do not know. There were certainly no churches open at that time. We met up with a few friends from the depot, and as usual Bill did not drink.

On Sunday morning when I appeared for lunch with a hangover I was met with the frosty intolerance that only the most religious can muster. This gave way to the fires of hell as his parents took it in turns to turn the heat up in the small dining-room with its religious symbols hanging starkly on the bare walls. I felt like the crucifix on the wall was going to fly off and stab me through the head. In fact, I felt like it already had. Finally I had to rush to the toilet to throw up. His parents had a look of triumph as I returned to the table. Maybe they thought a lesson had been learned. There had. If you have a hangover, don't wake up in the house of intolerant religious maniacs. I left soon after. Bill's dad was, it turned out, a reformed alcoholic. It explained a lot.

On the course we also had an ex-dustman, several salesmen and a motorcycle mechanic called Dan. Dan, later in the course, during the driving element, simply insisted that I move in with him and his very tolerant and lovely wife. I have never met a group of guys who were so generous yet wanted nothing in return.

In reality, there was another reason why I did not like staying on my own in the depot at weekends. The depot was reputed to be haunted. Of course, I did not believe that. Until my one and only weekend staying in the depot alone. After that I resolved to accept any offer to stay with classmates at the weekends.

At weekends the training centre was completely deserted. The only people who entered the building were the elderly guard squad, reserve constables who looked after the depot at weekends. I later found out that some of them would not go into the main building at night, even though they were meant to patrol the corridors on a regular basis.

It started with the sound of feet in the corridor, which, as I sat in my room, I initially put down to students returning to pick up notes they had forgotten. When I investigated, peering out of my room into the long gloom of the corridor, I could see no one.

Half an hour later I heard the sound of feet running right past my room. I bounded up and flung open the door, now slightly spooked. Again there was nothing. The footsteps had gone towards the toilets and showers at the end of the corridor. There was nowhere to go from there. With my truncheon in my hand, I searched every crevice of the bathroom area. My heart was pounding by now. The whole corridor seemed to have plunged in temperature.

That night, I finally drifted off to sleep. I was woken by voices. It was 3 a.m. The voices appeared to be directly outside my room. Again I flung the door open, this time with my study chair in my hands. The corridor was empty but what completely freaked me was that the voices continued for a few seconds, right next to me, as loud as if the speaker were two feet away, and then faded away. The atmosphere in the corridor was now icy. Completely arctic. There appeared to be a slight mist at head height. I had to keep rubbing my eyes to make sure it was not my vision which was going.

I had never experienced such a feeling of someone being there but not there. It was very, very odd. Even as a sceptic about the paranormal, I could find no logical explanation. A fellow recruit and a believer in ghosts afterwards attributed it to the restless souls of RUC men who, once killed in horrific terrorist acts, could not find peace, and for whatever reason had returned to where their journey to death within the force had begun. It was as if they had returned to a crossroads in their existence.

Whatever the truth, I had a very restless night and was very pleased to see the lads back on the Sunday evening. I never stayed a night in the depot at the weekend again.

The months leading up to the start of my RUC course had seen several more murders of RUC men. DC John McGarry was killed by an under-car booby trap in Ballycastle. Sergeant Samuel McCrum was shot dead in Lisburn. Sergeant Stephen Gillespie was killed when the IRA fired a rocket into his Land-rover and Reserve Constable Douglas Carrothers was killed by another car bomb in Lisbellaw.

In the student area of the city centre, Constable Edward Spence was shot at point-blank range by a terrorist close-quarter hit gunman. Two terrorists had been dressed in suits in order to blend into the area. One had taken advantage of the fact that the officer's hands were tucked inside his body armour. He had come up from behind and pushed Spence's hands deeper inside the protective vest while his accomplice shot the now defenceless constable.

Although in some ways detached from the vicious world outside the training centre walls, we had to be constantly aware that the moment we put on the green uniform we had become targets to be murdered by the IRA.

On my first evening in the depot I heard the sound of an explosion as a coffee jar bomb was thrown at a police station sangar in east Belfast. Throughout the training, due to the elevated position of the training site, the sound of gunfire and explosions in the city could regularly be heard at night. These attacks, unless they resulted in a newsworthy death, would rate only a brief mention on the local news. Very few made it into the English press. They were too commonplace.

On arrival at the English training centres, you are presented with a couple of pens, a pencil, a rubber and a pad of paper. In Belfast, the only difference was that on top of the small pile of stationery left on your classroom desk was a Ruger revolver and thirty rounds of ammunition.

The revolver was your personal protection weapon which was carried at work, but also, if you were sensible, was never far from your side when off duty. It weighed thirty-one ounces. A solid little lump of metal, seven inches in length. The short barrel of only two inches allowed it to be nestled in the back of one's waistband with comfort. Most officers carried the weapon this way instead of using the pancake-style holster issued.

The double-action trigger pull of twelve to fifteen pounds made it virtually impossible to fire accidentally. It could happen though, in bizarre circumstances. I once met a sergeant who when pissed would proudly show off a perfect groove running down his left buttock cheek. He had one evening run into the pub toilets to take a piss and while standing there had kept his left hand on his Ruger, stuck in his jeans waistband. With the relief of pissing, his left hand had somehow tightened and a finger managed to exert enough pull on the trigger to fire the weapon. The round ripped a trail across his arse, leaving him to stagger into a now silent bar room with blood gushing down his legs in torrents.

Many RUC officers had been attacked while at home, or going to or from work. A typical incident which proved the value of having the personal protection weapon with you at all times involved the son of a senior RUC officer. The son, also RUC, was cleaning his gun on the kitchen table. His father was out mowing the lawn. Two terrorists pulled up on the main road outside the house and opened up on the father with an AK47.

The son, hearing the gunfire, loaded his weapon and reached the front door just as one of the terrorists was striding across the lawn to finish off his father, who had been hit a number of times by the initial burst of fire. To the surprise of the terrorist, he himself came under fire as the son let off six rounds. The terrorist who was carrying the high-powered automatic rifle turned and ran, jumped on the motorcycle with his accomplice and made off. The terrorist was struck by one round and was later arrested. The father survived his injuries. I was later to provide regular soft target protection to that house. In typical Ulster style, the family refused to move after the assassination attempt and instead built a large fence around the garden.

My Ruger was to become my most intimate friend. It was with me at all times while I was in Northern Ireland. It slept by my bed, and during the day sat on the lounge table ready for that front door being smashed in. At an early stage I became determined that if an attempt was made on my life, or worse still a kidnap attempt, I would be in a position to empty the first six rounds at my visitors.

I was socialising one weekend off in a bar which had a snooker-room above it. It was not the best place in the world for an Englishman with short hair to be, but I was not going to let that stop me drinking with mates. As usual I took advice when it came to keeping my mouth shut, by not hanging the big 'I'm a Brit' advertisement around my neck through making my accent obvious.

I went upstairs with a lad called Gordon, started a game of snooker, and generally thought I was being the grey man in the corner. The problem with drinking in many Ulster pubs is that people have a built-in antenna to detect strangers.

Halfway through the game two men came to the top of the stairs, glanced in and moved out of sight. I saw the movement at the door and nodded to Gordon, saying, 'I think we might have some hassle here, mate.' As I said it, four men came through the door. One was reaching for a snooker cue. They were definitely going to go for it. My accent had obviously been overheard.

I flicked my cotton jacket back to show the Ruger revolver sitting in the pancake holster on my hip. 'Don't even think of it, you fuckwit,' I said. Gordon came out with a torrent of abuse in his heavy east Belfast accent. The men froze, unsure if I would use the weapon. I must have looked serious enough. It gave us enough time to get down the stairs and out.

'Thank fuck you had that with you,' Gordon shouted as we legged it. 'I left mine in the house.'

It became clear within just a few weeks of starting my training that the social life of an RUC officer was potentially dangerous to one's health in more ways than one. In the English training centre if you drank more than two pints per night you were noted as a problem drinker. If you got to the bar before 10 p.m., not enough time was being spent studying. In the RUC depot, if you could not pour four or five pints and a couple of shorts down your neck in the evening then it was clear you were some kind of effeminate lesser being.

With the increase in alcohol consumption, socialising outside the training centre brought added dangers. There were areas in Belfast it was risky to stop in even to buy a paper. To drink in a pub there would be suicidal. In previous visits to the province with SB, a standard part of the familiarisation tour with local SB involved driving into west Belfast.

The value of this exercise was, in my view, far outweighed by the risk, especially since by that stage of the day our RUC SB guides would be well oiled with Bushmills whiskey or straight vodka. I had visited the area without incident, but my mate, Detective Constable X, also from the SB office in England, had a close encounter with the potential dangers of the area which left him raging. As usual, large amounts of alcohol had been taken with lunch and by the time he clambered into the rear of the RUC SB man's car he had no idea where they were going and promptly fell asleep. He was with one other SB man from England and two local SB at the front. When he saw me again he described what had happened: 'Those stupid cunts took us into west Belfast. Not just the fringes, oh no, they had to drive us all the way up the Falls Road. I woke up as the car was boxed in at the front and side by black taxis. Those stupid bastards nearly had us killed.'

In a classic piece of complacency, the local boys had driven into the Falls as they had dozens of times before, but this time the sight of four men in suits had aroused suspicion. It did not help that the other English SB man had taken out his camera and taken a few happy snaps. They were nearly his last. Within minutes, the car was being shadowed by black taxis. At least one would have contained IRA men.

As the SB car did a U-turn to head back down the Falls, one taxi had gone directly across its path while a second had come up alongside. This was the moment that my mate had woken up, staring into the eyes of an IRA thug in the back of the taxi on the offside. Fortunately the driver's training had kicked in, and as his partner drew his personal weapon and pointed it at the men who were climbing out of the two taxis, he reversed out of the trap and screeched off down a side road. It was a close thing, and apparently, although trying to make light of it, the two local SB men were visibly shaken. Constable X was unimpressed. Even less so when a few weeks later the two British army corporals, Howe and Wood, were torn apart on live television in similar circumstances.

On weekends off from training we avoided bad areas, but that did not guarantee a safe evening. The IRA would send operatives into pubs and discos frequented by police and soldiers.

One evening at a disco in Bangor I noticed Sid, my milling partner from the first day, double-take and then walk over to a couple in the heaving crush of drinkers. One was a very attractive girl. The other was a clean-cut bloke who looked like a policeman. I saw Sid lean over and whisper something in the guy's ear. He then planted himself about an inch from their faces. They moved back. Sid was intimidating when he was sober. When drunk, he was just plain fucking scary. The couple moved back, and back, with Sid following. Finally they found the exit and left.

I had followed Sid, expecting a fight to start. When they were gone he turned and said, 'IRA.' He knew the couple well from the area he had previously worked in Belfast as a reserve constable.

In the training centre, I was getting a taste for drinking that in the future would nearly fuck my life up completely. My upbringing had been one in which drinking alcohol was an everyday event. Although my dad tended not to drink, my mother always had a bottle of wine on the table at mealtimes. From the age of fifteen she would have lagers in the fridge for me. Drinking from as far back as I can remember was a part of my life. Like many, I did not see it becoming a problem.

The first time I got really hammered was when I was fifteen and drank a whole bottle of Cinzano neat. That effectively put me off spirits for a long time. During my late teens and early twenties, every so often I would get off my face, but I was very fit and quick to recover. I socialised in a crowd of rugby club drinkers. It was a pattern of being pissed one night a week after the game, but it did not seem to do much harm. When I first joined the police I was an occasional drinker. I could take it or leave it.

After separating from my wife in my mid-twenties, my boozing habits changed completely. I had to be very conscious of stopping at a certain point or I would become aggressive. I would often sit up drinking with the lads in the section house until the early hours, even though I was on early turn the next day.

Around that time I went on the CID course, which did not help. It was a work-hard-play-hard course, with too much emphasis on the play. After a couple of hours' study it was expected that you would go down the bar as a class and drink on until the early hours.

My hangovers became severe. I was regularly having seven or eight pints in the evenings. It was starting to affect my work, and eventually I was called in by my Detective Chief Inspector. He realised, I know now, that I was doing the typical bloke thing when a marriage splits up. Hitting the self-destruct button out of guilt. Going overboard on the novelty of being a single man again. He had a few long chats with me. Built up my confidence again. After a few months of that I started listening to my body, and by the time I had applied for the RUC I had become an occasional drinker again. Unfortunately, the episode left me with the potential to become a heavy drinker and I had not come to the best place in the world to avoid heavy drinking.

In Ireland in general, if you 'like a drink', it basically means you go out and get pissed on a regular basis. Among a large number of people it is perfectly acceptable to go out and get utterly blocked, turn yourself into a gibbering, dribbling wreck, come within a drink or two of complete alcoholic annihilation, and then do the same the next day without a second thought. It is a binge drinking culture. Great in some ways, because people within drinking circles are generally not excessively judgemental.

A Special Branch friend recently told me of a SB Christmas function in England to which a couple of RUC SB had been invited. One of them had got so pissed in the pub that he had wandered off and was only found when there were shouts from the kitchen staff. They had walked in to find him pissing in the middle of the kitchen floor in front of all the waitresses. This did not surprise me or even disgust me: it was the kind of outrageous drunken behaviour I had become familiar with.

Drink was to become the potion that brought the evil twin out to play, the guy who was witty and charming after a few glasses and then transformed into an unpredictable, unstable animal. My evil twin was to come out to play more and more as my time in Northern Ireland went by. It's hard to say even now, but I had started the journey towards alcoholism.

Drink and lust are your worst enemies. In the depot on one of the walls was a poster of an attractive girl. In the background were three masked men with rifles. The caption underneath was, 'So you want to take her home? She wants you to meet her brothers.' In the early days, the honey-trap had been a successful tactic of the IRA: using women to lure horny young squaddies to their deaths. I was soon to learn how easy it was to be drawn into a risky situation, if you let your judgement become clouded by booze.

It was a weekend and I was staying with a friend in north Belfast. We hit several pubs in the city centre, finishing off in a disco in a rough spit-and-sawdust dive in the student area. We were both blocked. Smashed out of our brains on a cocktail of Bass ale and Bushmills whiskey.

One fact of life that a drunk man forgets is that if approached by a female in a pub when he is in that state, she is either more pissed than he is or, in the case of Northern Ireland, may be taking advantage of his temporary loss of reason. Brain out to lunch, and dick in the navigator's seat.

She was a dark-eyed student with curly brown hair and a wicked, crooked smile. My mate was chatting to another girl who had whirled off the dance floor into the path of his slurred patter. Within minutes the student was at my side, grasping the top of my arm, smiling into my unfocused eyes and smelling sweetly female and cosmetic above the smell of beer and fags. I felt flattered that she had picked me out.

'I heard you at the bar. You're English, aren't you?'

'Do ya want a drink?' I said, ignoring the question.

'What's your name?'

'Dave.' I was always 'Dave' when I was pissed.

'I'm Sinead.'

She accepted the drink and I basked in her attention, wishing I were sober enough to speak properly, wondering why she persisted when deep down I knew I was a drunken, stumbling mess. I listened to her as best I could in the pounding noise. She had spent time in Boston. Now she was back studying at Queens University.

At last the disco was winding up. I made for the door having seen my mate leave with his new friend. To my surprise, Sinead was still with me, grasping onto my hand as if I was some special prize she had won at the bar. I found my arm slipping around her slim shoulders as we fell into the cold air. She was whispering in my ear. 'Are you in the army?' Warning bells were going off in my subconscious, but as yet not breaking through the layers of booze which sat like an oil slick over my brain matter. 'No, I'm a bit old to be a squaddie.'

It was the first time in the evening she had actually asked me what, as an Englishman, I was doing in the north of Ireland. That was normally the first question. 'I'm on holiday visiting my cousin. I'm a fork lift truck driver in a brewery back home.'

'Sure. Go on, tell me the truth.' She was pinching my thighs and that crooked little mouth was only inches from mine as she pressed herself up against me in the noisy throng outside the pub. 'You could be an officer at your age, you don't sound like a fork lift driver.' She kissed me hard on the mouth. 'Let's keep a bit of mystery,' I said stupidly after she had finished sucking on my tongue. I wanted to be whatever she wanted me to be, as long as she did that again.

My mate had vanished, clearly forgetting that I was staying in his house. I told her so, looking confused as to what to do. 'Here, you're coming with me.' She led me away from the crowd like a large, drunken child.

I was in a lounge with no carpets, which had a threadbare sofa and very little else. Unlike the vision I had stumbled home with, the place was filthy and looked abandoned. There were no personal possessions that I could make out. She had left me sitting on the sofa with a glass of stinking red wine poured into a plastic mug. I could hear her in the hall, whispering into a mobile phone. At last I was beginning to sober up. What the fuck was I doing in a flat in the university area with a girl called Sinead, who quite clearly thought I was a squaddie? Who the fuck was she talking to at 2 a.m.?

As she came back into the room I told her, 'I'm out of here.'

'You're fuckin' going nowhere,' she said with a hard lashing hatred to her Belfast accent. As I roughly pushed her aside to reach the door she became tactile again, running her hands over the front of my jeans. When I swung the front door open, smashing her protesting hand in the process, she let out a torrent of abuse. I was a dirty Brit bastard. I was in her fucking country. I didn't fuck off back to it as she suggested, but I did grab the nearest taxi and made my way back to the relative safety of the RUC depot. The situation remained a big 'what if' in my mind.

I've always had a good survival instinct, even before I became a policeman. At the age of nineteen while hitch-hiking alone in France I had stopped off at Marseilles railway station. A guy had attempted to drag me and my rucksack into the entrance to an underground car park. He was in his thirties and clearly thought I would be easy pickings for robbery, or maybe worse. I never knew. I was very fit and aggressive when cornered, and I nearly took the guy's windpipe out after he had tried to floor me.

In those days I rarely drank. I would not have let myself be vulnerable due to booze, so if a threat came it was easier to deal with. I reflected for a long time on how drink had laid me open in Belfast to avoidable danger. I was embarrassed about the incident with Sinead, and stored it away in my memory as one to learn from. The problem with my developing social life was that lessons were soon washed to the back of the mind with a few whiskeys and beer.

Drinking in the training depot was also getting out of hand. We were known as a wild course who partied a little too hard. Towards the end of the time in training, we were all running too close to the wind.

After one disco I found myself in the women's accommodation with a visiting woman sergeant. It was a sackable offence to put a foot into the female area. As we fooled around on the bed, one of my classmates appeared from underneath it. He had anticipated that she and I were getting on, and had decided to surprise us. Three careers were suddenly on the line due to drunken stupidity.

I realised in the morning that I had to calm down, and that unless the whole course wound their necks in a little, we would all be in the shit. We had a bollocking for our general attitude and one fella was back squaded. We calmed down from that point. Focused on the end of the course, when life would become less carefree.

The classroom work in the RUC depot was very much the same as the drudgery of learning the law that I had experienced the first time around in the English training school. It was a necessary weapon in dealing with republicans who in many cases knew the legislation relating to terrorism inside out. Many thousands of pounds had been paid out in the courts to terrorists or their associates, on the basis that legal procedure had not been correctly followed during searches under the Northern Ireland Emergency Provisions Act or the Prevention of Terrorism Act.

The RUC had always had a strong ethos of discipline. It had to, in the face of such provocation. By the early nineties, the training had begun to incorporate issues of an ethical nature. To the credit of the instructors at the training school, they realised that bad behaviour by police fell into the laps of the paramilitary propagandists. Just a few individuals who were prone to dish out summary justice to suspects in the form of beatings or intimidation could very easily taint the whole organisation.

A typical class exercise would involve putting half a dozen recruits through a scenario which at the start involved an ethical decision. The purpose was to show how a bad decision at the outset of an incident could have far-reaching consequences.

One example I recall is a time we were shown an incident on video. In the scenario, we were viewing from the rear of a Land-rover. The make-believe situation was this: your sergeant, who has recently lost a brother to a terrorist act, is with you in the back of the Land-rover. He is verbally abused and taunted by a known republican suspect as the Land-rover drives by. The sergeant orders the police vehicle to stop, gets out and punches the suspect in the face, breaking his nose. The sergeant then tells the driver of the Land-rover to drive on, leaving the suspect bleeding on the pavement.

At this point the video was stopped. The instructors went round the group, asking 'What would you do?' Most people at that stage said they would do nothing until they had spoken to another sergeant back at the station.

The scenario was then developed further: you decide to let the matter rest. A complaint is made at the station. You are interviewed by your inspector. The Discipline and Complaints department is called in. Suddenly, your own job is on the line. Even in the training scenario, it demonstrates how it is easy to be drawn into a conspiracy of silence.

The training sergeants put a huge amount of pressure on recruits in these exercises. They left you torn between loyalty to individual colleagues who had gone astray, and what was clearly right in moral terms. Put that into the Northern Irish situation where by being moral you were in fact informing on a workmate in favour of an individual who has absolutely no moral problems with going out murdering a policeman, and the whole issue became an even bigger dilemma. It made you think about the big picture. About being drawn down to the level of the scum we were there to protect society from. At the end of the day, you would only discover what you would do when you were in that situation. At least the training meant that the issues would not be entering your head for the first time.

The training sergeants also went out of their way to jump on any sign of religious discrimination. I was once overheard in the bar using the word 'Fenian'. I was hauled in the next day, and for half an hour my job was on the line. I had been using the word in a historical context. Someone had picked up on half a conversation. With several close relations being of the Roman Catholic faith, I was certainly not prone to intolerance of other religions. Once I had explained myself, the sergeant let the matter drop. It did make me very aware, at least, of how careful you had to be in Northern Ireland.

At times it was hard to focus on classroom work, since so much of the training was centered around the use of firearms on the ranges and in operational scenarios out at the army training camps dotted around the Northern Irish coast. We were put through ambush situations and learned to respond to sudden threat scenarios. We were taught to patrol with the kind of caution necessary when patrolling Ulster's streets and countryside.

Apart from the Ruger revolver, we were trained in the use of the Heckler and Koch MP5 with its deadly 9mm parabellum rounds, which, unlike MP5s used on the mainland which were fixed on single shot, could also be fired in bursts of three. It had a muzzle velocity of 400 metres per second, a rate of fire of 650 rounds per minute, and only weighed seven pounds when loaded.

Its bigger brother, which was used in country areas, was the H&K 33. This had a muzzle velocity of 920 metres per second and a rate of fire of 750 rounds per minute. It fired vicious-looking 5.56mm rounds and was slightly heavier, at ten pounds, but still a very manageable weapon to carry.

The words of Section 3 of the Criminal Law Act were engrained by the firearms trainers in our heads. 'A person may use such force as is reasonable in the circumstances in the prevention of crime, or in the effecting or assisting in the lawful arrest of offenders, suspected offenders or persons unlawfully at large.'

Unlike certain, non-special forces, members of the military, policemen, who are closely acquainted with the criminal justice system and know how viciously it can turn on one of their own, take the use of firearms against suspects as a very big deal. As I was later to discover when confronted with the opportunity to kill with my weapon, the notion of standing in a dock facing a manslaughter charge acts as a very effective deterrent to the use of firearms except in the most clear-cut instances.

In the world outside the depot, the terrorism continued. In September of 1991 the IRA attempted to bring their biggest-ever bomb into Annaghmartin checkpoint in County Fermanagh. It consisted of 8,000 pounds of home-made explosive [HME]. Fortunately the tractor and trailer which carried the device became bogged down in a muddy field. As is so often the case, good luck prevented major loss of life at the checkpoint. In a further attack, Constable Eric Clarke, an Englishman and ex-soldier, was killed in a mortar attack on a Land-rover in Swatragh.

All killings fill you with disgust. One killing, close to the depot, was particularly callous. A black soldier from the Paratroop Regiment was shot by the IRA. The soldier was on leave at the time, merely visiting Ulster. The circumstances showed how vulnerable the security forces could be, even in a 'safe' area. The paratrooper had been on a previous tour in the province, but on this occasion flew into the city airport to finalise wedding arrangements to a local girl he had met and become engaged to.

On arriving at the airport, he recognised a taxi driver who had made regular collections from Palace barracks. He assumed that the taxi driver, working for a firm in the predominantly Protestant town of Holywood, would be sound enough. The taxi driver dropped the soldier at his fiancée's parents' house in east Belfast. The excited soldier no doubt told him of their plans to go shopping that day, and how long he would be staying. Unfortunately the taxi driver was an IRA man, put into the taxi firm in Holywood for just such an opportunity. The soldier had signed his own death warrant by trusting a taxi driver on the basis that he had done regular pick-ups from the barracks. That evening the IRA burst into the house in Belfast and shot the paratrooper dead in front of his future wife and in-laws.

As the course dragged on, it became natural just to want to get out and do the job. I was finding the views of a couple of recruits in the squad senior to ours abhorrent, to say the least. I was prepared for a degree of racial prejudice towards my Englishness out on the street, but I did not expect it from work colleagues.

Two of the recruits had been hostile to me from the moment they had first heard my accent. On one occasion, after a few drinks, the reason became clear. 'Englishmen shouldn't be allowed in this force,' one said.

'So you want to be part of the UK, but you don't think anyone else from the UK should serve here?' I replied.

The argument deteriorated into how, in their view, someone from the mainland could not understand the situation in Northern Ireland. Moreover, if you didn't hate Catholics you were not fit to be in the RUC. It was the only time in my service I heard this sort of bigoted talk from a person younger than forty.

It ended with one of the senior squad recruits saying, 'I hope you're the first to get shot out there.' I had to physically stop one of my own squad taking the sad wanker apart. Fortunately, his view was not the norm. Argument will never change bigots like that. It is too ingrained in their consciousnesses.

At long last we reached the passing-out parade day. It is the proudest day for any recruit. The drill display is second to none. Over the months of the course, we had been turned from an uncoordinated collection of individuals into a fluid, self-contained squad. The drill sergeant had done his work well, and we put on a great display for the relatives and friends who crowded the drill square to see their loved ones pass out to their new stations. It culminated in the throwing up of caps in the air and unashamed tears of pride in the achievement of reaching the end of the course.

My parents both came to the passing-out parade. The Parkinson's disease had really taken hold of my dad by now and he seemed to be in another world. The alternating side effects of either rigidity or tremors made movement extremely difficult. His voice had become an incoherent slur. He spent the day in bewildered confusion, while Mum was clearly conscious of the sympathetic glances of the other parents and relatives.

It was extremely hard to see the father I respected and loved reduced to that state by the ravages of the disease. I wished that I had been more aware of how his condition had deteriorated, but I had not seen my parents since I had moved to Northern Ireland. If I had known, I would not have asked them over for the passing-out parade.

Despite the sadness of seeing my father so ill, the passing-out day was still a great experience. I had met several of the parents over the weekends. I enjoyed seeing the lads surrounded by proud relatives. It was what the RUC was all about – a force to be proud of. It was also a time of uncertainty. In the last week, as if to drum in the reality of the task ahead, we had been told by the course commandant to have a good look at each other now. The chances were that when we next met, there would be one or two gaps in the ranks. There were not many RUC courses which went through that did not have recruits murdered in the first few months.

The passing-out parade was touched by tragedy. On their way home from the training centre, two of the RUC band were killed in a road traffic accident. It was sad news as we started on our careers. I was to become familiar with this seemingly endless cycle of tragedy.

The day after our passing-out parade, two soldiers at Musgrave Park Hospital were killed by a terrorist bomb placed in the military ward of the hospital complex. The device ripped through the recreation area used by military patients, while there was a rugby match on TV. Ten others were hurt in the explosion. The individual later convicted of the murders was a hospital porter. It was clear that the IRA would strike anywhere. No place was sacrosanct in their plans to murder.

FERMANAGH

An evening shift in Enniskillen sub-division. Training in Belfast seemed like years ago, but it was only a few months. The car radio stuttered into life with a call from Enniskillen control room: 'Unit for urgent call to Constable Belmont's house. He believes that there was a suspect outside his house trying to attach something under his car. It has fallen off onto his drive and the suspect has run away. No direction of travel.'

As the radio message came over the air on the so-far sleepy late shift, I was manning the town car with Tony. Terrorist attacks appeared to be becoming more regular. A three-kilo Semtex device with the added ingredients of shrapnel, bolts and ball bearings had been found by the road side in Belleek a couple of weeks back. The previous night, in nearby Lisnaskea, the IRA had been disturbed setting up an ambush for local RUC officers. A man acting suspiciously had made off from a van parked in the village. Inside were two horizontal mortars which were ready to be fired at a passing police patrol. When placed loose at the roadside the horizontal mortar could be unreliable, as in November of the previous year, when the deadly projectile from such a mortar had narrowly missed a security force patrol in Newtownbutler.

On other occasions, especially when the device was housed in a vehicle, the mortar was devastating. In March of 1992 it was this kind of mortar which killed Constable Colleen McMurray in Newry. To add to the horror of this attack, the scum who had come out of the pubs taunted, then attacked with bottles, the officers and ambulance men trying to save the dying policewoman. Such memories ran deep. They kind of used up your forgiveness reserves.

We were in a big, lumbering, armoured Sierra – the standard chariot of routine patrol in Ulster – just a quarter of a mile away from where we knew Constable Belmont lived. I couldn't believe our luck. The IRA was so adept at placing under-car booby traps that to catch a terrorist in the act was nothing short of a miracle. What's more, at this very second he was only a few hundred yards away, running like a scared rabbit.

Tony was driving. He was an excellent driver, far better at high speeds than I was, so I always let him drive. The two of us always worked well together. He put his all into police work and he reminded me of a couple of guys I had worked with in the English police. Very tenacious. Giving that bit extra for the job.

Tony had survived two cancer scares and was blessed with an unshakeable religious belief that I admired very much. His God had given him reason to have faith. I secretly wished I could have that certainty. Tony didn't stick religion down your throat, but he was true to his own principles.

'I'm putting one in the breach,' I said. It sounded corny, like a line from a bad script as I said it, but you don't want to spook a partner by cocking your weapon without warning him. I slid the cocking handle of the MP5 firmly back, releasing the 9mm round into the chamber, ready for firing. The MP5 was a weapon you could feel confident with. It was very accurate and virtually fired itself.

It was always hard to make that leap from the steady process of routine but wary patrolling, to sudden extreme danger. The RUC generally carry weapons with the safety catch on and no live round in the breach. That way, when the weapon is cocked, it is a conscious decision that the level of threat has gone up a step. The racking sound of the weapon is sufficient, then, to heighten the senses and create that surge of adrenaline which is essential for conflict. It also helps prevent negligent discharges, known as NDs.

Tony nodded as he concentrated on his driving. He stopped the car short of the address and we both deployed with MP5s in hand. He also cocked his weapon as he exited the car. The terrorist could be very close.

Less than a minute had passed since we had received the radio message from Enniskillen communications. I gave our arrival over the secure radio and asked for further information as we kept a visual containment on the area. It could be a set-up. Our training taught us that you don't go near a scene like this until it is fully checked out, but our proximity to the call made it a golden opportunity to confront a terrorist on a live operation. As far as I was concerned, I was paid a large amount of money to take risks. Our job was confronting killers. Killers who would always have the upper hand by virtue of the element of surprise. Suddenly, we were in a position to give them a surprise.

The house was too quiet. Constable Belmont should have been there, and would by now have acknowledged our arrival. What had happened in the minute or so since he had put the call through?

Tony and I moved closer to the front of the house. My MP5 was ready to fire. The safety was off, and balanced to react to the slightest movement. My senses had never felt so heightened. Could it be an ambush?

Suddenly, as our ear pieces spoke to us, Tony and I simultaneously cursed and looked at each other in utter disgust. It was one of the few times I actually heard Tony swear. Constable Belmont had rung back to say he had moved house the day before. He had moved in with his girlfriend and forgotten to tell the control room. Valuable minutes had been lost because of this fuck-up.

The correct address was only two minutes away at the speed Tony drove, but by the time we arrived the terrorist had long gone. Belmont was at the door looking agitated. He had been alerted by the security light in the drive coming on, and as he looked out he had seen a dark figure reaching under his car. The booby trap device had fallen from the car's belly as the IRA man had been spooked by the front of the house being illuminated. He had run. The device, intended to kill one of our colleagues, was lying just under the car. It was a black video box with a large magnet taped to one side. It was amazing that something so small and commonplace in appearance could be so deadly. It was still highly dangerous.

As other police cars arrived, we began the clearing of residents from houses. If the bomb exploded, it could cause death and destruction two or three hundred metres from the centre of the blast. Some people were reluctant to leave, but we patiently explained the potential danger. In this estate many work for the security forces, or are the relatives of police or military. Eventually, everyone within the cordon area was persuaded that it was in their best interest to leave, and go and visit friends or family for an hour or two.

The ATO (the Army Technical Officer, who carries out the bomb disposal) arrived and examined the device. It could have exploded at any time, turning the car it was sitting under into a fireball of showering, metal fragments. Within a couple of hours the UCBT [under-car booby trap] was made safe and the pieces taken away for forensic examination.

Tony and I were pissed off. If only we had not gone to the old address first we would have definitely intercepted the terrorists as they left the estate. There is only one way in to the estate and we could have blocked it off within seconds of the initial call. We had no way of knowing that the policeman had moved and he probably would have passed on his new address within the next few days. He had no idea he was being so closely targeted. It was just bad luck.

Becoming a target could happen in the most random fashion, such as an overheard piece of information about where you live. Generally the IRA would latch on to a specific routine: drinking in the same pub, or having a hobby which took you to the same place every week. They would then watch you for several weeks or months, building up a pattern, working out the best place to make the hit, calculating escape routes and the risk of being caught. That they had traced Constable Belmont to his girlfriend's home was a measure of how up to date their information could be.

If you drank in the pubs around town you could assume that anything you said, however banal it was, would be repeated and eventually reach the wrong ears. In a small town, where everyone knew something about everyone else, gossip flowed like the vodka and beer in the favourite watering holes. A typical police evening out would start with blokes talking out the side of their mouths in whispers. A couple of hours later, anyone within ten yards was party to the conversation.

UCBTs were a constant source of concern. During this period, throughout the province, the IRA had a fifty per cent success rate with the cowardly device. Some time before Constable Belmont's lucky escape, I was first on the scene where a UDR soldier had found a one-and-a-half pound device under his vehicle. He had climbed into the car outside his house at 4.50 a.m. on a dark and wet winter morning. The estate where he lived on the edge of Enniskillen contained both Protestants and Catholics, living without antagonism. Attacks like this served the IRA purpose of creating mistrust between the two traditions.

The night before, on his way home from the UDR barracks, he had bought a torch so that he could check under his car more thoroughly, and as an afterthought that morning he had picked the torch up off the passenger seat and leaned out of the car to have a cursory look underneath. What he saw froze him solid in his driver's seat. Hanging below him, right under his arse on the underside of the vehicle was a UCBT. Gingerly he lifted himself out of the seat and legged it inside to phone the police.

On arriving I had a quick look so that the make-up of the thing could be described to the ATO, then we cordoned off the area. It was the classic box design, bound with black masking tape and fixed to the underside of the car with a magnet. Again, after four hours in which the mixed religion community sat on the brink of having their homes wrecked, the device was defused successfully.

Days after this attack a colleague from Enniskillen station had a similarly lucky escape when he discovered a device under his car. He had just bought the vehicle, which had a very distinctive number plate. The most recent attack on Constable Belmont, the third in a few months, showed how desperate the IRA in Fermanagh were to have success with the under-car booby trap.

The IRA had not always been unlucky with the UCBTs they planted in County Fermanagh. In May 1991, Reserve Constable Douglas Carrothers had been killed by a bomb placed under his car in the village of Lisbellaw. The memorial plaque in the Elim Pentecostal Church in Brookeborough states 'murdered by terrorists'. The simple abrupt truth of those words brings home, I think, the true evil of the terrorists' actions. The three subsequent targets of UCBTs in County Fermanagh were lucky not to have the same epitaph. Elsewhere in the province, other victims were not so lucky.

When off duty I would generally check my car, but every so often in the first few yards of driving I'd remember that I hadn't, or think that I had not been thorough enough. Then I would remove my arms from the steering wheel (I always thought I could cope with losing my legs, but never all my limbs) and clench my buttocks, praying that the car would not go 'bang!' It was generally true that if the blast took your arms and legs off there would be little chance of survival. If your arms were placed close in against the chest there was a slight chance that the blast wave might not catch them, just your legs.

The most survivable UCBT was when the device was placed in the wheel arch to prevent detection by a target that the IRA would have noticed, through surveillance, only checked the underside of his or her car. It was a cat and mouse game. Even now, working far from Northern Ireland, even in the middle of some European city, I find I instinctively drop my car keys by the driver's door, swoop down and have a quick check underneath. Then I will look at each tyre in turn as if checking the tread, in fact doing a sweep of the wheel arches. However ridiculous or unnecessary it seems I just can't stop doing it, it was so much of an everyday routine.

———

Enniskillen is the main town in County Fermanagh. It is a place of strong loyalty to the Crown, steeped in a history of conflict that runs back to the early plantation settlers of Ulster. It has a proud military lineage. The Inniskillin Dragoon Guards and the Royal Inniskillin Fusiliers were formed in 1689 to defend Enniskillen against James II. Since that date, local men have served in campaigns all over the British Empire. The Skins, as they were known, had fought at Waterloo, in the Boer War and on the killing fields of the Somme.

In 1992 the 5th Inniskillin Dragoon Guards merged with the 4/7th Royal Dragoon Guards to become the Royal Dragoon Guards. The Inniskillin name was lost. The Fusiliers had already been amalgamated into the Royal Irish Regiment. It was an emotional day, even for an outsider such as myself, to watch the Inniskillin Dragoons lay up their colours in St Macartin's Cathedral.

The town also has a large Roman Catholic population who in the past had undoubtedly suffered poor treatment from some of their Protestant neighbours. In recent times, and certainly in the years I spent in the town, I could see no clear evidence of discrimination. The Housing Executive estates were no better or worse whether they were predominantly Catholic or Protestant. They were certainly slightly better, in terms of appearance and cleanliness, than the council estates I was familiar with in England.

The middle classes of the two religions lived in the same streets. Even within the supposedly bigoted world of the RUC, I was friends with several local policemen of the Roman Catholic faith who had many stories to tell of past prejudices, but very little criticism of the current situation. One thing was certain. If you did come out with bigoted language in the RUC, you would be jumped on from a great height by the authorities. Individuals occasionally spoke of such-and-such playing the 'green card' to obtain a position or advancement. In other words, he had used his religion as a Catholic to put pressure on the hierarchy. Most people knew that such talk was utter crap. Any bigots within the force had to keep their thoughts to themselves and their mouths firmly shut.

The physical landscape of the town is dominated by the brooding presence of Lough Erne. It is a huge and unpredictable water mass. In moments, the surface can go from smooth as a mill pond to angry ocean-sized waves. It is even said in local folklore that the Lough must claim a certain number of victims each year. In my time in Fermanagh this proved to be the case, with a couple of suicides, a fisherman and the odd tourist being drowned in the murky waters.

A particularly sad case was one of a German tourist lost overboard whilst pleasure cruising with two friends on the Lough. The body was not found for a week. I remember looking at the bloated purple remains in the morgue as the post-mortem was about to be carried out. Reflecting what a dangerous place the Lough could be. Moments of pleasure could so easily turn to terror and death.

The land surrounding the Lough is of the same temperament. In the claustrophobic badlands of South Armagh's lanes and twisted clan mentality, when violence comes it is not unexpected.

By contrast, in County Fermanagh there is a sense of a tranquil, steady country life. There is a balanced, if at times fragile, harmony between the two communities. This makes it all the more shocking when that balance is upset and the idyllic peace of the countryside flares into bitter violence. In reality, centuries of land disputes and an underlying current of religious distrust mean that the peaceful overview is always likely to come tumbling down. Terrorist incidents did not occur on a daily basis as in some parts of the province, but when they did they were often extreme in nature.

On my arrival at Enniskillen I had been posted into one of the four sections covering the day-to-day policing of the town. To say I was treated warily at first would be an understatement. There was a rumour going around among some of the more geriatric elements that I was not only

English, but an English Roman Catholic. It was the leftover mindset of people still stuck in the prejudices of the 1970s, when the numbers of killings were at a peak, and suspicion between the two religious communities was at an all-time high. It wasn't long before I was confronted with this.

'So what foot do you kick with; are you a Prod or a Taig?'

I bit my lip, still at this stage trying to be patient. I was to learn later that it was far easier to tell people nothing. If it worried them, it was far better to keep them guessing. 'Try and cope with the concept that I don't have a religion. We don't go to church in England much. Think of it like I play golf, but I don't belong to a particular golf club.'

That did not go down well amongst some in a hard Prod farming community. I might as well have said I was second cousin to the Devil. My partner in the car that day, a bigoted old fart, persisted.

'Well you must have been christened one or the other.'

'Let me put it this way. I don't believe in churches, but I do believe in a controlling deity. A big shiny force for good, up there somewhere. In other words I'm a Deist. Will that do you?'

'Yes, but are you a Protestant Deist or a Catholic Deist?'

The bloke was serious. He just couldn't get it into his head that it was possible to be born without a religion stamped into your genetic make-up. Sad. This form of obsession with religious identity was not the normal way of thinking. It appeared only in the older generation of RUC officers, and then only to a small degree. After a lifetime in England being totally unconcerned about religion it was hard to get used to, or indeed listen to.

Fortunately, in over five years I probably only met a dozen policemen who really were concerned about the religion of their colleagues, to the extent that working with someone of Roman Catholic faith would have been a problem for them. Ninety-nine per cent of police clearly understood that the fact they and their families were being murdered by persons of the Roman Catholic faith was totally irrelevant. They were being murdered by gangsters, with an out of date revolutionary ideal which made it acceptable to murder to achieve one's aims. Only on the fringes of society, where the thug mentality ruled, did an individual's religion come into play.

I found the reaction of people to police in crime-ridden estates in England not all that different from the reaction in Ulster. The difference was they did not regularly try to kill police in England. It boiled down to hatred of authority. In Northern Ireland, they could claim that the RUC was a Protestant tool of oppression. In fact, like anywhere, it simply enforces the law. If the Garda were patrolling South Armagh, or west Belfast, they too would very soon be seen as a government tool of oppression. Criminals and terrorists do not like law enforcement. The situation is only complicated when the more gullible in society listen to the propaganda spouted out very successfully by the political representatives of the law breakers.

The nights out were getting wilder. There were a few younger lads living in the station. The need to get your head showered and take your mind completely away from work was always there.

There were many decent girls in Enniskillen, but in the places we drank we were not going to find decent girls. There was a particular breed of woman in Northern Ireland who seemed only to go out with policemen. Money and flash cars had a bit to do with it!

Female visitors were barred from the station at night, but the rule was not seriously enforced. One morning I paused in the corridor as I saw T's door open a crack. He was gazing up and down the corridor like a cautious animal.

'She still in there, then?'

T looked horrified.

'How the fuck do you know?'

'Because I smuggled you both in last night in the car,' I said. T couldn't remember meeting the girl, let alone coming back with her.

We were out any night we were off or starting late the next day. Along with 'blocked', we had another phrase for being severely drunk: 'Enniskillen drunk'. I still use that as a measure as to when I'm moving into a dangerous level of intoxication. After two or three in the morning in a pub in Enniskillen, the whole pub could be so drunk that people were falling back off stools and nobody would bat an eyelid. I was starting to find that I was going into work with a hangover more and more. It was a bad sign. The taste for drink was creeping up again.

As a section uniform officer your role was to answer everyday calls, patrolling with two or three in an armoured car. You would regularly check the mortar base plates (places identified as possible sites for a mortar attack to be launched on the station) and, several times a day, at times and places allocated during the briefing, two cars would RV to carry out a vehicle check point (VCP).

The purpose of the VCPs was to disrupt terrorist movement and, at best, to discover munitions in transit, or terrorists engaged on a live operation. There was, of course, an element of luck in this, because before the road was used the IRA would send a clean car ahead to warn of any VCPs in the area. Sometimes luck was with you. In a random stop, one of my depot colleagues opened a boot to find half a dozen AK47 rifles. By all accounts this was fortunate for him, since he had not been too proactive up until then and was on the point of being hauled in and threatened with dismissal if his work rate did not improve. One good stop like that could make you flavour of the month for a long while.

Doing snap VCPs out in the countryside was an effective but dangerous tactic to combat terrorist activity. They could also be a constant source of frustration. In the early hours one morning we set up a checkpoint several miles from Enniskillen. On many occasions you could set up a VCP for twenty minutes and not have a car come near you. This time, one emerged out of the misty gloom before we had everybody in place. The stopper circled the red torch lens. The car appeared to slow and then reversed at speed away from us, swinging around in a gateway. We scrambled to the two cars. The car that had made off had obviously turned off its headlights, and by the first junction the police cars had to split.

I hazarded a guess and headed towards Kinawley, but by now we were just chasing shadows. The darkened narrow lanes in Fermanagh, with the border so close, worked against us over and over. The frustration was that you would never know if it was a terrorist operation or a drunk driver who had slipped away. It was an example of a typical and weekly occurrence.

In the main the checks were fruitless, but you knew that they did limit the IRA as to when and how they transported the weapons and explosives to kill policemen.

Patrolling had its differences from England. The first time I was driving and a 999 call came over the air for a serious RTA out of town, I flicked the two-tone horns on. We were in the unusual scenario of being stuck in gridlocked traffic in the town centre. My observer that day was a wily old

Fermanagh Reserve man with a zillion years' service. He was a huge, placid fella, who sat in the passenger seat of the car like an enormous bear dressed in an RUC uniform. He ran a farm as well as working as a full-time reserve. Basically, the man never stopped working unless he was sleeping. He had a very ponderous, mumbling manner of speech.

'Cub,' he said (anyone younger than him was a 'cub'). 'Cub. We're not in London now. Let's not be telling them we're coming. We'll get there soon enough without all that racket.'

He was right. The IRA had used RTAs as decoys to bring police into ambushes. It was still hard to get out of old habits, but I was learning slowly.

Ambushes were a very real danger. Many of my own colleagues in the police or serving in the UDR were in the security forces as part-time members. In normal life they were especially vulnerable to attack.

A typical example occurred in early 1992 while I was serving in Fermanagh. A fifty-year-old part-time UDR corporal, who in his day job was the county dog warden, was lured to the town-land of Scardens Upper, near Belleek. A four-man IRA ASU had forced a local farmer to ring in with a bogus report of a stray dog.

The wily dog warden was not one to rush blindly into a call, and it took a second call from the farmer to convince him that the report might be genuine. Even so, he took appropriate precautions. Although part-time UDR, which I was later to find out did not guarantee reliability, this individual was extremely switched on.

The corporal had previously been targeted by the IRA. In 1978, he had been one of a group of Protestant workmen working for the local council who were ambushed by an IRA gang near Garrison. One of the workmen had been killed and the corporal himself wounded with a bullet in his arm and shrapnel in his shoulder. His previous experience had made him wary. As he drove up to the farmhouse he kept his personal protection weapon, a Walther P5, to hand. He had cocked the weapon ready for immediate use.

It was most likely the intention of the IRA ASU to hold and torture the UDR corporal prior to killing him. Ropes ready to bind him were allegedly later found in the search of the farm. He would have known a great deal regarding local men who were in the security forces. In a few hours of pulling finger nails or burning the eyelids with cigarette butts, the IRA interrogators would have extracted valuable information. I have seen photographs of IRA victims tortured over several days to gather intelligence. Evil and barbaric are insufficient terms to describe what they did to those poor bastards. To achieve their aim, the ASU hiding at the isolated farm house planned to take their target alive.

Twenty-one-year-old IRA volunteer, Joseph McManus from Sligo, approached the corporal's dog warden van which had tentatively entered the farmer's yard. He instructed the driver to get out of the van, pointing his weapon at the victim's face. The UDR man knew he was about to die, either in seconds or in the next few minutes. His previous dealings with the IRA had taught him that they were merciless adversaries. He raised his self-loading pistol, and as he did so, the IRA man shot at his suddenly non-compliant victim. The UDR man fired three rounds at the terrorist. The post-mortem would later show that the first round struck McManus's hip and then deflected off the bone straight into the heart, killing the terrorist instantly.

The corporal's problems were only just beginning. The remainder of the gang, on seeing their comrade go down, opened fire on the van. In an exchange of gunfire, during which the terrorists fired dozens of rounds and the corporal continued to return fire despite having to reload after a stoppage, the intended victim managed to drive off his attackers. He sustained serious bullet wounds to the legs, eight hits in total, but remained conscious until the first police officers arrived at the scene. Fortunately the first at the scene were CID officers, which ensured the crime scene preservation was done correctly right from the start.

The remainder of the terrorist gang were picked up by the Garda and charged, initially, with possession of two Kalashnikov rifles and a Webley revolver which were found discarded nearby. Even with that impressive armoury they had been seen off by a fifty-year-old man armed only with a self-loading pistol. They had seen their youngest recruit in the ASU shot and had abandoned him to make their getaway, only to be caught by the Garda hiding face down in a storm ditch near the scene. It was not a glorious episode in the history of the Irish Republican Army.

In November 1992 the two men, James Hughes and Conor O'Neil, pulled out of the storm ditch by Gardai, were found guilty of the attempted murder of the part-time UDR man at the special criminal court in Dublin.

One of my duties, a few days after that murder attempt, was to guard the remains of Joseph McManus as he lay in the mortuary in Enniskillen. It was said that Protestant mortuary attendants had sewn a Union Jack into the chest cavity after the post-mortem, but that sounded a bit far-fetched. Loyalists can have very active imaginations.

The body was returned to Sligo for the funeral, where the priest, a Father O'Shea, stated that it was not a priest's role to condemn someone who had been seen as doing wrong! The terrorist's father, who was a former national chairman of Sinn Fein, expressed pride in his son. That was all well and good if he really believed that it was right to murder and torture human beings to reach a political goal. At the end of the day, you reap what you sow.

———

Until I moved to Ulster, terrorists were not like real people to me. The characters I had interviewed while serving with SB, plucked out of the neutral and antiseptic airport environment, were just individuals we matched up to their files. We expanded those files if the suspect would actually talk to us; sounded them out as potential informants.

I would always dig into their past to see if there was a criminal history which could be of interest. Sexual offences were the best. These details would be passed on to the security services for use as they saw fit. An IRA man would be very loath for it to be common knowledge among his fellow terrorists that he had a conviction for abusing young girls. It amazed me to discover how many of the 'hard men' on either side had deviant tendencies shown up by past criminal convictions or intelligence reports.

Now, in Northern Ireland, I knew where the terrorist lived, not solely by his address on a piece of paper, but by what type of motor he drove. What colour his garage was, how many kids he had and where they could be seen playing. I stopped him on his way to work or going down the shops. If I went to the sports centre I could swim past him in the pool. Even more bizarrely, he would know where I lived too. Very soon some of the terrorists knew my first name. They would nod at you in pubs. All the time, you knew they could be plotting to kill you. It was unnerving at times, and at all times it felt unreal.

My first search of a terrorist out on patrol came after a few days in Enniskillen, when I was detailed to accompany a UDR patrol. The duty was known as doing RUCLO: RUC liaison officer. I had very little warning regarding the patrol I was going out with since the duty came up at short notice.

I was to go out with the part-time UDR in a two-vehicle Land-rover patrol. The unit I was to work with were known as the 'dole patrol'. They liked to call themselves 'full-time, part-time UDR'. In other words none of them had jobs, so they could work each and every day in their UDR role and be paid for it.

Nothing on earth could have prepared me for the shower of shit I was about to go out with. My previous experience of the army had been through my brother who had served in the Grenadier Guards. I had a huge respect for the military. Suddenly I was sitting in a Land-rover with a bunch of men who seemed to view the whole thing as an opportunity to skive and mess about for a few hours. Police had to accompany each UDR patrol because of the past exploits of the particular unit I was working with. Only the corporal appeared to be making an effort to remain professional. He had, in fact, been full-time UDR in the past, which was completely different in its level of professionalism.

The men I went out with that day chatted in tight little groups at the few VCPs they did, presenting a great sniper target. They smoked in public view. Raced each other in the Land-rovers, and then sulked when I told them to stop it. I then had to instigate each VCP, as they had decided not to talk to me. I had eight hours of that shit.

At one point I recognised a well-known and dangerous terrorist as a back seat passenger in a car. I brought all the occupants out one by one and searched them with the assistance of the patrol corporal. The rest of the 'dole patrol' stood back sulking, not even aware until halfway through the search that one of those stopped was a local suspect. They were either completely uninterested or else had an appalling knowledge of local players.

To top it all, after I had finished the patrol I stupidly did not check my kit bag until the following day. Numerous items had been stolen. I had a good memory for faces. The wasters in that patrol were always around the town, getting pissed in the rougher loyalist pubs, screeching up and down Belmore Street in their sad little Vauxhall Novas.

They all paid a price for their actions in the long run. All of them regularly committed traffic offences. I made sure they went to court or received fixed penalty tickets at every transgression. Some of them were used to being treated leniently because they had army IDs. That soon ended when it was known they had stolen from police while on patrol.

In the short term, I remained shocked that utterly useless bastards like that could be permitted to wear an army uniform. It was a sad little element of a generally decent regiment that in Fermanagh alone had seen twenty-four of their men murdered by terrorists since 1971. They were a disgrace and an embarrassment to the vast majority of full-time UDR, and very many of the part-timers, who were extremely professional.

The range of weapons devised by the IRA in order to kill policemen was huge. As well as standard firearms, car bombs and the under-car booby trap, a particularly worrying weapon was the coffee-jar bomb. It was an improvised hand-grenade which was easily made, with up to two pounds of Semtex. It was also easy to carry and conceal. When the jar was thrown it set off the impact detonator as the glass shattered. We were fortunate in Enniskillen when a supply of these bombs was found, ready for use, by workmen renovating a pub. They had been stashed in the pub toilet. This chance discovery very likely saved the lives of police officers in the town – maybe my own! Throughout the province, several soldiers were killed by coffee-jar bombs either on patrol or when they were hurled into security force bases.

The PRIG (Projected Recoilless Improvised Grenade) could be fired direct at police vehicles, including Land-rovers, and was highly likely to kill the occupants. The projectile was fired from a simple tube with a trigger mechanism which rested on the user's shoulder. To balance the tube on the shoulder, and prevent recoil, two packets of digestive biscuits were placed at the rear end of the tube. A food tin containing the Semtex charge was fired from the front of the tube. It was extremely simple, again easy to carry, and deadly.

The mortar bomb was an ever-developing weapon which posed a constant threat. The horizontal mortar could be fired by either command wire, or even a simple flashlight unit. Again, we were lucky in Enniskillen; a horizontal mortar was located hidden in bushes on a road we used several times a day. Why it had not fired successfully was a complete mystery to the ATO who came to defuse it. We breathed a collective sigh of relief, but I had the feeling that we could not continue to escape attack.

There were mortars of all sizes, with varying ranges and trajectory characteristics. Perhaps the scariest mortar of all was the 'barrack buster', which, with a couple of hundred pounds of explosive, could destroy a whole police station and anyone unfortunate to be in it in one hit.

The quest for more firepower by republicans terrorists is unrelenting. Rocket launchers such as the RPG 7 and the Sam 7 have been on the IRA wish list since the 1970s. The only known deployment of a Sam 7, which has the capability to bring down helicopters, was against a Wessex helicopter in Kinawley, Fermanagh in July 1991. In this case the missile did not lock on to the target.

Although the IRA seem more comfortable at times with their own improvised devices, they are willing to try any new weapon they can get their hands on. In February 2000 police in Dungannon seized a RPG 22, the updated version of the RPG 7. Its 72.5mm calibre rocket can penetrate forty centimetres of armour and over a metre of reinforced concrete. The new weapon was found near an army base, ready for use by republican dissidents.

With the constant level of threat to police personnel, I was sometimes surprised that more police officers had not lost it. How had they stopped themselves from taking out a form of summary justice on those individuals in the community who made every working day a lottery as to whether one would get through it alive? In 1996, the RUC was to admit that fifty-five RUC officers had committed suicide since 1970, forty-seven of them with their own personal protection weapons. By the year 2000, that number was to reach around seventy. When the stress of the terrorist war became too much the results were invariably tragic and dramatic.

In 1992, the case of Constable Allen Moore demonstrated how close to the edge some officers could get. In this tragic series of events, the officer concerned was to go right over that edge. The catalyst for Constable Moore's breakdown was the funeral of a colleague who was shot dead by his own wife in tragic circumstances. After attending the funeral in Comber in the afternoon, Moore returned to the grave and fired a number of shots over it with his own Ruger revolver. Local police were alerted and Moore was eventually arrested in his own car, initially for drink driving. His revolver was taken from him.

When released, Moore had consented to go into the care of another policeman to sleep his hangover off, and prepare himself for a police medical examination that day. The police authorities believed that they had done enough to curb the officer's extreme behaviour. But Moore's disturbed mind was, by now, set on a particular course. He slipped out of his minder's house and collected a legally held shotgun from his own home in Bangor. He then drove to the Falls Road in Belfast, where he bluffed his way into the Sinn Fein centre, pretending to be a journalist. There, he removed his automatic shotgun from a sports bag and opened fire, killing three of the people in the centre.

For a while Moore was on the run. I can recall descriptions of his vehicle being put over the air on the police radio. Nobody could tell what he might do next. Eventually he did what so many RUC men have done before. Sitting in his BMW on the banks of Lough Neagh, he turned the shotgun on himself and took his own life. He was as much a victim of the conflict as any policeman shot on the border by an unseen sniper.

The ever-present availability of firearms; the tendency to drink too much; long, stressful hours and a certain tolerance to violence caused by constant exposure to traumatic scenes made the life of an RUC man a dangerous cocktail. In one incident, not well publicised, mobile support unit officers were playing cards in a mid-Ulster station. Drink had been taken, and with emotions running high over comments made by one officer sitting opposite another, the aggrieved, extremely pissed-off policeman emptied the six rounds of his Ruger revolver into his colleague's groin area. The injured officer lived, but only by virtue of prompt medical treatment. The attacking officer's career came to an abrupt end as he was charged with serious assault. Flare-ups were not uncommon, although they would normally be resolved by fists, rather than shots being fired.

The stresses of working in Ulster could also be seen on the military. When I later lived and worked with military units in the Belleek area, it was clear how pent-up frustrations caused by the Northern Ireland environment could be blown out of all proportion.

My first experience of this was in 1992 in Fermanagh, shortly after a thousand-pound bomb had devastated Fivemiletown The First Battalion Staffordshire Regiment, called in to secure the RUC barracks while it was demolished and rebuilt, had only been there a few days when an eighteen-year-old soldier cracked. He shot his company sergeant major seven times with his SA80 rifle, killing him in front of the remainder of his platoon. Bizarrely, when this case was brought before the local court in Enniskillen, the soldier was found not guilty of murder. His defence was provocation by the sergeant major he had killed. Juries in Fermanagh were renowned for strange judgements. This was certainly one of them!

I learnt very early on in Enniskillen that it was not uncommon for a police colleague to go missing for a few days. On these occasions the man would not appear at a briefing, and a few raised eyebrows would signify that he was off again on an alcoholic bender. I had one friend who went for a pint after work and sobered up three days later in Surrey. He had no idea how he'd arrived there, apart from that, in the fourth pub he went to, he recalled meeting a friend of a friend who was a lorry driver, bound for Scotland en route to the ferry at Larne.

Sometimes men would turn up to work drunk, in which case they were thrown in the back of an armoured car or Land-rover until they sobered up. Drinking on duty was less common. It was not something I witnessed until I later worked in Belfast. In Fermanagh, the inspectors were relatively tolerant of the men who had major drink problems. For some there was no hope of redemption. Others would slip between the two worlds of being a born-again Christian one month and a drinking, gambling, whoring monster the next. It was a hard drinking environment, with the inevitable tragedies that come through alcohol abuse.

On one afternoon, while on patrol, I met a local inspector at his holiday caravan near Enniskillen. He was extremely hospitable and for once I broke the no drink on duty rule by having a drink with him and his wife. A few days later the same inspector was found dead at home in Enniskillen. He had gone out for a few drinks after coming back from his caravan break, fallen asleep downstairs the worse for wear, and overnight had choked to death on his own vomit.

To walk into certain pubs in Enniskillen was to be greeted with a bar full of local peelers. Some of them worked in out stations such as Lisnaskea or Kesh and only came into Enniskillen to drink. Many I only ever met when they were smashed out of their brains. If I did bump into them when in uniform, they inevitably failed to recognise me.

Licensing laws in the town were largely irrelevant. If licensees was brought before the local JP for breaking the laws, they would be fined one pound by that particular resident magistrate. It made putting together a court file rather pointless. Half the legal profession in the town could be found drinking after hours. The majority of people had what could be described as a very European view of drinking – all day and all night – putting County Fermanagh well ahead of its time. I personally never bothered to walk into a pub until after eleven in the evening because there would be no bugger there until then. On many occasions I did not leave my own watering hole until five or six in the morning.

This state of affairs greatly annoyed the large Christian element in the town, who constantly complained to the sub-divisional commander about the lack of enforcement when it came to the drinking laws. The occasional officer would arrive in the town and attempt a clampdown, but mysteriously would find himself posted, in quick time, to a border station. The border stations had their pubs but were harder to regulate. To clamp down too heavily on the village pub in a nationalist area would have created tremendous bad feeling, just where the police needed all the goodwill they could get.

The roads in Fermanagh, in fact, claimed more victims than the terrorist campaign. Up until July 1992, twenty people were killed in eighteen months on Enniskillen's roads. Not all deaths were due to drink. There was a culture of driving at great speed on roads which were designed, in the main, to take agricultural vehicles. Some deaths were, however, due to an old-fashioned view regarding drink driving. Although it was frowned upon to get into a car totally legless, most men I knew would drive a car after five or six pints of beer without even thinking about it. Policemen could be the worst offenders, but circumstances made that almost inevitable.

A story that made the local papers when I was in the depot was enough, I thought, to put any policeman off driving while drunk. A policeman from Newtownards station was driving home one evening when he hit a man crossing the road. He was so pissed that he did not notice the man land on his bonnet and remain there. He didn't hear the victim screaming; one of the man's legs had been caught up in the wheel arch of his car. The policeman carried on a few miles to his home, parked up in his drive, and went to bed. Neighbours came out after hearing the man's screams, found him still stuck to the front of the car, and called the ambulance. The victim lost his leg. The drunk policeman went to prison.

Even that story did not change some habits. Many police lived a mile or two outside Enniskillen on 'safe' estates. They drank in Enniskillen, and there was no way they would trust a local taxi driver to regularly take them home and get to know their habits. It was too much of an invitation to be targeted.

It was fair to say that very few people walked in the town. The incessant Fermanagh drizzle didn't encourage that. Driving when half pissed was simply the norm. What made it less hypocritical was that unless a driver was totally smashed out of his head, he would be generally given the chance to be driven home or else park up his car and collect it in the morning. If the police had prosecuted everyone in Enniskillen driving over the legal alcohol limit, there would not have been many left in the county with a licence.

One regular and serious offender who had been let off several times in the past would not take the numerous warnings not to drive home when pissed. On a very windy, rainswept night, this individual, a local car salesman, decided to drive through one of our VCPs. The VCP had been set up to warn motorists of a large tree lying across the road. He drove straight into it and was killed instantly.

In Northern Ireland as a whole, over the course of 1992, the security situation deteriorated. There were bombings in Belfast and smaller towns such as Lurgan and Bangor. I was near to the Bangor bomb, showing a friend from England around with the assurance that Bangor was a quiet place where nothing ever happened, when the bomb went off and wrecked the main street.

The sound and feel of a bomb going off, even when you're a quarter of a mile away, is unforgettable. It gives your whole system a violent jolt. A concentrated shudder flows through your limbs and ends up in the chest. Afterwards, there are always a few seconds of silence. An eerie moment before the scene becomes animate again. Fortunately in the case of Bangor no lives were lost, although in a subsequent attack on the town a part-time policewoman lost a foot in a blast, which was detonated by a terrorist as she walked up to the vehicle containing the bomb.

Despite a 'ring of steel' around Belfast, a 2,000-pound bomb was placed outside and blew up the police forensic science laboratory on the edge of the city. This was a devastating blow for police morale. Many court cases were disrupted because of the destruction of the evidence held at the lab, although not as much evidence was lost as the IRA had perhaps anticipated.

In May a huge bomb at the Cloghogue checkpoint killed Fusilier Andrew Grundy. He died warning his colleagues of the imminent danger. Lisnaskea was blown up in August, and it was only by completely sealing off the town with permanent vehicle checkpoints that Enniskillen avoided being destroyed by the IRA campaign against the towns of Northern Ireland.

Private Paul Turner was killed by a sniper in Crossmaglen. He became the 3,000th victim of the conflict. RUC Constable Jim Douglas was shot while unarmed and off duty in a Belfast bar. At the end of the year we were faced with the tragic murder of Alan Corbett in Belcoo. In the twenty-three years between 1969 and 1992, the death toll as a result of the troubles worked out as one every third day.

I was becoming restless again. Patrolling the streets of Enniskillen was a limited horizon, and since I wished to work in one of the border stations, I knew I would have to serve for a period in one of the mobile support units. My health was suffering through the lifestyle of working in the town. I was putting on weight due to not being able to train as I had always previously done. During the depot training, I had ripped one of my ankle tendons. I had been excused PT for the last month of training and had gritted my teeth through the drill display, but since then had not been able to run on the ankle without it ballooning up.

It didn't help that I always worked in armoured cars. I had little exercise at work. When I wasn't working, because I couldn't train I was often in the pub. It was a vicious circle that I knew I would have to get out of. The mobile support unit do a large number of cross-country foot patrols. They were allocated training time as part of the shift. It was an obvious solution to help me get back on track, but also to gain a broader view of Northern Irish police work.

The MSU were dedicated anti-terrorist and riot squads. They were made up of younger men who had made a conscious decision to be part of a hands-on unit. MSUs throughout the province carry out searches, undertake cross-country patrolling, arrest terrorists on behalf of CID and are called to all events where there may be potential for public disorder. To carry out such work the MSU men have to be fit as well as switched on regarding anti-terrorist legislation. In Fermanagh, many of the officers originated from the county and so had great local knowledge, which, once you got to know them, they were keen to pass on.

I put in my request for transfer. Luckily a vacancy was there due to recent moves of MSU men out to border stations. This was a pattern I hoped to follow. I was transferred straight into a mobile support unit, based in a separate block within Enniskillen RUC station.

One of the first notable events was a massive search operation at a republicans village in Tyrone. Over 100 policemen from the MSU units in Enniskillen and Omagh were involved, and twice the number of army personnel. At the 5 a.m. briefing we were designated areas to search, which ranged from gardens and fields within the village to specific houses and outhouses.

An hour later we were waiting at the heli pad in an army base in Omagh. One by one, our transport, three Chinook helicopters, landed. The rear doors opened, and in two lines the lads from my MSU streamed up the tailgate into one of the vibrating bellies. Within seconds we were arranged either side of the aircraft with a third line sitting between us in the centre on the floor. A couple of excited explosives dogs barked themselves hoarse as they sat in the centre of the mass of police and army.

I counted over seventy people squashed into the metal shell as it heaved itself upwards, and away over the roofs of nearby houses. I was right next to a window. The three Chinooks skipped across the countryside at around 100 feet, oblivious of the huge loads of men they were carrying. As we approached the village they seemed to be jumping the hedges, they were so close to the ground.

In less than fifteen minutes of leaving Omagh, we were running into cover positions as startled locals started to twitch their curtains to see what was going on.

After clearing each area for booby traps we set about the search tasks. For the first time ever while I had served in Ulster, I felt that I was in an occupying army. The village was completely nationalist and strongly pro-IRA. As some of us searched and others gave cover, sullen groups, burning with silent hatred, would gather. Only the very young kids ran in amongst us, laughing and thinking the whole thing was great value.

We moved on to the village sports field and playground. An army explosives dog found some ammunition down the road from our location. The sullen crowd moved off to have a nosey down where the activity was. Some of the local kids brought out a ball, and a game of footie started. For twenty minutes half of our unit kicked a ball around with the local Under-10 team, which swelled from five members to twenty as soon as word got round. We knew we were safe enough playing alongside the kids. Nobody was going to take a shot at us in those circumstances. The game ended abruptly when a few of the mothers appeared and rushed into the opposition's defensive line, slapping heads and cursing at them. They, as far as their parents were concerned, had been playing football with the devil. We called it a draw and got back to our next search.

An hour later we were all flown out of the village, a few munitions recovered. No arrests. A good game of football ruined by angry republican mums. I put it down as one of those odd days, with many contradicting events, that you had in the RUC.

I was to have many happy months with the MSU. Initially, however, I had to learn to cope with the sheer mind-numbing boredom of static VCPs. As I started duties with the MSU, the threat to towns throughout the province from IRA bombs reached an all-time high. The commercial centres of several large towns were literally blown to pieces. The authorities in Enniskillen were determined that this would not happen to the town, and, to combat the threat, twenty-four-hour checkpoints were put into place to prevent a device being driven into the town centre.

This 'ring of steel', a phrase borrowed from the precautions placed around Belfast, was to continue for several months, with the two Fermanagh MSUs doing the bulk of the operation. For a sixteen-hour shift you literally stopped every vehicle coming into the town. The checkpoint duties were mind-blowingly tedious. Between three of us assigned to each checkpoint, we would check the cars and vans or give cover to the checker.

During the shift, you were lucky to get two forty-five minute breaks. Mostly we had to eat packed lunches while we worked. After sixteen hours of that I understood the meaning of extreme boredom. After three months doing those kind of shifts we were all becoming zombies. Some days I was waking up to start it all again at 7 a.m. and finding I had slept with my boots on.

Men would try anything to relieve the boredom. One lad had a tiny radio taped onto the stock of his MP5 with a wire to the ear piece running up the inside of his jacket. We would have passing conversations about sex as we changed points, and then resume them thirty minutes later. Every passing female would be scrutinised, then verbally ripped to bits or given graphic praise.

I remember a story from Belfast, where they were doing similarly long, tedious hours on static points. An unknown peeler in the city was coming up on the radio every ten minutes with the words, 'I'm bored!' Regular as clockwork, the forlorn little voice continued all the way through the shift. At some point a very senior officer had been listening in the Belfast communications control-room when he overheard the bored constable. He grabbed one of the controller's headsets and announced over the airwaves: 'Officer who is stating he is bored, this is Chief Superintendent "Blah", please identify yourself to the control-room.'

There was a brief pause. The whole of Belfast was listening. Then the voice replied: 'I'm bored. But I'm not stupid!'

On another occasion, a Belfast officer stopping traffic on the Queens Bridge in Belfast, into the umpteenth hour of a freezing shift, was pounced on by a senior officer who ripped into him because he was using a Maglite wand torch with a red end attachment, rather than the police issue torch. He was also told to remove a scarf because it was not uniform issue. The man listened to the senior officer in disbelief, wrapped the scarf around the torch and chucked the whole lot in the River Lagan, going sick on the spot. The continuous use of static VCPs were not great for morale.

In the case of Enniskillen the long hours paid off. The town was one of the few not to be successfully bombed. As the threat eased, so did the static checkpoints, and we returned to the varied duties that an MSU carries out. It was realised that once you have permanent VCPs the IRA would simply change strategy. They were too predictable, and tied up men when they could have been used more productively on other operations.

We were dropped by helicopter to carry out searches in remote areas. Set up snap VCPs on the more remote border roads. Patrolled in soft skin cars right down on the border, proactively looking for the terrorist rather than waiting for him to find us. It was a lads' world. Only one female on our unit.

Out of respect for their own security, I will not go into personal descriptions of the unit, but one key characteristic ran through the whole team: a sense of fairness when dealing with suspects. No matter how much individuals were detested for their terrorist associations, they were treated well in the searches of their homes or vehicles, and never mistreated after arrest. Many of the men I worked with had lost friends or relatives to the violence. It never, on any occasion, resulted in excessive force being used, or suspects being set up with planted evidence. Looking back on the provocation, and how easy it would have been to take the law into our own hands, I still find that remarkable.

In January 1993 we heard the tragic news that a young lad who was in the senior squad to my own during training had been murdered on duty. Michael Ferguson was only twenty-one years old. A real decent lad to chat to in the training centre. Not a bad bone in his body, the kind of bloke you meet and just know he is 100 per cent. Michael, who was of the Roman Catholic faith, had followed his father into the police. That in itself had taken a lot of guts. It was never easy for a Roman Catholic to join the force, because he risked being persecuted by elements in that community.

Michael was shot in the head at close range in Londonderry city centre. His colleague had gone into a shop on a call. Michael had been giving cover outside. A young terrorist had simply walked up and placed a gun to his head, pulling the trigger. The vulnerability of all of us carrying out police work was really brought home. You just never knew. The most mundane call could be a prelude to death. To the terrorist, Michael had just been a uniform. I honestly do not believe that someone who classifies himself as a human being could have looked into Michael's eyes and pulled the trigger. Maybe those individuals were so debased by violence that they should not even be counted as human beings.

A month later I had another reminder of the need to be forever vigilant. I was visiting Gough barracks in Armagh, where some of my initial course were undergoing further training. We stayed in the bar late, chatting about what we had been up to over the last year. Comparing experiences. It was a good evening. I, at some point, started to chat with a reserve constable who worked in the barracks. As the drink loosened tongues, he confided in me that he was under heavy threat from the IRA; he had a girlfriend who was a Catholic. The conversation moved on and we were the last to leave the bar. I found myself an empty room in the barracks and slept off far too much Bacardi.

A couple of days later I was watching the news. Reggie, the man I had been talking to, had been killed by an under-car booby trap after a night out to a bar with his girlfriend. While they were in the bar, the device had been planted under his car. His girlfriend had been following him in her own car when the bomb exploded. He lost both legs in the blast and died later.

On 12 December 1993, terrorists claimed two more police officers' lives in Fermanagh. Constable Andrew Beacom and Reserve Constable Ernest Smith were on mobile patrol in Fivemiletown. As their police car came to a junction in the small town, terrorists on either side of the road opened up with automatic weapons. The policemen had no opportunity to return fire. One of them had tried to reach around to the back seat where his MP5 lay. It was a brutal and ruthless attack. Constable Beacom's wife was one of the first on the scene, having heard the shots.

I did duty at the funerals a few days later. It was another wet, dismal Ulster day. It is impossible to give words to the atmosphere of utter sorrow that hung over that small town. In another country there may have been immediate reprisals against republican sympathisers. In Northern Ireland, the victims of violence seem to transcend that human need for revenge. So often I looked at the wives or parents of murdered policemen and felt in awe of their capacity to rise above the crime that had been inflicted on them.

After a murder, one of the more pleasurable tasks we carried out in the MSU was arresting suspects wanted in connection with terrorist offences on behalf of CID. Our task was to lift one of the men believed to be involved in the Fivemiletown killings.

We went with CID officers to a building site. I had been fully briefed on the grounds for arrest. Like many IRA men, the suspect was employed in the building trade. He was identified by one of the collators who was familiar with him. He pointed out the man, who appeared resigned to the fact that at some stage he was going to be lifted, although his hands were shaking as he lit up a fag.

I confirmed his name and then said, 'Listen carefully to what I'm saying. I arrest you under section 14 (1) (b) of the Prevention of Terrorism (Temporary Provisions) Act 1989, as I have reasonable grounds for suspecting you have been concerned in the commission, preparation or instigation of acts of terrorism.' I was effectively arresting him for murder, but all arrests under the

Prevention of Terrorism Act are done using the above wording. I then cautioned him with the caution that at that time was specifically used in Northern Ireland: 'You do not have to say anything unless you wish to do so, but I must warn you that if you fail to mention any fact which you rely on in your defence in court, your failure to take this opportunity to mention it may be treated in court as supporting any relevant evidence against you. If you do wish to say anything, what you say may be given in evidence.'

He made no reply to the caution. It is drummed into the volunteers that they should say nothing.

On the journey to Castlereagh holding centre I had briefed the two reserve officers not to speak at all. As in all cases, whether criminal or terrorist (and in my book they merged together anyway), we were prohibited from talking about the matter for which the suspect was arrested. In this case, if the suspect spoke himself about other matters, it would be an attempt to gather information for his own ends. I knew that when he hit that interview room he would be giving the detectives the silent treatment. I made sure that he did not have the chance to get any chatting out of his system on the hour-and-a-half journey to Belfast. He asked to smoke. That was denied. He even tried some casual conversation. The lads did as I asked; completely blanked him. We left him alone with his thoughts. Did not talk amongst ourselves, and completed the transfer of the prisoner in complete silence. He was handed over for interview.

As on many occasions, we had the disappointment of later hearing that the man had been released without charge. An unfortunate fact of life in Northern Ireland was that it was harder there to obtain enough evidence to charge. Witness statements are difficult to obtain in a land where they can be your death warrant. If there was no direct forensic evidence, all a suspect had to do was sit and be silent for a few days. It was demoralising to see so many guilty men walk free.

The social life in MSU became more extreme as the workload increased. When you work for hours upon hours, in often filthy conditions and with the high risk of being killed or injured, there is a tendency to go mad when a couple of days off come along. Going mad invariably involved drinking huge amounts of alcohol. With a couple of mates from my initial training course, we would often hit the seaside town of Portrush on a Friday afternoon, wallets bulging with overtime money, and not leave until lunchtime on the

Monday. Portrush had the attraction of buzzing little harbourside bars during the day, and great nightclubs to keep us entertained into the early hours. If you wanted to talk, rather than have your ears assaulted by noise, there were a couple of hotels which did regular lock-ins.

It was the perfect place to unwind and forget day-to-day stresses. Also, of course, to meet girls. The north-west of the province had the best-looking women in Northern Ireland. The Protestant-Catholic thing seemed to cease once you hit Portrush. In a culture where sex often had to be an awkward contortionist session in the back of a car, due to so many youngsters living at home, Portrush was great because most visitors were in B&Bs or staying in the huge caravan parks sprawling along the coast.

The first time I went to Portrush I was told that you would have to be minus a dick not to score in the town. As I woke up the next morning sleeping across a table in my mate's caravan, very much alone, I did have to have a little look to make sure it was still there! At least it was clean and I wasn't going to spend the next few weeks worrying if I had caught crabs from some mangy beast who looked like a goddess after ten pints.

I was eternally grateful for a built-in safety valve when I drank: I didn't get horny, just sleepy. It prevented many of the unsociable diseases that some of my friends went home with, and saved me from waking up with the trog from hell. I might have had a snog early in the evening, then perhaps arranged a date for lunch the next day, when I wouldn't be gazing through beer glasses. Then if it was worth following up, well, then we still had one more night. Once I had reached a certain stage in the drinking, more beer and then immediate sleep became my priority.

Northern Ireland was a very small world when it came to gossip. It always amazed me that you could be slow-dancing with some good thing in Kelly's disco on Friday, and on Monday night someone in Belfast would give you a blow-by-blow account of what you had been up to. I was to learn very quickly that everybody knows someone who knows you, or knows of you. I had girlfriends at various stages, and one thing I was sure of – if you did stray, it would not be long in getting back. I limited my sexual adventures to the times I had no girlie back home who would cut my bollocks off! Ulster girls do not mess about if you treat them badly.

Even staying away from one-night stands, I made a few bad choices. One girl, who was, it turned out, a compulsive police groupie, only wanted sex

118

if she was in a car completely naked in a farm track in the middle of the countryside. If it was in a hard republican area, all the better. It got a bit freaky the day she grabbed my revolver from the glove box and asked me to shag her while holding the gun to her head. 'Fuck this for a night's entertainment,' I thought, as I pulled my socks on and drove her home.

That year I attended the inquest into the SAS killing of the terrorist Seamus McElwaine in 1986. It was held in the courthouse in Enniskillen, and for me summed up the twisted nature of republicans thinking when it came to the use of violence.

As an MSU officer it was my job to sit in the dock with the SAS men involved in the shooting, who were brought over from wherever they were serving in the world, and gave evidence from behind a screen. The purpose of the proceedings was for the facts to be presented to the jury, and then the jury to present a finding to the Coroner on the facts of the death.

It has been said that McElwaine was responsible for up to a dozen murders. He was a dedicated and ruthless killer who had been in the IRA since boyhood. In April 1986 he had been preparing another killing, having placed a 800-pound landmine in a culvert on a road near Roslea. The landmine was discovered by the army by chance, and the SAS were put in to watch the firing point. When McElwaine and one other terrorist approached, both armed, the SAS men opened fire. Both IRA men were shot, but McElwaine was killed while the other survived his injuries. The circumstances of the shooting were disputed by republicans who claimed that both men could have been arrested.

In a perfect world, all armed and dangerous killers would be arrested and brought to trial. But to arrest a ruthless individual who has killed many times before, without thought and certainly without mercy, is not as straightforward as some believe. The SAS men I heard in court gave their evidence professionally and with great honesty. They saw a threat to their own lives and acted accordingly.

The jury saw it differently. They were not there to provide a verdict on guilt or innocence. They were there to summarise the facts. They did completely the opposite to what they had been instructed to do by the Belfast Coroner. The finding they produced showed clearly where their political sympathies lay. Much to the annoyance of the Coroner, their spokesperson launched into a finding which in summary said that the IRA man had been unlawfully killed by the SAS soldiers. It was nonsense, but great propaganda for the IRA.

To me it was simple. A prolific murderer had gone out to kill, and while armed had been finally confronted by soldiers. In those moments, it was no different from troops facing each other on a battlefield. McElwaine died as he had lived. By violence. If he hadn't been killed, no doubt many more would have fallen victim to his chosen path for political reform.

Although I was enjoying work, the long hours and constant reminders of the potential early end to life were creating an abusive side to my own character that was not pleasant. I was by now drinking far too much on a daily basis, virtually the whole of my social life revolving around pubs and late-night drinking. I was either on an enormous high, or else grumping about the place in a severe depression. I had begun to flare up more easily, looking for a punch-up during arrests rather than talking the person away from conflict as I normally would have done.

It did not help that I was living for a while in the station complex. Never removing myself from the police environment. Always thinking of the mortar with my name on it, flying over the station wall and into my pokey little room. There were some days when I just lay in bed all day, not getting up until the evening, to go to the bar. I would leave the station complex like a furtive animal. Always looking over my shoulder to see if I was being followed. I was, for a period, acutely aware of my English accent. How easy it would have been to target me with the lifestyle I was living, yet I kept on hitting the same bars day after day.

I was not alone. Other single men stuck in the complex, away from their families, formed the same patterns of behaviour. We egged each other on in our drinking. If I did not wish to go out then Pete would come hammering at my door. If Phil was not in the pub I would go and drag him out from amongst the empty pizza boxes and fag packets in his stationhouse room. It is easier to justify a bad lifestyle when you have company!

One weekend I was in Amsterdam on a stag party extravaganza with a police friend from England and his mates, and for good measure had brought along a couple of close friends from the RUC. I was the best man.

We did the usual tours of the bars and the red light district over the three nights we were there. It was noticeable that when we tried the coffee shops, the lads from Northern Ireland would have nothing to do with dope. It was so far removed from their culture. The police lads from England, many of whom had been students, got stuck into the chance to smoke legally. In my mood at that time, who knows what I could have taken. I smoked dope until I was sick, then smoked some more. I drank, as everyone did, but always took it that little bit too far.

By the time we left on the Monday morning I was a complete wreck. Pissed for three nights on the trot. Even the lads from the RUC thought my behaviour had become extreme. Separated from the others, I had woken up in a gutter that morning, covered in vomit, lumps of the cannabis resin I had been chewing still stuck in my teeth. I had had at least one fight. There were bruises on my face and cuts on my knuckles. I was a complete mess. After that weekend I shook for three days as I went off booze.

It probably did me a favour, because it acted as a turning point in my lifestyle. I was becoming a different character, and not liking that character in the slightest. For the next few weeks I hardly drank. I bought a bicycle and started to train again. I moved out of the station into a rented house. I even took up golf! I had resolved that it would be the last time I woke up in a gutter covered with puke. You have a choice with stress: ignore it, and it will eat you up. Face it and accept the signs, and it is there for the beating.

I had done many stints out in border stations while in the MSU, mainly filling in for sickness in Belcoo or Kinawley. Both were good stations, with good lads in the station sections, but because each station had two sangars the long, tedious sangar duties were shared with the military. This meant that a great deal of time was spent within the station complex. I certainly did not want that.

In the other border station, Belleek, I knew things were run differently. I noticed that on one section in Belleek the lads were always in great form when they went off to work in the helicopter. They were never off sick, which is always a good sign. They were a tight little team, all lads I liked. When one of them left for another station, I held little hope that I would get the posting, since I was well down the waiting list for a border station, let alone the plumb station of Belleek. Fortunately, the man initially put forward to go on that section was neither liked nor trusted by the lads. They had a big say in who came to work with them, and my name was thrown in. Out of the blue I was off to work in Belleek. I had dreamt of working there from the moment I had arrived in Fermanagh. The day I heard of my posting was a damn fine day.

BELLEEK

Belleek RUC station is the most westerly police station in the United Kingdom. It is also the closest RUC station to the border with the Irish Republic. It is separated from the southern side by five metres of river, which run along the station's rear wall. The very fact that it was manned twenty-four hours a day during the entire period of the troubles was an enormous irritant to the local IRA in Fermanagh and South Donegal. The area was constantly patrolled by the military, and in the period I served in Belleek, by joint military and RUC patrols.

We lived with, but slightly apart from, the army within the station complex. Police occupied one half of the ground floor and all of the first floor, while the army lads had a rec room and a couple of operations rooms on the ground floor. Only the key army personnel, being the officer in charge of the platoon, the sergeant, the Int. man and the medic were encouraged to come over to our half of the building. Generally, we never went into where the squaddies lived. You needed clear boundaries in order not to start annoying each other.

The geography of the station made it ideal for a potential attack. The rear wall is clearly visible from woodland across the river on the southern side. In one of the first uses of an RPG-7 rocket launcher by the IRA in 1972, prior to the construction of the later, more robust rear wall, a rocket had been fired from the south. It penetrated the building and struck Reserve Constable Robert Keys in the chest as he walked down the central stairway. He was a married man with six children. He was killed instantly.

On turning left out of the station, a narrow lane called Cliff Road took patrols first to a large field which served as one of the helicopter landing sites, and then, a hundred metres further on, to a border crossing point. The crossing point was marked, and obstructed by concrete posts to prevent a vehicle being driven down the lane. It would have been simple, otherwise, for the IRA to trundle a mortar down the lane and leave it just out of sight of the police station, primed to fire. With typical ingenuity, born from the fact that they have all the time in the world in the 'long war' to address a problem, local IRA were to overcome the obstacle of the concrete posts. Just prior to the 1994 ceasefire, they did trundle a mortar down that lane, very nearly bringing about the deaths of the whole station party.

To go right took patrols down to 'splat corner'. This corner had been the scene of the 1987 sniper attack on Lance-Corporal Thomas Hewitt of the Royal Green Jackets. The twenty-one-year-old soldier had been posted to Belleek only a few days when he was hit in the head by a round, fired from the 'battery' area in the Irish Republic. This vantage point, overlooking the Belleek Pottery bridge, is a hill with a tumbledown fortification on the top. Overgrown and neglected, it was the perfect spot for IRA snipers to pick out targets in Belleek Main Street and was the chosen firing point in the murder of Lance-Corporal Hewitt. Due to this and other attacks, the corner, which has to be crossed from the police station access road to enter into Main Street, became known by security forces and local civilians alike as 'splat corner'.

The murder of the young soldier, newly arrived in Ulster, was especially tragic because he had a pregnant wife at home in England. Every time I ran across Main Street while on foot patrol the murder served as a reminder of the ability of IRA snipers to operate from the south.

Across the border were the towns of Ballyshannon and Bundoran. They had long been favourite bolt holes for on-the-run (OTR) terrorists. Ruthless killers from Tyrone and Belfast could enjoy the holiday atmosphere of Donegal while plotting murder in the north. There were also local terrorists from Sligo, Cavan and Donegal. Even within Fermanagh there were a few who were very active IRA members, but were more inhibited in their actions because of daily contact with local security forces.

In short, there were a lot of people out there in the Belleek area who were planning to kill us. The population in the area of the police station was predominantly Roman Catholic but, as in most parts of the north, that did not mean the locals supported terrorist killers. The locals were, I was to discover, one of the reasons attacks on the station did not have the level of success that its geographical vulnerability suggested they should have had. The local people were extremely decent. Although, before the ceasefire of 1994, basic fear of the paramilitaries may have prevented them from being openly friendly to police, they were not, with a few exceptions, hostile. In fact, behind closed doors the majority were extremely hospitable. However isolated the terrorists believed they were making us feel with their campaign, while local people continued to give us their discreet support our reason for being there was justified.

———

I looked around the helicopter landing area within the military barracks in Enniskillen on my first day of work with the Belleek station party. There was the skipper, the 'big man', who I will call Billy; another constable by the name of Jim, and two full-time reserve cons, Tom and Alan. They were all top drawer. Excellent policemen. Strong individual characters.

They had asked for me to come onto the section, which was flattering but part of the way things had to be done when serving in a border station. The conditions under which police lived on the border made it essential that the station party got on as well as humanly possible.

Belleek station was a very close environment. The police area consisted of an ops room, a sergeants' office, a kitchen and a small radio room, where the armoury was located. All day-to-day activity such as eating, relaxing, planning of patrols, answering telephones and writing reports took place in the ops room. It was lavishly furnished with two threadbare lounge-style chairs and a swivel chair from the desk. The walls were a mosaic of area maps and peeling yellow paint. Wires for electrical equipment ran in crazy patterns, tacked to the wall. The carpet showed the wear and tear of a thousand pairs of boots returning from cross-country patrols. If it hadn't been so ragged the carpet would have got up and walked off, it was so alive with muck.

Upstairs we each had a room, which was a luxury by border station standards. In other stations you took the room of one of the guys from the previous shift, so if your room partner was particularly unhygienic you would have to spend the first hour of duty cleansing the pit in which you would be sleeping for the next few days. We only went to our rooms to sleep, apart from Alan, who went through spells of disappearing up to his den. He was a private kind of guy, and I suppose it helped him cope with the constant feeling of being targeted.

In the attic area of the station was a secure area to which only we had a key. It was used by Special Forces teams who would arrive at the station in the rear of transit vans at night, and take up residence in the attic for days or weeks. They had absolutely no contact with ourselves or the regular army. Completely self-contained in the metal rafters of the building, they would silently leave the station complex in the dead of night. Sometimes they were away for hours, often for days. It was a good indication that the threat level had gone up when a team moved in upstairs. Nobody would ever discuss or speculate as to why they were there, but their presence was reassuring. It showed we were not just being abandoned when the chances of an IRA operation were high.

Billy the sergeant was a keen sportsman and represented the RUC. He was Mr Sociable. A real party animal off duty, but totally professional when at work. He ensured that Belleek was a 'dry' station, never allowing cans of beer to be smuggled in as I had seen in a couple of other border stations. Most of all, he was a great one for looking after the blokes' welfare.

The two reserve cons, Tom and Alan, were as competent as any regular constable and more able than many. They were both extremely funny. Jim was a big country lad. Generally quiet, his tranquil nature hid a passionate temper when he was rubbed up the wrong way. Both he and the skipper had survived the mortar attack on the training centre in Enniskillen in 1985. He was absolutely dedicated in his police work; slow but extremely methodical, yet very fast to react in a threat situation. His mother lived alone on a farm in a predominantly Republican area. For years she had been intimidated to give up the land. To visit her, Jim would park his car miles away and then cut across country during the night. It was known locally that her son was a peeler, and if the area IRA had known he was at home they could have had a hit team at the house within a couple of hours. Even then, he would often sleep in an outbuilding with a shotgun by his side.

The police personnel in Belleek were divided into two sections of five men. One section went into work for three or four days while the other section took their rest days. At the conclusion of the duty period the sections changed over. This changeover was accomplished by helicopter, using one of a dozen or more helicopter landing sites, sometimes up to two miles away from the station.

We would bring everything we needed for the few days on duty. Escorted by military, we would make our way into the station with our rucksacks packed full of supplies for the next duty period. Marks & Spencers did very well out of myself and Billy. We both took the view that if you were locked up for a few days you may as well spoil yourself with the grub. In fact, everybody benefited since we took it in turns to produce meals.

There was always keen interest from the other lads at what Billy and I had in our rucksacks. 'Mmm. Do we have salmon *en croute* for the weekend?' Jim would drool in his country accent as he gazed into my or Billy's rucksack. His culinary knowledge had come a long way for a big country lad who had been brought up on spuds, and plenty of them! Jim could eat until a normal human being would virtually have died or burst open. Yet not an ounce of weight ever showed on him. We all walked off the huge feeds with the patrols or stints in the gym, but when we could not finish what was on the plate Jim would shovel it into himself and still not show any sign of getting bigger. I don't think the gym was an area he ever discovered in the station. His only exercise was the long range patrols.

At all times the police in Belleek, as in other border stations, were assisted by military units who remained in the station for up to six months. Although their day accommodation was in the station, as described previously, they lived outside and to one side of the station with sleeping accommodation under a mortar-proof canopy in Portakabins. The canopy would have offered little protection if a device had landed within the compound. That must have always been on their minds as they curled up at night with their porno mags and pictures of the girl back home, but they never complained about that side of things. British squaddies don't moan about danger. Bad grub or the post not arriving on time, and they could gurn for Britain, but the possibility of a 400-pound bomb landing on your head was not even worthy of comment.

Once in the station you were effectively on duty twenty-four hours a day. With the size of the living space, you were always in each other's faces. Hence the need to be sure you were not landed with a disruptive individual. We all had to get on. If we did not, then the whole morale of the station was in jeopardy.

The skipper grinned at me as the big bird whirled down onto the landing strip in an eye-squinting flurry of dust and furious noise. He lifted up one of my ear defenders and shouted in my ear. I couldn't make out a word he said, but I grinned back anyway and shouted back that I couldn't hear a fucking word. He got the drift and gestured that we would talk later.

I felt happier than I ever had since arriving in Northern Ireland, running into that chopper with my pack in one hand and my H&K 33 rifle in the other. I was now with a group of blokes that, on first impressions, I liked 100 per cent. They all appeared competent and committed to the job. I was never disillusioned of this first impression. Tom was grinning at me in the chopper. He was happy because he had someone new to slag, especially since I was an Englishman. He was a real comedian, brash on the surface but with a heart of gold. Alan was more withdrawn, but still very good-humoured. He was to be my main patrol partner. Jim just looked on impassively. He could look very serious and then come out with the most odd or funny comment of the day. He normally worked with Tom.

The load-master shifted from one side of the big vibrating monster to the other. We sat with our packs on the floor and our rifles between our knees. I saw a note passed to the load-master and then on to the pilot. I should have guessed. They were informing the pilot that it was my first flight into Belleek.

The chopper banked hard right, out over the lough. After a half-mile of skimming the lough surface, the pilot brought the machine up and continued in a steep climb until we were above the cloud base. It was like breaking through the clouds in an aeroplane, except this was no cosy pressurised cabin. It was breathtaking. The noise. The cold. The feeling of just hanging on the clouds in the incredible brightness and blue. I realised that there was sunshine in Fermanagh after all. It was just several hundred feet up.

Then the plunge began. Nose down. The chopper dropped like a stone back through the clouds. This was for my benefit. The best value funfair ride I've ever had. They were paying me to take it! As we approached the water we levelled out. Everyone was grinning, although Alan had gone green. It turned out that he dreaded having a new face on board the chopper because he invariably suffered more than the intended victim.

As we swooped past Rosscor army base the chopper buzzed the sangar.

We were so close that you could see the startled squaddie fall off his stool. The approach from then on into Belleek was where it became tense, since this was the point that an attack on the chopper was most likely. The loadmaster shifted from one side of the aircraft to the other, checking the route in, while we prepared ourselves for the drop off.

On the first day we swooped into the HLS closest to the station. The area was very exposed to the south. As with all changeovers, the military were surrounding the landing site. The outbound section were ready to dash on board. We jumped off and ran with our rucksacks and rifles to the nearest cover point or else just lay flat out in the field, while in seconds the chopper gathered up its grateful police cargo and set off towards Enniskillen. We then sorted ourselves out while the army covered us. Packs on, and then all into decent cover to get our bearings before we set off for the station. Then, after a few nods to the squaddies, we set off fifteen to twenty yards between each man.

The last thirty or so yards we would normally run, bags of spuds bouncing about in our rucksacks, then through the gate. Our army protectors were always the last to reach the safety of the compound within the walls, although I soon noticed how the skipper would make a point of accompanying the last man back into the complex.

Sweating buckets. Into the ops room-cum-lounge-cum-dining-room where we spent the greater part of the next three days, when not on patrol. I was the new boy so I put on the first brew of the shift. The first of many. I was introduced to the station goldfish, Bill and Ben. I had arrived in the strange world of Belleek RUC station.

The RUC station in Belleek had been fortified in stages against terrorist attack. A sangar protected the entrance to the station, which was accessed via a search area and two huge metal gates which were worked electronically. The walls of the compound were twenty feet high, topped with corrugated iron or mesh. Another sangar with slit rifle ports ran along the rear wall overlooking the south. This sangar was not manned at the time, and contained a makeshift gym for the squaddies.

The station building had been strengthened with a mortar-proof roof. Unfortunately the walls had not been strengthened to the same degree, and were showing signs of buckling under the roof's immense weight. That was not very reassuring. When the station was finally demolished after the 1994

129

ceasefire, the ease with which the building tumbled down when the JCB went to work on the walls was disturbing. We had put far too much faith in that mortar-proof roof. If the station had suffered a direct hit from a mortar, it would have come falling down around our ears, in the words of one site engineer, 'like a pack of deadly concrete playing cards'.

The first thing we would do while we had a brew in the ops room was to establish which patrols we would carry out over the next few days. The patrol routes and timings would come down from the permanent RUCLO in the army base in Enniskillen, so we would check these against patrols done by the previous section to make sure that we were not setting up a pattern in timings or locations visited. Often we would have been, so the times would be changed. Sometimes it was good to bounce back out of the station almost immediately to ensure that the changeover time was not seen as an opportunity to move munitions around by the local suspects. On other days we would arrive and not go out on patrol until the early hours of the next morning. 'Keep them guessing' was the order of the day, and fortunately we had a skipper blessed with good common sense and an awareness of the dangers that lurked outside the station walls.

As well as foot patrols, we carried out 'eagle ops'. A chopper would pick us up at a pre-arranged grid reference and take us to a remote area. After an hour or so it would return and drop us several miles away. Once or twice I stopped the same motorist I had stopped five minutes earlier, twenty miles down the road. That certainly puzzled them. Patrols could last twenty minutes or many hours. Variation was the spice that saved your life!

At the end of a twelve-hour patrol, with choppers due to pick us up several miles from the station, inevitably the rain would be pissing down and the weather closing in. It was amazing how often, when the army control asked what the conditions were like for pick up, they were given by the army patrol commander as fine – even if the cloud base was two feet above our heads! The choppers always managed to get through, even in the most atrocious conditions.

It did not take much to unsettle the local IRA units, and luck could be a huge factor in creating a situation where the terrorists would become spooked by something that did not fit into the normal pattern of events. Terrorist operations invariably try to take advantage of the predictable: the police patrol which always collects papers from the same garage each morning; the foot patrol which uses the same barn in a rural area for a lay-up. To counter this, the RUC man's day must be one of breaking patterns. Sometimes this occurs because you remember to do so, and on other occasions through good fortune.

On foot patrols it was good to be paranoid at times. Better to be paranoid than slack, and end up dead. On patrols, the army lads would be watching how you reacted, and I noticed early on that if you were extremely cautious it was picked up by them. I carried a reel of fishing line in my rucksack, and on several occasions when we were on a break from patrolling in some isolated wooded area it proved invaluable.

Many of the lay-up points had been used by previous regiments. Not all squaddies were diligent in not leaving traces of army use. Military debris, like foil from ration packs or fag ends, gave terrorists who were covering the same ground as us a gigantic clue as to where the patrols took breaks. On previous occasions throughout the province soldiers had picked up fag packets or porno mags left in isolated places only to discover when they had an arm or hand blown off that they were booby trapped. We could not call out ATO for every strange object in a wooded clearing we came across, so on every recce of a potential lay-up site I would gently loop my fishing wire around any unusual items and give it good pull from a hundred yards away. The squaddies liked it because they always hoped something would go 'bang'. It also made the newer lads completely switched on to any out-of-place item we came across.

On the morning of one changeover, in a combined operation of Fermanagh and Donegal PIRA the terrorists took over a house belonging to a local delivery man. The house was on the southern side of the border. Together with his family, the man was held hostage at gunpoint. The terrorists took his blue delivery van and carefully modified it, placing steel plates around the interior and cutting a letter-box-sized flap in the rear door. From a distance, the flap was invisible. They then mounted a heavy calibre machine gun on a tripod in the rear of the van, so that the barrel could be put through the flap when the gunman inside was ready to fire at his target – us. If troops or police returned fire, the shooter inside the van would be protected by the steel plates.

At the time that this van was being prepared as a reception for myself, Billy, Alan, Tom and Jim on our way into work, I was lying in my pit in my own house, near Belfast. I had a blazing hangover, probably the first time I had got myself into that state before a changeover day in Belleek. I was fighting a winning battle against the drink dependency I had been breeding in my system during my time with the MSU, but occasionally I would still overdo it. I was rediscovering my fitness, losing weight and generally feeling reborn, but every so often I'd slip back and let the drink take control of an evening.

I knew we had a relatively early changeover that day, but I was determined to leave it to the last possible moment before emerging from my bed to start the hour-and-a-half journey to Enniskillen. I wanted to feel human again. Let the axe through the middle of my brain evaporate. I went back to sleep.

The phone rang.

'Where the fuck are you. Are you still in your pit?'

It was the skipper. I had forgotten that I was meant to pick him up in his house in Belfast.

'No, I'm just up,' I lied.

'Were you on the piss last night?'

There was no point lying about that, because he was going to see the state of me when I eventually got in. I had devil-red eyes set into puffed-up, smoke-irritated sockets. Not pretty. As you get older it can take a day or two to shake off the effects of a bad hangover. I knew my body would be poisoned for at least half of the three-day duty and I was completely pissed off with myself.

Billy bollocked me. Quite rightly, because if we didn't leave immediately we would miss the chopper. You don't keep choppers waiting. We agreed that he should go on alone and I would do my best to make the pick-up time. I dragged myself out of bed feeling like I had let the boys down, unaware that my oversleeping would contribute, by sheer good fortune, to our lives being saved that day.

I missed the pick up. The others had gone up to catch the chopper, but Jim had remained to go into Belleek with me by vehicle. Normally this would be a complete no-no, but on this occasion one of the armoured vehicles we kept in Belleek had come into Enniskillen station for servicing. Jim had the car revving at the gate as I pulled in. He had already signed me out an H&K 33, and within minutes we were on our way via the Kesh road towards Belleek. It is a road of fast, straight lengths and then sudden tight bends. Perfect for

132

an ambush. A few years earlier, before the changeover into work was done by helicopter, two of the Belleek men had been blown off the road by a landmine. A large crater was left in the road, but the device had not exploded directly under the car so they found themselves upside down in a field, still alive.

The road for the last few miles runs parallel with the border, with several access roads and tracks heading into the south. The geography is so in favour of the terrorist that it would be very hard to commit a murder on this part of the border and not get away.

A murder on this road had led to the IRA in Fermanagh and South Donegal being temporarily disbanded in 1988. A twenty-one-year-old local Protestant girl, Gillian Johnston, was shot dead in her own driveway while sitting in a car with her fiancé. He was badly injured in the attack, during which the IRA gunmen had fired over thirty rounds into the couple. The IRA later described the killing as a 'mistake', alleging, wrongly, that the family had connections with the UDR. The local IRA had served their penance and now, six years later, were up and running again.

Twelve heavily armed terrorists were involved in the ambush that at that moment was being set up in the village. They had at least two men positioned on the battery with rifles trained on Main Street. They had a team scouting the road into the town, and the now armoured van was in position at the bottom of the street ready to reverse and then fire on the patrol as it turned into Cliff Road to reach the RUC station. Cliff Road, which led from Main Street up to the station and then on to the border crossing point, provided a perfect killing ground. For fifty yards there was nowhere to go on each side apart from through people's windows. The squaddie in the sangar would have been unable to return fire for fear of hitting members of the patrol. Rounds fired back at the firing point would have been deflected by the steel plates in the van. We had been set up for a spectacular ambush. One that intended to kill as many security force personnel as possible.

Unknown to us, the chopper that had picked up the rest of the boys was running late. It had taken off from Enniskillen and gone to another nearby army base to refuel. Due to this delay, as Jim and I reached the outskirts of Belleek we saw the chopper coming in to the field where the outgoing section were waiting. We paused briefly to speak to the lads from the other team.

'Anything strange or startling?' I said to one of them.

133

'Nope. All quiet. Have a good one.'

It couldn't have been further from the truth. The village was heaving with IRA activity. You couldn't blame the outgoing lads for not seeing what was going on; there was probably nothing to see. Just a well-known blue van in amongst other well-known vehicles in the village. If there were men hanging around on the street corners, then it was no different from many other Northern Irish small towns in which a regular sport seemed to be standing on corners watching traffic go by.

We drove off down the hill. We were both wearing civvy jackets over our uniforms. I had the H&K 33 visible, resting on the dashboard. My hangover had worn off earlier than I had expected, and as always when heading into work I scanned the sides of the road looking for anything out of the ordinary. Part of the training for border stations was reaction to ambush. We had all recently spent three days up in a military camp in the north-west, running through drills after simulated ambushes. It was an intensive training period which involved loads of team work. Instructors would set devices along the roadside, jump out firing weapons or throw thunder flashes. The final series of exercises had taken place at night to add to the realism. It certainly added to the confusion, and I had had a lucky escape when one of the police vehicles nearly reversed over me. I got away with a knee which swelled to the size of my thigh, and probably missed being wiped by six inches. I was thinking about the training as we headed down the hill towards where the blue armoured van was waiting.

The IRA do not like things that break from the norm. Suddenly, having seen the outgoing patrol leave and a chopper swoop in with the new section, the IRA dickers who were monitoring the situation were faced with a completely new scenario. A plain, armoured car coming down Main Street with men in civilian clothes carrying weapons. It was so out of the ordinary that it put enough doubt in their minds to temporarily abort the attack, and witnesses were later to report that the blue van had shot off back across the pottery bridge into the south.

The danger was not over for the patrol. The military team seeing the lads back into the station initially headed down Main Street. It had been the intention of the military patrol commander to go to the bottom of the street and run across splat corner. Fortunately, a squaddie at the head of the patrol, a lad who had recently been posted out to the platoon, took a wrong turn into a side alley, so the patrol came in behind the shops, and a relatively safe route into the front of the barracks. No member of the patrol came into the view of the sniper who was still lying out on the battery in the Irish Republic.

Some time later the IRA unit must have realised that they had panicked too easily on seeing the break from routine. We were to learn that the IRA team stayed in the village until early evening. The van was moved back into position, ready for a patrol to emerge. The panic caused by the sudden appearance of plain-clothed armed men had worn off. They waited for the next killing opportunity.

We did have a patrol of the village detailed for 3 p.m. that afternoon. The skipper cancelled it. There was a football match on Sky TV. We never went out that day and the first thing we knew of the ambush was when the delivery man and other hostages were released and contacted the local Garda. Ballyshannon Garda rang to tell us what lucky bastards we had been. The family and anyone who had arrived at the house had been kept hostage by masked men all day, until after tea time. They had spoken of one man coming back to the house looking wet and frozen. That had been the sniper. Due to a series of events that had thrown the changeover out of the predictable routine, and a good match on the telly, some of our lives were undoubtedly saved. We were indeed a bunch of lucky bastards.

There was no such thing as a typical patrol with the army. Although we had our own tasks, which might mean taking a statement in an isolated location, checking up on a ongoing domestic dispute or just showing a presence in a particular village, to many soldiers the purpose of some of the patrols must have seemed mystifying. That sense of a lack of purpose could lead to them making their own entertainment.

On patrols near the border, you had to be particularly aware of where any satellite patrols were operating. A farmer complained to me one day that he had just been stopped in the south by Brits. When the patrol leader called his team on the radio, operating out of sight towards the border, they swore blind that they were still in the north and had not been near a road. Calls started to come in to Belleek station from the south saying that a British patrol was operating there. We called the patrol in to our location, and again they denied going near the south. The lance-corporal was a scouser, and even his accent had been mentioned by some of the callers. The patrol members were interviewed by military investigators but continued to deny ever crossing over to the south. In the end no action was taken. Going over the other side and doing VCPs gave some soldiers a real kick.

Information that the station was on the verge of being attacked was always filtering through to us. The information would rarely come from local Special Branch, who told us very little. More often it came from the first-rate intelligence collators we had in Enniskillen. They were generally spot on with their predictions. At times snippets came from the locals. From them it was never too specific, just a quiet warning to be careful over the next week. Those hints were appreciated. By saying even that much they were risking their lives.

The isolation of the station ensured that, if attacked, it would probably be some time before assistance arrived. A station takeover was one possibility that we considered seriously. Although we were heavily supported by troops, if their accommodation suffered a direct hit from a barrack buster there is no doubt they would all be wiped out. Anyone out in the open in the compound would also be killed by the blast. The police officers, and any army personnel left scrabbling around in the remains of the main building, could then consider themselves really in the shit. The frightening aspect of the MK 15 barrack buster's power was that the station walls actually made it more dangerous by not allowing the blast wave to escape; it became concentrated, and twice as deadly.

An IRA unit had managed to break into Ballygawley police station in 1985. Two police officers, Constable George Gilliland and R/Constable William Clements, had been shot dead at the gates of the station as they were being opened. Other officers within the station had escaped out of a rear door. The IRA team were believed to have taken guns and documents from the station before making their getaway. A bomb they had planted during the attack later destroyed the station.

This episode showed what a determined terrorist was capable of.

In Belleek we never took it for granted that having a large number of troops with us ruled out the possibility of such an attack. Whether on guard in the ops area or asleep in bed, a weapon never left my side. On patrols I took the H&K 33 for its long-range capabilities. Within the station, I carried

136

around the H&K MP5. That would be more effective in a gun battle within the station complex. I tried to develop a plan for every eventuality, and ran through movements time and time again to impose them on my memory. At night, with the sole night guard answering the phones, I would dream up situations and then react accordingly. If any squaddies had looked in the narrow, armoured-glass windows they would have thought I'd completely lost it.

The time spent feeling that one might be attacked and killed at any time has left a definite imprint on my own mind even now, over half a decade later. When I dream, I invariably have nightmares which involve being attacked in the house. My wife tells me that she knows when I am having these dreams because I let out a constant noise, like a distressed animal. I wake up in a clammy, frozen terror and cannot rest again until I have searched every room in my home. I never had dreams like that before I served in Northern Ireland. If that proves to be the only psychological legacy of being a constant target, then I have got away extremely lightly compared to many other RUC men.

———————————

With the constant sense of an impending attack it was good to have the chance to take the initiative. The skipper came off the phone in his office one lunchtime with a glazed but happy expression on his face. He looked like he'd had sudden and unexpected sex – I knew that look after seeing him at a few wild weekend parties in his house. 'They want us to storm a house,' he announced.

We were all on the edge of our seats. This kind of operation was normally carried out by the specialised firearms unit, the RUC SSU or by the military. He went on to explain. 'Enniskillen have got info that an ASU is camped out in this house prior to carrying out an attack on the station.'

We had been expecting some kind of attack on the station for a while. One plan that had come to our ears was that they planned to mount a mortar on a boat and launch an attack from the river running behind the station. I am sure that all possibilities had been considered and tested, but now at last we had positive action.

The house in question belonged to a local republican suspect and was situated just on the northern side of the border. An indeterminate number of IRA men were currently at the house. It was to be their forward base for an attack on Belleek station. Whether this was to be a gun attack or an MK 15 mortar we did not know. That in itself did not matter too much: the important thing was that they were there. Because it would take too long to bring a specialist firearms unit down from Belfast, we were going to have to deal with it ourselves.

The skipper spoke to the platoon commander on the military side, who picked five of his most capable lads to come with us. Tom was asked to stay behind to do the ops room, but not because he was less able. He was the only one married with a kid; I'm sure that had some bearing. The plan was that we would approach the isolated farmhouse by road. Its location was in our favour in that it was at the end of a road which then came to a border crossing point impassable by normal vehicle. The incoming section, who had been waiting in Enniskillen for the changeover until this blew up, were to fly in by chopper with more military and act as a cut-off if the terrorists tried to make off from the house. Waiting on the other side of the border were Gardai Special Branch officers. They were the only Garda unit that were routinely armed. It all looked splendid in theory. As always, reality has a way of spoiling the best of plans.

We stopped the two armoured cars a few hundred yards short of the farmhouse. The military lads took each side of the hedgerow while we secured the road. We informed Enniskillen that we were in position and moved up slowly to where we had a visual containment on two sides of the property. Like clockwork, two choppers from Enniskillen appeared chattering over the hedges and dropped their loads on the far side of the house.

The lads brought in by chopper confirmed they were in position. They seemed to have gone a long way past the farm, but we moved in closer and I brought one of the vehicles up as a forward control point. It was not textbook stuff, but when it comes down to it, with limited time and the knowledge that the terrorists had fifty yards to run before they were safe over the border, you just have to get on with it.

The skipper and Jim reached the house and took cover, waiting for the other units to confirm they had moved up and were also in a good containment position. I was manning the Forward Control Point (FCP) behind them. A chief inspector kept coming up on the net demanding 'sit reps' and blurting out orders based on his absolute zero knowledge of what was happening at the scene. He was a well-known fuckwit, a pain in the arse, and the last man you wanted chuntering over the radio in that situation. He was eventually persuaded to button it until we had more information.

The house was completely contained by now, by police and military from my section. The troops and lads brought in by helicopter were nowhere to be seen. They had effectively gone missing. They were not replying to my radio transmissions. I began to have a bad feeling.

Our skipper was a dynamic character who did not pussyfoot around. Jim was the kind of guy who would have charged twenty terrorists with a sheath knife in his hand. With the military lads they did an entry on the house and very quickly established that the terrorists had recently left. There was bedding laid out in rooms. Tea recently brewed. Even a roll-up waiting to be smoked. Then the shots started, out towards the south. Our attention was now diverted from the house towards the hedges. Suddenly two of the inbound section appeared like bolting rabbits from the undergrowth, grinning sheepishly.

Slowly the missing patrol rendezvoused at the farm. It had indeed been a huge and potentially lethal fuck-up. The inbound police and military had been dropped near the wrong farm, a good three-quarters of a mile away from where they should have been. Initially they had believed they were as close to the farm as we were and had it contained. Only when they were a little closer did one of the patrol realise it was not the well-known suspect's farmhouse. To top it all, they had stumbled over the border as they made their way back to the correct location. The Garda Special Branch, seeing armed men dressed in dark clothing coming through the hedge, had opened up on them! Luckily their shooting was about as good as the whole operation. In the confusion, probably alerted initially by the sound of the helicopters, the IRA men had made their escape.

In the debriefing the chief inspector from Enniskillen enjoyed slagging off the whole episode. It was so easy to be wise after the event. Sometimes operations go right, and other times they are doomed to go horribly wrong no matter how well you think you have it planned out. At least, I reflected, we had thwarted the attack and given the terrorists a scare. No police or military had been injured, which was the best result of any operation.

Personally, it increased my confidence and admiration for the lads on my own section even more. They had not hesitated in storming a house which they believed contained IRA men. On our side of the operation, we had all worked together effectively as a team. The day could have had a far more tragic ending than it did. That was the measure of a good day in Ulster – nobody gets hurt. No one dies.

We were fortunate with the various regiments that passed through Belleek. It was harder for them stuck in the station complex because, unlike us, they did not have a break every few days. They were in all the times I patrolled with them, impeccably polite with the locals, and incredibly keen to go out and patrol the area despite the dangers. A very few did crack under the strain. One squaddie on my shift shot himself in his side while on duty in the sangar. It was a survivable if somewhat messy flesh wound. The guy had been so desperate to escape home he had turned the rifle on himself. The majority were happy to be in Belleek. It was their professionalism, after all, which helped keep us alive, and for that I will always be grateful.

I loved patrolling the Belleek area. The scenery varied from forest to sprawling peat bogs to tight little hedged fields. The area was littered with decaying, fallen-down cottages, and the occasional abandoned manor house from the pre-Irish Famine era. Prior to the famine which swept Ireland in the mid-1800s the population in Fermanagh had been far greater, but after it was decimated by starvation, disease and emigration, the tiny homesteads had been left to be reclaimed by nature. For those who remained life was harsh. There were still a few homes without electricity or mains water.

On one border crossing point we had regular dealings with a character called Danny, who seemed to be permanently at war with his neighbours. He lived in a two-room cottage and drew his water from a well half a mile away. The lighting was provided by candles and his only source of heat was a peat-burning stove.

The rooms were absolutely stinking. He slept on a mattress covered in old newspapers and the remainder of his clothes. Whenever we were up there arbitrating in the latest showdown with the family of inbreds who lived on the hill opposite, we would be offered tea in metal mugs which hadn't been cleaned

140

since the 1950s. Danny would throw big lumps of fatty bacon into a frying pan full of fat and filth which sat permanently on top of the stove. He never seemed offended when we turned down the chance of tea and bacon butties.

Danny was finally connected to a piped water supply, and had his home wired for electricity towards the end of my time in Belleek. I expect he is still feuding with his neighbours.

Other homes were basic but absolutely spotless. On patrol one afternoon I was beckoned into the isolated home of a man in his seventies. He was delighted to see the patrol coming up the road and had the kettle boiling over the range and ancient hearth before we had reached the front door. His house was immaculate, although it could have been a star attraction in a folk museum showing how people lived in the 1940s. I sat, fascinated, while the old man told me how he had fought in the Second World War, and had been wounded in the desert campaign. He proudly showed me his campaign medals. The man had recovered from a shrapnel injury and returned to Fermanagh and his wife, where he had lived ever since from his smallholding; he was still more or less self-sufficient.

In recent years his wife had fallen victim to Parkinson's disease. We had a common bond there, so it was good to talk about my own father's struggle with the illness. His wife was bed bound, so she now lived a mile away with their daughter's family. He walked down every morning to see her. Otherwise he would sit in his little cottage with his memories, or tend his vegetables. I was the first person from England the old man had spoken to since 1946.

There was very little crime reported in the area. Long-standing land disputes could flare up into cases of criminal damage, but in the main locals sorted out their own problems. There was the odd punch-up in the pubs in Belleek, but it was rare for an official complaint to go in. Any call we did receive had to be treated as a possible set-up. Even RTAs would only be attended by us if they were serious, meaning serious injury or death. When we did attend the scene we would ring a friendly local and ask them to have a drive past the area first to make sure the incident had really taken place. The good side of that type of policing is that people did not bother you with trivia, as they do on the mainland. We did not get called to cats up trees. I am sure the locals realised we had enough to worry about without wasting police time with utter crap.

The method of policing a border station leads to an odd lifestyle. For three or four days you think of nothing but staying alive and policing the local area. On days off you were, in the case of all my section who lived in the Belfast area, literally a hundred miles from that life. Although I was still prone to the odd piss-up with the lads, I was basically living a healthy lifestyle, running, cycling and windsurfing on my days off. Enjoying being more or less single and able to do what the fuck I liked in my own home. My walls were painted white. There was no fluffy nonsense on the shelves. My windsurfing board lay across the middle of the lounge. My bike sat unmolested in the kitchen, and the only cooking device I had was a microwave. For a while it was good to be a single bloke again. The lads would go home, live our normal lives for two or three days then usually meet to travel in to Fermanagh together and catch the helicopter to work, where real life would once more be put on hold.

Sometimes you didn't have to even reach work to be reminded of the constant terrorist threat. Myself, Billy the skipper and Alan were driving into a village one day, en route to Enniskillen, when an IRA barrack-buster mortar went off in front of us. Seconds earlier the terrorists had placed the van containing the mortar outside the RUC station. They had made off on a motorcycle, and as they did so, and as we entered the village, the device detonated, sending the explosive cylinder soaring over the station. Fortunately the mortar only partially detonated, but the blast from the explosive charge that sent the mortar into orbit ripped through the narrow street, shattering the windows of the houses and in many cases showering elderly residents with glass.

We climbed out of our car cautiously to assess the scene. It was rare to arrive first. We were armed with just our personal protection weapons, but we initially kept them out of sight, since the chances of a second attack on security forces arriving at the scene was high. We were in civilian clothes, so again we had to be wary of showing weapons in case we were mistaken for terrorists.

We were so familiar with the way all of us worked that we just fell into necessary roles automatically. I telephoned Enniskillen RUC control-room from a phone box to give an immediate assessment. I was quite happy that the box was not booby-trapped, since at the time of the explosion a little old man had been making a call. He was still standing transfixed, staring at the burning van and the scene of devastation. I prised the receiver from his

142

fingers and shooed him to one side. By talking to the comms man in Enniskillen we established that the RUC station was not manned that afternoon. It was a part-time station and as such an easier target for the IRA.

We still had the very real threat that the partially exploded mortar could go 'bang' big style. There were a large number of residents milling about by now and a few in the houses opposite had injuries from the flying glass. We helped evacuate the older residents across fields to the rear of the houses and set up a cordon. By now people had sussed we were police, and since the other police heading for the scene were aware of our presence there, it was not so crucial to keep quiet about who we were.

When uniformed police arrived we were able to hand over a cordoned crime scene complete with identified witnesses, and a full assessment of damage to the scene as well as the location of the partially exploded mortar. All that on our way to work! I heard later that some of the locals had told the uniformed police who arrived at the scene that the SAS had been in the village at the time of the explosion. This, it turned out, was because they had heard my accent, and assumed I and the other two lads were army in plain clothes. They should have realised that if the SAS had been lying in wait, the IRA unit would not have made their escape that day.

As the threat of a mortar attack on the station grew, we increasingly changed our patrol times to night, and put in place an ambush on the border crossing point where we suspected the device would be brought over. During 1994, in the run-up to the September ceasefire, the IRA tried the barrack-buster mortar at Newtownbutler, Tempo and Rosslea RUC stations. The IRA craved desperately to have success in Fermanagh. Fortunately, during this period their plans to destroy a station and kill all the police within were spoiled because they had not perfected the mortar design.

It was during my time in Belleek that news came through of the Chinook tragedy. In June 1994 a Chinook helicopter containing the top anti-terrorist officers from the police, army and security services crashed into the Mull of Kintyre. In one dreadful accident the lives of twenty-five of the most able men in the fight against terrorism and an experienced helicopter crew were lost. It was a bitter blow to the whole force and the most terrible personal tragedy for the bereaved families. I was at home when the news of the crash came through but as I returned to work a day later the mood was still solemn. The loss of those men made our work far less safe. It will be many

143

years before we know how many lives their work in the shadows of intelligence gathering and covert operations saved.

As usual, the squaddies at Belleek already had a theory about the crash.

'It was a mobile phone,' one of them announced to us as we had our first brew and discussed the crash.

'Oh yes, and how the fuck do you know that?' said Jim.

'Well, when one of the RUC men's wives was told of the crash and that her husband was believed to be dead she apparently said that couldn't be the case since she had been talking to him on his mobile, and he had said that they were just reaching Scotland. They reckon that the mobile phone interfered with the chopper's instruments.'

I never heard this theory mentioned again in reports of the causes of the accident, and I suspect it was one of the rumours that emerge after these kinds of tragedies. In truth, a mechanical problem not yet admitted to may prove to have been the cause of the crash. Having complete and utter faith in the chopper pilots who took us to work in Belleek, I found pilot error very hard to believe as the ultimate cause.

The truth may never be known. The one certainty is that it was a dark day for the RUC. It is tragic that these men, whose work against terrorism was to contribute to the 1994 ceasefire by their bringing about the near-defeat of the terrorists and forcing the IRA leadership to take the ceasefire option, did not live to enjoy the relative peace.

I had become good at lying still by now. My H&K 33 pressed into my shoulder. One round in the breach and my eyes straining in the darkness for movement down the lane. My fingers teased the hard plastic of the safety catch, hoping this would be the night that we would catch the individuals so intent on our murders. I felt it would be a perfect kind of justice for them to be ambushed as they made their way to ambush us.

Of course, it was not officially known as an ambush: we would not have been allowed to carry out such an operation. It was known as a 'lay up'. We were there to observe the border crossing point. In reality however, away from the niceties of language, we all knew we were there to arrest and, if they resisted with force, to kill an IRA ASU.

144

This went on for many weeks. We did not put the lay up position in place every night. That would have eventually compromised the whole thing. As it turned out, the IRA were to have a partial stroke of luck. Sod's law came into operation. One weekend the skipper and I both took the weekend off. The lads in the station did not have the manpower to commit to several hours of watching the border. By chance, the IRA picked this weekend to bring in their barrack-buster.

Jim, Tom and Alan were settling down to what looked like a quiet weekend in Belleek. There was already talk of the ceasefire, although we knew that Republicans Sinn Fein were strong in Fermanagh as well as South Armagh, and it was clear that this local grouping of IRA men were not happy about giving up the armed struggle.

It was this group of individuals who were to form the nucleus of the Real IRA and Continuity IRA who would carry the long IRA war into the millennium. It was like-minded terrorists who would later carry out the Omagh massacre. At the time of writing in 2000, they represent the main threat to the peace process in Northern Ireland. The leader of this faction, a former IRA quartermaster, has had reports of his attempts to continue the violence detailed in the press, north and south. The latest was a trip to the Balkans to set up an arms deal, under the cover of working for an aid agency. Despite this strange open forum on his activities, he is still free, with the Garda apparently unable to find enough evidence to detain him.

In the summer of 2000, the Continuity IRA set off a 250-pound car bomb in Stewartstown, only fifteen miles from the Drumcree protests. Fortunately nobody was killed. There was huge damage, yet it was hardly mentioned by the press, who were anxious to portray the whole of Northern Ireland as infected solely by Orange madness. Subsequent events have underlined the increasing threat from the Real IRA. An bomb attack on a railway line in London. Two 80-pound bombs left at an army base in Londonderry. A mortar attack on Armagh police station and a rocket attack on the headquarters of MI6 in London. A major success for the Real IRA in terms of loss of life or massive destruction is clearly not far off.

In 1994, these dissidents were dangerous extremists on the verge of breaking away from the IRA. Over the next few years they would grow strong enough in numbers, and their own arms supplies, to ensure that despite the talk of peace, another republican terrorist army would carry on the killing. I

145

recall how after the ceasefire was declared there were leaflets distributed by republican Sinn Fein in South Armagh calling Gerry Adams and Martin McGuinness traitors to the republican cause. It challenged them to come to South Armagh and explain to the rank and file what the ceasefire was all about. As far as I know, the IRA's yesterday's men did not take up the invitation.

While the lads in Belleek lounged about and watched Sky TV, the IRA unit were putting in place their next plan to kill the Belleek station party. As with the failed ambush plan they had set in place, a large number of terrorists, probably up to twelve, were involved. The problem they faced was how to move a MK 15 mortar close enough to the station to be fired without being seen by military in the sangar. The plan they came up with admittedly was ingenious.

The designers of the mortar had to overcome the problem that in bringing a mortar down Cliff Road to the RUC station from the border crossing point, concrete bollards which were arranged close enough to prevent a vehicle passing between them had to be negotiated. The solution they hit upon was to mount the mortar on the detached bucket scoop of a JCB digger. The scoop was then fitted with an axle and wheels, and large lifting handles were placed on the sides. The explosives were packed into a modified gas cylinder and placed in a metal firing tube welded to the bucket base. The arming device was attached to a light switch. With over 200 pounds of explosives, the weight of the device was immense, but it could be lifted by four or five men on either side just high enough to clear the bollards. To pull the mortar, two large poles were also welded onto the bucket. As mortars went, it should have won an engineering prize!

A local witness would later tell us that while out for a stroll up Cliff Road he ran into the IRA gang setting up the attack. He described the men as all being masked and carrying long arms. It was a well-planned and determined operation. The man was taken hostage and tied up on the crossing point while the terrorists lifted the mortar over the bollards and started to move it the couple of hundred yards to the firing point.

It was at this moment that Jim took an army patrol out of the rear gate of the station to do a routine mortar base plate patrol. The route they had decided on was straight up Cliff Road. As they clambered through the undergrowth and over a garden wall adjacent to Cliff Road, it is likely that the IRA unit heard the army patrol moving towards them. They had put the mortar in place and even armed it, but instead of taking up ambush positions and waylaying the patrol, something they certainly could have done with the numbers and fire power they had, they simply legged it up back towards the crossing point. By later accounts, they rushed past the hostage they had taken in blind panic. Jim and his patrol turned the corner into Cliff Road and discovered the mortar sitting there looking at them.

The lads and military did a great job in evacuating the station and clearing all local residents. All the time they did this, they faced the possibility of the mortar exploding at any second. This would have meant instant oblivion for anyone within a couple of hundred feet from where it landed. As soon as any locals were out of the danger area, they drew back to a safe cordon distance. An ATO officer attended the scene and did his stuff with the device.

It soon became clear how lucky the lads had been. The skipper and myself went back into Belleek the next morning. I managed to have a chat with the ATO officer, who was still at the scene. He confirmed that the mortar had been primed and ready to fire. It hadn't done so. The officer could find absolutely no reason why the device had not initiated within a few minutes of being primed. When pressed, he said: 'It was an act of God. By rights that station should have been flattened, and everyone in it.'

A few days after this attack, myself and Tom went up to a local doctor's house in the village. The much respected doctor had passed away and it was our intention to offer our condolences to his wife and leave. With the house full of locals and family prior to the burial, his widow would not dream of us not coming in, and we were able to pay our respects to the doctor in the bedroom, given a drink and treated with complete civility. It struck me at the time that this was the true nature of country people in Ireland. Terrorists could throw as many mortars at us as they wished. Our position was completely justified while we had the support and respect of decent people like that. In the final analysis, the terrorists were just murdering scum.

With the IRA activity as intense as it was in the Belleek area, the whole talk of a ceasefire hardly seemed credible. We knew even then that any ceasefire would be a tactical ploy to allow the IRA to gain strength and rethink tactics. The IRA do not call ceasefires when the campaign is going well, only when they are under pressure. It was frustrating to think that they were being given time to revitalise their strategy.

A sub-plot to the intended destruction of Belleek RUC station occurred a few weeks later. The mortar that the IRA had used that time vanished from the station compound in the dead of night. Its disappearance coincided with the return of the serving regiment to their base in the north-east of England. I've since been told that the mortar is now the centrepiece of the regimental museum!

The year had been a violent one, throughout the province. 1994 saw the deaths of several RUC officers. Constable Johnston Beacom of the Markets neighbourhood unit in Belfast was killed when a rocket was fired at his Land-rover from an alleyway off the ironically named Friendly Street. He was a married man with three children. An off-duty officer, Jackie Haggan, was shot dead while watching greyhound racing in Belfast. He was shot once in the head, then again as he lay on the ground. The murder was witnessed by his pregnant wife. In Londonderry, Constable Gregory Pollock became the 296th RUC victim of the troubles when he was killed by a horizontal mortar, fired into the Land-rover he was travelling in.

Throughout the province atrocities committed by the loyalist terrorists continued, in particular the murder of six men watching a World Cup match on TV at O'Toole's bar in Loughinisland.

Locally, more officers in Fermanagh were fortunate not to lose their lives when a soft-skin police car was attacked on the main Belfast Road. Two terrorists on the back of a lorry opened up on the car in a line of traffic. By chance, also in the police car with the three officers was a Sinn Fein councillor being taken up to Belfast for questioning. He, as well as the three RUC men, was injured by gunfire in the attack. It was ironic that the terrorists very nearly succeeded in killing one of their own. One of the policemen managed to return fire and the driver reversed out of the ambush, saving his colleagues. The attack had an international flavour. A bus containing fifty Scottish tourists was hit by rounds in the attack, as well as a car containing two Dutch tourists and a local Chinese resident. It is doubtful that the tourists returned to Northern Ireland in a hurry!

Despite these events, at the end of August the ceasefire did take place. In Belleek, on the last day of the month, it was hard to focus on the fact that from the next day we could be back to normal policing. We were to discover, however, that the local IRA units still had one final message for us.

On 31 August we avoided the Main Street in the village. Again, Billy's

148

sixth sense regarding potential danger was kicking in. Late in the evening we carried out a cursory patrol of the immediate station area – the last before peace descended.

We again kept out of the Main Street and stuck to the rear of the shops.

With less than an hour to go before the ceasefire came into effect, we returned to the station. All the time that we had been out on patrol, a sniper had been in a position overlooking the village, hoping for a final chance to kill one of us. The IRA man, who was waiting on the battery area across the border, would have been aware from the noise of the gate clanging that the patrol was back in the station. He was clearly frustrated, having missed his last opportunity. As we entered the station the sniper unleashed the firepower of his weapon into the station compound, which was visible from his firing point. A dozen or so rounds flew overhead. The crack of gunfire split the quiet of the night. Jim, as usual the first to react, ran to the back sangar hoping to be able to identify the firing point. The attack was over in seconds. The rounds had struck the station fence and passed fifteen feet or so above us. With a deflection the sniper may have got lucky, but our luck held all the way to the ceasefire.

It was a clear message from the local IRA. They neither approved of nor supported the ceasefire. They had been prepared to take our lives in the final hour. Only prudent patrolling at that late stage had prevented us from coming into the sniper's sights. I have no doubt that had the chance of a shot offered itself, the IRA man would have taken one of us out. The 'peace' to my mind had very little credibility.

One of the rounds fired that night was found the next day, embedded in the bedroom wall of a local doctor's house. Again, the terrorists had risked the lives of decent local people to make a statement of their discontent with the idea of a peaceful terror-free society.

After the sound of gunfire had ceased, the police switchboard in Belleek had come alive, with residents of the village ringing in to see if we needed assistance in the station. That was the true nature of the Belleek area; those conversations with the decent people of the village, so pleased to hear that we were all safe, remain my lasting impression of the village.

The main result of the ceasefire at a local level was that we had the pleasure of getting to know the locals far better than had been possible before. For the first time we were served openly in the shops, and when off duty even made a point of turning up in some of the local pubs. It wound the few hardened republicans in the area up a treat.

The culmination that year of this newfound relationship with the public was a Christmas party. Over 100 local people turned up at the station and, with drink supplied by local publicans, partied the night away. It was as if a cloud of fear had been lifted.

In some cases the fraternisation went a little too far. When I decided to check my room halfway through the party, I discovered that a police sergeant from another station had stumbled upon the unlocked door and was now bouncing one of the local girls across my mattress.

'Get off my fucking bed,' I said, trying not to laugh at the horrendous sight of his fat arse going up and down into the ample folds of a girl I recognised from a nearby village. The thought of there being two Catholic priests, a bank manager and a local teacher from the village downstairs made the whole thing even more comical. 'Sorry, Rick,' he said, and the two of them slid onto the floor where they kept humping away. I gave them another couple of minutes then came back and kicked them out, this time locking the door behind me.

On the morning of New Year's day I was out on patrol in the village with Alan at 3.30 a.m. when one of the local publicans asked us to give him a hand in clearing his pub. The place was still heaving. Traditionally we gave the pubs in the village a lot of leeway with opening hours, and, to be frank, on New Year it wouldn't have bothered me if the locals had stayed there all night. They did many other nights of the year. The licensee either genuinely wanted everyone out, or perhaps felt pressurised to look like he was making an effort to close because our patrol was outside.

I asked Alan to stand just inside the door to watch my back, and then went in and politely asked each group to leave. It took a while, and there was some slagging, but the result was that the whole pub of a couple of hundred people cleared out. That would have been unthinkable before the ceasefire – one policeman clearing out a pub in a supposedly republican area!

It was sad that in general you couldn't contemplate a relationship with any of the local girls. Even at that stage it was clear that the ceasefire would not be permanent, and any locals involved romantically with policemen could expect little sympathy from the IRA. It was a shame, because some of the girls were great crack and gorgeous with it.

Like many parts of the west of Ireland, at one time or other there had been some Spanish blood injected into the gene pool, and not just because of shipwrecked sailors from the Spanish Armada, although that may have happened in one or two places if they were not all clubbed to death on the beaches. In fact, during the sixteenth and seventeenth centuries the Spanish had landed several small armies on Irish soil. Since most of the plots and alliances that sent them there came to nothing, most simply vanished into the interior and assimilated with the locals. It was quite common to sit outside a pub in Belleek or Garrison and see some dark-skinned girl with jet-black curly hair who looked as though she would be more at home in Andalucia than Fermanagh or Donegal. We looked, we admired, but the sad fact was that if you fell for one of the locals and ended up marrying her, when the violence began again she would be unable to return home without her life being in danger. I wouldn't have wished that on anyone.

Only after the ceasefire did the Police Authority authorise the building of a new RUC station in Belleek, to replace the crumbling heap that would have been our tomb if the IRA had succeeded with their plans. The fact that the new Belleek station was built to the most rigorous standards, as far as being mortar proof went, was a pretty fair indication that the ceasefire was not being seen in all quarters as permanent.

The new station was built over the next few months. Workers lived on site and we were housed in filthy Portakabins while the rebuild took place. We now really did feel under siege in the station! Vast quantities of building materials were brought into the station each day. The place was overrun with workmen who lived in their own accommodation from Monday to Friday, then were bussed out for the weekend. Huge blocks of concrete were brought in and assembled within a massive metal frame. The new station would withstand a direct hit from an Exocet!

The living conditions and disruption put a different kind of pressure on our little team. It was a time of adjustment to a new way of policing the area, and strangely it felt like we had lost something good in our way of life. It was clear that things would not be the same again.

The sergeant, Alan and myself wanted out of the station. Although the new structure was going to be incredibly secure, the rebuild was a good time to move on. I was to leave Belleek for Belfast before the rebuild was fully complete. I have never seen the new, completed station, but I'm sure the police there now must sleep far better in their beds than we did in the old station.

Belleek was a turning point for me, in that it made me fit and focused on police work again. I was running every day, playing hockey and rugby, and enjoying life with a great new girlfriend. It brought me back from the potentially alcoholic bad lifestyle that I had developed in the Mobile Support Unit. I would never again go down that path. Most of all, I had worked in a team of men who were second to none. We had been lucky not to be killed or seriously injured in our time in the station, but now that time was over, and it was time to move on.

BELFAST DAYS

There we were, in the city centre police car, looking at President Clinton on stage. We were parked outside the Virgin Megastore in Belfast. The crowd stretched away down Donegal Place towards the stage in Donegal Square. It was a heaving mass of expectation, warm with excitement in the November chill. On stage was the President of the United States with Van Morrison. 'There's something you don't see every day,' I remember saying. 'What? Van Morrison?' my partner Tony murmured. 'Yeah, dead on, fucking Van Morrison,' I replied.

Tony was a good lad, one of the younger elements in my section. He had joined the police in the previous four years and was still dead keen. Like me, he loved arresting people, and was one of the regular faces who hauled their catches in front of the custody sergeant. Also like me, he was completely sceptical about the peace process.

It was very bizarre, because despite all the continued talk of peace and the public hand-shaking with terrorists, it was clear to us all that this was a farce. The peace process, by November 1995, was moving far too slowly for the republican movement. As it turned out, even as we stood and watched Clinton, preparations for the February 1996 bombing of the Docklands area in London were being made by the IRA in South Armagh, allegedly with the full knowledge and approval of Gerry Adams and Martin McGuinness, amongst others.

Some of the crowd that day may not have known that the peace effort was doomed. Others did, but enjoyed the carnival atmosphere anyway. It was, after all, a historic day for Belfast. There had not been many reasons to have such a public party over the last thirty years.

Van Morrison sang his 'Days Like This', which had been the soundtrack of a TV commercial showing two boys from the two main communities enjoying a day on a beach together. A year from then, with that song still widely played, it would be easy to reflect that if 'Days Like This' was the anthem of the new peace, it should now be shown as the soundtrack of a video showing the explosion at Docklands, the riots at Drumcree and the bodies of republican drug dealers pissing out blood from gunshot wounds to the head onto the floors of Belfast bars.

Around this period I went to a Van Morrison concert in the grounds of Killyleagh Castle. To my mind, it summed up the times to see that one of the security men employed by the organisers was a well-known terrorist from the Markets area in Belfast. He was a man who had individually murdered policemen, and yet there he was frisking unknowing members of the public.

The 'drug dealer murders', throughout 1995 and into 1996, were worrying because they were taking place not in the estates but in very public view, right in the city centre. When I first started policing in Northern Ireland, drug use was minimal. When I was initially posted to Enniskillen RUC station, I had suggested to the sub-divisional commander one day that we should have a local divisional drugs unit. I had previous experience of setting up such a unit in England in order to target street-level dealers. His response was that there was no drugs problem in Northern Ireland, and never would be one on the scale of England.

In a very few years the availability of drugs had rocketed, I believe partly because there was no structure of localised drugs units to feed information up to the force drugs squad. Paramilitaries on both sides moved in to take advantage of the huge profits that could be made in this lucrative trade. Terrorists had years previously carved up the city into areas of influence in respect of extortion rackets. Now they simply did the same with drugs.

By the year 2000, loyalist paramilitaries involved in the drugs trade were using terrorist methods even in the small towns of the province. In the September of that year, an under-car booby trap placed under a van in the High Street of Bangor seriously injured the head doorman of a club in the seaside town. He had taken a public stand against dealers using the bar.

In 1996, one of the numerous murder scenes, a large American-theme pizza restaurant, was a place I used while off duty because it was so safe. I had taken my brother and his family, visiting from England, there the day before. The next day I was looking in the windows, as I set up a tape cordon

154

around the place, at the body of an INLA member who was shot at close range several times by a fellow member of INLA. Supposedly the organisation was split by a disagreement as to whether or not to declare a ceasefire. The victim had been arrested in the Republic of Ireland in 1995, and without the permission of INLA members in Belfast had allowed his lawyer at the Special Criminal Court in Dublin to read a statement declaring an INLA ceasefire. In reality, it was just an internal power struggle. Watching the pool of blood spread over the floor, where I had stood not many hours earlier with my brother and young nephew, I resolved to review the places I regularly used in the city.

We did our bit that day to help things go smoothly for Mr President. We ferried worried-looking Secret Service agents around to locations in the city where they were to mingle with the crowds. I don't think I had ever seen a fawn-coloured knee-length raincoat in Belfast before, so with those on, and of course their little Secret Service pins on the lapels, they did look a bit conspicuous.

There would have been no threat to President Clinton from the republicans elements. So much of Sinn Fein's efforts were geared towards keeping America sweet. There was a more realistic threat from extreme loyalists, as in unionist circles the US administration was perceived as pro-republican.

Security was as tight as if the President were visiting the Middle East. Andy and I had watched the presidential motorcade come down the motorway from the airport. The M2 was completely closed for the event, and all the highly polished RUC traffic cars were at points along the route. Due to a traffic problem on the flyover link, our minging, mud-splattered armoured Sierra had found itself on the opposite carriageway as the presidential limo cruised past. We had a great view, and could almost feel the senior officers in the procession cringing as the battered old workhorse we were driving came into view.

The day had been a triumph of planning for the senior officers and operational office at Musgrave Street RUC station. Plenty of reasons to pat themselves heartily on the back and knock back large measures of Bushmills whiskey at the end of the day.

The only small hiccup came when a notorious inspector, who went through life permanently half-pissed, tried to lead a bunch of school children who were standing on the fringe of the crowd around the Markets area in a little song for the President. To the horror of the other officers present, the President's limo actually stopped. Unfortunately the children of the Markets were not playing to the same script. As the merry inspector waved his police cap around, wildly conducting the improvised choir, one of the kids grabbed the cap and made off with it. The inspector tried to give chase and chaos broke out in the crowd. The motorcade rapidly moved on. The inspector played no further part in the day's events, probably retiring to the bar for the rest of the day. He has since retired from the job.

I had applied for a transfer from Belleek RUC station to Belfast with the logic, at the time, that the whole method of policing Belleek would change. No longer would we be choppered in for a few days at a time. The military that lived in the station with us would be withdrawn. The tight comradeship of the station would be lost as it reverted to a sleepy country hollow.

It was also a question of money – it would be a lie to pretend that it was not. We earned a good salary in Belleek because we had built-in overtime of over 100 hours a month. It was hard-earned, but certainly made the long hours and risk more palatable. That too was likely to go, so if I was to return to a normal police salary (Belleek probably added £400 per month onto my wages), it would be preferable to live nearer my home in Belfast.

I recalled talking to a policeman who had served for over thirty years in Fermanagh, whose first posting as a young constable was to Belleek before the troubles. He had reminisced: 'There was very little to do in the station. We lived in of course, not because it was dangerous; all single men in those days lived in. There was a lot of cooking and cleaning. Every day, the sergeant would give me an envelope and off I would go on the police pedal cycle to meet the probationer from Kesh, who would start out from his station at the same time. We normally met after about seven miles. He would hand me an envelope from the sergeant in charge of Kesh station. After months of this we got curious, and one day when we met up we decided to look in the envelopes. Two blank pieces of paper! The sergeants had been doing this for years to keep the probationers busy. It was that quiet.'

The thought of that kind of environment made me shudder. If Belleek was to return to a normal opening station, with no army and a small number of police keeping it ticking over, I knew that there would be plenty of local men who would jump at the chance of working there. As far away as possible from the police authorities based in Enniskillen. Belleek always had the reputation of being a far-flung outpost. It was, after all, the most westerly British police station. Its isolation was one of the attractions of the place.

I was, as it turned out, totally mistaken. By the time the transfer came through it was becoming clear that things would not be changing in Belleek. The peace was far too fragile. Local IRA were too closely linked with breakaway republican groups. But by then it was too late. In many ways I also thought Belfast would be good for my career, so rather than try and renege on the transfer I resolved to throw myself into the faster-paced life of Belfast city centre.

The sergeant, Billy, and Alan my patrol partner left at about the same time as me. Only two of the five on my shift at the station remained. We had a couple of wild leaving drinking sessions, one of them in a village within our area, which annoyed local suspects no end. Then that was it. In early summer, I started at Musgrave Street RUC. I was about to have a huge culture shock.

Belfast is a city carved up into orange and green areas, with the majority of Protestants living to the east of the city centre and Catholic residents to the west. Within that huge generalisation, you find a large Prod community around the Shankill Road and to the north-west, and on the east side of the River Lagan, the nationalist Short Strand area bordering on hard Prod land at the bottom of the Newtownards Road. It is forever shifting, as residents in small enclaves, such as the several encircled Protestant communities in west Belfast, start to feel uncomfortable and move on. In some areas there is a permanent under-current of ethnic cleansing. It affects both communities and is instigated by a very few individuals. Unfortunately, the fear factor is huge. The current situation on the Shankill Road has complicated matters further. A feud between the UFF and the UVF has created divisions within the Protestant community, splitting the upper and lower Shankill and forcing many Protestants to move home because of threats from other Protestants. Working-class Protestant areas are commencing a trend of violent self-destruction. The city centre, on the other hand, has never appeared as calm and prosperous as it does today.

The Belfast of the year 2000 has changed beyond recognition from the Belfast I first saw over ten years ago. Apartment blocks have sprung up overlooking the Lagan, rubbing shoulders with international hotel chains and huge construction projects such as the domed concert hall. The west side of the docks has become a tastefully designed office area, and more recently a vast ice-skating arena and science park complex is appearing out of the rubble of the east docks. New clubs and restaurants seem to appear on a daily basis.

Belfast has become buzzing and cosmopolitan, a rival to any European city. Even five years ago, although the foundations for much of this rejuvenation were being laid, it was not apparent that the whole momentum would survive such a fragile ceasefire. House prices in parts of west and south Belfast have almost doubled in recent years. Many buyers are from the south of Ireland, where a property in Dublin can cost more than in London.

Belfast has re-invented itself, despite a dark history and an appalling international image. Around 250 security force personnel have been murdered in Belfast alone during the modern troubles. Well over a thousand civilians have died in the Belfast area as a direct result of the conflict. To many people's minds, Belfast will always be associated with news stories such as the Shankhill butchers and the murder of the two British corporals, and images of burning vehicles and running battles with police and army. That those memories are now giving way to modern and positive images is an enormous credit to the decent people of Belfast.

Every July a period of madness takes hold again, when loyalist elements set up barricades in protest at the restrictions put on them to march traditional routes. What has become a predictable few days of violence and disruption over the last few summers is in reality small scale in the context of a thirty-year terrorist campaign. A greater tragedy would be if a few dissident republicans who believe violence is the only way to achieve their aims drag the city back to those dark times. Just prior to St Patrick's Day 2000, with most of Northern Ireland's politicians over in Washington, the RUC seizure of 500 pounds of explosives in two vans outside Hillsborough prevented republican terrorists from sending a brutal message to the absent politicians. One of those arrested at the scene had been released under the terms of the Good Friday Agreement.

I came into Musgrave Street station a couple of days before my first shift so that I could get my bearings and unload all my gear, to save time when I started work. After being used to the half-dozen rooms in Belleek station, the main building in Musgrave appeared to be a maze of grey dusty corridors. In this station in particular, the spending priorities towards overtime budgets against building improvements were clearly apparent. The place was dirty, peeling and musty. Thirty years of neglect had taken their toll.

I found the locker-rooms where the officers changed. They were in old Portakabins under a mortar-proof cover. It looked like a refugee camp. On top of the lockers, every conceivable item filled the space to the ceiling. Boots, bags, empty crates of lager. A spade, part of an engine. Even items marked as court exhibits.

A couple of policemen walked past me as I strolled about getting my bearings. 'How's it going?' I said. I received a half-grunt of acknowledgement back. It was very different from Fermanagh. Down there, within two minutes they would have asked enough questions to write a potted history of my life.

I was thinking about those court exhibits just flung onto the top of lockers. I always thought that elements of the legal process were strange in Northern Ireland, such as officers retaining exhibits themselves to look after rather than placing them in a secure property store, where they could be monitored. Also, officers in Ulster retained the original court file: all the original statements and contemporaneous notes were kept in one bundle. In English forces, once submitted the original file was kept by the process unit. If it was lost the whole case was down the pan.

There was a lot of potential for disaster in the RUC system, yet nobody seemed too concerned to change it. There was always a strange determination within the RUC not to do things the 'English police way'. To be fair, files were not lost too often, but even losing things occasionally was annoying and totally avoidable.

Original files could disappear for reasons other than carelessness. There was often talk of cases being 'squared' by CID or by senior officers. In other words, the file would disappear and the case never reached court. The reasons for this could range from a charged individual being an informant, and therefore being done a favour because of his value, or, at the most irritating end of the scale, pure nepotism. A mate of a senior officer having his drink-driving case dropped.

Towards the end of my time in the city, this situation improved with the introduction of an English-style paperwork process unit, put together by a very capable sergeant who was later to be killed in tragic circumstances, not related to police work. In functional terms, the unit did much to take the pressure of dealing with files away from the men so they could concentrate on being out and about and doing the job.

Looking up, I noticed that the roof of one of the Portakabins was covered in loose glass. I found out later that this was made up of shattered bottles of spirits. Every time there was a locker-room drink, or a party in the station, the empty bottles would be hurled up onto the roof, smashing to pieces and adding to the mountain of glass.

I realised that there were no spare lockers in the hovel in which my new section changed, so I went up to the administration office. It was a building of shut grey doors. The admin staff looked a little surprised when a strange policeman appeared. The whole place had a closed feel to it. I told them I was starting in a couple of days and needed a secure locker. 'Most officers keep their stuff in their car until one becomes free,' someone helpfully suggested. I thought back wistfully to when you arrived at a new station in England. Nice shiny new locker; orientation tour of the station with at least a sergeant. Practically a starter pack of goodies to welcome you. I tried ops planning to see if they knew how one achieved ownership of a locker. The same blank looks.

'Fucking Brit,' I heard as I walked out the door. I paused and looked back at the guy. He realised I had overheard him and intently scanned the papers on his desk. I let it go that time but had him clocked for the future. That sort of abuse was not uncommon, but you had to get used to it. If you flared up every time some arsehole abused your nationality, life would have been a permanent fight. The majority were okay; if they slagged you for being a Brit it was done to your face, in a jokey upfront kind of way. That was fine. Part of the banter you expect as a policeman. The snide little racist bastards who simply hated the English, regardless, were few.

This locker thing was becoming an issue in my head. One thing I detest is piss-poor organisation for the welfare of police, and I was not going to drive around for weeks with all my kit in the boot of my car. The security implications of that were horrendous.

At last I ran into the store man – the first friendly face so far. He turned

160

out to be a real gentleman. Within half an hour he had humped a locker from nowhere into the changing area, and advised me to stick two padlocks on it. I knew he was right in that respect. A friend of mine who had transferred to a west Belfast station from England had, in the first few days, complained to an inspector when his cap was stolen. The next day he came to work and found his locker burst open and every piece of uniform he possessed gone. Vanished forever. There were ways and means of getting even in the RUC, but official channels were not the wisest.

I offloaded all my kit and drove home. Having been a known quantity down in Fermanagh, I was back to being a nobody. The whole process of getting known and, more importantly, respected was to start all over again. I began to wonder why I didn't just pick a place and stay there.

Musgrave Street covered the main part of the city centre up to where Donegall Pass RUC took over, with a small strip of streets being covered by Queen Street RUC. We policed the small red light area near the BBC building, and heading west, almost up to the start of the M1 motorway. We covered the Markets area, which had always been a hotbed of terrorist activity, and also the docks.

The section put out three vehicles containing two or three men. One of the vehicles would be an armoured Land-rover. The section also had to cover all the security points guarding the station and the Courts. This task was generally done by reserve constables, but the regulars did their bit to alleviate the tedium of sangar duty. Some of the reserve men were happy enough. Stick them in a sangar for eight hours with a barrier button to press, a flask of coffee and a copy of *The Sun* and they were in reserve constable Heaven. It was seen as a nice easy day, but that was not always the case.

Not many months after I had transferred back to England in 1996, one of my more laid-back reserve constable friends was sitting doing duty in one of the sangars. He was reading his paper on his lap, perched on a stool, when he sensed a car stopping outside on the busy road. As he glanced up he saw a man hop out of the passenger seat and throw a long tube up onto his shoulder, while resting his elbows on the car roof. The rocket, fired at such close range, went straight through the bullet-proof glass of the sangar and out the other side, exploding as it hit the wall behind. My ex-colleague had thrown himself to the floor a split second before the rocket had been fired.

That saved his life, although he was wounded in the leg and his hearing was badly affected because of the proximity of the explosion.

Also out on the ground was the Markets neighbourhood unit, a tight, hard-working bunch who concentrated on the one area. They did all the day-to-day enquiries in the Markets area. They had a mammoth job breaking through the fear factor of local residents who had great reason to fear intimidation from local paramilitaries. On foot in the city centre were members of the neighbourhood policing unit.

One of Belfast's Mobile Support Units would also be routinely tasked to cover the city centre if not involved in operations elsewhere. Taken as a whole, that was a lot of manpower. It was still amazing on certain days how difficult it was to find a policeman in the city apart from the regular section.

With so many policemen, and even a couple of policewomen on the section, it took longer to get to know everyone than in the RUC stations I had been used to up till then. With two sergeants, an inspector, permanent gaolers, reserve constables to do security and the regular constables, the section numbered well over twenty. There were in that total only ever four or five regular constables, and we did all the files that the city centre generated on each shift we worked. Each day, as a regular, you would work in the main town response car or the second car. In other words, anything that happened within the city centre on your shift you would go to, either to deal with personally or as a back-up to the first car tasked.

I thought I had come back into a normal policing world of responding to calls, making arrests and doing files for court. I had on one level, but the station I had been posted to proved to have a strange and at times secretive atmosphere, where policing at times seemed to be the secondary consideration.

The station was run from the operational planning office by an individual sergeant, who I was told had complete power over the day-to-day running of the station. The divisional commander was largely irrelevant. If you wanted overtime or a posting to another station in the division, you had to be 'in' with ops planning. It was related to me how, when a new divisional commander had arrived one year, he had brought his own ops planning sergeant with him. A few phone calls were made, and within a day the old ops planning sergeant was back in place.

Certain individuals within the neighbourhood unit did appear to receive the bulk of the overtime. A simple check of the overtime figures confirmed that. The station was full of whispered rumours, generally only telling half a story. The suggestions of wholesale masonic influence were possibly far-fetched, although a few masonic rings were flaunted openly.

What was clear from my arrival in the station was that there was a huge amount of self-interested back-scratching going on amongst a small circle of people. Ensuring certain characters received the majority of overtime may have seemed a small annoyance. Overlooking the fact that they often left early but still claimed the full shift would again be seen as a petty issue. Over a period of time, however, that works out as a huge advantage in money and time off. It created an atmosphere of simmering jealousy and resentment. The majority of policemen who faced the day-to-day stress and danger on the streets looked on that kind of practice with disgust.

The more I heard, the more I consciously had nothing to with certain members of the neighbourhood policing unit. They were known within the station as the 'toads'. The toads were made up of some RUC bandsmen who would be an operational liability elsewhere, because they were constantly called away for police band duties. Some were good policemen, and others should have stuck to their instruments. The RUC was peculiar in that under old recruitment practices, a man could have been taken on solely on the basis that he played a musical instrument well. That was not an official written policy, yet it was transparently the case. The police brass band, and to a lesser degree the pipe band, were considered of huge importance amongst the police hierarchy. On completion of training the individual would be given a 'soft' station such as Musgrave Street, with a posting to the neighbourhood unit so that he could attend all the concerts and practice sessions.

This was still going on when I joined the force in 1991. A member of my squad who played the pipes was offered a station down the road from his home. All the other single men were sent to the far corners of the province. To his credit, that individual eventually dropped out of the police pipe band so that he would have more chance of a career in the police.

As well as bandsmen there were all the station hangers-on; lazy and good-for-nothing creatures who had some influence with the ops planning department. They were always there for their morning Ulster fry-up in the canteen, gossiping like old women. They had time to gossip. On section

163

there was no such luxury as sitting around consuming grease at that time of the morning. Section received all the initial calls to incidents. There were very few quiet days in the city.

A typical character in the 'toad band' was a full-time reserve constable who ran a garage in addition to his police duties. Every morning he would arrive at the station in his police uniform, have his big greasy fry-up and then drive back out of the gates. I finally discovered that he was away to his garage, sometimes with the cars of senior officers, to do a day's work. He would then return to the station in time to have a cup of tea in the canteen and slide off home. It was a petty form of sanctioned corruption; sanctioned by virtue of the fact that the senior officers were aware of it but let it continue. Often because it was to their advantage.

There were similar stories from Queen Street station which worked closely with Musgrave Street. A long-serving constable there told me of an officer related to an influential sergeant, taken on as a reserve constable. He was another who would appear at the start of a duty and then not be seen again until the end of the day. He was also by all accounts a very old man. If the rules had been correctly applied, he would not have been recruited due to his age.

One officer was so disgusted at these abuses of the system that he told me he kept a log of the goings-on in case he was ever dumped on. Then he intended to use it as a bargaining tool. The rumours went up a scale with allegations of officers, long since retired, making a fortune out of ripping money off from the social club. Whatever the truth of these stories, the atmosphere it created was a rotten one, more frustrating to me because I knew that it was unique to that city centre station. When you mentioned Musgrave Street to men from other stations, there would be a shake of the head. The perception was one of drunk sergeants and dodgy practices.

On one occasion I was overheard chatting to the inspector about whether it was worth making waves about certain issues. A senior constable approached me and warned me off.

'Richard, there is nothing they would not do if you threaten them and their little ways. Nothing they would not do.'

I had no reason to disbelieve him.

Before long, I was doing licensing checks one evening shift, driving one of the skippers around for the first time. We went into a couple of pubs down by the docks. It was the same routine in each one. A few stilted pleasantries and a glass of whiskey would appear in front of the sergeant. We would linger on, a second glass would be put down, and only then would we move on to the next. If an alarm went off on a pub premises overnight the sergeant would always attend. After a while I became used to the skipper disappearing for half of the shift.

When I had first put on the RUC uniform in training I had been intensely proud to be part of a force which I would still rate as the best in the United Kingdom. In Fermanagh I had come across characters in the ranks who were odd, but at the same time still proficient and competent policemen.

Belfast bred a different kind of peeler. Extremes of environment create extremes in behaviour. It was a place of huge contrasts in policing terms. From the relative safety of areas such as Strandtown in east Belfast, which operated as near as anywhere to the way a mainland station worked, to the besieged outposts of the west. Attacks on the security forces there were a daily occurrence, and police could not go out without army back-up.

In the city centre, many of the policemen had worked for years in harder stations and the mental results of that were clear. Drink problems were commonplace. One reserve constable on my section came to work every day with a bottle of whiskey in his bag, carefully laid out next to his sandwich box. By the end of the day half of it would have been drunk. Others drank from mineral water bottles at breakfast time which contained vodka. These men never appeared drunk, because they were not drunk in the normal sense. They were simply topping up all the time, dependent on a certain level of alcohol to carry them through the day.

Behind every alcohol problem, if you dug deep enough, there was a story. A shooting that resulted in a death. The loss of a friend or family member. Being personally attacked or targeted by terrorists and missing death by moments or inches. Usually a combination of all these things. RUC men were, after all, only human, and the pressures of the events that occur over a thirty-year career can be immense.

By this stage I was rarely drinking, and perhaps seemed extremely unsociable for not taking part in the locker-room parties after work. Heavy drinking sessions were simply off my agenda. I was in a stable and happy relationship. Other priorities were taking the place of a wild social life. The memory of how easy it was to live a destructive, abusive lifestyle, as I had been prior to being posted to Belleek station, was fresh in my mind. It would have been easy to be judgemental about the officers who drank on duty, but I had been there. If anything was failing, it was the support system around these men, who were suffering so much stress that their only escape was booze.

At times their behaviour reached extremes that I could hardly believe did not end in them being sacked. A couple of senior constables on an evening beat of the docks appeared back at the station blocked and in the company of two sluts they had met in a pub. They took them off for a private party in one of the court cells.

The best way to avoid the shit hitting the fan if that kind of incident became common knowledge was to stay away from drinking on duty altogether. It was hard, because every night shift saw a few cans being passed around on at least one of the nights, usually in the early hours of the morning at an impromptu barbecue. Every morning a few of the night shift lads would linger on for a few drinks.

My getting back to 'normal' policing was interrupted by the events that were to become an annual feature of Northern Irish life. The summer of 1995 saw the seeds sown for several summers of violence. The confrontation at Drumcree began in the July. Drumcree was to become a huge symbol of loyalist opposition to what was perceived as too many concessions being given to the republican movement.

The images of marching Orangemen do not do any favours to the unionist cause when they are broadcast on TV around the world. Unionists as a whole do not appear to give a damn about that. Unfortunately, with the triumphal nature and anti-Papist overtones of the majority of the marches, they appear to be something out of a past, bigoted world.

Orange Lodge leaders may argue that the processions have more to do with religious worship, but my time in the Mobile Support Unit told me a different story. It was all about flaunting dominance; a tribal dance which began as a good-natured pageant, but then, fuelled by copious amounts of alcohol and mass fervour, inevitably led to intimidation and violence.

When policing band parades in Enniskillen, the behaviour I witnessed as the processions paused outside particular Catholic pubs and played 'The Sash' made me extremely uncomfortable about my role. Clearly intimidating to Catholic residents, it was permitted to go on despite the potential for creating public disorder. Although I knew that very few of my colleagues were anti-Catholic, the practice within the force of allowing Orange marches to go through Catholic areas must have created the impression in the minds of Catholics that the RUC was there to protect Orangemen. When that image is removed then the RUC may start being perceived as an unbiased police force.

In the years that I lived in Northern Ireland, the majority of people I associated with, both inside and outside the police, came from the middle ground of the community. Predominantly, though not exclusively Protestant maybe, but certainly not anti-Catholic. Contrary to the image portrayed by the media that every Protestant is out there marching with an Orange sash on the twelfth of July, in reality not one person I knew took an active part in the marching season. The Northern Ireland people I knew were forward-thinking, cultured, and focused well ahead on the Northern Ireland they wanted for the new millennium.

The shuffling, moronic individuals who pumped themselves up with booze to go and wind up the local Catholics were an anachronism in the modern Ulster. It always struck me how many physical and mental misfits there were in the parades. If they weren't limping, they were twitching. Many were curiously small men with blotchy, drink-ravaged faces and lank, unwashed hair. They were all universally appalling at marching. It was, aside from the sinister overtones, a sad and comic spectacle.

Although they probably genuinely believed they were part of a huge Protestant movement, they were not. They did represent many thousands in a population of 1.5 million, but that, I think, puts the numbers in context. They were vocal and at times dangerous, as are all large crowds inebriated with drink and the moment. They certainly were not, in my view, a majority. The Protestant majority were sitting at home watching TV. Mowing their lawns. Taking their kids out. At work, if they could get there during the violence. They were doing the stuff that normal hard-working people do around the rest of the UK. They were taking their summer holidays to escape from the province over the summer madness. More importantly, they were generally as disgusted with the loyalist violence as they were with the republicans.

The Orangemen had traditional parade routes and were determined not to change them. In some areas, shifts in population created a situation where the fact that the area they marched through was now predominantly Catholic. One such area was Drumcree, near Portadown. In 1995 the RUC decided to re-route the parade at Drumcree. This led to a three-day stand-off between police and Orange supporters. It was apparent that serious public disorder could develop and to avoid this a deal was achieved with the local Catholic residents' group to allow the parade to go through.

This stand-down by the security forces was seen by the Orangemen as a great victory. They tried the same tactic on the Ormeau Road in Belfast, threatening to muster all Orangemen from the province to force the parade through. Again, senior police officers, no doubt fully supported by the Northern Ireland Office, backed down. The parade was forced through the Catholic area. Public disorder was to break out in Belfast. It was a strange kind of peace we were experiencing!

The difference between the public disorder I had experienced on the mainland and that in Belfast was the sheer scale and underlying hatred shown towards the security forces in Ulster. The majority of these situations in the UK contain a small element of hard-core troublemakers, and they take longer to build up to extreme violence. In the Markets area, within minutes of a riot starting cars had been hijacked and torched and petrol bombs would be bouncing off the Land-rover bonnet. During one disturbance a ten-year-old with an amazing throwing arm nearly took my head off with a brick when I had to jump out of the Land-rover to clear an obstruction. It skimmed my left ear, missing the back of my head by inches. The mini rioters could run and disappear down the alleyways like whippets.

At the height of the trouble the sound of gunfire could be heard distinctly through all the other sounds of destruction. Rounds occasionally struck the Land-rovers but in the main did not penetrate the armour.

During those moments I would reflect on the incredible differences in policing I had seen, not only in Northern Ireland but also on the mainland. My days in Belfast, a small part of a police career that saw me increasingly linked with events in Ulster: an association that began when taking holidays in the province in the late 1980s. As an outsider, you either grow to love Northern Ireland or learn to detest it. As a place it has always been good to me, although there were many moments when the sadness in the midst of so much potential made me want to say 'Sod it' and head back across the water. Fortunately the good always outweighed the bad. The extreme badness of the minority had a way of highlighting the great decency of the majority. There were times early in my service when I was not so convinced of that.

There were some great characters in the station. The RUC was unique in that constables who had joined before a certain date could carry on working until they were over sixty years old. On my section we had Old Ben who had done forty years' service. Ben was constantly falling out with the bosses, and because of this was still doing routine patrol at the age of sixty, out there mixing it on the streets alongside probationers with a year's service.

Ben had joined the RUC during the IRA border campaign of the late 1950s. With a glint in his eye, he could tell you of the day that they had mortared the Garda 'by mistake' near the Fermanagh/Donegal border town of Pettigoe. He had a medal for bravery, capturing armed terrorists during the early part of the modern conflict, and was one of the best shots in the RUC even in his advanced years. The men he had joined up to serve with had, in many cases, been young soldiers during the Second World War, and certainly did not mess about when it came to dealing with domestic terrorists.

Ben had the biggest fists I have ever seen. He had boxed for the RUC during his early career, and even at sixty I saw him, during a vicious punch-up in the city centre, land a punch that lifted a twenty-year-old off his feet and over a bench. He did, however, have an annoying habit of falling asleep at traffic lights. You would have to nudge him when the light turned to green! Ben was fascinated by the way I did contemporaneous notes on everything, a habit I had picked up in the English police, and at that stage only just coming in as a requirement within the RUC. He would wink at me and ask how the book was going; he was convinced I would one day write about working in Belfast. He was more perceptive than I was, since the idea was not to come to me until a long time after.

The terrorists were still out and about, but at times it was a frustrating task knowing what they were up to. I always made a point of checking all the tucked away places within the city centre as part of routine patrolling. In a rear yard behind some shops, we once came across a parked up car with four evil-looking blokes inside. They were just sitting there, apparently doing nothing, which generally means people are up to no good. As my mate covered me with an MP5 I instructed the men to get out of the car. They said absolutely nothing. Offered no explanation of why they were there, in the middle of the afternoon, tucked away in an alley in the red light area. They all gave their details, and continued the silent routine as I searched the car. If there was a space I looked in it. The RUC search training is second to none, and it was with a great sense of disappointment that I finally admitted defeat. It was completely clean, even registered legally to one of the men.

The checks on their names and dates of birth came back over the radio. They were four top IRA men from west Belfast. Two were part of an interrogation squad, dangerous and evil men to the core. They were certainly planning something. Possibly waiting for a weapon to arrive. Maybe a drug deal about to go down. Annoyingly, there was nothing we could hold them on. A few months earlier we probably would have detained them just for being who they were, under the Emergency Provisions Act, but with the climate much changed, along with the guidelines over using the terrorist legislation, we could only log the occurrence and let them go. To this day I wonder what they were up to. At least by disrupting it we may have prevented some attack.

It was at times amusing to watch the reaction of police officers as the signs of normalised policing crept into the Belfast stations. We received our first marked police car, complete with stickers and a big yellow stripe down the side. When it arrived in the yard colleagues circled it warily. Someone chucked me the keys. 'Here, you'll be more used to panda cars,' he scoffed.

The changes were not well received, but not because the men were against change. It was simply the case that nobody trusted the peace. Anything that made a police car easily identifiable on the day in the future that the IRA decided to start killing policemen again was not appreciated.

There are many different and quite separate worlds within the small city centre area of Belfast. The red light district was a small but active part of the Belfast scene. I sat, crewed up with Tony, near the BBC building one day with one of the girls in the back of the car, generally having a chat. She was telling us how she worked for a month then rested for a month. At the moment she was saving for a conservatory for her house in Glengormley. She was moaning because she had to forgo her month off, as the conservatory was going to cost four grand, and told us about one Northern Irish politician.

'X comes down here regular you know. Just for a hand job. Then there's a peeler from your own place.'

'Oh yes?' I said, hopefully.

That was more interesting than some politician, but she refused to give us a name, although we both had a good idea who it was.

The girls were generally very protective of the names of clients. In the small world of Ulster, secrets are not kept for long. This made it all the more amazing to me that anyone would use the services of girls doing business out on the streets.

It was a small enough problem, so the police didn't bother the girls, and instead concentrated on scaring off the odd kerb crawler. Wholesale pimping was not common then, although that may have changed as paramilitaries become involved in a wider range of rackets. Most of the prostitutes were married housewives earning a little or a lot of extra cash, depending on their age and looks. Some were taking home a grand a week tax free. Others were lucky to make a couple of hundred. All this was going on within yards of where the middle classes danced on tables in the frantic party atmosphere of Larry's piano bar.

I had to give some serious thought as to where my career was going at this stage. I decided that I would either go for promotion or specialise again in CID. The problem was that the culture of CID in the RUC was very different from that in England. There were two types of CID men that I had come into contact with in Belfast. There were recent entrants in their late twenties or early thirties, some of them now detective sergeants, who were efficient, keen, and more importantly had a good relationship with the uniform branch. Then there were the long-serving detective constables who spoke to uniform like they were stupid, permanently reeked of alcohol and bluffed their way through the law, having probably never updated themselves on legislation or procedure since the early 1970s.

It was embarrassing to be at a call where you knew CID would attend, doing your bit to look professional and interested, and then watch two half-pissed, gum-chewing half-wits turn up to take over the case. CID had one or two excellent senior officers, some first-rate new detectives, but there were a large number of ignorant bastards left over from a different era.

Once you were in CID you were effectively there for the rest of your career. I decided that I would give it six months and then, despite my reservations, go for CID, and after another year look for promotion. It had been a basic principle of mine that I would only go for promotion when I had covered all the departments and roles that I was interested in as a constable. It had nearly reached that stage. I was confident now in virtually any policing situation. There were very few things now in police terms that I had not dealt with, but I still wanted to have a complete year working the city centre environment. I settled my mind again on day-to-day policing.

1996 saw the breakdown of the ceasefire with the bombing of Canary Wharf in London's Docklands. Two men at work in a newsagent's shop, Inam Ul-haq Bashir and John Jefferies, were killed when the huge device, contained in a modified flatbed lorry, exploded at South Quay on the ninth of February. The 3,000 pounds of explosives caused millions of pounds' worth of damage to the area. The subsequent police enquiry, and the trial in 1998, revealed that the men behind the attack were from South Armagh. One man from Crossmaglen was convicted in June 1998 on charges connected with the explosion. Many others involved with the IRA operation remain free, doubtless to plan further attacks as the Good Friday Agreement unravels. The same Good Friday Agreement which ensured that the man convicted of planting the bomb on South Quay would be freed in the year 2000!

Despite the sudden and dramatic breakdown of the ceasefire, Belfast still had an air of normality. The feeling was that IRA operations would be run as a campaign on the mainland for a while, to put pressure on the government. We carried out normal policing tasks. Arresting thieves and drunks. Breaking up fights. Dealing with road accidents, but now with one very wary eye over our shoulders. The violence was inevitably going to start again in the province, but probably not overnight.

Unfolding events confirmed our feeling that the mainland would become the focus for the terrorists. Edward O'Brien, an IRA volunteer from Wexford, was killed by his own bomb as it exploded prematurely on a bus in central London. In June the centre of Manchester was torn apart by a huge explosion.

A notable event of that year was the thwarting of an IRA bombing campaign after months of police and security service surveillance. The police operation culminated in the arrest of several gang members, and the shooting dead of Diarmuid O'Neill, the IRA quartermaster. O'Neill was a native of London but of Irish descent. He was one of a new breed of IRA terrorists; he spoke with a London accent, and although involved with republican politics from an early age, the full extent of his involvement only became clear as he was seen and filmed covertly with known terrorists operating on the mainland.

His death at the hands of the Metropolitan police firearms unit, SO19, remains controversial amongst nationalist circles. A jury has since passed a verdict that O'Neill was 'lawfully killed'. There are now calls for a public enquiry into his shooting.

It is easy for some to ignore the indiscriminate deaths of members of the public which would have occurred if the gang's bombing campaign had not been thwarted. When a police officer puts his life on the line by taking up a weapon against violent and unpredictable men, with the knowledge that if those men have a weapon to hand they will use it, the split-second decision made by that officer to open fire must be respected. Only that individual officer is in a position to fully perceive the threat to his own life or the lives of colleagues. Hesitation can mean death. A heavy price to pay for going beyond the call of duty.

It was not until October of 1996 that terrorist violence returned to Northern Ireland on a scale to match previous attacks. The IRA managed to plant two car bombs inside the army's Northern Ireland headquarters in Lisburn. A soldier was killed and many injured in the subsequent explosions.

Security at the headquarters had always been surprisingly lax, even at the height of the conflict. I had been allowed in there once while on a holiday trip to Ulster in the late eighties, to meet a friend who was part-time UDR. I had been given unescorted access to meet him at a location in the complex on the strength of my English accent, and the fact that I said I was a policeman on the mainland.

———

It was family illness which in the end brought me back to England. Both my parents had become seriously ill. Despite my feelings for Northern Ireland and the wish I had to make it my permanent home, the prospect of not being close to my parents in their final few months was not something I was able to cope with.

My father had been mentally destroyed by Parkinson's disease. He lived in a confused world where the past and present were jumbled. He rarely recognised family members, and had lost all power of coherent speech. It was distressing to see him so physically and mentally wasted. Inevitably, there would now be a rapid decline. It was worth being back in England and able to visit more regularly, even for the very few moments when recognition would come to his disease-frozen features. A smile would break through that rigid mask in which Parkinson's envelops its victims. There were sometimes flashes of the mischievous sense of humour he used to have. Those moments were becoming very rare.

My mother, too, was rapidly deteriorating. Her turn to alcohol in later life, perhaps as an escape from my father's illness, had taken a dreadful toll. She had smoked all her life, and now, when she was not smoking, she was hooked up to a nebuliser to aid her breathing.

The years I had spent away in Northern Ireland played on my mind at this time. I felt I had neglected my parents over the last five years, but deep down I also knew that you cannot live your life for your parents. Driven by very mixed feelings I applied for the second time in my life to Sussex Police. Musgrave Street had soured my own impression of the RUC, but I knew I could at any stage have moved away from there.

With a sense that I was making a big mistake, I went through the two-day assessment for Sussex Police. This was my fourth assessment to enter a police force: my first had been with Sussex and my second with the Met, which I had been offered but turned down, and my third with the RUC. It did not get any easier with practice, and the testing process, both physically and mentally, were many times more demanding than when I had first joined Sussex. After a nervous wait at the end of the assessments I was offered a position with the force where I had begun my police career. I was soon to be on the move again.

Several colleagues tried to persuade me not to leave the RUC. I think they realised that once my parents had passed away I would regret leaving Northern Ireland. Men who were normally very reserved in praise, such as my inspector, were saying nice things about me. He wrote on my application for Sussex:

> Constable Latham is a mature officer . . . his range of experience in
> both forces and in various units is very much evident in his practical

> policing role in Belfast. His work is invariably of a high standard, reflecting both his experience and education. The officer is always neat and tidy in appearance and is respectful to his authorities. He is an articulate man who can relate to the public and his peers alike. He is a man from whom others would take the lead and would seek advice and guidance. The officer can be relied upon to carry out all his duties with professionalism, tact and diplomacy requiring the minimum of supervision. He conducts himself at all times to the highest standard. I would have no hesitation in stating that this constable would be an asset to another force and a loss to this one. I would be sorry to lose this officer if he is accepted.

Coming from an officer I respected, I was extremely touched by the inspector's assessment. It did make me think twice about leaving the RUC. Even in a few years the force had become an integral part of my identity. As I left work for the final time, I tossed an RUC plaque and tie onto my car passenger seat. I had been presented with them at the briefing. I felt like a part of me had been cut away.

It was with very mixed emotions that I started packing for the move to England. Policemen as a rule do not leave the RUC. If they do leave, it is either because they are thrown out or, late in service, some leave to set up businesses. Once you leave, the protective structure is dismantled. You will always be a hate figure in the eyes of some nationalists. Always a potential target should the murder of policemen as an IRA strategy return.

Sadly, I stuck my RUC plaque and tie in a box with other bits of memorabilia. It was a large part of my life, now stored in a box. It was amazing how much crap you could accumulate in five years.

The removal lorry rolled up outside. I had never felt attached to a house before. We had moved around a lot when I was a child, because we had always rented or had lived in provided accommodation. This had been my home as a single man over a period when everything had been going well. There was not a bad memory attached to it.

I had the same bad feelings all day. If I could have changed my mind at that stage, I would have taken everything back into the house and stayed.

A SAD JOURNEY

The summer of 1996 promised to be another period of conflict sparked by the stand-off at Drumcree. As my colleagues in Belfast prepared for the anticipated public disorder, I found myself putting the final few items into our car in preparation for moving to England. The prospect of giving time to my now very ill parents was positive. On the other hand, I did feel sad about leaving the province. I had lived for the last year in a house on the north-east coast. From the kitchen window on a clear day, the dark line of the Scottish shore, less than twenty miles away, was visible. Out of the back window the Mourne Mountains loomed in the far distance. On days off I would walk the rocky, unspoilt coastline or cycle the lanes of the Ards Peninsula as far down as Portaferry. I windsurfed on Strangford Lough. Drank pints of Guinness in ancient pubs. It was the kind of environment which should have made Ulster a mecca for tourists. Thirty years of conflict, ironically, had kept the countryside safe from over-exploitation. There was much to miss.

When I had arrived in Northern Ireland I had only one suitcase. Now I was leaving with my wife (I had married a few months earlier) and a removal van full of the bits and pieces acquired when one finally becomes a grown up.

It was a huge step for my wife too. She had never lived outside Ireland, and she was aware that the cost of housing in the south-east of England meant we would be buying a smaller house, and that our standard of living would decline. I had the impression that many in England still believed that Ulster was essentially a poor area, the population living in red-brick terraced housing in Belfast or shabby rundown cottages in the countryside. In reality, the disposable income of working people in the province was higher than the rest of the UK.

For many years, up until very recently, house prices were half the price they were on the mainland. Mortgages were therefore lower and more money went into the pocket. That was reflected in the great social lives people enjoyed, despite the ongoing conflict. Cars were exchanged for new models sooner. Northern Ireland had the highest percentage of BMW owners in Europe.

The security situation created wealth because there were over 12,000 policemen on very good salaries. The military operation created additional trade. Whether in building or rebuilding, there had been a large amount of wealth generated by the conflict. After the 1994 ceasefire, small businesses took off as people developed more confidence in the future. Talented individuals, who were the product of the best education system in the UK, were returning home from the mainland and abroad. The tourist industry started to come back to life. If you were unemployed, the benefits system was the same as the mainland but there was also a booming black economy.

As I wrote earlier, having spent years going into council, or as they are called in Northern Ireland 'housing executive', homes, I realised it was the case that the provided accommodation in the province was of a higher standard than it was in England. Poor or rich, old-fashioned values of cleanliness and order in the home were very apparent in many of the houses, even on notorious estates. Some of the younger generation lived in shit, and made life miserable for their neighbours, but that was so much the norm on council estates in England that it would not even be worth commenting on.

We were in fact lucky to get out of the province on the day we had planned. The furniture van had gone on ahead a couple of days earlier. As we drove to Larne for the ferry to Stranraer, there were barricades literally being erected by loyalist groups on the road behind us. Another couple of hours' delay and we would have been stranded in the province for another week, since the ports were soon blockaded and the ferry services stopped.

It was a sad journey through Scotland and down to the south coast as we left friends and family behind. The Orangemen's barricades were the prelude to a week of intense rioting, the worst anarchy to hit Northern Ireland for many years. The RUC were, at some points, trapped inside the police stations. As a police friend told me afterwards, they lost count of how many baton rounds they had to fire to turn back the mobs. Officers could not reach their homes because of the loyalist gangs. For several days they slept in the stations. All this I watched on television from the safety of mid-

Sussex. I felt a sense of having deserted the place which, when I moved there, I had intended to be home for the rest of my days.

Within three days of returning to Sussex I found myself working on the central sector of Brighton police station. It was the station I had most wanted to be posted to after my initial training in England, for the naive motivations you have at twenty-one years of age. It was odd to be in Belfast one day and in central Brighton the next.

Although I should have been pleased with the posting, I eventually had to admit to myself that my whole outlook on policing was changing. This gradual change was to result in an eighteen-month period in Sussex police, before I decided to quit the job altogether.

I had come from the relatively low-tech environment of the RUC to the computer-dominated, customer-orientated world that English policing had become. The RUC had been on the verge of bringing in a computer system for general use just prior to my leaving, but daily incidents were still written up by hand in a large ledger book called the C6. In English police stations there were terminals and laptops on every desk, and for every conceivable function.

Procedures within the RUC had hardly changed for decades. It was a huge change from the world of hard talking, if at times blunt sergeants and inspectors to the new model first-line managers, spouting management speak for all they were worth. I had never heard the word 'proactive' used so often by so many supervisors.

Being proactive in the English police environment was to prove extremely difficult. The political correctness of the job made it virtually impossible. Policemen lived in a permanent state of concern over saying the wrong thing to female colleagues and admin staff. The nick was becoming a banter-free zone. A typical incident nearly put one of the WPCs in the shit. She was sitting in a car with a lesbian police sergeant when two males in Brighton's West Street started kissing in full view of the police car. 'Oh my God! That's disgusting,' was all she said. She then had to sit for the next half hour and explain the comment in analytical detail, with the lesbian sergeant debating whether or not to make a complaint against her.

179

In dealing with the public, the job had become a minefield. If you targeted known black criminals then allegations of racial discrimination would follow. Paying attention to constantly offending white criminals resulted in solicitors turning up at the station bleating about harassment. Any complaint generated an investigation, which on top of the other crap police had to deal with was added stress.

In amongst it all were some good PCs and the odd good boss. If they were good they were also not stupid, and it became clear that many who had put their all into good solid coppering in Brighton over the years had realised the tide was turning in favour of the criminal and the yob. They took the chance to leave and go into squads or move into other departments.

On the outside, the exterior of the police station had been panelled with plastic bits to make it look like a trendy office building. The interior of the nick was now all fluffy and cuddly. Open-plan areas, the computer terminals and pot plants. An officer could waste thirty minutes going through his e-mails at the start of a shift after the briefing. Paperwork, which was bad enough when I initially left Sussex despite numerous attempts to reduce it, seemed to have doubled in quantity. That, to a major extent, was the fault of the criminal justice system, which required the same information on files over and over.

It all looked very slick on the surface, but at the end of the day someone has to go out into the cold and nick criminals. A hard core on my section could do that. I worked with lads such as Big Al, Mad Tony and The Bear. All of them could handle themselves well in rough situations, but unfortunately that did not apply across all the sections. Police response was a bit of a lottery. It depended upon what time of day it was and who was on duty.

Brighton had become a town of beggars, squats and drug users. It had always had a seedy side. The difference now was that it was all out in the open. You could not walk fifty yards in the town centre without falling over a wino in a shop doorway, or a *Big Issue* seller with obligatory DSS-financed dog. (It was the case that if you were living on the streets with a pet dog you could make a claim for dog food.) The beggars were extremely intimidating, and especially targeted the commuter rush to the central railway station.

Very little seemed to be happening to stop this general decay. The first impressions were that the police were doing bugger all to prevent it. As time went on and I became more disillusioned with policing methods, I realised that this impression was not wrong. A few individuals were throwing themselves wholeheartedly into tackling crime, but the sheer quantity of work left officers bogged down with paperwork.

The fear of receiving complaints, the awareness that your supervisor would crucify you for an error made in good faith, the lack of back-up in manpower terms, led to a negative mindset. Many young coppers would drive past incidents or aggressive groups of lads kicking over bins and being a general nuisance because it was not worth the hassle of being drawn in.

People tended to complain with no thought that the officer was only doing his or her job. I saw drunk and unreasonable individuals walk in with clearly bogus complaints against officers and be entertained like VIPs with tea and biccies in the inspector's office. How different it was from the three drunk and abusive youths I once saw walk into a front office in Belfast demanding to see the inspector to make a complaint. As they became increasingly more violent and aggressive, the Inspector appeared with his baton and chased them out of the front office and halfway up the street!

In Northern Ireland, at least you could be confident of support from a decent majority of the population. In England it seemed that very few had a decent word to say about the police. Certainly little respect. The lack of manpower and escalating crime rate was a result of many factors. The net result was that the policeman's job was becoming harder, as public support decreased.

There was a complete lack of appreciation of the day-to-day threats that an officer faced. I remember two middle-class couples coming out of a wine bar in central Brighton sniggering at the stab-proof vests we were now wearing as a matter of routine. They did not have a clue. Over a few months in Brighton I went to dozens of incidents where knives were being used. Saw several of my colleagues attacked with weapons. The number of firearms being carried was on the increase. If those people, climbing into their Volvo to head back to their £300,000 house in mid-Sussex, had to witness just one of the violent incidents we were sent to in a day, they would have shat themselves.

Several officers I knew were waiting for the results of tests for HIV infection having been stabbed by needles. When you searched druggies, they would leave needles inside their pockets so that the sharp end would pierce your search gloves. We dealt with the shit at the very bottom of the gutters. Saw the dark and messy side of life, a side which very few saw. In return for the working with filth, the unsociable life-shortening shifts, the risks to health and the danger of physical injury, I had twats in Volvo estates sniggering at my protective vest!

Another annoying perception of the police, which I found had increased in England, was that all coppers were corrupt. It was complete bollocks. We went out of our way to follow procedures which were in many respects overly fair to criminals. I came from a generation of policemen who would not accept so much as a fiver from a member of the public, even if you had gone well out of your way to help that individual out. Unfortunately, serious corruption amongst a very few individuals, in positions within regional crime squads, had provided confirmation in the public mind that no policemen could be trusted. With big corruption trials involving Metropolitan Police officers about to hit the public domain, that belief will be impossible to erase.

Somewhere in the back of my mind a little voice was asking me if this was all worth it. The court system was failing victims, we as police did not have the resources to do the job properly and the atmosphere we worked in was increasingly anti-police.

During the summer of 1996 we started to come across individuals from the north-east and Liverpool and Manchester checking out the Brighton area as an expanding market for their drugs businesses. They had chosen the south coast because they had heard the police were soft on drugs. They were right. We were soft on crime generally. It did not look good for the future.

I was a great believer in the zero tolerance method of policing: clamp down on small misdemeanours and the big issues would be partly solved. Tackle the petty vandalism, remove graffiti every time it appeared, take the begging off the streets and the atmosphere of crime is reduced. Begging can all too easily lead on to assault and robbery. A regular method used in robberies by down-and-outs was to threaten the victim with a syringe filled with their blood. Decay leads to further decay. Individuals graffiti where they see other graffiti.

It is well documented how the zero tolerance approach has worked wonders in New York, where the idea had first been put into practice. In several visits to that city in 1999, I walked around Manhattan in the early hours of the morning with no feeling of threat. The same year, over a couple of shopping trips in Brighton after I had left the police force, I was hassled several times by aggressive beggars and witnessed two punch-ups involving young drunks. I did not see a single police car, let alone a copper on the beat.

Unfortunately, within the politically correct minefield of English policing the wholehearted adoption of a zero tolerance policy was never going to pick up momentum. It will take the crime rate to become far worse and the general lawlessness of cities to reach a desperate stage before someone has the guts to take a grip of the situation. The current deplorable level of morale within police ranks in the year 2000, the failure to attract recruits, and the huge number of resignations shows that that time is still a long way off.

There were some early indications of the way things had changed. I was out with a colleague on Brighton seafront when I saw a number of dodgy characters hanging around the sea front toilets. Men in macs and baggy, brown corduroy trousers. Not the professional gay types who had made Brighton famous for the strength of the 'pink pound' in the area and the gay night life. These were just seedy, dirty bastards.

'I'm just going in to check the gents,' I said, expecting him to follow me in, so that if there were offences taking place we could corroborate each other. He was a young and permanently worried-looking probationer. An even more perplexed look came over his face at my suggestion.

'The guidelines are that we shoudn't check the toilets,' he said.

'What?' I honestly thought he was joking. 'What fucking guidelines?'

'Yes, it upsets the gay community. It is seen as infringing their rights.'

'You've got to be fucking joking,' I said.

He wasn't. That really was the policy of the bosses in Brighton. I have absolutely nothing against homosexuality. Like any other sexual preference, as far as I'm concerned you can do anything in the privacy of your own home. This, however, was a licence to have sex in public.

I knew for a fact that gay men did not restrict their activities to within the cubicles. Any holidaymaker with children could walk into a public toilet and be subjected to the sight of men having sex. If I had sex in public with a woman, I could expect to be nicked for indecency. It was pandering to a minority at the expense of the less vocal law-abiding majority. Political correctness gone mad.

Two coppers on the beat while I was in Brighton checked some notorious toilets and heard noises coming from one of the cubicles. They burst the door open to find one man on his knees doing the business on the one standing. With the shock of the policemen's sudden appearance, the man with his mouth full promptly had a heart attack. He stopped breathing, at which point one of the policemen gave him mouth to mouth. Although the man died, the policeman received a commendation for his actions, detailing the circumstances. With the piss-taking that followed, I know he wished he had never gone into those public toilets that day!

During another incident, I arrested a demented naked man with a knife running up the street in the middle of the afternoon. We took the knife off the man and grabbed hold of him. As myself and my partner Paul, The Bear, placed the cuffs on him, all I could hear around me were people abusing us for having the man face down on the back seat of the car. We were using a minimum amount of restraint to stop a very violent person from biting us, yet I had naive little voices in my ear telling me that I was going to be on video. That they were going to make a complaint. I had had enough of that shit.

Brighton was certainly a town full of mad people, perverts and druggies. Any woman who walked around there alone in the evening was naive or stupid, or mad, a druggie or a pervert herself!

In common with Worthing, people died lonely deaths in pokey one-bedroom flats, only to be discovered when the smell started drifting in to the neighbours. I lost count of how many sudden deaths I attended. Those where a doctor could not instantly establish cause of death, and police were called. Some stick in my mind, like the elderly man found one evening in the street. I went with the body back to the mortuary and searched it myself while waiting for an on-call mortuary attendant. The old man was in an appalling state of neglect, although you wouldn't have guessed immediately since his outer clothes were okay. His socks may have been on for months. I peeled them off just to see if I could. Underneath the socks he had curled-up yellow toenails an inch long. I found that all his underwear was practically stuck to him.

Since we had no reports of him missing, I went back to his flat to search for details of relatives. In his wallet there was a single photograph. It was him, a few years earlier, with his arms around two girls in their early twenties. It was a happy, smiley, family scene. The flat was a stinking mess. I found out from neighbours that he had had a bust-up with his daughters four years before and not spoken to them since. He had gradually gone downhill. I noticed from a balance slip in his pockets that he had thousands in the bank, yet he died like a dog in the gutter from self-neglect and misery.

Gradually I was reaching the conclusion that the risk and day-to-day hassles involved in being a policeman were not worth it. The justice system simply smacked offenders on the wrist and sent them back out on the streets to commit further burglaries, robberies and assaults. I knew that if I had to deal with a serious offence committed against myself or my family the courts would not provide any form of justice, and the temptation to take the law into my own hands would be overwhelming.

The courts had become an ordeal for the victim, with the odds in favour of the criminal. I felt complete sympathy for individuals who did not want to give witness statements. The police service could not protect them against intimidation. Better to walk away now than spend the next fifteen years being frustrated by something which I could do nothing about.

I was also feeling uncomfortable that I was now unarmed. A call came over the PR one evening. A man with a handgun had been seen in a burger bar near the sea front, arguing with a female. The street ran down to the sea from a busy main road. It was summer, and the whole area was swimming with daytrippers. We tried to contain the scene, as best we could, by placing police cars at the top and bottom of the street, but with just two in each car and other cars tied up on emergency calls all over Brighton, it was a virtually impossible task. I moved closer to where the man had been seen, with Tony, one of the lads on my section. We had no decent description with which to ID the gunman. Without locating and identifying him, we had no idea if the containment that we were trying to put on was in the correct area.

'Bet you wish you had your MP5 now,' Tony said. He was spot on. I felt vulnerable without my weapon. What was I going to do? Shout 'Stop! Or I'll shout "stop" again!'?

Out of the uninterested crowds a shabby woman in her forties appeared. She was rough-looking, and the worse for wear with booze. 'My boyfriend's in there,' she said, pointing into a fish-and-chip shop. 'It was me who called you. He has a gun.'

As I looked in at a dishevelled figure in the takeaway, I saw the man, now aware of us outside, trying to stuff a handgun down the side of the red vinyl benches which ran along one side. Being plain pissed off took the place of my earlier feelings of vulnerability. I still had a PR 24 baton which could inflict some damage. Tony and I burst into the chip shop. I brought my baton down hard on the suspect's right arm, closest to where the barrel of the gun was visible. He was then dragged down, nose to the floor, with Tony kneeling between his shoulder blades. He was a big, flabby, smelly specimen. I retrieved the weapon and tried to clear it. It was an imitation. The fucking bastard! After a drunken argument with his girlfriend he had told her he was going to go out and waste a few people in the street. She believed he might do it, and had always presumed that his toy gun was real, so she had phoned in the 999 call. We nicked him and carted him off to the station. The armed response team turned up about ten minutes later.

I decided that it was only a matter of time before one of the many firearms sightings which were reported each week turned out to be a genuine lunatic on the loose with a gun. If that happened, the thought of being helpless to defend either myself or the public was too much. I applied for firearms training and, while at Brighton, completed the Sussex Police firearms course which allowed me to be an authorised firearms officer (AFO) on division.

Despite having done initial and frequent refresher training in the RUC, it was a requirement to train again within my new force. I was counting the weeks before the course started. Then, with a couple of weeks to go, my mother died. She had been in and out of hospitals and care homes for over a year. I sat with my brother and sister in the hospital near Shoreham, watching her painfully gasp for breath as her lungs finally gave up. Her death, although expected sooner rather than later, left me feeling crushed. I had arrived at the hospital with a new nightgown and fresh toiletries for her. I was not mentally prepared to watch her die that day. The only consolation was that after a painful struggle, she appeared to reach out with the happiest expression on her face. Whatever she had seen so close to death filled her with joy. Her breathing eased, and then just faded away. She was gone. The problems in the later years of her life could have destroyed anyone. To watch your life partner eaten away by an incurable disease is a cruel fate. Despite the inevitability of the destruction of her health through the lifestyle which had taken a hold of her, I still felt bitter that she had left us so early. It was not her fault. She had become a victim of fags and alcohol; they had led to a change in her which she was powerless to control.

Regardless of her physical infirmity, in her head my mother was not an old person. She was still at times full of fun, and forever interested in other people's lives. I felt as if we had been robbed of at least ten years of her company. She would never see the child my wife and I were planning. That, more than anything, hit me hard. I should really have withdrawn from the firearms course, but I felt it would at least keep me busy and focused elsewhere.

The course was tough, and completely different from the firearms course I had completed on first joining the RUC. In the RUC, the course was just another part of the training that everyone would pass. You had to pass the course, because every officer needed to carry a weapon. If you were crap at shooting you were taken away and coached until you got it right. Eventually the instructors would find enough holes in the target to pass the recruit. If you were unsafe, the worst consequence would be that you were only allowed to carry the Ruger revolver. On the mainland, there is a high attrition rate on firearms courses. One slip and you were out.

We were trained in the Sig Sauer P226 self-loading pistol, a far less forgiving weapon than the Ruger revolver. The Sig fired 9mm parabellum rounds. It had a fifteen-round magazine capacity, which took me a long time to feel comfortable with having been so used to the Ruger. Fortunately we were also trained in the H&K MP5 carbine, an old friend.

On a basic level the courses were similar: learning drills on the range and letting the muscle memory necessary for firearms use develop. I found it annoying that there were slight differences in the drills, because often I would be carrying out a drill taught on the range in Sussex and then switch back to an element of the drill learned in the RUC firearms training. It was the same for some of the ex-military lads, but in my case I had been operating with different drills for so long, and until so recently, that they were still right up there in my subconscious.

I was never unsafe. I just wasn't as smooth as I knew I could be, which on reflection was probably down to my mind being distracted by the death of my mum. I kept running over her last few words to me. My own inability to say anything during her last moments of consciousness. I had been a sobbing wreck. What you should have said always comes afterwards. For the first time, having been involved in so much death during the course of my police career, did I really understand the true nature of bereavement. I had passed dozens of death messages to relatives, thinking I did it well, but only now did I understand the emotions that were ignited by death. How the sense of loss was so huge it made you physically ill. How as a grown man you could cry in a way that you had not done since childhood. I had periods of uncontrolled sobbing while I was alone. Pent up anger which I found hard to release.

Fortunately, those kinds of feelings do naturally heal, but for several months I was in extremely bad form. Withdrawn and inwardly bitter. My decision-making process seemed to have slowed down. At certain stages on the course I was ready to dump it. Uncertainty over whether I would have the guts to walk away from the police force kept me going. At least it was better than going through druggies' socks in the cell block!

Aside from work on the range, in the RUC the course concentrated on how to react if ambushed, move and cover exercises out of the killing zone, whether the environment be rural or urban. The bulk of the firearms training in Sussex was geared towards putting a containment on a scene. As an AFO on division we were expected, in an ideal world, to contain the scene until the specialised firearms team arrived to make an entry if required. We could also be expected to carry out searches of buildings, or areas, to turn imprecise information on the location of the suspect into precise information regarding his whereabouts. That might be in a room, a cupboard, up a tree or in the boot of a car. This involved long hours, numerous scenarios, plenty of self-criticism ('If you've fucked up, say you've fucked up'), and repeated tongue lashings from the instructors.

Some of the instructors were a little too into the whole weapons, fast cars and black romper suit thing for my liking. They were the ones who were in your face swearing and screaming when you made a tactical error. Others, who probably had less to prove, took the casual but firm approach to instructing that I had been used to with the RUC. Different instructors suit different students. They were all competent; it was just a case of different styles.

I completed the course and went on to do a developmental course with enhanced training a few weeks later. Deep down, though, I realised that I was still extremely distracted by my mother's death. I was certainly depressed by it, and as a result my concentration and general enthusiasm were not up to their normal levels.

I was on the verge of quitting the police altogether when the opportunity of a move to the airport-based Anti-Terrorist Unit came up. I grasped the opportunity, but with the knowledge that my time as a police officer was coming to an end. In my own mind, I had already made the decision. I was missing the RUC, yet I knew it was highly unlikely that they would recruit again in the foreseeable future. I missed living in Northern Ireland, and was in the strange position of being an Englishman who considered Northern Ireland more home than England.

My wife and I were now split between Sussex and the province, making regular trips back to see our friends and my wife's family, who had now moved down to Dublin. She was not enjoying living in England, yet we still had to consider my father, who was now in a nursing home for the elderly and mentally infirm. There was rarely a sign of recognition when I visited. He had reached the dreadful stage of either sleeping or staring into space. He was lost in a world that I could not reach. Those were not easy visits.

One of the last operations I was involved in before leaving Brighton was policing a 'reclaim the streets' protest in the town. It was a dimension of English life that had passed me by in the years I was in Ulster, because that type of anarchist-inspired street protest simply did not exist there. The main participants were what we at the police station called 'fraggals': whites, with dirty dreadlocked hair and layers of dirty clothes, preferably green. The aim of the protest was to block the traffic. To cause mayhem, as a way of objecting to cars. In reality it was a way at having a go at everything and everyone who stood for authority.

Hundreds of police in riot gear were deployed as several thousand protesters attempted to bring Brighton to a standstill. One of their chief objectives was to destroy the CCTV cameras in the town which 'infringed their human rights', regardless of the fact that the cameras had led to dozens of arrests for serious crime. Regardless that police themselves had to be more restrained because the cameras were recording them as well. As far as the protesters were concerned, they were the symbol of an authoritarian 'big brother' state.

The protest became nasty when demonstrators sat down to block certain streets, and police, with carefully rehearsed techniques, set about removing them. Scuffles and fights erupted. I was hit by a spotty combat-jacketed youth, with a punch which had so little force I hardly knew I'd been hit.

189

Unfortunately the guy behind me did not know that, and a split second later his PR24 baton came down with a crack and knocked the irritating little protester unconscious. He was dragged away in a bleeding heap by his mates. This kind of violent, anarchistic protesting was a complete revelation to me. Something that had developed over the years I had been away, and had not in any shape or form touched the province. I had only vaguely been aware of protests surrounding such projects as the Newbury by-pass. The violent eco-warrior generation had certainly arrived!

Towards the end of the day, when most of the trouble had died down, I spotted someone who was wanted on warrant at a table outside a bar. As I nicked him, with my partner Tony waiting by the car, the whole pub poured out. It was full of fraggals. They tried to 'unarrest' him. I held on, and eventually had to draw my baton to keep back a mob of around twenty fucked-off anarchists. Tony had beaten a path to me by this stage and together we held the crowd back. As more police arrived, it turned into a full-scale beating match. 'Did you have to nick that fella today?' one of the inspectors asked me as I was helping to load the tenth prisoner into a van. 'Yep,' I grinned. I hadn't had so much fun since Belfast.

The work on the Anti-Terrorist Unit based at Gatwick airport provided a good breathing space for me in which to make a decision regarding my future. The unit was well run, with a firearms range and first-rate instructors on site, completely self-contained in the police station building, while regular uniform patrol and CID for the airport worked from offices in the airport terminal buildings. The shift pattern had built-in training time when sections overlapped, so there was ample opportunity to get fit. Within a few months of joining the unit I was running seven miles around the airport perimeter on most shifts, or spending a couple of hours in the gym being coached by L and B, the team's 'body beautifuls'. It was the most stress-free environment I had ever worked in. I had become a policeman who did not have to worry about the fucking mess it was all turning into on the outside.

The lads on my team were excellent, because the unit attracted highly motivated and fit individuals, many with military experience. There were several faces from my early days in the police, who for one reason or other had become fed up with normal policing and had graduated into firearms and then the Anti-Terrorist Unit.

The unit was fundamentally there to counter any terrorist threat to the airport. The IRA's mortar attack on Heathrow airport confirmed that the IRA saw the bombing of an international airport as a legitimate target. In many ways, the tactical patrolling of the airport was similar to the patrolling I had done in Northern Ireland, on a smaller scale. We carried out VCPs, did sweeps through the terminal buildings, and checked potential mortar base plate sites within an area of up to three-quarters of a mile from the runway and terminals. To go into greater detail would be inappropriate. I have no wish to compromise the specific details of anti-terrorist operations and procedures at the airport. The threat is probably as high now as at any time, since the new republican terror groups have intensified their campaign.

As I tried to settle into English policing again, events in Northern Ireland continued to demonstrate that terrorism had not gone away. In February 1997 Lance-Corporal Restorick of the Royal Horse Artillery was shot dead by a sniper near Newry. Individuals later convicted of his death in 1997 have since been released under the terms of the Good Friday Agreement. In April, a reserve constable, Alice Collins, was shot in the back while carrying out duties at the courthouse in Londonderry. In May, Darren Bradshaw, an off-duty policeman, was out with friends in a crowded, well-known gay bar in Belfast city centre. Republican terrorists singled him out and shot him dead. In June of that year another off-duty officer, Greg Taylor, was beaten to death by a loyalist mob who had grievances over the RUC handling of a loyalist parade in a nearby village. Taylor was recognised as a policeman and set upon. Two other RUC men present were lucky to escape with their lives. In May 1997 two constables patrolling Lurgan were shot dead by republicans terrorists: Constable John Graham and Reserve Constable David Johnston were murdered only a short distance from the RUC station by close-quarter assassins. When, in July 1997, the IRA declared another ceasefire, the chances of it being a lasting cessation of violence did not look good.

After the murder of the loyalist Billy Wright in December 1997, 1998 began with a spate of killings amongst paramilitary groups. Most could be attributed to internal feuds or disputes over drugs territories. It took the Omagh bombing of the same year to remind the world that terrorism affecting the mainstream population had not gone away.

The atrocity of Omagh, where twenty-nine people and two unborn children were killed by a terrorist bomb on 15 August 1998, must rate as one of the most evil acts in post-war European history. A 500-pound car bomb exploded amongst shoppers on a busy Saturday, less than forty minutes after an initial and inaccurate warning had been received on the presence of a bomb. The scene of carnage was well documented at the time by amateur cameramen. Some of the less graphic, but still disturbing, footage was shown on national TV.

The event was so shocking that for a while the Real IRA did reinstate a ceasefire. Sadly, this republican breakaway group have now returned to an active campaign. It is now only a matter of time before there is another Omagh. The inquest into the Omagh bombing in September 2000 only served to act as a bitter reminder of the fact that nobody has been brought to justice for the killings. While concessions are handed out after each terrorist outrage, the killings will go on.

I left the police force when an opportunity came up in the travel business. Working at an airport can give you a wider perspective on the world. My fourteen years of policing was over. I realised that there really was a life away from police officers and police stations.

My father died peacefully in his sleep in 1999. It was a great release for him. For us all.

I spent fourteen years as a policeman, or a peeler as they are known in Northern Ireland. The majority of that time was served in the English Special Branch, or as a constable in the Royal Ulster Constabulary. By the time of publication of this book, that force may well have been thoroughly trashed by the recommendations contained in the Patten report. The last recruits to be joining the RUC, under that name, have already passed through Garnerville, the police training centre.

To put the matter simply, it appears from the sidelines that the IRA have bombed and murdered for so long that the Government has lost the will to continue the fight against terrorism. At this moment, a fully armed terrorist group have been allowed into the political process. The breakaway republicans are still planning terrorist atrocities. They appear to be growing in confidence – confident enough to have fired a missile at the headquarters of MI6 in September 2000! The institutions put in place by the Good Friday Agreement have broken down once, and may do so again because the IRA do not wish to give up their weapons. If a complete handover of arms takes place, all well and good. In the meantime the RUC, the organisation that never lost the will to combat political terror, is slowly and clinically being sacrificed.

In 1996 Ronnie Flanagan took over as the Chief Constable of the RUC. An articulate, forward-thinking officer, well liked by the rank and file, he may prove to be the best thing to have happened to the force in recent years. There could be no better man at the top to guide the force through this difficult period. The restraint that officers have shown as the murderers of friends and family have been released back into the community is remarkable.

I sometimes do not believe that people in England can fully appreciate what is happening in Northern Ireland. As one Northern Irish ex-colleague said to me recently, 'You can literally be walking through the city centre and see the man who has killed your brother, husband or father a very few years ago, heading into a bar for a drink with his mates.' The law seems to have been turned on its head. Still the weapons issue drags on. The situation would be farcical if it were not so tragic. When faced with the waves of Sinn Fein propaganda, intimidation of communities and evasive responses, the Chief Constable's sane and articulate response through the media has been striking. He remains the voice of reason in the whole uncertain situation.

At a stage when my work took me abroad often, frequently visiting the USA, Northern Ireland frequently came up in conversation. I realised then how successful the Sinn Fein propaganda machine has been in painting the RUC as a jackbooted, Nazi-type organisation.

In the latter part of 2000, a new Investigation Department under the direction of the Police Ombudsman was set up in Belfast to take over the police's previous role of investigating complaints against themselves. The investigators are civilians with the same powers as police. It is interesting that a major part of the recruitment campaign carried out by Price Waterhouse Cooper took place in Australia, South Africa and the USA. The message, rightly or wrongly, that this will send out to many is that to achieve fairness the recruits had to come from abroad. Whether, say, an individual with an interest in Irish matters, possibly of Irish descent and living in the USA or Australia, has had a balanced diet of media coverage from the province over the last decade or so is an interesting question. Ex-policemen recruited from those countries are, I would guess, more likely to be looking through nationalist eyes at the whole situation. On the other hand, it may be a great educative process for many from abroad, and show that the force is not made up of Catholic-torturing demons!

Six months on from the creation of the Investigation Department of the Ombudsman, the jury, as far as RUC men go, seems to be still out. In conversations regarding the new process I was surprised by the lack of any strong feeling following the introduction of this ground-breaking system. This may be in part because very few cases have completed the full investigative process. It also stems from the fact that the majority of officers did not view the previous system of police investigating police as being in their favour. There was distrust of the officers in the previous Discipline and Complaints Department. There will be the same distrust of the individuals tasked to interview police under the new system.

The Police Ombudsman has a staff of over one hundred, divided into three departments. The largest is the Investigations Department with more than sixty staff. Well resourced, and with so much riding on success, the Police Ombudsman is able to offer large salaries by Northern Irish standards. It will have no problem attracting talented, well qualified individuals. Headed by Mrs Nuala O'Loan, a solicitor and former lecturer in law, the public profile presented through the media in Northern Ireland has been, up to now, impressive. To be seen as impartial from all viewpoints in the province is a hard act to pull off. To have come this far, without having cultivated the complete distrust of any particular faction or interest group is one achievement on a very long journey.

One purpose of this book is to add some balance to what has become another part of history. It is not an attempt to paint the force as whiter than white. All organisations have faults. When I have encountered situations of prejudice or bad practice I have written about them. It is the personal experience of an individual, both good and bad. I had the advantage of being able to compare mainland policing with Northern Ireland.

The guys I worked with were remarkable in that they were constantly even-handed, despite the immense provocation and threat from extremists. My experience was one of a remarkably tolerant police force. Most of all, a consummately professional police force. Far higher in calibre of recruit than the police forces on the mainland that I have had dealings with and in a completely different league from all the foreign police organisations I have seen during my travels overseas.

Autumn 2000, and I was back in Ireland on holiday. I drove out of the imposing gates of the Slieve Russell Hotel in County Cavan with my family and took the road into the north to have a look around Enniskillen. En route I drove into Kinawley, where I had peered out from the sangar for many hours while with the MSU, with the constant expectation of having a large mortar fired at me. I tried to see it through civilian eyes. The area still looked grey and threatening, despite the fact that it was a gloriously sunny day. Enniskillen proved to be hugely different. Buildings which I remembered as tatty and worn were now brightly painted. New developments of luxury apartments lined the Erne waterways. It had a cosmopolitan feel to it that made one feel that the town had moved on from its terrorist-ridden past. Foreign tourists strolled around. People ate outside at a couple of cafés. A big change from the place I had policed nine years previously. It emphasised how ridiculous the whole continuation of the armed struggle by a few dissidents was.

We drove up to Belfast, and again were amazed by the number of tourists strolling around the city. When our journey took us back down to Dublin a few days later, the differences between the two cities were not as obvious as they had been ten years before. Both were exciting, vibrant places. Despite loyalist feuding and deaths on the Shankhill a few weeks earlier, those events could be seen for what they were; the result of increasingly bitter gang warfare while ex-terrorists and recently released prisoners kept up a continual battle for control of the drugs and extortion rackets. The question was whether that virus would spread and threaten the stability of the whole province.

8.

ON THE VERGE OF PEACE?

Northern Ireland remains a place of great contradictions. The past never lets go of the present and has a way of overtaking it. With so many Northern Irish politicians having previous links to the violent terror groups of the past, many see it as only a matter of time until the relative peace is shattered. What will result if that scenario unfolds remains unclear.

When I joined the RUC, there were a few individuals who talked about making preparations for the 'big day', meaning the day when the British Government tried to hand the North back to the South of Ireland. Several people I knew, both in the RUC and in civilian life, saw a future which could deteriorate into a Bosnian-type nightmare. A future in which ethnic cleansing and civil war were just around the next political corner. They were not haters of Roman Catholics. To them, it was to be a war against IRA-supporting republicans.

As individuals, these people were full of contradictions. They wanted to be part of the UK, yet they loved to see the England rugby team beaten by Ireland. They could support Liverpool or Man. United as their football team, yet if England were playing Germany they would enjoy seeing England beaten. The biggest lunacy of their thinking was seeing the Queen as a unionist pin-up, while at the same time speaking of fighting the Crown forces in order to remain British!

Whether or not a rogue element of the current generation of policemen in Ulster will go down that path is a matter of debate. From my own experience, I know there was ample opportunity to skim off ammunition from day-to-day handling of firearms because, as previously described, the checks to prevent abuses were not in place. Weapons training provided another opportunity. On a fifty-round shoot, if you decided to hold back a couple of rounds in your pocket it was not going to be noticed. I could not say whether many took advantage of that.

There was, I was told in my first week of training, reputedly a gun shop where, on production of your warrant card, rounds were sold at a pound a time. This was seen by most as a handy way of replacing individual rounds of the thirty issued for the Ruger revolver. Very helpful in the event of an ND which had occurred and not been reported, or the rounds simply being lost. It would have been, though, an impractical and expensive way of stockpiling ammunition. Hardly a means of preparing for revolution.

More realistically, there are officers who would have contacts within the extreme elements of loyalism. Not as many as in the early years of the troubles, but still a hard core with Orange sympathies exist. With those links, the availability of firearms and explosives would be certain. The real question is whether the will to become involved in an all-out struggle to prevent the gradual break from the United Kingdom is commonplace.

The type and calibre of person recruited into the RUC over the last ten years creates, in my view, a virtual certainty that the police as a whole will not be drawn into violent opposition to the current changes being imposed on the force. As in the rest of the UK, police recruits are now predominantly middle-class in background. The selection procedure is, and has been for several years, extremely rigorous. Even to arrive at the final interview stage, a candidate must go through tests and examinations, which are marked strictly on merit. The old days of nepotism, when having 'contacts' was a vital element of selection, have long gone. The majority of recruits over the last ten years would be of a high standard, and not generally from backgrounds which perpetuate sectarian views.

Another factor is the high salaries of police officers over the last decade. This has ensured that the standard of living enjoyed by policemen is way above the average. Mortgages, smart cars and a comfortable lifestyle are hard to walk away from and are certainly not worth giving up for a decline into anarchy.

Changing circumstances could very easily alter this assessment. Thirty years of terrorism has kept the level of criminal activity in Northern Ireland, aside from terrorist-related crime, very low. If a massive increase in crime occurs, whether due to the numbers of criminals released into the community under the Good Friday Agreement, or simply as Northern

Ireland catches up with the mainland, then the consequences will be far-reaching for the province. If the numbers of the Northern Ireland Police Service are cut to the level of English forces, then the same issues affecting the mainland will be evident in Ulster. There is a very good argument to say that perhaps the numbers of police in the province are about right to provide adequate protection for the public, while on the mainland numbers are ridiculously low. Remaining officers will find themselves under immense pressure. With police pay for new recruits already eroded by the loss of housing allowances, the result will be a gradual loss of morale, an inability to retain officers and a lowering of the standard of recruit. Under those circumstances there would, perhaps, be a greater likelihood of policemen being drawn towards the extremists. The forcing on the RUC of a quota system, by which fifty per cent of candidates will be from Roman Catholic backgrounds, will create additional resentment. A belief amongst the RUC that sub-standard recruits from republican areas are being permitted to enter the force will be the inevitable result.

Early indications during 2001 are that these trends are well underway. Many officers speak of being totally demoralised by the new atmosphere in policing. Sickness absence in the RUC is higher than most other UK police forces. Crime of all kinds is on the increase. Sectarian conflict, rather than diminishing with the scaling down of the terrorist war, appears to be spiralling out of control. Each news report from Northern Ireland is a litany of pipe bombs thrown through windows and sectarian intimidation. In some parts of the province the army has been recalled back onto the streets to help the over-stretched RUC cope with the violence. It has a familiar ring to it.

Despite these negative signs the recruitment drive carried out in 2001 attracted over 8,000 applicants. Common sense alone dictates that from that number of applications, the standard of recruits, whether chosen under a quota system favouring Roman Catholics or not, will be high. Disillusioned as the current personnel in the force may be, there are thousands of willing potential recruits anxious for their opportunity to join the force.

If it is unlikely that the RUC would oppose the introduction of policing changes inspired by the Patten report by violent means, does it follow that Ulster is at last on the verge of peace? Unfortunately Northern Ireland has been on the verge of peace for so long that a drift one way or the other is

199

overdue. The trend towards a sustained renewal of a terrorist campaign by dissident republicans, combined with an increase in paramilitary gang crime, points to an ominous future.

The loyalist feud on the Shankhill Road during the summer of 2000 led to more than 250 families fleeing their homes. The scale of that displacement of persons was unusual. Significantly, the families who fled were Protestant families being intimidated out of their homes by fellow Protestants. The loyalist gang warfare has provided another dimension to policing Ulster, and will place added pressures on communities where paramilitary influence is on the increase. To sit and watch the evening news in Ulster shows how punishment-style beatings on both republican and loyalist estates have become a daily normality.

As Ulster drifts in a state of uncertainty from 2000 to 2001, the events in, and related to, the province have taken on the characteristic sense of impending crisis which afflicts Ulster politics. Despite a surge of police activity in Ireland by the Garda directed against dissident republicans, the Real IRA in particular shows all the signs of a terrorist group on the rise. The Real IRA formed in 1997 after splitting from the Provisional IRA. The group had a strong foundation with the IRA's quartermaster general and top bomb-maker being one of the dissidents forming the nucleus of the leadership. With members increasing, even since the Omagh bombing, in South Armagh, Fermanagh, Londonderry and the border counties of the Republic, the terrorist group's ability to mount attacks increases each month. The regular attacks on security bases in the province and devices left on railway lines have the appearance of low-key operations, part of the preparation and training of new volunteers for bigger events.

Despite the arrests carried out by police in the Republic, little damage has been done to the Real IRA. The pro-active policing actions of the Garda contrasts pointedly with the way terrorists were permitted to run free prior to the 1994 ceasefire. The ability of the Garda to seal all border roads during the foot-and-mouth crisis of 2001 was particuarly ironic, when compared with the previous token efforts over the last 30 years at closing off the border to terrorist movement. Unfortunately, the majority of Real IRA suspects detained under the anti-terrorist legislation in the south, including suspects for the Omagh atrocity, have been released without charge. Should more be charged, as the enquiry into Omagh appears to be making progress, the question of whether they will ever be convicted in court has been made doubtful due to a television documentary naming the suspects. Good lawyers should have a field day with the new human rights legislation now in place. The subsequent trials may well fall apart if it is successfully argued that the suspects cannot now receive a fair hearing.

In September, the attack on the high-tech headquarters of the Secret Intelligence Service on the south bank of the Thames was an audacious response, from the dissidents, to the close attention they will be aware that they are receiving from the intelligence agencies. With millions of pounds now channelled into tackling terrorism, and with massively expensive covert surveillance operations in place, the British authorities were still unable to prevent the Real IRA firing a missile at the MI6 building.

The year 2001 has seen bomb attacks from the Real IRA on the mainland: mortar attacks at army bases in Armagh and Londonderry; bombs repeatedly placed on the railway line between Belfast and Dublin. Luck has been on the side of the security forces. It is only a matter of time before a similar attack results in a large loss of life. A tragedy on the scale of the Omagh bombing is, many feel, only a few weeks or months away.

The Provisional IRA remains a highly dangerous force. In many respects, it suits the IRA and Sinn Fein to have the Real IRA bogeymen threatening to bring down the peace process. History may show more links between the two groups than is currently realised. When the groups do clash, the Provos are quick to assert dominance, as in the murder of dissident republican Joseph O'Connor. O'Connor, a Real IRA member, aged twenty-six, was shot dead by gunmen outside his Ballymurphy home in October 2000. Although Sinn Fein and the IRA have denied responsibility, it is generally accepted that it was an IRA killing. To claim responsibility would completely invalidate Sinn Fein from further involvement in the political process. To many observers, it has reached the stage where it is unlikely that there would be any circumstance in which the British Government would exclude republicans who pay lip service to peace. The Real IRA have not been slow in stating that it was the IRA who carried out the murder. Of course, in the political world, uncomfortable truths are easily swept to one side.

On the international scene, the IRA still has in place a sophisticated empire of money laundering, drugs supply, smuggling and counterfeiting. In a probe by the US General Accounting Office, an investigative arm of

Congress, the involvement of the IRA in a vast international criminal network was detailed. It did not tell anyone anything that was not widely known, but it was good to see it confirmed by an independent source. The less sophisticated crime operations of the Real IRA, Continuity IRA and INLA were identified as province-based, with a developing international involvement. Yet it is clear that, like all criminal empires, the potential for rapid growth is massive. Perhaps the step President Bush took in May 2001 of banning Real IRA activity in the US, and listing the group as a terrorist organisation, will go some way to slowing down the development.

The IRA is still committing murders. Five years on from the first appearance of the convenience murder gang known as DAAD, whenever a dispute arises as to the amount of cut from drug dealing operations DAAD go in and assassinate the troublesome dealer. The removal of drug dealers by assassination has continued to be a regular occurrence. The strategy is clearly a risky one for the IRA, constantly taking the peace process to breaking point. The need for control over the paramilitary world, clearly transcends the danger poised to IRA credibility in the peace negotiations.

On the political front, the Unionist First Minister David Trimble has come under increasing pressure from his own Ulster Unionist party regarding the IRA's failure to hand over any weapons and the changes proposed to the RUC. The general unionist perception would be that enough concessions have been made to Sinn Fein. Should David Trimble be forced to stand down, negotiations with the Taoiseach in Dublin, and representatives of Sinn Fein, would become less likely to succeed. A complete collapse of negotiations may take Ulster back to the brink of an all-out terrorist war. With military bases removed and the RUC morale at an all-time low, the decent law-abiding majority in the province will be more vulnerable than at any time in the last thirty years of conflict.

With such factors in play, Ulster being on the verge of a peaceful era of forgiveness and tranquillity appears unlikely. In a society where hundreds of killers and potential killers have been released back into the community, where loyalists have found their patience exhausted and now at breaking point due to the concessions given to republicans negotiators, prospects for peace are no longer looking good. The scaled-down military presence, the weakening of the police, the dismantling of the whole protective structure, can only lead to an increase in paramilitary crime and general intimidation and disorder. In those circumstances, in spite of a majority in the community who are law-abiding and desperate to see the peace process succeed, the weakening of the structures which have saved Ulster from all-out civil war over the last thirty years could, it may be argued, prove to be fatal.

Northern Ireland has become the classic example of a world where the lunatics in the asylum have taken control. The root cause of this is clearly the Government's wish for peace at any price. The price is now seen to be no handover of weapons from the IRA, dissident republican terrorists increasing in strength, an increasingly frustrated and fragmented loyalist community and the streets of Ulster awash with released terrorists. It would be strange, in many respects, if the next year does not see a descent into violence and anarchy on a par with some of the worse years of the conflict.

It would be impossible for me to sit down and write a completely impartial account of policing in Northern Ireland. All I can do is present what I saw as the truth of the situation. My own feelings for those who try to achieve political aims through murder and intimidation are, I hope, feelings shared by the vast majority of the population.

In terms of length of service, compared with the majority of police officers in Ulster, who serve thirty years or more, my contribution was small. It is by virtue of the fact that I am an ex-policeman that I am able to write this book. For the officers who for many years have endured constant threat to their lives, intimidation, and the tragic loss of family and colleagues, I have only the deepest respect and admiration.

My view and experience will be different from that of many others. I would not try and pretend to be the voice of the ordinary policeman, because my experience is from my own perspective, as an Englishman in the Ulster community. I believe that the English will always be seen as outsiders in Northern Ireland. I know English people who have lived in the province for thirty years and still feel they have not been fully accepted. I know some who will feel I have no business writing about Northern Irish matters. It is because of such attitudes that I feel I do! Many may disagree with my interpretation of events. I make no apology for that. We all see each situation from a different perspective. The force has obviously moved on since my period of service. It does not mean that there is no value in examining the past.

This is my own view as a private individual. My own history. On a larger scale, the history of the last thirty years of terrorist conflict will be written by examining the stories from all the different viewpoints of those involved in the war. Thousands of lives, caught up in tragic and extraordinary events. Policing in Ulster was one face of those complex events. There are very few accounts of what it was like to serve as an ordinary policeman in the RUC. This is one of them.

RIVERSID...

RIVERSIDE LANE

GINGER BLACK

[signatures]

MOMENTUM BOOKS

Riverside Lane
First published in Great Britain in 2016 by
Momentum Co.
www.momentumbooks.co.uk

1 2 3 4 5 6 7 8 9 10

Hardback ISBN 978-1-911475-00-2
Paperback ISBN 978-1-911475-01-9

A CIP catalogue record for this book is available from the British Library.

Typeset by Octavo Smith Publishing Services
www.octavosmith.com

Jacket design by Matt Willis
sclef.co.uk

Printed and bound in the UK by TJ International

To:

Jan
Nicolas
Jonathan
Jim
Josephine
Frederick
Benjamin
Freddie James
Louisa
Felix
Jeremy

... and to you, for reading this book to the end.

ACKNOWLEDGEMENTS

Special thanks to Wendy Leavesley and Shelley Phillips for the superb film they made for our website, and to Anna Kierstan, who patiently proofread the final draft.

Our gratitude goes to Jeff Prestridge, YTL Hotels, Denise Ellis, Kevin Snook and the Monkey Island Hotel for providing the inspiration for so many beautiful scenes in the book. We are indebted to Tim Moore and Mitch Albert at Momentum Co., and to our talented editor, Jasmin Kirkbride.

Finally, eternal thanks to our husbands Nicolas Thum and Jonathan Lockwood for believing in us, and to our wonderful children for all their kindness, patience and understanding during the writing of *Riverside Lane*. We could not have done this without you.

Thanks to everyone who helped make *Riverside Lane* a success with their support on www.kickstarter.com:

Alan Jones, Alex Rowe, Alice Gellatly, Allan Donaldson, Amanda, Amanda Barron, Amanda Guinan, Amanda Pepper, Amanda Spilman, The Amber Zone Clinic, Andrew Carpenter, Andrew Howells, Andy Brown, Angela and Alan Hearn, Angela Elbourne, Angela Smith, Angie Parkinson, Angus Fowler, Ann McTaggart, Anna Kierstan, Annabel Thum, Anne Baraniecki, Anne Manson, Barbara Zanin Amblard, Barrie Mair, Benjamin Thum, Bray Hair Studios, Brenda Blake, Caroline Power, Carolyn Morgan, Catherine Ryan, Cecilia Del Favero, Charlotte le Butt, Charlotte Overton, Chris and Linda Binsley, Chris Coles, Chris Collis, Christian Graham, Christina Scandelius, Christopher Brain, Claire Burnett-Scott, Claire Murray, Corrine Curtis, Dan Hop, Daniel Murphy, Danny Sheehan, David and Adrienne Robinson, David Gulliver, Debbie Roberts, Deborah Britton, Denise Snook, Diane Burnham, Diane Coyne, Dr Adrian Haffegee, Duncan Fox, Elaine Leigh, Emily Russell, Emma Bong, Emma Child, Emma Eversfield, Felix Thum, Fiona Bruzas, Forest Bridge School, Francesca Carpenter, Freda Thum, Freddie James Lockwood, Frederick Thum, Geoff Revell, Gillian Mason, Glynis Moore, Graham Barker, Gregory Reczynski, Gwyneth Edwards, Hannah-Rose Dutfield, Hayley Bull, Heather Barron, Helen Carpenter, Helenn Glasson, Henrietta Mitford, Henry Carpenter, Henry Gewanter, Hitec Laboratories, Iain Garden, Ian Yeldham, Inger Breitenstein, Irina Lenchits-Evans, Iveta, Jack Fisher, Jackie Richards, Jacqueline Brear, Jacqueline Giles, Jade Anderson, James Del Favero, James Senior, Jane Balmer, Jane Kierstan, Jane Smith, Janet Pengelly, Janette Verrall, Jayne Wells, Jean and Alan Spilman, Jean-Luc Reyes, Jeff Prestridge, Jen Brown, Jennifer Stacey, Jenny Morgan, Jeremy Pengelly, Jessie Clapp, Jim Pengelly, Joanna Wong, John Bowman, Jon Withers, Jonathan Lockwood, Josephine Thum, Julia Haythorn, Julie Graham, Juliet, Justus, Karen Drake, Kate Green, Kathy Fabry, Kathy Hammad, Keith Parsons, Kristin Gould, Laura Miller, Laura Withers, Laurence Holloway MBE, Leonidas Koumantakis, Lesley Collins, Lincoln Jopp, Linda Leigh, Lindsey Davenport, Lisette Sens, Liz and Malcolm Morgan, Liz and Tim Smith, Liz Morgan, Lola Bowman, Lora Burnett, Louisa Bateman, Louisa Forward, Louisa Thum, Lucy, Lucy Maxwell, Lydia Casadei, Lyndsey Holmes, Lynn, Lynne Kennedy, M. Rawlings, Mandy Herne-Smith, Margaret Burnett, Margaret Kivell, Maria Wrigely, Marie Oldham, Mark Spilman, Massoud Entekhabi, Maureen and Cedric Simmons, Maureen Norton, Meri Leak, Michael Kelly, Michael Powell, Mike Charleton, Milly Ayliffe, Miranda Absalom, Mollie J. Lockwood, Monkey Island Hotel, Monica Cornforth, Monica Wyatt, Neil Simpson, Nicholas Trigg, Nick Pengelly, Nicola Hussey, Nicolas Thum, Nigel Anker, Norma Thomas, Patsy at Rosemead Surgery, Paula Ray, Pauline Moore, Pendle Jackson, Peter & Lin Hughes, Phil Jacobs, Pierre Silavant, Polly Ingham, Rachel Evans, Rebecca Fox, Richard Cowles, Robert & Claire, Robert Dauney, Robyn Meboroh Collinson, Russell Forgham, Ruth Simons, Sally Hamilton, Sam Murgatroyd, Sara Del Favero, Sara Edgar, Sarah Fossella, Sarah Swain, Sarah Yorke, ShakeIt, Shelley Phillips, Sian Webster, Simon and Pat Davis, Sinead Sillars, Siobhan Bailey, Slimane Beiji, Sonia Allison, Sophie and Tom Eastwood, Sophie Chubb, Story in Bray, Susan Childs, Tessa Collinson, Thalia Kenton, Thomas Gartenmann, Tonya Dorney, Trevor Meboroh-Collinson, Tricia Welch Bland, Ulrike Wefelscheid, Vicki Owen, Vivenne Wray, The Wendy House, Wendy Morgan, Wendy Wright, Wraysbury Dive Centre, Yvonne Linley, Zita Crewe.

A NOTE ABOUT BRAY

Riverside Lane and its residents are fictional, and the novel is set in the twenty-first century. However, the authors wished to imbue it with the glamour of Bray's bygone age.

The quintessentially English village of Bray, Berkshire, is a feast for all the senses, from the aromas of its renowned culinary delights to its charming, timber-framed cottages, medieval church and splendid riverbank.

Today the peaceful village is best known for gastronomy, and lays claim to two of the restaurants in Britain awarded three Michelin stars. Wind the clock back, however, and you can hear the ghosts of Bray's glorious, decadent past: the clink of china as Edward VII takes tea on the immaculate lawns of the Monkey Island Hotel ... the haunting strains of Elgar's *Violin Concerto*, floating downstream from the Hut, where the composer often stayed and worked ... an echo of jazz as stars of the silent screen dance in the looming shadow of another world war.

You might hear the whirr of a movie camera at Bray Studios in the 1960s, as Anthony Head makes another Hammer classic, its grandiose style – death, sex and colour – making Bray the horror capital of the world ... you might see Diana Dors, "the British Marilyn Monroe", cycling through the village in hot pants ... you might also see Sylvia Anderson gliding by in a Rolls-Royce Silver Shadow, every inch as elegant as her alter ego, Lady Penelope in *Thunderbirds*.

The history of Bray can be traced back thousands of years. Ancient artefacts such as Neolithic axes and late Bronze Age swords have been found in the river, and Roman coins were discovered near the vicarage. Bray Church dates back to the early medieval era, and may be known best for *The Vicar of Bray*, an eighteenth-century satirical song about an infamous sixteenth-century cleric, who changed his views eagerly with every shift in the political and religious climate in order to retain his office.

In the 1920s, the Bright Young Things, that gilded generation of party-lovers, frequented Bray's fashionable nightspots and restaurants and put the tiny village on the global map. In an epoch synonymous with hedonism, aristocrats and film stars descended on Bray's hotels and the "clubs" of Ferry End to indulge their passion for cocktails, jazz and dancing. "Are you married, or do you live in Bray?" became a teasing query among the London social elite as they skipped from lunches to tea dances to parties and on to the nightclubs, returning home at dawn when ordinary folk were going to work.

"To feed and dance, always to be moving, that is the thing. We daren't risk more than an hour or two in sleep, in case something happens while we aren't there," declared one reveller, encapsulating perfectly the spirit of Bray's golden age.

ONE

ADUSKY GAUZE VEIL lifted to reveal the soft pink light of dawn. The sun recast the Earth in a glorious patchwork of fields, and a cacophony of birdsong stirred the residents of Riverside Lane from their slumber. Cherry and magnolia trees formed a guard of honour over the lane, which lay tranquil, deserted and calm.

High above, skimming the rose-coloured clouds, a British Airways jet descended over the River Thames. Luca Tempesta checked his seatbelt and reached for his cigarettes, curling his fingers around them with the zeal of a junkie. He flipped the packet, prompting disapproving looks from a couple playing chess beside him, and thought about his meeting with the Russian academic. He had felt bound by reckless honour to visit his wife's friend and mentor in Moscow, despite the risk. The man had deserved to know what happened to Natasha, but it gave Luca even more to hide.

The scent of freshly ground coffee permeated the cabin, reminding the American of his caffeine-addicted wife; he missed her clear, analytical mind and ability to rationalise situations. He thought of her final moments, and her terror as the net had closed in. She had paid the ultimate price for her loyalty. He stretched his legs into the aisle, seeking a comfortable position for his tall frame, and quashed a familiar feeling of dread that he knew served no purpose. It was imperative that he maintain a cool head; he could not afford the luxury of surrender. He turned his attention to a photo of Kingfisher House. Luca's agency partner, Maria, had found the place through a movie-industry fixer who knew an Englishman in need of a roof over his head in California.

"It's a house swap," Maria had explained. "You'll move into his pad in rural England, and he'll have your beach house in Malibu. The guy's got himself talked into buying a slice of the Hollywood dream, investing in a movie about a sex addict. It's gonna bomb, so there's no danger of him overstaying his welcome." The arrangement had cost Luca a fortune in backhanders and bribes, but it had been worth every dime for the simple guise.

"There's no paper trail," Maria had explained, "no contracts, no money, no nothing. It's all done on trust – a 'gentleman's agreement'. Jeez, only in England could such an arrangement be sealed with a handshake."

Six weeks had passed since Clive Buchanan's letter had dropped into his agency's PO box, the final proof – just as the fixer had claimed – that they had found the last man on Earth who wrote letters and sent snail mail. Luca scrutinised Clive's flowery, turquoise handwriting on the crisp, white card: *If Ivy Midwinter isn't in my shop, Village Antiques, and if my son Sam isn't at home, the key can be found under the potted verbena to the right of the orangery.* Luca, who did not know a verbena from a violet, felt such archaic security arrangements reinforced Maria's point that the tiny village was the antithesis of Los Angeles. She had found the perfect place to keep him safe and untraceable.

The house itself looked like the set of a horror movie, with turrets, a wine cellar and a back lawn stretching down to the Thames. *Simply marvellous for an early evening aperitif,* Buchanan had written. Luca wondered what the Englishman would make of the beach house in Malibu, from which Maria had erased all trace of his former life.

"The place looks like a gleaming show home," she had told him. "We've scrubbed it clean. All your belongings are in storage. There's no clue you were ever there."

The announcement was made that it was time to disembark, and Luca waited to leave the plane last, scrutinising the passengers as they filed onto the waiting shuttle. None of them seemed particularly interested in him. Meet-and-greet signs were held aloft in the arrivals area. He scanned the barrage of banners for his code name, exchanged passwords with a grey-looking driver and then followed him wordlessly out of the airport and into a black Mercedes.

The first stop was Village Antiques, where the house keys were handed over by an old woman named Ivy, who glared at the cigarette pack in Luca's hand.

"Look after the place," she said curtly, "and no smoking inside. It's an old house, steeped in history."

In the car, Luca resisted the urge to check his messages. The mystery emailer who had been hassling him, and who seemed to know so much about his life, was a problem for another day. For now, he needed to get into character and listen to the driver's tour of the neighbourhood: it might save his life at some point.

The Village was postcard-pretty with ancient, timber-framed cottages and a war memorial decked in poppies and pansies, which fluttered in the breeze. The driver waited as a shiny van boasting a ROYAL APPOINTMENT warrant blocked the road to deliver artisanal cheeses to a beige brick building with no nameplate. The dappled sunshine, along with his jet lag, made the Village seem surreal to Luca. He rubbed his eyes as three chefs in white, starched hats appeared from nowhere and circumvented the traffic, holding a tray of iced lobster aloft. Maria had told him about the Village's famous eateries. It was the sort of place where you could buy a bowl of snail porridge, but not a carton of milk. They passed a cricket pitch and turned into the exclusive enclave of Riverside Lane, which would be his home for the next three months.

There was no burglar alarm at Kingfisher House, and the entrance was adorned with stuffed animals. Leaving his luggage on the marble floor of the hallway, Luca made straight for the oak staircase, bounded to the upper floor and walked purposefully down a dark corridor before ascending wrought-iron steps into the attic. The room had far-reaching views across the Village and the town beyond, just as Maria's floor plan had shown.

He forced open a window, and the sweet fragrance of freshly mown grass drifted in with the breeze. Satisfied that the place would meet his requirements, Luca strode downstairs, guided by the natural light from the French doors, and stepped out onto the wet terrace. At the end of the garden, glinting in the light and replete with the day's rains, flowed the Thames. Luca walked slowly through dappled sunbeams to where ash and alder stood to attention, and willows bowed low to the water's passage. Nothing could have prepared him for this. He lived right by the ocean back in Malibu, but that suddenly seemed plastic where this river felt real. The beach was a little gaudy; the riverbank, a gift from nature. A single scull sped by, and Luca longed to be on the water, in that boat. As the river flowed along on its determined journey to the sea, his frenetic mind stilled a little. He sat on the pontoon and lit a cigarette.

"Beautiful, isn't it?" A woman's voice broke the silence, and Luca turned to see a pretty redhead walking towards him across the lawn. The sky had opened into an endless blue, and the garden greenery flattered it. A whoosh of breeze sent the leaves chattering, and the woman's dress flew up around her waist to reveal a shapely pair of legs.

"Whoops," she giggled, trying to hold down her skirt. "That's a bit gusty around the gusset! You must be Luca. I'm Clive's friend, Cecilia Honeychurch."

The beauty of the surroundings and the gentleness of the woman threw Luca off-balance in a way that all the danger of recent months had failed to do. He hesitated for a moment, then stretched out his hand.

"Luca," he said, "I've just arrived from Los Angeles."

"I know," Cecilia laughed, proffering a Tupperware box. "That's why I'm here. Do you have everything you need?"

"Well, I'm not sure I would put it quite like that," he replied, taking the box and opening it, "but at least now I have a cake!"

To say that Cecilia Honeychurch was furious with Clive was an understatement. What was he thinking, leaving a Fortnum & Mason hamper for his American guest, who would be tired and hungry and in need of more sustenance than a bit of Patum Peperium and some marmalade? That was the trouble with Clive – he always missed the bigger picture. Cecilia's mind wandered to their final parting, sweet kisses and vague promises of commitment when he returned from his soul-searching in California. Big talk of film company *soirées* and glamorous parties. It would be the making of him, he had insisted. *Him*, reflected Cecilia, always him. Most people who needed to regroup went for a long country walk and looked at something green, but not Clive. He had to do everything on a grand scale, fly off to another part of the world and invest in an industry he knew nothing about.

It had been out of character for the man Cecilia loved to take such a risk. Clive liked the safe life, or so she had believed; but either she was wrong, or she had never really known him in the first place. Worse still, tucked away in the deeper recesses of her consciousness was a cruel, tiny voice telling her she had wasted the best years of her life on him. But if Cecilia needed to confront the reality that her relationship was a bad fit and that, at forty-two, she had been worn down by commitment-phobic men, she was not ready to do so yet.

Dismissing her rising discontent, she had smoothed down her long, curly hair and pressed the doorbell at Kingfisher House, her arrival heralded by seven imperious chimes from the grandfather clock in the hallway. Getting no reply, she strolled to the back garden and found the American contemplating the river. He looked intense and solitary, and Cecilia immediately regretted disturbing him for such a silly reason as strawberry shortcake. She had half-expected a sun-kissed, sharp-suited Hollywood executive with a chiselled jaw, but the man before her looked dishevelled and slightly menacing, with a deep scar running down his right cheek.

A gust of wind had sent her dress billowing around her waist, and that had broken the ice. When she introduced herself – still flushed from the wind catching her skirt – as Clive's "friend", she surprised herself with the lie. It had tripped off the tongue so easily, and caught her off guard. *Friend?* Where in Heaven's name had that come from? Lover, devotee, follower, more like. What a bloody fool she had been. The American invited her into the house, and Cecilia noted that it was as cold as a tomb inside.

Bustling around the kitchen, she felt the intensity of Luca's gaze as he slouched against the wall, flipped his cigarette packet open and boldly appraised her body. For a split second she felt a little afraid, but something in his expression made her trust him. The man looked haunted – and Cecilia had always had a soft spot for troubled souls.

She fired up the Aga, ramping up the thermostat to full before working her way around the house, turning on all the radiators. That would serve Clive right; let the bugger face a massive utility bill when he got home. It was a small, silly revenge, but when facing the ravages of an unrequited love, even the tiniest triumphs count.

"It's like a museum," said Luca, and Cecilia noticed that his eyes twinkled when he smiled.

"Oh yes, that's the way Clive likes it," she replied, casting out an expansive arm. "The older and more ancient, the better. I think it's his way of making himself feel young again. Of course, it's not cheap, such casual decay. What may look like threadbare grandeur to you is, I am assured, the ultimate in shabby chic, the last word in English unassuming good taste. All very Clive ..."

She trailed off with a forced grin. Talking about Clive, and being in his home among his books and his clutter, was starting to make Cecilia feel sad. She did not want to be downcast. This poor chap needed looking after, and a miserable face was not going to do either of them any good. Luca opened the fridge to find it empty, and Cecilia rummaged through a cupboard overstuffed with sticky relishes and Duchy delicacies.

"Sam's supposed to have sorted all this out for you," she said. "He is hopeless."

"Sam?"

"Clive's son. He lives in the boathouse out there." Cecilia pointed out the kitchen window to a daub-and-weave building at the bottom of the garden. "He's supposed to have given you a welcome,

16

but things like this ... well ... they're not really Sam's forte. You know, brain the size of a planet, but not one iota of common sense. I'll tell you what, the Aga is going to take an age to warm up; why don't we head down to the Crown? I'll see if he wants to join us."

Sam did not want to go to the pub, nor did he want to meet his father's houseguest – but there was a chance the American would pay for the drinks, so he agreed. He turned up his music and ignored Cecilia's attempts to draw him into the conversation. She gave him a "look", however, so he removed his headphones.

"So what made you choose our little village for your holiday?" Cecilia asked brightly.

"England's always interested me," Luca replied. "Y'know, The Queen, afternoon tea, Shakespeare."

"Will you check out *Hamlet* while you're here? It's in town, and I've heard it's fantastic."

"Sure," mumbled Luca, "I'm a big fan of cigars." Cecilia's confusion turned to laughter, and Luca joined in with what Sam thought was forced gusto.

"And there are two famous restaurants nearby you might like to try."

Luca nodded. "I've heard that one of the chefs is a bit of a mad-professor type. Always creating new culinary inventions." Sam groaned inwardly at the ensuing chatter. The last thing he needed was another foodie pontificating about how marvellous the Restaurant was; it was bad enough being forced to listen to his father, and anyhow, the American would never get a table.

They stepped into the comforting embrace of the pub where Felicity, who lived across the lane from Kingfisher House, was serving. Sam reckoned she was the real thing, and sexy, too, in a tired, older rock-chick sort of way. He could see her checking out Luca, who was certainly no looker but could probably more than satisfy Felicity in the dosh department. Sam glowered and Cecilia elbowed him in the ribs.

"Make an effort," she hissed. He shrugged his shoulders. "You know exactly what you're doing, Sam. Snap out of it and make the poor bloke feel welcome."

Sam did not want to make an effort. He was feeling anxious. What if Luca wanted to talk every minute of the day? He was not equipped for socialising; it only made his "problem" worse. He needed to make it crystal clear that he was not available for chitchat, so he kept up his scowl despite Cecilia's chiding. All of it was lost on Luca, who appeared not to notice anything was amiss. At least the American had done the decent thing and bought a round of drinks, and Sam would ponce a meal off him later. If he had to put up with the inconvenience of a stranger invading his personal space, it was only fair that the man shell out, especially as Cecilia would probably not be feeding him so often now that Dad had gone.

Sam felt sad for Cecilia, who was putting on a brave face. He would have liked to talk to her about his father, but touchy-feely stuff was not his thing. He had known his old man would cast her aside one day; Dad thrived on courtship, but ran a mile at the first sign of commitment. Sam was the opposite: he loathed the chase, but longed for somebody to settle down with. It was humiliating to have a Casanova for a father, and so few notches on his own bedpost.

The door opened and a small, rotund man entered with a magician's flourish, waving an umbrella like a conjurer's stick. He had an orange face and wore a brightly patterned jumper. Sam groaned and inched further down the bar; if anyone was going to send his "problem" into overdrive, it was Frank Fielding.

"Raining cats and dogs out there," Fielding announced in a strong, suave voice that belied his stature. He extended a hand to Luca.

"Frank Fielding's the name." The American paused for a heartbeat, then shook it vigorously.

"Luca," he said. "On holiday from Los Angeles."

"A-ha, fresh from La-La Land!" Frank accepted a drink from

Felicity as he spoke. "I know it well. What do you think of our beer? I know you Americans prefer to drink weak, pissy-tasting beer, but we Brits favour warm, beery-tasting piss. You'll soon get used to it." He raised his glass in welcome, then invited Luca to dinner with great insistence, wandering away without even waiting for an answer.

"Frank is an ex-game show host," Cecilia whispered in Luca's ear. "Had his heyday in the Eighties; he's a bit faded now."

Sam smiled through gritted teeth. This felt like an ideal time to throw light on the house-swap malarkey that, to his mind, was just a bit too convenient. Cecilia had warned him not to air his conspiracy theories in public, but what the hell.

"So, you know this character who organised Dad's house swap, do you?" he asked.

"Sure, but not that well," Luca replied, tapping his cigarette pack as he spoke. "He's a friend of a friend."

"And how do you know this 'friend of a friend'?"

"Oh, Sam, stop giving our guest the third degree." Sam scowled, irritated by Cecilia's interruption as she switched the conversation, "Did you have a lovely break in Russia, Luca?"

A look of steel passed over Luca's face. "Russia?"

"Yes, Ivy Midwinter said you'd been to Russia." Sam watched the cuckoo attempting to take over his father's nest carefully, and the man definitely missed a beat before smiling broadly.

"Well, there's nothing like Moscow in the springtime!" he declared, his blue eyes crinkling in the corners. "That woman is a real Miss Marple. I'd heard the English like to gossip, but she seems to know more about my vacation than I do!"

"I think she's more like M," Cecilia laughed. "With the church and Village Antiques as her mission control centre! She seems to manipulate the great and the good of the Village, so she must know where all their skeletons are buried."

"Evidently," Luca muttered, then turned to Sam. "What d'you reckon? You must know her well, what with her working for your Dad."

Sam ignored Luca's question and munched on his Cornish pasty. Cecilia filled the gap by chattering about her catering business. The American was evidently transfixed by her charms, and who could blame him, Sam thought. It was true his father was pretty invincible in the game of love – but watching those two share private jokes when he had only been gone forty-eight hours, Sam could not help but wonder if his old man knew what he was doing this time around.

Luca bid Sam and Cecilia goodnight, then lingered outside the pub, chain-smoking and watching the dawdlers undertake the strange English ceremony of the long goodbye. He got out his brand-new, contractless phone and dialled Maria's number. On the other side of the world, Maria picked up her phone in an instant. Luca whispered into the mouthpiece.

"I'm here, all good. I need you to run a check on Ivy Midwinter, the old broad who runs Buchanan's antique shop. She knows I've been in Russia, and we need to find out how."

Switching off his phone quickly, Luca inhaled the cold night air, which hung heavy with the smell of damp earth. He was extremely tired; an insidious fatigue seeped into his bones and froze his soul. He lit a cigarette and used the glowing butt and a waxing moon to illuminate his path back to Kingfisher House. His weariness meant he did not notice the eerie hoot of the owl or the shrieks of warring cats as he passed through the churchyard. Nor did he hear the soft, echoing footfalls of the person following along behind him, tracking his movements.

TWO

AMANDA JONES PUNCHED Frank Fielding's number into her phone and waited. She wanted to write a piece on the gorgeous Premier League footballer who had moved to the Village, but her editor had insisted she cover Frank-has-been-Fielding and some boring story about him joining forces with a fat-cat financier.

Amanda knew it looked bad that she had never secured an interview with the popular entertainer. She had applied to his agent and doorstepped his wife Bianca, but to no avail. The man was a media tart, so his refusal to take her calls was clearly personal. Surely he did not still hold against her the vituperative piece she had written about wannabe Bianca DeSilva two decades earlier? How could she have known the woman was having an affair with the king of primetime television, and would end up as the new Mrs Fielding?

Amanda hoped that if she could keep her editor sweet on this one, the feature might act as her stepping-stone to the nationals. Dreams of a regular, juicy income from selling exclusives on footballers and celebrity chefs lifted her spirits before the telephone ringtone changed subtly and her heart sank.

The call was re-routing to Frank's indomitable assistant. The journalist rolled her eyes as a prim, measured voice announced: "Ivy Midwinter, how may I help you?"

Amanda slammed the phone down. That frigid ice maiden was never going to give her access to Frank. She needed a drink. Wandering into her kitchenette, she opened the fridge door, lifted a half-empty bottle of Chardonnay to her lips and took a large swig. With a heavy heart, she dialled her answer service to face the demon messages that flashed at her accusingly.

"Please call Sainsbury Visa."

"Please call Lloyds TSB."

"Please call Julie at NatWest *urgently*. We need to talk to you about illegal activity on your credit card."

It was all right for the Frank Fieldings of this world, Amanda reflected bitterly. He was part of a selfish generation that had it easy – soaring property values and retirement at sixty on a fat pension. Amanda, on the other hand, would be working until she was practically dead, and only if some politically correct gerontophile firm would give her a job in her dotage.

She returned Julie's call, drumming her pink manicured nails against the kitchen table as she waited to be connected.

"Miss Jones," said the banker, "you made a balance transfer of three thousand pounds, then someone tried to withdraw another five hundred from Oxford Street last Saturday, is that right?"

"Yes, that was me," Amanda replied in a small, tight voice.

"Oh, but surely you realised you were already over your credit limit? We thought your card had fallen into the wrong hands."

Amanda did not know what to say. Of course she knew she was overdrawn, but it was hardly her fault if the frigging machine kept coughing up cash. Her debt mountain was becoming ever more vertiginous, and she had become adept at dodging phone calls and hiding unopened bills. She was astonished that the Oxford Street machine had actually paid out, and had laughed as she fingered the notes gleefully. She was not laughing now; she felt foolish, and more than a little afraid. A stylish yellow Selfridges bag berated her from the hallway, a summer coat folded delicately among swathes of gossamer paper within. Maybe Amanda had known, on some subliminal level, that it would never truly be hers.

"Well, I thought the bank would exercise some caution and withhold funds if there was no money in my account."

"If you are unable to make good your monthly repayment, I will need to refer you to the default department," Julie said, entering into a well-rehearsed spiel. Amanda cut her off mid-flow and wandered into the living room. She would deal with it later, when she felt stronger. Hot tears sprung up at the unfairness of it all; she had spent the last twenty years believing that if she worked hard, paid her taxes and contributed to society, she would be all right. Not exactly a champagne lifestyle, but with at least enough money, a nice house, a car, a few designer clothes. She was not sure how much she owed, but suspected it was around sixty thousand pounds. Short of selling her modest apartment on the less salubrious side of town, she could see no way out of debt.

Amanda caught sight of her reflection in the mirror. A brittle, pale, angry face gazed back, deep furrows appearing between the brows and crow's-feet tiptoeing around the eyes. Her signature flowing, dark locks – once Amanda's crowning glory – were now in need of a fresh tint to hide the grey. Leaning closer, she wondered if ebony was too harsh for ageing skin, and whether or not she should start opting for chestnut or auburn highlights.

She took another swig of wine and stared bleakly at a poster on the wall in the hall that declared: MONEY CAN'T BUY YOU HAPPINESS. Ivy Midwinter's pinched old face popped into her mind. Money! That might thaw the crone's cold heart! She was always shaking tins under people's noses, and – if the rumour mill was true – had almost singlehandedly saved the Village's church from toppling into ruin, as well as providing considerable financial support to the local dropout centre. Amanda would offer a substantial donation to Ivy's beloved church in return for an exclusive interview with Frank.

She gathered up her handbag and car keys, and smiled. For all her pious superiority, perhaps Frank's sanctimonious old sword-bearer was no better than her after all. They both shared the same motivation: filthy lucre.

Ivy Midwinter had barely lifted her eyes from the computer screen when an ancient maritime bell announced the arrival of a new customer at Village Antiques. She was surrounded by gleaming cabinets of walnut and mahogany, displaying the jewellery, medals and small pieces of silverware Clive Buchanan had collected on his travels. Each item was polished and tagged with a brown card label, tied neatly with raffia and bearing the price in Ivy's precise hand.

Though she feigned obliviousness, Ivy was fully aware of Amanda Jones wandering around the shop, waiting for the opportunity to engage her in conversation. One of the benefits of being a little old lady was that people frequently underestimated her. With her greying, gamine crop and petite figure, she looked delicate and frail beyond her years – when, in truth, she was a sprightly, doughty sixty-five-year-old. Ivy's formidable energy was, it was said, attributable to her veganism and abstention from alcohol. She walked several miles a day, eschewed her portable television for a daily newspaper and had no family or social life beyond the church. Mostly she enjoyed peaceful evenings at Sunnyside in the company of her piano and her only pet, a venerable tortoise called Peter the Rock. As her fingers flew ecstatically across the keys, her beloved Bach would sustain her against memories of the past. Ivy's demons were buried deep, but when guilt swelled up and threatened to suffocate her, she turned to God for forgiveness and to her piano to forget. For Ivy Midwinter had a secret she shared with no other living soul.

"Lovely stuff," Amanda enthused, gesturing at the antique shop's wares. Ivy nodded curtly and continued with her computer endeavours. "My name's Amanda Jones –"

"I know who you are," Ivy said, and Amanda glanced over her shoulder.

"Learning how to use the computer, are you?" she asked.

The older woman's expression was like liquid nitrogen. One advantage of having worked for one of the finest minds in Britain was to be better versed in technology than most people half her age, but Ivy understood its limitations, too. She had spent over half her life working in a business where nothing was written down, and meetings were held in whispers. Those had been dark and difficult days during which, despite having access to the very latest equipment, an agile mind had been one's best computer.

Seated primly in her chair, coolly appraising the woman who had come to poke about Clive's shop, it occurred to Ivy that the journalist's appearance might be something of a gift from God. She was obviously looking for a story, and Ivy was well positioned to give her one – though not quite the interview she was hoping for.

"Miss Jones," she said, "as you clearly have no intention of making a purchase, might I enquire how I may be of assistance?" The two women exchanged a look of mutual understanding, and Amanda stuffed a twenty-pound note ostentatiously into the collection tin on the counter.

"My editor is on my case to write a piece about Frank Fielding's links with the financial guru Bill Lewis," she said. Then, waving her chequebook in the air, she added: "I would like to make a further donation to the charity of your choice in exchange for a fifteen-minute interview with your famous employer."

Ivy respected the journalist's candour, and relented a little. "In that case, make it out to the church, please, and I shall do my best." She paused to accept the cheque from Amanda and raised an eyebrow at the amount. "But you're on the wrong scent. If you're looking for a scoop, you should be pursuing the American who has swapped houses with the proprietor of Village Antiques. That's where the real story lies."

A chill wind glided through an open window, and Amanda hesitated for the briefest of moments.

"Do you mean Clive Buchanan, from Kingfisher House?" she asked, with a glint in her eye. "Who's the American? Can you tell me a little more?"

"He goes by the name of Luca Tempesta. And he's got a secret."

"What type of secret?"

"I don't know yet. But if you can find that out before I do, then I'll grant you an interview with Mr Fielding." Ivy's smile was like a glimpse of weak, wintery sunshine as she stood to indicate that their chat was over. "Good day, Miss Jones."

Ivy bolted the door behind the journalist. Returning to her desk, she locked the drawer and squeezed her eyes shut. "The blind will see, and those who see will become blind," she intoned, blinking furiously to dispel the strange dots that had started presenting themselves in her vision. They were becoming more frequent; Ivy knew she should visit an ophthalmologist. She hoped it was not un-Christian, but the thought of being unable to read her beloved sheet music upset her more deeply than any of the memories from her past. The Victorian marble clock, which comforted her hourly with its sweet Handel music, proclaimed that there was just enough time to deliver the cheque to the bank and get back to the Village for Evensong.

Standing at the bus stop with the melodious clock chimes still echoing softly in her head, Ivy caught sight of Luca Tempesta walking through the churchyard. Handel, she thought, had been sent to law school by his father, just like this American. The former had abandoned his studies and blessed mankind with the "Hallelujah" chorus; the latter, according to Ivy's preliminary investigations, had abandoned his to set up a private-detective firm; then, some years later, he had apparently disappeared from God's Earth without a trace. Except he had not disappeared. He was here in the Village, living in Clive's house, next door to Frank, smoking Russian cigarettes. And Ivy Midwinter planned to find out why.

THREE

MOLLY MULHOLLAND SKIPPED down Riverside Lane towards the church. A gust of wind sent a squall of blossoms spinning in delicate pink leaves around her slender frame.

"Look, Cecilia, it's confetti!" she cried, dancing beneath the cherry tree.

"And you, my darling, are as beautiful as a bride," Cecilia laughed, squeezing through the antiquated gate. She was weighed down by a basket of culinary delights bought from the farm shop that morning. They were on their way to the house of the local MP, Hugh Willoughby, where Cecilia was to prepare canapés, beef Wellington and bread-and-butter pudding for sixteen guests ahead of Hugh's select-committee meeting. She had chosen the menu with care, with the aim of satisfying his wife Joy's penchant for fresh, organic produce as well as Hugh's fondness for British food – or "school dinners", as he referred to her stodgier feasts.

Watching Molly scamper ahead in the tall grass before stopping to inhale the fragrance of a lonely crop of freesias, Cecilia felt privileged to spend so much time with her lovely godchild. She was not sure, however, that Joy Willoughby would feel the same way.

"Will you get married one day, Cecilia?" Molly asked, her mind still stuck on blossom-confetti.

"Oh yes, I suppose so ... one day," she sighed. "I need Mr Right to come along and sweep me off my feet first!"

"What about Clive? Mrs Willoughby says you've 'missed the boat on that one'! What does she mean, Cecilia? Did Clive go to California by boat? Can we catch the next one so we can visit Disneyland?"

If Cecilia was stung by Joy's unkind remark, she hid it well, and picked the blossoms gently from Molly's light-brown mane.

"Boats are like buses," she said, "there's always another one following along."

"You're so pretty, Cecilia. You can marry my Daddy, and then you'll be my second Mummy." Cecilia kneeled to look into Molly's earnest eyes, and pulled her into a hug from which she found it difficult to let go.

"I can never be your Mummy," she whispered against the girl's cheek, "but I promise I shall always be your friend and never leave you."

Cecilia felt a clutch to her heart as she released the child. It had been eighteen months since her best friend Esther had succumbed to an aggressive cancer that had advanced swiftly and cut her life short by decades. It had happened so fast that they were all still feeling the shock. Cecilia and Esther had been inseparable as children, playing together in the ramshackle den at the bottom of Cecilia's garden – fun and games in their imaginary castle blossoming over the years into teenage confidences and, ultimately, the worries of womanhood.

All Esther had ever wanted was to marry her soulmate and raise a family. It had seemed like an eternity before Ted, a handsome, dishevelled musician, wandered into her arms for keeps. They had tried for years to conceive a child until, on the final round of IVF, they had struck gold: Molly came into the world, the final piece of Esther's dream life. Who could have known such joy would be so fleeting, that within a few short years Esther would be gone?

"Mummy would be so proud of you, Molly." Cecilia smiled sadly and then, as if to reassure her further, added: "She's everywhere, you know. She's the wind in the trees, the sunshine on your face and the stars in the night sky." Molly stood and gazed outwards as a soft breeze stirred the tall grass, prompting a blackbird to take flight, singing out an intruder warning to its nesting young.

"Why is wind invisible, Cecilia? Is it Mummy's soul? Oh, look, there's a pretty yellow butterfly!"

"It's a sign," said Cecilia, with conviction. "Mummy loved yellow."

Kids were so wonderful. Cecilia had not, like Esther, hankered after a family of her own, but rather assumed she would just have them one day. She was a romantic – and that, she decided, had been her undoing. She had skipped blithely through life thinking everything would fall miraculously into place. Cecilia had wanted to discuss the possibility of having a family with Clive, but the right time had not presented itself; if she was honest, she had always known what his answer would be. It had even crossed her mind to "make a mistake", but she wanted Clive to commit to her through choice, not obligation. She had not noticed the passing of time, but now she could hear the clock ticking relentlessly. She had paid a high price for leaving it down to Lady Luck.

A ferocious black cloud eclipsed the sun and, for a brief moment, Cecilia felt chilly and sad, but then Molly laughed and the sun burst through the clouds again. She hoisted the basket onto her arm, straightened her back and stepped forth. Her life philosophy was simple yet effective: one could choose to be happy, or one could choose to be sad. Esther was gone, Clive had abandoned her and she was alone. It was painful, but the hurt would pass, and Cecilia Honeychurch was determined to be happy.

Molly ran ahead, flinging Pooh sticks into the river, racing to and fro and yelping with delight as the branches gathered momentum and dashed away on the upsurge towards the lock. Catching up with her, Cecilia set down her basket and took out her sketchpad. Joy would have to wait.

Leaning against the footbridge railings, she tried to find a subject to draw. (Molly was the only person Cecilia did not feel self-conscious drawing in front of, nowadays.) The opportunity was too good: Cecilia had a birds-eye view of the splendid houses flanking the river along Riverside Lane. She caught sight of Frank astride a motorised lawnmower, his stout little body bumping from side to side as his dog chased and yapped behind him. A scantily clad Bianca sat in a deckchair by the house, with a phone tucked under her chin.

Beneath the boughs of Clive's willow tree, Luca Tempesta sat in a boat, still as a heron, and Cecilia strained to get a better view. He seemed crumpled and careworn, yet exuded the quiet confidence of a man capable of taking charge in a dangerous situation. A girlish, thrilling fantasy sprang to her mind: Luca and Clive, manly brawn and edgy attitude pitted against old-school English elegance and charm, fighting for her honour. The daydream made her blush and pull back abruptly from the railings, stuffing her unused sketchbook back in her bag.

"What's wrong. Cecilia?"

"Hurry, Molly, we're going to be late for the Willoughbys' dinner party!"

"You're bright red!"

"I'm just a little hot, that's all!"

Rosamund Braithwaite's afternoon tea with Joy Willoughby could not have come at a better time. It had been too long since Basil had had a day out of the house, and her own unaccompanied trips were few and far between, with Basil nearly always finding an excuse to join her. Devoted as she was, Rosamund could not deny the *frisson* of freedom as she crossed the footbridge to visit her old friend.

She threw a stick for Mungo, and the Labrador hurled himself into the water with enthusiasm. He was a recent addition to the family, and, while adorable, he was irritating to have about the house until he had been exercised. Rather like Basil, Rosamund thought naughtily. Of course she loved her husband. Not many women could say that, after forty-two years of marriage, their spouses still had them on the pedestal of their youth; but contempt is born of familiarity, and Rosamund did find herself longing for moments alone. Just one opportunity every once in a while to bend over without Basil goosing her, one bath without him cheerfully joining her "for a chat", one moment without her constant guilt at rejecting his ardent advances.

Perhaps a little volunteer work might fit the bill. Rosamund could talk to Edmund, Joy's brother, who had set up the Port

Sanctuary; maybe there would be a slot for her there? Of course, Basil would have something to say about it, not least because it was the charity that Frank Fielding supported. Rosamund liked Frank, and she certainly admired the time and energy he devoted to the less fortunate, but Basil was not so keen.

She checked her navy ballet pumps for mud and held a large bunch of narcissi aloft as she rang Joy's doorbell. She knew something was amiss as soon as her friend opened the door.

"Come in, come in," Joy said distractedly. Rosamund followed the cooking smells to the kitchen where she found Cecilia – apron on and blouse asunder, revealing a pretty lace bra – waving a chocolatey wooden spoon at a little girl who was eating what looked like fudge from a glass mixing bowl.

"Hello, Cecilia; Molly, dear, how are you?" said Rosamund. But Joy caught her arm and chivvied her along.

"Don't let's linger in the kitchen; it's complete chaos and far too hot," she said. "Hugh has a work 'do' tonight. It couldn't have come on a worse day, but such is life." She closed the drawing-room door firmly behind her.

"Whatever's the matter? You seem upset."

"We've been burgled!" said Joy in a stage whisper, "They've taken all my rings! I don't know how I'm going to tell Mother. Family heirlooms, all of them!"

"When did this happen?"

"Before we got home last night. Hugh had a function to attend, and I joined him, thank goodness. I might have caught them in the act!"

"But what about Myrtle, is she OK?"

"Oh, you know Mother; she never hears anything. She slept right through it."

Joy stood up and bellowed impatiently: "Mrs McConnell, could we have some tea in here, please?" Rosamund felt awkward when Joy addressed people in such a fashion. She was unfailingly charming to her and to Basil, but unnecessarily sharp with others, including – and of this she did disapprove – the poor housekeeper.

When Kathy McConnell returned with a tray, Rosamund over-compensated for Joy's curtness.

"How delicious," she said. "There is nothing quite like a cup of tea that somebody else makes, is there?"

"Unless it's far too strong, like this one," Joy interrupted. "We shall need more hot water. Rosamund takes her tea black and very weak."

"I am sorry to be so awkward," said Rosamund, catching the housekeeper's eye and hoping she understood. Kathy smiled and headed off for the hot water, passing Hugh in the doorway as she went.

"Hugh, the police will be here in a moment, do put a tie on, will you?" snapped Joy. Rosamund wondered whether husband and wife might need a moment alone,

"I'll just pop up and say hello to your mother," she said. "Won't be a tick."

Passing through the kitchen to collect a jug for Myrtle's narcissi, Rosamund picked up a follower in Molly. The girl accompanied her to Myrtle's room, leaving Cecilia with her canapés and Joy and Hugh to their discussions about the impending police visit.

"I have had the most amusing email from Frank Fielding," said Hugh. "He appears to be under the misapprehension that I can somehow help him onto the next honours list."

Joy burst into laughter. "I imagine that's why they've invited us to their ghastly dinner party this Saturday. Well, I have heard it all now: *Sir* Frank Fielding! That'll be the day!"

"Stranger things have happened," said Hugh, "but what strings he thinks I can pull from Environment, I don't know!"

Joy snorted with derision. "Can you imagine what a field day the press would have with Bianca as 'Lady Fielding'? And then if they found out it was you who had put him forward?" She shuddered.

Hugh wished Joy would visit him more often at Westminster, but she stayed determinedly away – which he thought odd, given that his wife had encouraged him to stand for Parliament in the first place. Joy had channelled all her energy and business acumen into getting Hugh elected, but after the initial thrill, disenchantment had set in as it became evident he would never reach the giddy heights of Chancellor or Prime Minister. Joy had distanced herself further from the Commons when their son Tom had declared himself gay two years earlier, as if the mere mention of his sexuality would somehow taint her husband's career.

Though Hugh had tried hard to see his wife's point of view, he could not understand why their son's choice of partner had upset her so. There were a million ways a child could disappoint, but not by being true to themselves. Gazing sadly at Joy, he was just summoning the courage to say as much; but as so often happened, he was interrupted before he had time to formulate the words.

"Don't stand there daydreaming," she barked. "Have you got the valuations? The police will be here any minute, and I need that list."

"Mrs Willoughby's kitchen is so much better than yours, Cecilia." Back from Myrtle's room, Molly was leaning against the black granite island, marvelling at the state-of-the-art utensils and enunciating the names on the shiny appliances as if to emphasise their magnificence.

"Oh, Molly, do stop being so consumerist and help me whisk the cream for the bread-and-butter pudding," exclaimed Cecilia, exasperated at the relentless chitchat that was distracting her from the job.

"I'm not a consumerist," said Molly indignantly. "I heard Mr Willoughby shout 'bloody consumerist' at a fat politician on the television, so I'm definitely not one."

"I'm pretty sure Mr Willoughby would have been yelling about communists, dear, not consumerists."

"What are consumerists and communalists anyway?"

"A consumerist is someone who pays too much attention to the material things in life, and a communist is ... well ... I'm a bit too busy to explain that now." Molly spun around on the barstool, her legs flailing as the ride gathered momentum, catapulting her onto a nearby sofa with much unrestrained mirth.

"Is everything all right in there?" Joy's commanding voice resonated from the drawing room. Cecilia ran her hands through her tousled hair in frustration. She knew Joy was on edge after the burglary, and she needed to calm Molly down or they would both be in hot water.

"Molly, do shush, you'll get us into trouble," whispered Cecilia. The kitchen was heating up quickly, and she was at a critical stage with the pastry. She had peeled her clothes down to the bare minimum, but it had not cooled her off.

"I'll tell you what, I've got a jigsaw in my bag; why don't you wash that chocolate cake off your face and then play with that?"

Molly beamed, tearing out of the room and leaving the kitchen door ajar. Joy's truculent voice echoed down the hallway.

"But it's not that simple, Rosamund!" she shrieked.

"I'm sorry, Joy. Perhaps I am being dim. Tell me again, why exactly did Hugh break the window?"

"Because my rings had been stolen ... but there was no sign of forced entry. I can only assume that Mother, or perhaps Kathy, had left one of the French doors unlocked, and the burglar just let himself in."

"And so?"

"And so, if there is no sign of a break-in then we can't make an insurance claim! God only knows how Hugh got from that to thinking it would be a good idea to break the window himself, but break it he did ... and the lock! If the police find out that he falsified the crime scene, it will be all over the papers, and his career will be up the spout. All for a bloody glass pane. Oh, if only he had spoken to me first, but no, he knew better, and quick as a flash his fist was through the window. What was he thinking, yanking at the lock like a navvy?"

Cecilia strained to hear more. She could not quite believe the Willoughbys had tampered with the crime scene.

Just at that moment, Molly burst back into the room, Mungo

in tow. "I found this naughty dog in Myrtle's bedroom," she cried, "eating the food you left her on her tray! He's gobbled the lot!"

The dog dived under the table, with Molly in pursuit. Cecilia had to shoo Mungo out of the kitchen or Joy would, quite rightly, go nuts, so she got on her hands and knees to grab him and was rewarded with a luxuriant lick.

"They're dog kisses," said Molly knowledgeably.

Cecilia relented. "Oh, you are so handsome," she said, burying her face into Mungo's soft, brown fur for a moment. "Quite the most handsome chap I have ever seen. Come here, you rascal, give me a big cuddle!"

"How very kind of you to say so! Don't mind if I do," said Hugh, stooping low and peering in delight at the trio under the table.

Joy entered the kitchen a moment after her husband, snapping irritably.

"Oh, put your tongue away, Hugh, you're as bad as Mungo, slathering everywhere – and get that wretched dog out of here!" Having Cecilia around the house unsettled Joy. It made her miss their daughter Penny, and something about the younger woman's easygoing nature made Joy feel uptight and old. She looked at her now, with her shirt undone and only her sunflower apron protecting her modesty. All that yellow made Joy feel quite bilious.

"When you've finished the canapés, I think you and Molly should be running along," she said. "I can manage the rest. But tidy up and do the bins before you go."

The doorbell rang, but Joy left Kathy to answer. She could hear her offering the policeman tea and stepped out to speed the matter along.

"Do come through," she said haughtily, showing a nervous-looking officer into the drawing room. Rosamund called Mungo and gave Joy a reassuring hug.

"Must dash," she said, seeing Rupert's name pop up on her phone. "I've just spotted a missed call from our prodigal son."

Joy waved her out and opened the door to the kitchen where, to her exasperation, Hugh was now sitting at the table with Cecilia and Molly, enjoying a large piece of chocolate fudge cake.

"Hugh," she hissed, "could you come in here and witness all of this, please?"

"I'm sure you don't need me, Tinkerbell," he said, laughing. "You can more than handle it all by yourself."

Joy was perfectly aware she could handle the police interview alone, but she did not want to: she wanted Hugh to take control. Just once, she did not want to be the coper, the doer, the voice of reason. But she was not well versed in the art of asking for help, and her vulnerable side was too well hidden for Hugh to see it, so, as she always did when she needed a little understanding, Joy lashed out with judgment.

"Well far be it for me to interrupt your little tea party," she retorted, surprised that she felt hurt not to have been included. "Why don't you let me go and sort out the godawful mess you have made, and you just sit there and eat cake!"

"You sound like Marie Antoinette!" said Molly. "We're learning about her at school."

FOUR

LUCA PLUGGED INTO his iPod and set off on his run. Furious black rainclouds raced him along the towpath as the music projected vivid memories onto the cinema screen of his mind. Natasha, standing outside the library at UCLA, sipping tea from a polystyrene cup, her nose tucked into a book on Russian art, her body full of sharp angles and her skin luminously white. She looked intense and solitary, oblivious to the light mizzle that fell on her chestnut hair. Luca remembered how he had felt compelled to speak to her. She had given him an enigmatic smile and waved her soggy book aloft, the words *objet d'art* rolling sexily off her tongue. She had reminded him of the exotic double agent Mata Hari.

Everyone had said they were too young, that it would not last; but caught up in the carefree madness of youth, they had ignored family mutterings about being "as different as night and day", preferring to think of themselves as yin and yang – complementary opposites. Luca wiped the sweat from his forehead and left the towpath, quickening his pace towards the Village.

When the angry heavens at last released their ammunition, the American lifted his face in surrender. Natasha had loved the rain. His cheeks stung and her lovely face, a pale ghostly spectre, lingered somewhere beyond the raindrops. He let out a defiant shout and sprinted towards the Crown, where flames from the lighted hearth shone through the windows like a beacon.

"Evening, Luca!" grinned Felicity from behind the bar. "You look like a drowned rat! Here, take this towel and I'll pour you a glass of water."

Since his first evening with Cecilia and Sam, Luca had taken to punctuating his days with an early evening run and a visit to the pub on his way home. A crowd of pensioners were evidently given to the same habit, arriving on the dot of six and leaving at the next chime of the grandfather clock. Frank Fielding was a regular too, with his own beer mug and his favourite corner table, from which he held forth on world events.

Today Luca was early, and the bar stood empty. He took up his usual position, back to the wall and facing the door, and waited for the locals to arrive. He knew from experience that provincial watering holes were a good place to gather intelligence. Drink loosened tongues, and it had not taken long for him to drum up information from the village gossips. Ivy Midwinter, it seemed, was a religious zealot who harangued people for money for church conservation. Her life was clothed in secrecy, however, with rumours abounding that she had once worked for the British government. It did not make Luca feel less uncomfortable that Maria had been unable to ascertain how the old woman knew about his Moscow stopover. He did not like loose ends.

Bottling up his angst, Luca ordered some food. He tried to keep to a healthy diet, but Felicity insisted he sample the chef's trademark beer-battered cod and thrice-cooked chips. While he waited, she chatted amicably to him, explaining that Clive Buchanan's son Sam, had an obsession with conspiracy theories and high-tech security.

"He's bonkers," she told him in an excited whisper. "You'd think the Village was a hotbed of international intrigue from the ring of steel around Kingfisher House. Nothing ever happens in this bloody place, nor ever will. Unless, of course, you can come up with any interesting suggestions."

Luca changed the subject, but made a mental note to get to know Sam better. His CCTV surveillance would suit his purposes, making visitors think twice before paying any surprise visits.

The American had spent his first day in the Village installing discreet cameras around Kingfisher House. One peeped unobtrusively from the ear of a snarling stuffed fox at the front of the house, and another, poking from the spout of a Margaret Thatcher teapot, was trained on the back door. His meticulousness had paid off. Reviewing the film later, he had been surprised to see Ivy Midwinter snooping about the kitchen, examining every surface with the cold dispassion of a homicide investigation team. The fact that she had a spare key was a problem Luca needed to address; but for the moment, he felt glad that he had at least secured the attic with a simple but extremely strong padlock.

Establishing the villagers' habits and routines had been a shrewd move in more ways than one. A priority since his arrival had been to find a secure and accessible place away from Kingfisher House to store what Maria termed the 'ICE pack' (In Case of Emergency). Frank's early-evening pontifications in the pub had suggested a solution.

"You can never be too careful in show business," he had expounded, after boring his fellow drinkers with accounts of his expensive new Internet security system. "My whole life is on that computer: memoirs, ideas, scripts ..."

Luca, who knew that people who spent a fortune on Internet security often cut costs protecting their premises, began to listen more carefully. He had seen it many times before. Celebrities, corporations, even banks, safeguarding information with sophisticated encryptions and firewalls, only to be left stunned when criminals broke in and stole their hard drives.

The following morning he had woken before dawn and scaled the gates of the Fielding's imposing property, The Waterfront. Skulking in the shadows, he quickly confirmed his suspicion: he could be in and out of that property quicker than a New York minute. Just as he was about to head home, Frank's wife had burst out the door with the sunrise and set off on her morning run. Luca tailed her, enjoying the sight of her statuesque, Lycra-clad figure as he jogged easily behind her. He had feigned a loose shoelace at the war memorial, and she had played into his hands by inviting him to dinner – providing the perfect opportunity for him to hide his stash and get to know the neighbours.

Felicity delivered Luca's fish and chips to him and began rinsing glasses.

"Keeping up to date with all the local news, are you?" she said. "Well, you'll find everything you need in there. Read the local rag and you'll get an insight into what makes this village tick!"

Luca looked at the headlines. A garden-gnome thief had been apprehended, and the Queen was starting some ceremony called Swan Upping. Back home, dawn was breaking over downtown Los Angeles, a vortex of crime, hustling, drugs and sex; yet here, on this infinitesimal pinprick on the world map, folks were locking up their sheds to safeguard their pixies and the Queen was preparing to protect the swan kingdom.

"I see the local crime fighters have their hands full," Luca quipped, raising the glass with his left hand, leaving his right free for the weapon British authorities would not permit him to carry. He was not a man who relaxed easily, despite feeling he had parachuted into a chapter from *Alice in Wonderland*.

The English were a strange bunch. It took Luca days to figure out why everyone talked about the weather all the time. It wasn't as if it was even interesting: there were no tornados or hurricanes to make it newsworthy. Then he realised he was making the mistake of thinking it was the weather they were talking about, instead of it being simply their way of reaching out. In another era they might have said, "How do you do", but this had somehow been replaced with "Nice day", or "Lovely weather". It meant: "I want to talk to you."

The second thing Luca figured out – and this took less time – was to always agree with a weather greeting. It was social suicide not to. If somebody said "Lovely day", all he had to do was smile and nod. Even if it was cold enough to freeze the balls off a brass monkey. The fact that the Fieldings were throwing a welcome party for him the following evening was proof of Luca's seamless integration into the Village, and he couldn't help but feel proud.

As he finished up his chips, the pensioners entered the Crown with a whoosh of brollies and Rainmates.

"Lovely evening for ducks," said a grey-haired, elderly woman, taking off her raincoat. "Oddly, it's not too cold, though. Must be the cloud cover, I suppose." Luca almost laughed into his beer.

"What can I get you?" he asked instead, smiling and nodding.

Sam was beginning to feel a sneaking respect for Luca. He had feared the American would invade his personal space, but he had barely spoken a word since his arrival. There had, however, been a lot of mysterious comings and goings at Kingfisher House, which Sam – who already regretted surrendering his spare key to his father – had played back repeatedly on his CCTV. A few days earlier, dark-suited men had turned up on the doorstep with several large boxes. Sam had followed their progress keenly on his computer, but was left with more questions than answers. Torn between wanting to keep the American at a comfortable distance and the torture of ignorance, he had eventually wandered over. Trying to look nonchalant, he enquired if the delivery was for his father. Despite a propensity for conspiracies, he had accepted Luca's explanation that the box contained nothing more exciting than a new television.He popped the kettle on and thought about his father, a man who still wrote on a manual typewriter and sent faxes. Little wonder Luca felt the need for a new television set: the one at Kingfisher House was probably black and white. He felt concern for his father, who, for all his Old World charm, might well be chewed up and spat out by the hurly-burly of Hollywood. Somehow, Sam just could not imagine the man getting far without Cecilia's good sense to guide him. Since Sam's mother had left to run a vineyard in the Dordogne with her new lover, he and Clive had grown to rely on Cecilia's warmth and kindness, and although he was loath to admit it, she had become something of a maternal figure to him. That was the trouble with his father, Sam reflected: he always put himself first. He had not considered what effect losing Cecilia might have on his son.

Sprawled out on his leather sofa, he felt a sense of satisfaction that, unlike his father's chaotic home, The Boathouse was gleaming and spotless. Sam did not go in for possessions. The place needed no adornment with such a spectacular view.

The buzz of the intercom startled him, and peering into the camera he was astonished to see the scarfaced American standing on The Boathouse's doorstep. He ignored it for a few moments, then flipped the entrance switch and enjoyed a warm glow at Luca's surprised awe as he came through the door.

"This place is like something out of James Bond!" Luca exclaimed. "All you need is a Persian cat."

Sam was chuffed. He liked the idea of being an evil mastermind, it was so much better than the reality of being a spotty youth with a weird mind and an irrational lust for every woman who moved. He slid his fingers up and down the touch panel for effect, and a barrage of lights hit the room as Nirvana's *Smells like Teen Spirit* bellowed out from the speakers.

"Dad likes old things," he shouted above the noise of clashing guitars and a thrilling drumbeat. "I'm just the opposite."

"I can see that," said Luca.

Sam turned the music down and dimmed the lights.

"I have the Buchanan 'fish finger fortune' to thank for all this," he said. He did not normally entertain, and whilst it felt good to show it off a little, he felt it necessary to explain himself. "But I don't plan to squander my inheritance on antiques and movies like my Dad. I've got plans to save the planet." Something in the American's expression made Sam feel like an adult, and Luca clearly liked gadgets – another point in his favour.

"Clever stuff," said Luca, and Sam watched him scan the bookcase, which was stuffed with titles on mathematics, psychology and psychiatry. He picked up a skull from the table and watched as the brain detached and scattered into tiny pieces. "This all looks pretty heavy. D'you understand it all?"

Sam nodded as Luca placed the bits back onto the table carefully. "It's a model," he explained. "You can take it apart and reassemble it, and it maps the brain in tiny detail. I have a strong personal interest in the brain." It was difficult to read Luca, but by the look on his face he seemed to be judging Sam in a new and better light; so the boy continued, blurting out cathartically: "I suffer from synaesthesia. I don't actually invite many people into my home because of it."

"Didn't Jimi Hendrix have that?" Luca asked. "I read somewhere he used it to describe chords and harmonies as colours. Even invented his own chord for *Purple Haze*."

Sam nodded. "When I hear a word, I taste it. Some taste delicious, and others foul. I even dream with taste in my mouth. One of my earliest memories was singing nursery rhymes at four and getting the flavour of bacon and eggs." Luca laughed, and, encouraged, Sam continued: "I've learned to live with it now, but when I was much younger I'd choose friends on the basis of whether their names tasted of strawberry jam or Brussels sprouts."

"What does my name taste of?" Luca asked.

"Bananas."

"That figures."

"Unlike ordinary people, when I eat, the region in my brain that deals with words and sound lights up. I'm just wired differently." Sam slumped on the sofa. It was the most he had talked about himself in years. Luca joined him, pulling up the coffee table as a leg rest; while Sam thought this unusual, he did not feel the need to object.

"The brain is fascinating," Luca said, stretching out and yawning. "I've heard stories of people waking up from comas able to speak entirely different languages."

The teenager's eyes shone brightly. "Yeah, Dad told me about a bloke who became a mathematical genius after he was mugged, and he could see the Pythagorean theorem everywhere. He's an acquired savant now, almost superhuman!"

"Speaking of your father, how's he getting along? Everything OK at the beach house?"

Sam had received a letter, but was not going to tell Luca that the place was so high-tech his father could barely work the kettle, or that he had been cautioned for "loitering with intent" in Beverly Hills when he was simply taking his "daily constitutional". *Apparently people are not allowed to walk the street for fun in affluent parts of Hollywood,* he had written in his trademark turquoise ink.

"Great. Just great!" Sam lied, before changing the subject. "So, what sort of agency do you run?" Luca looked surprised. "Dad says you run an agency; what is it, advertising? Celebrity lookalike?"

"Gumshoe." Sam, who was none the wiser, raised a quizzical eyebrow. Luca laughed. "I'm a private detective. In the States we're known as 'gumshoes'."

"Wow! A real live LA detective in this village!" Sam grinned widely. It was better than he could have imagined, but Luca caught his eye warily.

"I'd appreciate it if you kept my profession to yourself though, son. I'm here because I'm kinda burned out. I need to recharge my batteries. You know, England in springtime, fishing, boating, afternoon tea – it might just help me to get my life back on track."

"I can just imagine!" enthused Sam. "You must have been involved in some incredibly dangerous cases."

"Not really," said Luca offhandedly. "It's just a small-time agency. Divorce, parking tickets, that's my kinda thing."

If only Sam knew how fast Luca's heart was beating under his cool exterior: had he said too much?

A few doors down on Riverside Lane, Ivy carefully folded the dossier on Luca Tempesta and placed it into a brown paper envelope, sealing it shut. The report had arrived that morning, slipping silently through the letterbox from a source she had known a lifetime ago, before Clive Buchanan, before Frank Fielding, back in the days when she had worked for Nigel Bond.

Ivy had spent the morning at Village Antiques, and the afternoon tending the churchyard garden. She had resisted opening the report until the hour she reserved for dealing with correspondence; Ivy's life was highly regimented, and allowed for no flexibility, spontaneity or surprise: just as she liked it. At precisely four o'clock, she had returned from church, left her outdoor shoes on the mat and donned her slippers. As the kettle boiled, she unlocked the back door leading to a small garden fronting the river and, slipping on a pair of gardening clogs, had taken her tea and the dossier into the sunshine.

Her garden, a replica of the kitchen garden at the convent of her youth, was completely given over to vegetables planted and staked in perfect rows with not a weed in sight. As Ivy sipped her tea under the shade of the crab apple tree, which wore a spring wardrobe of pink blossoms that bobbed and ruffled like lace, Peter the Rock approached from the cabbage bed. Ivy had become so engrossed in the document that her tea had grown quite cold, and she had completely forgotten to give her beloved tortoise his daily bath.

What she had learned troubled her. Ignoring Peter the Rock's plaintive stretches, she moved inside to her piano. Some people deserve to suffer, she thought, as she pressed the tips of her fingers into her eyes then began to play Bach's *Miserere*. The penitential psalm was appropriate to her frame of mind.

When she next looked up through the net curtains, Ivy could just make out the sky darkening as the coming night stretched out its long, gloomy fingers. She closed the lid of the piano and rubbed her eyes to dispel the images of musical notations that had begun to haunt her; then, glancing at the clock, she understood that the time had come to hand over the dossier. What would Nigel Bond make of it, she wondered? Ivy kissed the omnipresent silver cross that hung against her heart and scuttled out into the night.

FIVE

FRANK FIELDING SQUEEZED the Nissan Micra into the double garage beside his Range Rover and Bianca's powder-blue Mini Cooper. The twelve-year-old Micra was a strange vehicle for a celebrity to knock about in, but Frank loved the anonymity it provided. Unlike the Range Rover, which, sporting Frank's catchphrase SHoW TiME as a number plate, was a mobile advertisement for 'brand Frank Fielding'.

"Evening, ladies," he said, pausing to enjoy the view as he let himself into the kitchen where his wife Bianca and her best friend Felicity were busy preparing for the dinner party. "What are you two beautiful witches cooking up?"

"Casting a spell on Hugh Willoughby, so he clears the way for yer gong, Frankie!" his wife replied.

"And conjuring up a love potion to seduce the sexy American that's just moved into Clive's pile," cackled Felicity.

Frank grinned. "You'll blast him into outer space with what you're wearing tonight, Felicity!" She rolled her eyes as she stooped to kiss him on the cheek.

"Go on," she said with an amused sigh. She was used to Frank's one-liners, and every time she suspected they could not get any cheesier, he would surpass himself with a worse one.

"Yes indeed, he'll be in orbit – because your backside looks out of this world in those jeans!"

"Oh, babe, what are you like?" laughed Bianca, puckering her lips for a proper kiss.

"And *you*," said Frank, kissing his wife and stepping back for inspection, "should be renamed 'Summer', because you look so hot in that dress."

She laughed heartily. "Get upstairs and get changed – the guests will be 'ere in a minute!" Frank pottered off obediently, chuckling to himself as he went,

"... And wear that black silky shirt I got you for Christmas," his wife called after him. "You look good in that!"

"I want to be gone by ten-thirty at the very latest," Joy Willoughby commanded her husband. "So *do not* do that thing where I catch your eye and you pretend you haven't seen. Ten o'clock, ideally."

She wished she had chosen different shoes. The Willoughbys were walking to the Fieldings' dinner party. It wasn't far; they lived across the river, a little upstream from their hosts, but there was a convenient wooden footbridge with an inconvenient tread that never failed to ruin a stiletto. Joy hurried to catch up with her husband.

"Why don't you take your shoes off?" he asked.

"You do come up with absurd suggestions," she said tersely. "Speaking of which, why exactly did you accept this wretched invitation?"

"I'm sure we'll have a lovely time," he smiled, taking her hand as she teetered beside him. Joy snatched her hand away and smoothed her skirt; then, checking her heels for damage, she teased her hair into a gentle bouffant – unnecessarily, as she had had the forethought to apply extra hairspray. Frank Fielding appeared at the doorway,

"Welcome!" boomed the little man with the big voice, ushering them into an elegant hall. "Out of my way Hugh, so I can get my hands on your lovely wife."

"Frank," said Joy, allowing herself to be kissed, then turning to greet Bianca just as Frank went for the other cheek.

"Whoops!" he said as their lips brushed. "Bit early for that, Joy, but throw your keys in the bowl later and you might get lucky."

"Oh, Frank, what're you like? Don't tease," said Bianca, taking Joy's limp hand and leading her through to the terrace. "You look lovely tonight, Joy. I do like those shoes – very Theresa May."

Joy felt herself stiffen. She was sufficiently self-aware to know that the less comfortable she felt, the haughtier she became, but since fitting into these circles was not one of her ambitions, she fell back on a lifetime of training and smiled graciously.

"Thank you, Bianca," she said. "Goodness, that dress is striking. We're not going to lose *you* tonight, are we?"

Bianca laughed and handed her guest a Kir Royale. Joy preferred her champagne unadulterated, and was about to say so when she spotted the inferior brand and kept her counsel.

"Bianca!" interjected Hugh, grabbing the hand-tied bouquet on the chair beside him smoothly and presenting it with a mock bow.

"Oh, Hugh! How lovely." Bianca stood on tiptoe to kiss the politician, and squashed against him slightly more than his wife felt was necessary to thank him for the flowers that she had bought for her husband to bring along. She removed a tissue from her handbag and handed it to Hugh, gesturing for him to remove the offensive red lipstick now applied to his cheek.

"Cheers, me dears!" said Bianca. "Must go and do some kitchen things!" She dashed off, leaving her guests to enjoy the view of the Willoughbys' own splendid property – known as The White House – across the water.

Luca tucked an envelope into his inside pocket and straightened his tie in the mirror. Satisfied that he looked the part – scrubbed and clean, hair tamed, trussed up in one of Clive Buchanan's borrowed silk ties – he did a quick security check, glanced over his shoulder and headed into the night. Pulling up his collar against the cool of the early evening, he strolled up the path to The Waterfront, where he was joined by the bearded biker he had seen talking to the vicar and riding through the Village on a Norton Commando.

"Harley," said the big man, thrusting out a gigantic paw. He had a pleasant face, the wind of the open road etched upon it in a hundred broken capillaries.

The door swung open, and Frank's voice boomed theatrically: "Come in! Bianca is preparing a feast for the gods."

Showtime, thought Luca, as he switched on a smile and walked through the door. He felt the reassuring weight of his ICE pack, containing a false passport and cash, in his breast pocket. Maria's words echoed in his mind: "You deserve an Oscar for all your award-winning performances." Who should he be tonight, he wondered fleetingly as he scanned the room.

Photographs adorned the walls: a pouting Bianca from her modelling heyday, a beaming Frank with various celebrities. A white grand piano stood to the left of a vast fireplace, over which hung a Baroque-style oil painting. Frank beamed down like the Laughing Cavalier, flanked on either side by his two lady loves, Bianca and their daughter (both of whom, Luca suspected, had been height-adjusted to show Frank in a better light). On Bianca's lap sat a small, fluffy, white terrier.

"Luca!" Bianca shrieked, appearing at the top of a galleried landing in her bright red dress.

"It's the red-carpet *magnifico!*" announced Frank proudly. "My *coup de foudre!*"

"Oh, do stop talking Latin, Frankie," replied Bianca, turning mid-stair to show off a pair of smooth, tanned legs before clasping the American tightly to her bosom, which was artfully presented on a platter by the very latest in bra technology.

"Come!" she gushed, taking Luca and Harley by the arm and propelling them into the drawing room, where Felicity lounged, catlike, on an opulent pink and cream armchair. Felicity slunk over and embraced Harley, her bright, glitzy costume jewellery pealing like bells, then turned and planted a lingering kiss on Luca's cheek. Aside from pink lip gloss, her face was free of artifice; she wore her brown hair pulled up into an immaculate ponytail, with raisin-sized diamonds in her ears. She was older than her youthful body implied, and Luca suspected she was sliding into an age when women fear their beauty is fading. He noticed her eyeing his lack of a wedding ring.

"Anyone ever tell you look like Robert de Niro?" She joked.

Luca laughed a little too loudly, and turned his attention to a formidable-looking woman and a debonair man stepping in from the terrace through elaborately curtained French windows.

"This is Luca Tempesta, a guest of Clive's at Kingfisher House," said Frank, introducing him to Joy and Hugh Willoughby. "He's over the jet lag and straight into the gin and jag!" he quipped, and began topping up their drinks.

Joy covered her glass. "No, thank you, I shall save myself for the Meursault we brought along. I am so looking forward to trying it," she said. Then she turned to Luca. "How is dear Clive? Such a gentleman, we do miss him. Whatever possessed him, getting involved in this film project, I've no idea. It seems so out of character."

Luca ignored the question, but observed Joy with interest. He knew the type: steely determination to climb to the top of the tree, but unhappy with the view once she got there. He could tell by the way her mouth turned down at the corners that she was not getting what she wanted from life.

"Come far?" Hugh asked, and Luca smiled inwardly, knowing from his excursions at the Crown that this was English-speak for "What do you do for a living?". Etiquette required acquaintances to find a roundabout route to establishing someone's livelihood.

"Los Angeles," offered Luca.

Hugh probed further: "Must be jolly exciting, working in the hub of the film business."

"It can be."

"A friend of mine worked out there and said the traffic was murder at rush hour." Here we go, thought Luca. Traffic was another favourite line of enquiry.

"No worse than London," he replied, smiling.

"Do you drive to work?" Hugh enquired with the air of a man about to complete a crossword puzzle.

"I work from home." And so it continued. Luca could tell that Hugh was relishing the challenge, and he had to admire his determination.

"Nice to have that flexibility. You must be self-employed."

Their conversation was eventually interrupted by Frank, carrying a plate of canapés and wearing an apron in the style of a woman's naked body with ENJOY MY CUPCAKES emblazoned across the front.

"Hands off, Hugh! Don't touch what you can't afford," Frank minced, prompting much hilarity, and Luca moved away.

"Scoff's up!" cried Bianca, ushering them into a magnificent dining room. Felicity sashayed in, and took her seat at the table first. She was irritated that Luca had disappeared just as she was about to nobble him to be her chaperone.

"'E's been chatting to Cecilia in the kitchen," Bianca hissed into her ear. "Don't know where 'e is now; hope 'e's not stuck in the loo, the lock's bust." Cecilia's golden head popped around the doorway. Her cheeks were rosy, and golden tendrils framed her pretty face. She wore a white cotton dress and a cardigan buttoned up to her throat.

"Just whipping something up in the kitchen. Won't be long!" she called out.

"Looks like your boys are laying on the entertainment for the evening, Felicity," Hugh noted, gesturing cheerfully towards the window. Eight pairs of eyes looked out beyond the topiary, past Harley – who was enjoying a smoke against the wall – to four mock-Georgian windows showcasing the four perky white derrières of Felicity's sons. She sprang from the chair, cursing under her breath, and pounded the window.

Harley turned and smiled, then boomed: "Cool it!" in a voice so loud it shook the glass. The bottoms vanished.

"I'm so sorry," said Felicity. She was not easily cowed, but her four sons had run her ragged of late, and these exhibitions made her want to weep. It was not the shock of it that bothered her – they had all seen far worse – but the evident lack of control she had over her offspring.

"You've got your hands full there, Felicity," laughed Hugh. "Real live wires." Joy stared rigidly at her wineglass, appalled by the children's behaviour. Felicity and family were a disgrace to the neighbourhood. Her own twins, Penny and Tom, would never have behaved so abominably. She caught Hugh's eye, and he smiled reassuringly.

"Oh, they're lovely boys," said Bianca, giggling, "and tell them from me that's the best view we've had all evening." Felicity smiled gratefully and looked to Harley through the window.

"'Thanks," she mouthed, and the big man shrugged his shoulders. She was so thankful her friend was there. Since divorcing Dave, she had spent too much time trying to pay off her monumental mortgage and not enough taking care of the boys, who were becoming increasingly feral by the day. Thank heavens for Harley, who had moved in and was paying a generous rent as well as keeping the lads on a tight leash.

Felicity had not expected life to be so hard. She had married Dave, the boys' father, because she had needed financial security; but she soon tired of her older husband, and ditched him three years after their wedding. She had expected him to be devastated, and assumed he would stump up for his family in perpetuity, but he had celebrated his seventieth birthday in Honolulu by marrying a much younger clone of herself. Felicity had been forced to accept Dave's paltry settlement because of his threats to take the boys away. He was still meeting the costs of their upbringing, but when their youngest turned eighteen the payments would stop. The irony was that, for all his threats, Dave had only seen his sons a handful of times since the divorce.

She tapped on the window for Harley to return. He flicked his cigarette butt into the bushes and headed back inside.

Bianca thought it was going well. Harley looked hilarious, seated next to Joy in a sort of Mrs Thatcher-meets-Meat Loaf scenario, and dear Frank had grasped the nettle and was on the old bat's right. Bianca was loath to admit it, but she was intimidated by Joy Willoughby. She was so grand and rich and had – as she never failed to point out – *earned* her wealth, not married it, as Bianca had done. Frank pushed his chair back to make a toast.

"Raise your drinks, shut your mouths and everyone, please observe," he announced in his deep baritone. "May we get what we want, get what we need, but never get what we deserve!" He raised his glass to his guests. "Oh, and of course, welcome to Luca, our new friend from across the pond."

"Hear, hear," said Hugh, raising his glass to Luca's empty chair.

"Where is 'e? I hope 'e's not locked in the loo!" exclaimed Bianca as she went to sit next to Frank, only to be headed off by Hugh. She shrugged and moved to the next seat, catching Felicity's eye across the table. But Hugh followed and pulled out that chair, too.

"Bleedin' 'ell Hugh, I nearly hit the deck then!" Bianca cackled. "Make yer mind up, will you? Where d'you want to sit?"

"Dear lady," Hugh replied, "I was simply trying to pull your chair out for you. I am happy to sit wherever you put me." Bianca felt stupid. She looked across to see Joy smirking.

"I knew that," she said, hastily taking her seat next to Frank. "Only jokin'!" But the confusion had wrong-footed her, and she did not like it.

Her Dad had always taught her to lash out when her back was against the wall, so she downed her wine in one and glowered across the table at Joy.

"So," she said, pulling her tummy in and sticking out her chest. Her red jersey dress clung to her curves and served as her armour against the world. "Quite the trendsetter, aren't you?" Joy looked perplexed, and Frank a little lost. Bianca took another glug of Cabernet Sauvignon and spelled it out: "You know, Madonna, Demi Moore, they've both followed in yer footsteps ...? Cougars, marrying men ten years younger than them, like you did, Joy!" To Bianca's satisfaction, Joy looked horrified. "That'll teach you to make me look stupid," she thought, and to compound her insult she turned to Hugh. With the full dazzle of her orthodontically perfect smile and surgically enhanced breasts, she engaged him in conversation. Frank stepped in to soothe Joy, who asked frostily: "Is there any chance of a glass of that Meursault we bought along? I would so like to try it."

"Of course," said Frank, patting her hand as if she were a child. "Babe," he asked Bianca, "where is the wine the Willoughbys brought?"

"In the risotto!" Bianca replied.

Frank had no idea what had got into his wife. She had been drinking since early evening, but she did not normally get lairy unless somebody picked a fight with her. It had been her idea to invite the Willoughbys – part of her campaign to put Frank in the running for a gong – and a welcome party for the American had provided the perfect excuse. Now, less than halfway through the evening, she was insulting Joy, and Luca, who had barely uttered a word since his arrival, appeared to have vanished.

Frank knew Bianca had not put the Meursault in the risotto, because Cecilia had prepared it; but he also knew not to contradict his wife in her current mood. So he filled Joy's glass with table wine and enquired after Penny. Joy's face lit up at the mention of her daughter. Frank glanced at Bianca, who was all over Hugh, and gave her a disapproving look.

"... And of course, when she gets back from her travels – she's been paying her own way, mark you, no sponging off the Bank of Mum and Dad for our Penny – she hopes to read medicine at Oxford." Frank had heard all this before, as had most of the Village, and an image of his own daughter flashed into his mind. He wished Tallulah would take responsibility for a few of her bills now that she was of age, but she was showing no signs of independence – or, indeed, ambition.

He smiled brightly. "You must be proud of her."

"Penny has her faults, but she is *such* a hard worker, and so determined. Far be it from me to get in her way when she has her mind set." Joy held out her glass to be filled, and Frank obliged with the Cabernet Sauvignon he wished Bianca had chilled. "She'll be home soon," Joy added.

"I wouldn't hold your breath, Joy!" Felicity piped up from the end of the table. "Most kids bleed you dry, then head off into the sunset without so much as a backward glance – isn't that right, Harl?" Harley cleared his throat to answer, but Bianca interrupted.

"Give us a song, Harley – the one you wrote about Felicity, it's me Mum's favourite! I don't know why you're so bleedin' coy about it," she added, as Felicity raised her eyes to the skies. "If Frank wrote a love song for me, I'd be blabbin' it all over Facebook."

"*I Was in Love with the Vicar's Daughter*," reminisced Frank happily. "I remember it performed on *Showtime*, top of the Hit Parade in the Seventies. It was the hottest summer on record; I fried an egg on the bonnet of my Cortina."

Hugh, a junior MP with responsibility for national parks, appeared thrilled by this revelation about Harley.

"I suppose, in your line of work, Hugh, you meet more green campaigners and civil servants than you do music legends," said Frank.

"Absolutely," the politician nodded, "all very dull. Forgive me, Harley, but to learn that a bona fide hairy rocker such as yourself should have poetry in his soul is a wonderful revelation!"

"Speakin' of revelations from the house of God, yer old man the deacon did 'is nut, didn't he?" Bianca squawked at Felicity.

"Yeah, you could say he was not best pleased," she grinned. "I was fifteen, a pupil at the local convent and the 'vicar's daughter'. It got me expelled. Have you ever listened to the lyrics? Not exactly convent girl behaviour!"

Harley winked at Joy, who blushed crimson and rummaged busily in her handbag while Frank deftly changed the subject.

"Well, we've all sown our wild oats at some time or another," he said smiling at Joy reassuringly. "In my era it was turn on, tune in and drop out!"

"Yeah, but now it's more like, turn on, tune in and drop off," Bianca countered. Frank thought it a timely moment to head to the downstairs loo and check on Luca.

*

"Anyone for tart?" Cecilia asked gaily as she entered the dining room with the errant Luca.

"Oh, yes, the tart, that's me," offered Joy with more enthusiasm than she had intended. She had been perturbed by Harley's wink, and was relieved to be on safer conversational ground.

"We knew you married Joy for a reason," Frank quipped, and Joy and Hugh laughed bravely.

"Yeah, Frank calls me 'is 'sex object,'" Bianca joined in, beaming proudly at her man. "He asks for sex, and I object!"

Everyone laughed except for Joy, who shuffled uncomfortably in her seat. She had not had relations with Hugh for several months now, and what had started as a relief was rapidly becoming a nagging cause for concern. Hugh could sense her discomfort at the tone the conversation was taking and, ever the gentleman, he changed the subject.

"The economy is still in the doldrums," he said.

"You can say that again," replied Frank. "It does seem money slips through the fingers like sand nowadays."

"Yeah, but you've got that guy Bill Lewis advising us, 'aven't you, babe?" interjected Bianca. "So we'll be all right."

"It's not necessarily that simple," Frank replied, with unusual seriousness. "I had to talk to him only the other day. The latest investments he was so keen to sign me up for have failed to make a ruddy bean. And of course the overheads keep on going up."

This uncharacteristic outburst from Frank described feelings alarmingly similar to Joy's. Bill Lewis and his pesky investments had a lot to do with why she was feeling out of sorts. She found herself reflecting on the champagne reception Frank had held in honour of his high-profile financial guru. Hugh had been at Westminster and Joy, lured by an opportunity to mix with minor royals, had attended alone. Sophisticated, urbane and charmingly attentive, Bill Lewis and Joy had hit it off immediately. He had made her feel like a successful entrepreneur, a woman of substance, not the figure her husband so often appeared to see. She remembered him hanging on her every word as she told him about Sugar & Spice, the company she had built from scratch, which was now turning over three million pounds. It had been unlike Joy to accept lunch at The Ivy, but, dazzled by his virtuosity, she had agreed willingly. He had even sent a Rolls-Royce to spirit her into town, and Joy had felt like a royal herself.

Handing over a sizeable chunk of their nest egg to Mr Lewis had felt right at the time, and Joy had been reassured that captains of industry were among those investing with him. With the benefit of hindsight, however, she had known something was amiss, because she had never told Hugh. It had been easy to avoid the conversation, as he only ever expressed a cursory interest in the financial management of the household, but now Joy was not so sure. She glanced at her watch and tried to catch her husband's eye.

"Funnily enough, Lewis's name came up in the Commons only last week," said Hugh.

"In what context?" Did Frank have an edge to his voice, Joy wondered, or was she feeling her own anxiety at this piece of news?

"Well, I can't really tell you that, or I would have to kill you," said Hugh, smiling. "Suffice to say, he's very plausible, but I'm not sure there's an awful lot of substance there. I wouldn't get into bed with him, Frank; this recession is far from over, and from what I hear, he sails awfully close to the wind."

Joy felt queasy, but continued spooning mouthfuls of tart into her mouth: she did not want good food to go to waste. She caught Frank's eye, and they exchanged a look of mutual discomfort. Joy reckoned from his slightly cornered expression that perhaps she was not the only one to have been misled by Mr Lewis.

Luca, too, had observed Frank's awkward look, and wondered if – for all his cheerful bonhomie – all was well at Team Fielding. Celebrities in the US marshalled the full force of twenty-four-seven publicity machines, but as far as Luca could ascertain, the only person stage-managing Frank's affairs was Ivy Midwinter. The thought of the woman made him uneasy; Maria was still unable to establish how the old woman knew about his Russian stopover, and had signed off on an investigation. They could not afford any lapses.

He was relieved that none of the guests, except Felicity (who was playing footsie with him under the table), had taken an interest in his affairs; the party readily accepted the explanation that he was on holiday. Even Hugh had given up trying to guess Luca's job, and was too well-mannered to ask directly about it. Telling Sam had been a slip-up, Luca knew, and he wasn't about to make that mistake again.

The English guarded their privacy to the end. They sneered at stereotypical Americans offering up chapter and verse on their lives within five minutes of meeting, and pretended not to pry into the affairs of others – all the while surreptitiously trying to discover whatever they could and gossiping behind closed doors.

Luca observed the assembled company: eight people splashing around the tiny fishbowl of their lives, too caught up in the minutiae of their own affairs to notice the shark swimming among them. He reflected on the contrast between his old life and new one. Only last week he had been hugging the shadows in Los Angeles, a city where, beneath the veneer of glitz and money, the darkest of hearts beat steadily.

"So where's the wife?" Felicity interrupted his thoughts, looking pointedly at the white, tanless line running around his wedding finger. Luca was momentarily transfixed by her green eyes.

"We're separated," he said, trying to force a smile, but the look on her face told him she had not been fooled.

In the hall, Bianca launched into a drunken tribute to Frank's charity work, but Joy's shoes were pinching and their hostess was standing a little too close to her husband, so she said: "That is all marvellous, Bianca, but I am afraid we really must make tracks."

"You're keeping these good souls from their beds, babe," said Frank, putting his arm around his wife as he opened the door.

"Oh," said Hugh, "I nearly forgot! Did that chap Pete Walters catch up with you, Frank?"

"Pete who?"

"Walters, I think his name was. Yes, pretty certain, Pete Walters. He was at the cricket club the other day, asking about you."

"Asking about *me*?"

Hugh nodded. "He tried to engage Basil and me in conversation, but we were having none of it, just in case. You never know who you're talking to these days, do you? But then it struck me later, perhaps he was an old friend or something."

"Oh, do come on, Hugh," called Joy from the road. "It is jolly cold out here. Lovely dinner, thank you so much."

"Absolutely lovely," agreed Hugh. "Super time."

The door had barely closed before Joy sniped: "What a frightful evening. I thought it would never end."

SIX

THE FOLLOWING MORNING the bells pealed, calling the residents of Riverside Lane to prayer. Felicity and Ivy worked in companionable silence, Ivy laying out the hymn books and Felicity sorting through the choir robes. The vicar was preparing for the service in the sacristy. It was the fifth Sunday of Easter, and Reverend James cut a resplendent figure in the pulpit, wearing white robes and a purple chasuble.

As the last of the shuffling parishioners settled for their morning worship and Ivy stilled the organ, he said: "O Lord, from Whom all good things come, grant to us Your humble servants, that by Your holy inspiration ..."

Hugh Willoughby was not listening. He was quite at home, sitting in his regular pew at the front, positioned far enough away from the suspended Madonna that, should she crash down, he and his family would be safe – but where, perhaps more importantly, he could enjoy plenty of leg room, Joy could feel important and mother-in-law Myrtle could see and hear the proceedings.

"... Jesus Christ, our Lord. Amen," intoned Reverend James.

"Amen," responded Hugh, working out what time he would need to leave to meet Tom and Jake for dinner in town at nine o'clock. He wondered whether or not he would have to eat two meals, as he had done before, in order to please the disparate members of his family. Reverend James continued his address while Hugh debated asking again if Joy would join him for dinner with Tom.

"... And also with you," he said, joining the congregation on autopilot as instinctively as he changed gears in the car or accepted a cup of tea from his wife.

Reverend James thrust out his arms, his pink palms turned towards the congregation.

"Welcome!" he said in his sonorous voice, dazzling them all with a smile. There were responsive mutterings and awkward wriggles in the pews. Hugh once again admired the vicar, and reflected on how well he would do in the despatch box at Westminster. "We will begin by worshipping our Lord in song. Hymn number 136."

"All creatures of our God and King," sang Hugh enthusiastically, while Joy nudged him and Myrtle sniggered behind her order of service. "... Lift up your voice and with us sing!"

Hugh had always loved singing, but had never been very good at it. It was one of the many wonderful things about being British: one could sing out loud and proud in the house of God regardless of tone or tune, and nobody minded. Nobody, that is, except for Joy, who was now shushing her husband with an irritation Hugh knew from experience would give way to amusement if he persevered in his endeavour, increasing the volume with each verse. He was right: when he turned towards his wife and clenched his fists together beseechingly, singing at the very top of his voice – "DEAR MOTHER EARTH, WHO DAY BY DAY ..." – Joy was unable to maintain her composure, and Hugh's heart soared. The Sunday service would not be the same without breaking down his wife's defences at least once.

"Let us pray," instructed Reverend James in a sombre voice. Back in control but humanised, Hugh felt, by her affinity for holy laughter, Joy got to her knees. Her head was bowed, and her hands clasped so tight her knuckles whitened.

Myrtle, who could not kneel and remained in her wheelchair with her eyes lowered, watched her daughter with concern. Today was her twin grandchildren's birthday, and the occasion looked set to be marked by the absence of either's presence at The White House. Penny, of course, was halfway across the world, and who could blame her? Though Myrtle could see how it pained her daughter, she understood Penny's almost visceral need to get as far from her mother as possible.

"... O Lamb of God, that takest away the sins of the world, have mercy upon us."

Hugh had taken mercy on them by ceasing his singing, and now appeared lost in a world his mother-in-law suspected had a lot more to do with his children than with God. She sighed. It had been lovely watching him persist in his efforts to make her daughter laugh. Joy could be so terribly brittle with Hugh, and Myrtle lived in constant fear that one day it would be he who would snap. She did not mean to be like that; Myrtle knew that if ever a woman needed mercy it was Joy, who lived in self-induced torment at having driven her more worthy chick from the nest for having the wrong plumage and causing the other to flee in terror (clutching a handsome cheque from her father) when she realised she was to become the sole focus of her overbearing mother's fussing and clucking.

As far as her children were concerned, Joy's geese had always been swans, and her expectations of them onerous. Her life was ruled by pride, and she smiled bravely and refused to acknowledge – even to her own mother – that the repeated extensions to Penny's trip were anything other than positive, despite the fact that each month necessitated another secret transfer of funds (something Hugh would never have sanctioned had he known) in order to facilitate Penny's latest vacillation.

"... O Lamb of God, that takest away the sins of the world, grant us Thy peace."

Peace, thought Myrtle, allowing the words of the liturgy to soothe her. Felicity's angelic voice rose above the congregation and stilled her troubled soul.

"Sing, pray and walk in God's ways ..." sang Felicity. "... For whoever places his confidence in God, God will never abandon."

"Amen," muttered Myrtle, and squeezed her daughter's hand gently. As the service drew to a close, Luca slipped unseen into the crowded church and took a pew at the back – a worshipper in search of self-preservation, not salvation.

"Keep your friends close, but your enemies closer," Maria had joked in the email she had sent through that morning, with the

"Ivy Midwinter" file attachment. Its contents had explained much about the file's eponym and her reasons for trailing Luca; but still, he had to stop her.

"Make it clear you have something on her," Maria had urged. Luca hoped that Ivy's Russian connection was a coincidence; "Kuznetsoy" was a common name after all. But the old dear was out of her depth, and Luca was not about to stop her from drowning. As well as records of her dramatic past with the civil service, Maria had uncovered another deeply personal secret Luca felt certain Ivy was planning to carry to her grave, and this would be his leverage.

The sun streamed through the stained-glass window, bathing Reverend James in a transcendent light as he stood, glorious in his purple chasuble and stole, his back to the congregation, preparing the altar table for Communion.

"Behold the Lamb who bears our sins away," sang the congregation, and Luca looked up at the illumination from the stained-glass window. His gaze was returned by the Madonna, who stood holding the Blessed Infant beneath a glorious sky of lapis lazuli and a canopy of golden stars; but he ignored the muffled whispers of his conscience, zoned in on his target and waited. He had come too far to fall at the last hurdle.

"We invite all who have professed a faith in Christ to join us at the table," announced Reverend James. Pew by pew, beneath the watchful eye of the Queen of Heaven, the villagers took their places in the communion procession. Ivy crossed herself and joined the queue behind a skeletal old man.

"This is the body of Christ that was broken for you; eat," directed Reverend James as he glided along the line of worshippers, dispensing the holy wafers.

"Amen," his grateful flock responded. Luca moved silently to the aisle, genuflected and sidled up behind an unsuspecting Ivy, who was waiting blissfully in line.

"This is the blood of Christ that was shed for you; drink." A shuffling of feet, and the faithful moved forward to receive the sacrament. "The body of Christ ..."

Luca seized his opportunity, stooping until his mouth was against Ivy's ear.

"Back off, if you know what's good for you," he hissed. "God will be no protection against the demons I'll dig up to haunt you."

"Amen," responded the communicants, rising to return to their pews while the altar servers washed the chalice and paten for the next batch.

"Amen," whispered Ivy, as she moved forward to take her place at the altar rail. Luca's only sign that his message had got through was the old woman's tightened grip on her cross of St Christopher, and her rapidly blinking eyes. He turned his back on the vast granite statue of Jesus and smiled winningly at Joy Willoughby as he left the church.

Sam was pleased that Luca had left his binoculars on the garden table. The lens was astonishingly sophisticated, and afforded him a splendid view of the gas-guzzling *Ciao Bella* as it chugged downstream, belching oil leaks and phosphate-based cleaning products into the water. He would normally report the gin palace to the Environment Agency, but the gorgeous Isolda was on board, sprawled out on deck in a miniscule bikini. He adjusted the lens, bringing her lush body into sharp focus. The sight of her endless legs and buxom body glistening under layers of suntan oil gave him a thrill. He yearned to be the one rubbing cream into her skin, not her Russian sugar daddy.

Isolda's actual name was "Linda", but Sam's brain translated that into sauerkraut, a taste that did not agree with his discerning palate or his fantasies; so he had bestowed on her an exotic name. *Isolda. God's gift. Giver of God. God-given. Greek. Tastes of strawberries.*

It was galling to have fallen in love with a woman who had no respect for the planet, or for him. Sam had once engaged her in conversation in the pub car park, but she had flicked her hair in a way he thought magnificent and roared off in a Lamborghini Murciélago. Telling her the car emitted two hundred and ninety grams of CO_2 per kilometre had perhaps not been the cleverest of chat-up lines.

He checked his watch. He was not sure how it had happened, but since the evening he and Luca had mulled over developments in brain science, Sam had become enthralled by his new friend. The American was generous at dispensing fatherly wisdom, something Sam badly needed and a skillset sadly lacking in his own father. Clive had raised Sam to believe Americans were brash, vulgar philistines who lived on a diet of hamburgers and fizzy drinks. The British, on the other hand, had more discerning palates, his father would boast, especially in the Village – a culinary mecca.

"Don't ask yourself what Bruce Willis would do, Son," was one of his father's favourite sayings in sticky situations. "Ask what Sir Roger Moore would do!"

Sam was not so sure. It was, after all, the US that had saved the day in World War Two, and four hundred years had passed since the Founding Fathers had set sail for the colonies with language from the golden age of Shakespeare and the King James Bible. A lot had happened since then.

In homage to Luca, Sam had adopted a few Americanisms of his own, tagging "so" to the start of each sentence and using the present tense to recount his anecdotes. He had substituted "please may I have" with "can I get" in the pub, and believed it had gone down well with Felicity, who had given him a drink on the house. Americanisms, Sam concluded, made him sound confident and in control, switched on. Luca had laughed when Sam told him of his new allegiance to the Stars and Stripes, and returned the compliment.

"Actually, Britishisms are becoming increasingly commonplace in the US. English pronunciation is considered a mark of status, classier than our own," he had explained.

The best thing about Luca, Sam thought, was that he made him feel everything was possible. He was full of inspirational-speak; words that would have sounded corny and contrived with an English accent came across as "kinda cool" in a Californian drawl.

"Reach for your dreams, man, it's all out there waiting to happen," Luca would say. Sam booted up his laptop and turned his attention to his blog. He needed to kill time before Luca's return. *Motorists must switch to electric cars by 2050 if Britain is to meet CO_2 emission targets ...* He sighed, unable to focus on the important issues, picked up Luca's binoculars and trained them on the river again, hoping to get another ogle. The sound of crunching on gravel heralded Luca's return; Sam grabbed his laptop and rushed to greet him. He thought Luca appeared a bit on edge; the American eyed the binoculars sharply, and slipped them into his pocket.

"You look like I feel," Sam joked. "Anything I can help with?" In the absence of a reply from Luca, he ploughed on: "I hope church helped. I didn't have you down as the religious type."

"Following me, are you?" Luca admonished, and Sam shook his head. Then his face brightened; he knew a way he could help his friend.

"So, with a name like 'Tempesta', you must be Italian Catholic, right?" he asked.

Luca ignored him, but Sam continued: "There's a new confession app out, launched for people who don't want to confess their sins directly to a priest. Here, look: you log in under a secure password and tap in your age, sex and date of last confession, and it'll present you with the sins your demographic profile is most likely to commit: lying, dubious business activities, adultery, for example."

He sneaked a peep at Luca and noticed him flinch. Sam was not one to judge, but if he could only persuade Luca to get a few of his sins pardoned online, it might free him up to talk about Sam. He could even run some of his own naughty thoughts by Luca, a sort of confessor by proxy. Sam had been having quite a lot of them recently, and it would feel good to unburden himself.

"It's the first-ever mobile phone app to receive Roman Catholic approval," he continued. "If it cuts out the middleman, giving electronic absolution without the embarrassment of facing a priest, it's got to be a good thing, right?"

When Luca finally looked up, Sam was alarmed to see tears streaming down his face.

"Man, that's the funniest thing I've ever heard," Luca said eventually, and Sam exhaled with relief. Now that he had pulled himself together, this would be an ideal opportunity to return to the subject of himself. But before he could open his mouth to impart his news, Luca had jumped up from the chair and bolted to the door.

"Gotta go, things to do, people to see," he shouted over his shoulder. It was only after he slammed the door that Sam registered the look of steel beneath his laughter.

SEVEN

As THE RESIDENTS of Riverside Lane awoke on Monday morning, the Braithwaites' prodigal son Rupert stepped into a television studio in London's West End. Although he was new to the fame game, he had used his recent leisure time to study the subject from every angle and now felt poised for a stratospheric rise from ex-con to celebrity, following the publication of his book *The Sponsored Walk*. He scanned the Green Room. It would not do to show his awe in the presence of the Shakespearean actor Rudy Roper or the Kazakh supermodel Anya, whose coquettish grin Rupert returned with a confident, thousand-watt beam.

The actor, who pointedly ignored Rupert, reminded him of his father. Before retiring to the Village, Basil Braithwaite had toiled for decades at the family firm, but his son had known since childhood that hard graft was not for him. He sighed, reflecting with satisfaction that, contrary to his father's predictions that he would "amount to nothing", he was on the brink of success as an author and celebrity. Fame alone would not pay the bills, however, and Rupert had been forced to ask his parents for a loan.

"No can do," Basil had growled. "I am going to cash in my pension to fund a golden retirement. I'm thinking the QE2 might suit the Duchess." Rupert had rolled his eyes. "You may well laugh," Basil had continued, "but your mother will be the subject of all my munificence from here on in."

"Oh, darling, please don't take any notice," his mother had interjected. "Sometimes I'm afraid your father just can't help what he says."

It was around then that Rupert had begun to wonder whether or not his old man might be losing his marbles, and his thoughts had turned to power of attorney; he did not begrudge the old folks dinners out or even the odd weekend away, but threatening his legacy was pure madness.

To allay his nerves, Rupert focused on his antipathy towards his father. The old man had been too hard on him. He had never wanted to go into the City in the first place, and could hardly be blamed that the fund had gone bad. He had only been trying to save his clients from boring administration by ticking the box that said they had been alerted to the risks. Every fool knew about risk! Nobody ever got rich with their money just languishing in the bank, after all.

The green light flashed, and Rupert sauntered down the corridor; but to his dismay, instead of the usual host, the gorgeous Gemma, a prickly, middle-aged man sat on the studio sofa. A stand-in, it was explained. The presenter was cued in to start his introduction:

"The cover brags, 'From preschool to Pentonville via public school!', but surely that is something to be ashamed of, not to boast about? Today's guest is the author of *The Sponsored Walk*. Despite being afforded all the privileges money can buy, Rupert Braithwaite ended up in prison for fraud at the age of twenty-three. Today we will discuss whether or not there still such a thing as 'society'. Do we have the sense of duty and responsibility of our forefathers?"

The camera drew back, and Rupert opened his mouth to speak.

"Are you proud of ripping people off?" the presenter challenged. Rupert smiled; then, realising his mistake, he adopted a pained expression. The stand-in continued: "In your book, you claim as your heroes Victor Lustig, Frank Abagnale and George Parker – but those men were con artists and criminals!"

Rupert laughed nervously. This was not what he had expected; he had, rather, anticipated a little flirting and a lot of talking about himself.

"But at least *they* preyed on the rich and corrupt," his inquisitor continued. "Your tawdry little scam exploited the poor and the vulnerable. And now you expect us to dig deep and buy your book to further line your pockets?"

"I wouldn't exactly call it 'digging deep,'" Rupert replied. "It's only £8.99." He suddenly wished he had taken his agent's advice and done media training.

Smelling fear, the presenter continued his attack: "You represent a generation of young people who feel they are entitled to success rather than being prepared to work hard and earn it, do you not? And it's not as though you were without privilege. Money, status, the best public school – did none of these things teach you anything?"

Rupert had exactly five minutes of airtime. If he did not think on his feet, he could lose everything. Taking a deep breath, he turned to face the camera.

"Prison taught me more than public school ever could. I became a man during my incarceration," he blagged. He allowed a faint crack in his demeanour. "I read the Bible, talked to the priest and took advice from my parents, who have suffered so much because of my foolishness."

Now Rupert breathed easily. He had certainly learned enough to know when he was in control, and the power dynamic in the interview had just shifted. "I used the time to reconnect with my father," he continued, "and it is one of life's cruelties that just as I am free to live a better life, he has become imprisoned in a world I cannot share."

The presenter turned to the camera, explaining to the viewer: "Basil Braithwaite is a legend amongst old-school stockbrokers, and holds a CBE for services to charity." Turning back to Rupert, he asked: "Is he proud of you?"

Rupert smiled bravely as he recast his foe as an unsympathetic villain. "My father is suffering from dementia," he said. "I have written this book to raise money towards a cure and to create publicity for the terrible disease that causes untold misery around the world."

The clock showed forty seconds remaining; determined to have the last word, Rupert embellished his tale of woe. He opened his big brown eyes and looked pleadingly into the camera.

"Just as I have been granted my liberty, my father is losing his," he said. "Every day, he is forced to rely on his loved ones for the most basic tasks. It's a terrible burden on my mother, who is gradually losing the man she loves, and for me, his only son."

The break came, and the camera cut away. "Put that in your pipe and smoke it," Rupert muttered nastily, and stormed out to get Anya's number.

Meanwhile, back in the Village, Rupert's parents were enjoying a leisurely breakfast in their warm, sunny kitchen.

"Turn that bloody racket off, will you?" growled Basil.

Rosamund pressed the "mute" button on the remote and tried to ignore her husband's chomping from behind *The Daily Telegraph*.

"It's gone loud for the advertisements," she said. "I do wish they wouldn't do that." The television was a constant source of friction; if Basil had his way, their house in Riverside Lane would be a screen-free zone, but Rosamund enjoyed a little light entertainment and so resisted Basil's attempt to impose his will.

"It seems Hugh will be overlooked again in the next reshuffle," said Basil through a mouthful of muesli. "Don't suppose Joy likes that much." Rosamund sipped her coffee and said nothing. "It says here he went to a reception attended by Elton John and Gary Barlow, whoever he may be. Bloody ridiculous, if you ask me."

"More coffee?"

Basil nodded and continued his diatribe. "Why is it that nothing in this country is ever considered important until a bloody celebrity hijacks the cause?"

"Celebrities can do a lot of good," said Rosamund, heading to the fridge for milk. "They help raise awareness, and an incredible amount of money."

"Pandering to the lowest common denominator. They should–"

Something on the television screen distracted him. "Bloody hell, is that Rupert?"

"Where?" asked Rosamund from behind the fridge door.

"On the box!" Basil scrambled for the remote, but by the time he had found it and peered at the buttons, their son had disappeared from the screen.

"Are you quite sure, Basil?"

"Of course I'm sure! Surprisingly, given how little we see him, I am capable of recognising my own son."

"What was he saying?"

"How the hell do I know? You had the wretched thing on silent!"

Rosamund poured her husband's coffee. "Silly old me," she smiled, and Basil patted her bottom. Rosamund would not argue – there was no point – but she was confident he was mistaken. If Rupert was going to be on television, he would certainly have told her. She made a mental note to invite him for Sunday lunch. They had not seen him for months after his last visit, which had ended in one of the unholy rows that were not unusual for father and son since Rupert's release from prison. What had been different was that Rosamund, who usually tried to take a neutral position, had sided with her husband. She still quaked at the memory of Rupert storming out. He had called six weeks later to announce that his book was to be published, and Basil, who was not entirely sure what it was about, had imparted a few pearls of grudging wisdom, which Rosamund regarded as a peace offering.

"Quick, turn it up!" barked Basil. Advertisements over, the camera panned to the presenter.

"That was Rupert Braithwaite," he said. "Our thoughts are with his family during this difficult time. And now, the news."

By lunchtime, it was mayhem in Riverside Lane. Bianca watched from her window as Amanda Jones vied for position outside the Braithwaites' home. Frank was incensed at the tone the television interview had taken, and had ignored his wife's running commentary. He knew from his heyday how unpleasant it was to be a victim of unwanted media attention, and felt certain that Rupert's motivation had nothing to do with altruism and everything to do with furthering his career. He had not been surprised to hear the bombshell about his neighbour's dementia; Basil was a delightful, eccentric old buffer, but he could be very odd, and was sometimes so gruff and rude that one could be forgiven for thinking he did not like you. On occasion, Basil had appeared not to recognise Frank, despite the fact that they had lived next door to one another for six years. He was also clearly deaf, because whenever Frank called to him over the fence or out the window, Basil never, ever heard him.

Having spent fifty years in show business, Frank deplored the new phenomenon of instant celebrity; aside from its embodiment by talentless nobodies, it made him feel old and "past it". As he approached his seventies, he needed to resurrect his career – but he was short on money and short on time. All too often, he was passed over by whippersnappers and wannabes who thought Frank Fielding a laughing stock. Bianca, who was much younger than him, had ambitions for accolades from the Palace; but Frank knew that was nothing more than a pipe dream.

"Look at Amanda Jones, all dressed up like a dog's dinner!" Bianca called. "You'd think she was bleedin' *News at Ten*, not the local rag."

"Come away, babe," said Frank, "let's not get involved."

But Bianca could not drag herself away. All the while, on the television, dementia experts expostulated on Basil's demise, and Frank was filled with sad memories of his mother and concern for his poor neighbour.

"You should ring 'em, babe, give 'em some advice," said Bianca. Frank was relieved when the Braithwaites' number was engaged; as comfortable as he was in front of a camera, he was not awfully at home with illness and despair. He had a tendency to flip into game-show mode and try to jolly everybody out of things, yet there could be no jollying his neighbours out of the dreadful news of Basil's illness, nor of their humiliating exposure at the hands of their son on national television.The young man's sentimental pleas reminded Frank of his own father's disingenuous whining after his mother's Alzheimer's diagnosis. By the time the wretched disease had finished with her, she could not move, speak or see, and her world had become a single bed in a small room. Frank

73

sighed heavily. Then, suddenly, it hit him. He knew how to help his neighbours. He would do what he did best, and what they could never do: face the media. He would do it on their behalf. He bolted upstairs and changed into a bright jumper. A slather of Brylcreem and a hint of foundation, and Frank Fielding was camera-ready.

"Don't you speak to that Amanda Jones!" Bianca called to his back as he departed.

Basil watched his wife's beautiful, tear-stained face as they listened to his lawyer's sage advice. Bloody Rupert. He could not give two hoots for himself, but Rosamund did not deserve this; she had devoted her life to that boy, given her heart and soul, and this was how he repaid her? Struggling to understand how such a vile child could have sprung from such perfect loins, he joined Rosamund at the table and squeezed her hand.

"He's drawing us up a statement, and says we should keep a low profile and speak to nobody."

"How could he do this?"

"Don't take it so hard, Duchess," said Basil. "It does have its funny side. If our neighbours think I have dementia, I have the excuse to be as rude as I like! Plus, I can conveniently forget that our esteemed son is a jailbird!"

"Basil, you mustn't joke. Dementia is a terrible thing. Rupert should be ashamed for using it as a stepping stone to promote his bloody book."

"Rosamund Braithwaite!" cried Basil in mock horror. "There is absolutely no need to swear."

She smiled. "Well, if he has told the British public he is raising awareness of dementia, he can jolly well put his royalties towards finding a cure. Just because we are prepared to keep his lie a secret doesn't mean he shouldn't honour his promises."

"Good God, where's the remote?" Basil blustered. "Look, Frank Fielding's on the bandwagon now." The television screen panned to Frank in a luminous patterned jumper.

"I am deeply saddened," Frank said in a deep theatrical voice, "that my dear friend Basil Braithwaite ..."

Basil choked. "Dear friend? Bloody little has-been! *Dear friend*? Good God. Has the world gone utterly mad?"

"Do be quiet," said Rosamund, turning up the volume. "Listen to Frank."

"... We should allow them their privacy at this sad time ..."

"Oh, for God's sake, turn it off, Rosamund!"

"He's trying to help us."

"Well, he's not. He's fuelling their fire and making it worse."

"... cheap publicity stunt to sell more copies of his book ..." Frank continued onscreen. "He is nothing more than a con artist and an opportunist."

"To Hell with this, I need a drink." Basil pushed back his chair in disgust.

"But it's not yet twelve o' clock," objected Rosamund.

"Today is not the day for your finishing-school rules, Duchess. We are going to have a drink, and turn that wretched television off." He picked up a crystal decanter and poured them each a brandy. In the background, Frank Fielding continued his statement.

"... please give my friends the space they need, and say a prayer that they are able to come to terms with this dreadful sadness."

"A prayer?" shouted Basil, "A prayer! Good God, I've heard it all now!"

EIGHT

A FEW DAYS LATER, Bianca Fielding slipped out of the house at dawn. A kingfisher darted in and out of the water and a red kite hovered overhead, but Bianca was oblivious. Her iPod was turned up high and she thundered along the towpath, enjoying the cold air on her arms, sweat running down her back.

Early morning was Bianca's "thinking time". When she was running, she had all the smart answers, all the solutions, all the witty retorts and pearls of wisdom. Today she was thinking about Frank. It had been kind of him to address the journalists on Basil's behalf. She was proud of the way he had handled the media, stepping bravely into the breach and making such a lovely statement. She and Frank had been relieved to learn from Rosamund that Basil did not have dementia, and it had, as Frank had assured the press, all been a cheap publicity stunt to sell more copies of the book.

The Willoughbys' return invitation for that evening could not have come at a better time, Bianca decided as she pounded the footpath, feeling grateful that the media had not been so intrusive when she and Frank had begun their affair over two decades earlier. She wondered how celebrities managed today: liaisons conducted under a barrage of flashbulbs, their every kiss photographed, their actions analysed.

Frank had been at the height of his fame and still married to Jeanette when he had pursued Bianca. He was the king of Saturday night light entertainment, riding high on the success of *Showtime*; Bianca, a catalogue model, had used all her wiles and plenty of thought-provoking bedroom techniques to sink her fasteners into him. She knew he had indulged in the occasional extramarital romp over the years, but she had turned a blind eye, telling herself this was the price she had to pay for marrying a household name. She was not insecure – she was beautiful and younger than her husband, and as the mother of Frank's only child, Tallulah, she held the ultimate ace. After Tallulah's birth, she had withheld all sexual favours until Frank agreed to the snip. There would be no more Fieldings to usurp Bianca now. She and her daughter were sitting pretty upon the throne of Frank's love.

Popping in to the newsagent's to collect the morning papers on the way home, Bianca was assaulted by a rack of headlines declaring: FRANK FIELDING CALLS LOCAL CHARITY UNDESERVING.

"Oh bleedin' 'Enry!" she cried, her hands over her mouth in horror. "Bleedin' bloody 'Enry! That Amanda Jones has gone and done it again!"

Throwing a twenty-pound note onto the counter, she grabbed all the papers from the rack and, clutching them to her jiggling breasts, hared off down the pavement, desperate to return to her husband before he switched on the television. He did not deserve this. He had faced the media with the best intentions, wanting to help the Braithwaites in their hour of need, and that evil hack had twisted his words. After all he had done for charity, all those nights helping those poor, wounded military folk. He gave his time selflessly and generously without a world of complaint, and this is what he got for it.

Unlocking the front door and ignoring their little dog, Dubonnet, who was yapping for his breakfast, Bianca ran up the stairs and into the arms of her husband.

That evening, Bianca waved her champagne flute aloft and the Willoughbys' housekeeper Kathy refilled it dutifully. As the golden nectar flowed, Bianca tipped the glass to forty-five degrees and stuck her finger into the flow.

"Stops it going all fizzy an' spillin' everywhere," she explained. Kathy McConnell recharged the other glasses calmly with neither a bubble nor a drop spilled; she was proud of her steady hand. Bianca turned to Rosamund and, sucking her finger, said: "I learned that trick years ago, when I was modellin'."

Rosamund was about to respond when Basil chipped in mischievously: "Why don't you tell Bianca about your modelling days with Joy, Rosamund?" His wife began to protest, but was interrupted.

"You've got to be kiddin' me!" shrieked Bianca, "You two? Modellin'? Ooh, you dark horses." Kathy offered Mrs Braithwaite a canapé and a complicit smile.

"Thank you so much," said Rosamund quietly.

Kathy did not like having to serve Bianca and her publicity-hungry husband. Her own mother, who had spent a lifetime in domestic service in Edinburgh's New Town, had always maintained that true class showed in the way people dealt with the serving orders – and the Fieldings fell well short. In this regard, Kathy knew Mrs Braithwaite to be faultless, and Mrs Willoughby too, for, while she could be snobby, she understood boundaries and never overstepped them. Kathy played her part in the Willoughby household to perfection, behaving with a quiet subservience that fuelled her boss's self-importance and cemented her invaluable position.

The former pub landlady had been introduced to the Willoughbys by Joy's brother Edmund Pendlegrass some years earlier. Kathy had been seeking work in the Village, a place she felt more in keeping with her social standing than her own neighbourhood. As a friend of the family, she had expected Joy Willoughby to be a kindred spirit; but her superiority complex had been clear from the moment Kathy set eyes on that imperious face.

The Willoughbys had, in fact, been looking for a cleaner, and although Kathy needed a job, she was not prepared to demean herself with such lowly work. She had played the politician's wife like a musical instrument: Joy's shrewdness had been no match for her as Kathy pandered to her snobbishness, feigning an assumption that, given the grandeur of The White House, the vacancy was for a housekeeper. Kathy explained that while she was not prepared to clean, she would manage the household, ensuring it ran to perfection and overseeing chores such as gardening, deliveries and fresh flowers. Her winning card had been her expertise in managing formal dinners, and the revelation of a tenuous link to royalty.

"When I was in service in Edinburgh and the Duchess of Kent visited, we would always measure the distance between place settings and the angle at which the glasses were positioned to ensure everything was just so," Kathy had told a rapt Joy, and it had taken less than an hour to persuade the politician's wife to hire the housekeeper she had not known she needed. Before long the two women were talking support staff, and there was an additional budget for Kathy to take on a raft of cleaners and maintenance men. Kathy had even negotiated a higher salary to reflect the extra responsibility.

Kathy McConnell had not spent fifty-four years on this Earth without learning a thing or two. An unforgiving mother, cleaning jobs from the age of fifteen, a drunk of a husband and working as a pub landlady had all rendered her more than capable of handling the Joy Willoughbys of this world. She drew confidence from her friendship with Edmund, who had used the games room at the Rose and Thistle for Port Sanctuary functions. Life had been cruel, but Kathy knew her star was ascendant, and that she had been born for a far greater destiny than her current dreary existence implied. Soon it would be *her* sipping champagne from a cut-glass crystal flute, and when the good times rolled she would behave with all the grace and elegance of Rosamund Braithwaite (or "Mrs B.", as Kathy affectionately thought of her).

Kathy had studied Mrs B. carefully, and learned to mirror her polished elegance. She copied her phrases and expressions and emulated her mannerisms and style. Tonight, for example, her idol was wearing a plain shift dress in French navy, with a three-quarter-length sleeve and a boat neck. Simple diamond studs adorned her ears, and navy and cream ballet pumps graced her feet. Kathy thought her unforced elegance in the face of the tawdry media intrusion hit just the right note. Her sleeve was a flattering length, the neckline modest and stylish, and Kathy knew that tomorrow she would scour the second-hand shops for a similar ensemble. Her first port of call would be the charity shop where Mrs B. donated her castoffs. On more than one occasion, Kathy had purchased a genuine Rosamund Braithwaite hand-me-down that had instantly become her most prized possession, and while she had trouble taming her curly red hair into a neat bob like Mrs B.'s, that did not stop her from trying. She referred to her scrapbook, which contained newspaper cuttings of her idol attending various charity functions, mostly with Mrs Willoughby. Kathy cropped out her boss and carefully mounted Mrs B.'s beautiful face on the scrapbook's pages. The funny thing was, although she had versions of every outfit seen on the object of her admiration, Rosamund had never recognised any of them.

"Come on, Roz, 'fess up!" said Bianca, interrupting Kathy's reverie. "Tell us about the modellin'!"

Kathy winced. This was all wrong. She took a deep breath, and rather than feel irritated by Bianca Fielding – gold digger, rascal robber and common tart – she smiled. Kathy was playing the long game, and she planned to win. She knew Mrs B. was only being polite, and that deep down she, too, must loathe Bianca's vulgarity. It was only a matter of time, she told herself, before she and Mrs B. became the closest of friends. Frank chipped in, trying to salve his wife's gaucherie with a clumsy charm.

"Oh, I'm not surprised to hear you two ladies had your glamorous days," he said, before realising his mistake and adding: "That's not to say you aren't still lovely now, just ..."

Kathy smiled to herself; navigating social mores was not easy for the uninitiated, though she herself could negotiate such pitfalls blindfolded. A thunderous laugh startled her, and a soufflé crouton fell to the floor. Kathy bit her lip, restored it to the plate and offered the offending canapé to Basil Braithwaite, who accepted it greedily and barked: "Go on, Fielding, dig yourself out of that one!"

"Don't worry, Frank," Rosamund interjected kindly. "We know exactly what you meant. Basil is just stirring. Ignore him!"

"Good God," said Joy, moving to the window that afforded an unrivalled view of the river, where a solitary figure was rowing. "Isn't that the international man of mystery who's residing at Clive's?"

She bristled visibly as Frank joined her, putting a friendly hand on her back. "It certainly is," he said. "Did you know Bianca took up rowing for a bit? But she kept kissing the cox, so they asked her to leave." Kathy thought Joy's expression would curdle cream, but Frank appeared oblivious, chuckling at his own wit. "Mind you," he continued, "I think I'd fit in pretty well with the dawn rowers – you know me, always up for a bit of morning glory!"

Joy was unwittingly saved by Bianca. "What sort of modellin' did you do, Joy?" she asked, trying to suppress a smirk, "Catalogue? Catwalk?"

"Take no notice of Basil," laughed Rosamund. "Of course we weren't models. We learned modelling at school, which is rather different."

Bianca giggled. "School? You did modellin' at *school*? There was me, strugglin' with readin', writin' and bleedin' arithmetic, and you two learned *modellin'*?"

"Finishing school," said Joy tightly, and Bianca collapsed into squeals of mirth, which the other woman pointedly ignored. "It's where girls learn how to become young ladies."

When Bianca had at last gained enough composure to be comprehensible, she explained to her bewildered audience that finishing schools were also where transsexuals went to be feminised. "I read it in the *Sunday Mirror*," she said. "After the op! It's where they get kitted out with the boobs and makeup and stuff."

"Not a million miles from Lucy Clayton's, then," observed Basil with a smirk.

"Oh, do let's talk about something else," Rosamund laughed. "It was all a load of outdated nonsense."

"I disagree," countered Joy. "The things we learned have been very useful. When meeting royalty, for example; there is an absolute minefield of *faux pas* to make if you don't know the correct etiquette."

Bianca stopped laughing. An image flashed into her mind of

her resplendent in a Karl Bowman hat and Frank shaking hands with the Queen at Buckingham Palace. She and Frank had been delighted when Joy's note had dropped onto their mat a few days earlier, both seeing it as a thank-you to Frank for speaking out about Rupert Braithwaite. But for Bianca, it represented so much more: final acceptance into what she half-jokingly called the Riverside Lane "inner circle".

"Oh, Frankie, it's all down to you for smoothing the waters. We're on our way!" she had exclaimed gleefully, logging on to an expensive retailer and ordering a new ensemble for the evening. Sipping her champagne, Bianca hoped that Amanda Jones had not scuppered their chances.

"What are the dos and don'ts then? Come on, spill the beans," she said, and Joy seized the opportunity to show off her royal encounters while Bianca tried to commit some of the rules to memory: "Your Majesty", then "Ma'am"; no touching; never turn your back on the Queen. She knew that if she were ever to become Lady Fielding, she must stop larking about, comport herself with decorum and be on her best behaviour. In the spirit of "no time like the present", Bianca emulated the elegant way Rosamund was seated: ankles crossed neatly to one side, hands folded in her lap. But she almost toppled off the sofa. Instead of waving her glass in the air to make a point, she tried placing it gracefully on the table as Joy did, but then her hands felt odd and fiddly. Her phone made a yapping noise.

"Aw, that's Dubonnet," she said, "I recorded him barkin' for my ring tone. Isn't it sweet?" Joy grimaced, and Bianca fished her mobile from her bag and pressed the requisite keys with her long, red nails.

"Mobile phone etiquette," said Joy crossly, "is something sadly lacking in society nowadays."

"Don't worry, Bianca," said Rosamund, "you're amongst friends. Do you know what the Queen says when somebody's phone goes off?"

"No," said Bianca, apparently stupefied that Rosamund did know.

"She says: 'Oh, do get it,'" said Rosamund, doing an alarmingly good impression of Her Majesty, "'it may be somebody important'!"

"Yeah," Bianca cackled, her irrepressible fizz restored, "like anybody's more important than the Queen! What else did you learn?"

"No glitz before six," offered Joy, eyeing Bianca's outfit.

"But that's terribly old-fashioned now," Rosamund interjected, wishing Joy would think twice before she spoke. All the same, Bianca – who was often decked in diamante well before the sun was over the yardarm – appeared fascinated. Rosamund could hear Joy regaling her with the six-point rule.

"We were told to spin around in front of the mirror," said Joy, "and take off the first thing that caught our eye in the reflection. Every different colour, each pattern or stripe, each piece of jewellery or accessory is another point." She explained: "A busy pattern, like your trousers for example, would be at least a three, so everything else should be plain and modest. And you should never, ever wear more than six points during the day, maybe seven for a big night out." Rosamund did not want to be around when Joy totted up the points for Bianca's huge earrings, low top, busy necklace, animal-print trousers, high heels and countless bangles and rings. Spotting Kathy hovering in the background, she used the opportunity to catch her attention.

"Kathy," she said quietly, "how is Angus?"

She had heard from Joy's brother that Kathy's husband Angus had lost his job as a pub landlord and consequently their pub, accommodation and livelihood. Apparently the McConnells were now living on a rundown estate on the edge of town. All credit to Kathy's professionalism – she had never mentioned her reduced circumstances, and had continued to look beautifully turned out – but Edmund, who appeared to know all about Kathy's home life, had revelled in passing on the gossip.

"It really is ghastly," he had reported in a tone reminiscent of his sister's. "She's kept all those Morningside pretensions – you know, doilies, antimacassars, sugar tongs and whatnot – and her doorstep is scrubbed and gleaming. But it's plain her neighbours don't have the same standards." Rosamund could not picture Edmund, in his blazer and tie, in such an environment, and wondered how he had come to be there. "Apparently the locals throw their rubbish into her front garden. They push Angus over when he stumbles home drunk, and he's always covered in cuts and bruises. Bring back National Service, I say!" Edmund had concluded. "That'll sort out the men from the boys."

"Angus is just fine, thank you, Mrs Braithwaite," said Kathy, adding solicitously, "I've got some of your favourite elderflower cordial in the kitchen. Would you like me to fetch you a wee glass?"

"Oh, Kathy, how clever of you to remember," Rosamund replied with delight. "I would love that. Thank you." As she turned towards the other guests, she added, over her shoulder: "By the way, I do like your blouse."

Joy was desperate for the Fieldings to leave. After the dinner party and Frank's well-intended television interview, she had invited them as a favour to Rosamund, to acknowledge Frank's efforts at saving Basil from the media (even if he had somewhat missed the point), but they were now overstaying their welcome.

"I can't serve dinner much later than nine," she whispered to Hugh in the kitchen. "Whatever time do you think they're leaving? Surely they know six-o'clock-drinks finish at eight-thirty?"

Hugh laughed. "Of course they don't," he said. "That is, unless you've told them. I imagine they think they'll leave when the Braithwaites do."

"But Rosamund and Basil are invited to dinner!" Joy became shrill. "And I have as good as told them it is time to leave. I even plumped up the cushions, for goodness' sake!"

"A little too subtle for the Fieldings, I fear," said Hugh, still laughing. "Do they know the Braithwaites are staying on?"

"Well, no, I thought it would appear rude to point that out. I assumed they would know to leave when their welcome had expired."

Hugh raised his eyebrows. "I think that particular ship may have sailed, Tinkerbell," he said, returning to the drawing room. Joy, who had long since instructed Kathy to stop replenishing the glasses, listened to the laughter ringing down the hallway and could not help but wish that Hugh was not quite so in thrall to Bianca.

"Hughie, you are *so* funny!" she heard Bianca screech, and Joy swallowed hard. Her neighbour might not have been "finished", but Joy could not deny the woman knew how to hold a man's attention. It was easy to be snobby about Bianca's allure, but if she was honest she had to admit a small part of her was the tiniest bit jealous. She returned to the living room wearing an apron and waving a wooden spoon, in the hope it might act as a catalyst to the Fieldings' departure.

Frank, oblivious to Joy's hints, was having a super time despite the unsavoury press allegations that had almost caused Bianca and him to cancel. He was enjoying the opportunity to chat properly with his neighbours, and was grateful they had not bought up Amanda Fielding's vitriolic piece in the local paper (though Rosamund had quietly thanked him for stepping into the breach over the non-story about her husband's health). Nobody had mentioned the Braithwaites' convict son, either – Frank imagined it was just too upsetting to talk about – so all in all, everybody seemed to be back on an even keel, and the best of friends. Frank spent most of his life surrounded by women, so he was enjoying a bit of male camaraderie; Hugh was unfailingly charming, although Frank was a little surprised he had not mentioned the arrival of the police, whom he had spotted in the driveway before Joy drew the curtains. Basil, meanwhile, was terribly funny, pretending to be such a rude curmudgeon and disapproving of everything Frank said. He was pleased that Rosamund and Joy were chatting about fashion with Bianca; he feared people found his wife over the top, and he longed for her to fit into Riverside Lane's circles. Of course, she did not help her case sometimes, but tonight Frank felt proud and could not wait to tell her so. He glanced at his gold Rolex.

"Goodness," he said. "We should be going, leave you good people to your supper. Shall we walk home across the bridge together?" he asked the Braithwaites.

"Actually, we're staying for dinner," replied Basil.

"Oh, bugger, I didn't realise that," said Bianca, "but that's fine. Lovely. It's only egg and chips at home, Frankie. Whatever Joy has made us'll be much nicer." Had Bianca been a little more socially aware, or a little less drunk, she might have picked up on Joy's panic-stricken face, but she was insensible to it all. It took Rosamund to save the day.

"Basil, how many times must I tell you, dinner is just *you*. You and Hugh need to talk about your, er, investments – and I am, um, desperate for an early night." Basil looked bewildered, but soon picked up on the undercurrent from his wife. He stood obediently as she turned to Bianca. "Take no notice of Basil, he never listens to a word I say. I'd love to walk back across the bridge with you." Rosamund grabbed her coat, accidentally spilling the contents of her handbag onto the floor. Kathy dashed over to pick up the belongings, and Rosamund took the arm of a confused-looking Frank and guided him towards the door. "You must be exhausted," she said, looking over her shoulder and mouthing "back shortly" to Hugh. "Bianca told me you did overnight duty at the Port Sanctuary last night. You really are a saint. Come on, now, let's set off before it starts to rain."

The Fieldings having outstayed their welcome meant that Kathy left The White House far later than intended. She accepted Hugh's offer of a taxi, and felt a familiar stab of despair as the vehicle whisked her away from the Village.

Kathy knew Angus would be blotto by now, snoring in front of the television and waiting for his tea. The man revolted her. She had loved him once, but he had always valued the bottle above her. It had been down to her own hard graft that they had kept the pub for so long, and the life of a landlady had afforded her many benefits – not least that she had been so busy, she and her errant husband rarely crossed paths. They had enjoyed a good income and a fine home, and Kathy would never forgive him for drinking it all away. They had left the pub in shame, with nothing to show for a lifetime of hard work. Nothing, that was, except for Kathy's secret, which she guarded more fiercely than a tiger its cub: her ticket out of drudgery. She stroked her secret, and fed it, and spoiled it, and indulged it any way she could. One day, it would spirit her away into a world in which she would take tea with Mrs B., and Joy would welcome her into the bosom of her family.

She rummaged through her handbag and removed a cotton handkerchief, then spread it on her lap and gazed at it happily. It was so delicate, so ladylike. The lace edging was tasteful, and the embroidered initials – "R. B." – pretty and discreet. It would make a wonderful addition to her collection. Kathy held the handkerchief to her nose and inhaled deeply. Chanel No. 5: she recognised the scent because she often looked inside Mrs B.'s handbag and helped herself to a squirt of perfume. The fragrance, still vivid on the cotton, was classic and elegant, evocative of the life Kathy felt certain lay ahead. As they pulled up outside her house, the taxi's headlights illuminated two young men relieving themselves in Kathy's flowerbed. She collected her dignity and, with her head held high, opened the front gate and walked down the small, neat path.

NINE

I T HAD BEEN two weeks since Felicity had introduced Friday Night Happy Hour, and Kathy was first in the pub. Glancing at the clock, she noted that she had an hour to rest her tired feet before the 18.17 bus transported her home. If she timed it right, Angus would be long gone by then, propping up some bar, no doubt, and she could prepare a TV supper and settle down for her favourite soap. She ordered a Babycham and sighed.

"Long week?" asked Felicity, and Kathy nodded. It had started with an apoplectic Mrs Willoughby denouncing her for leaving the French doors unlocked. Then she had suffered the indignity of having to dance attendance on Bianca Fielding, who had inveigled her way into the affections of Mrs B. The image of the two women linking arms and heading off into the night still rankled Kathy.

She wondered how the barmaid, who lived opposite the ghastly Bianca, could afford to reside in Riverside Lane. When – as he inevitably would – Frank Fielding moved on to a younger model and Kathy's special secret was allowed to blossom in the light of day, she too would live close to her beloved Mrs B., and perhaps even befriend the new Mrs Fielding.

The door opened and Amanda Jones teetered in, looking around the Crown with her weasel eyes. She pulled up an adjacent stool and said, "Mind if I join you?"

Kathy did mind; she had endured the paparazzi camping out in Riverside Lane for over a week, and her heart had bled for the intrusion poor Mrs B. had suffered. It was just like when Princess Diana died. She also knew the journalist had only imposed because there was nobody more important to talk to. It was not the first time Amanda had tried to butter her up, and Kathy had learned to deflect her advances over the years; if the media wanted to know the goings-on at The White House, they would have to speak to Mr Willoughby's press office.

"Fancy a drink?" Amanda asked. Kathy demurred, explaining frostily that it was almost time for her bus. "Oh, don't worry," the journalist said. "I'm going your way later – I'll drop you home."

Outside, the rain tapped persistently at the window, and the cars stood at a rush-hour standstill. The bus was bound to be late, and the carrier bag of spirits she had purloined from the Willoughbys for Angus were dead weight. The thought of being whisked home in a warm car was tantalising.

"That looks good," Amanda persisted, pointing to the cocktails chalked up on the board, "Fancy an Amaretto Adventure?"

Amanda carried the jug to a table and Kathy followed, disquieted by her choice of drinking partner.

"*Slàinte*," she said, raising her glass.

"Cheers," said Amanda. "I like your hair. You've gone a shade darker, haven't you?" Kathy patted the bob that had turned to frizz in the drizzle.

"Just a little," she said, sipping the drink, which tasted like childhood sweets. "It's called 'Chestnut Dream.'"

"You're looking good," said Amanda. "With your hair like that, you remind me of somebody, but for the life of me I cannot think who it is." They were interrupted by a loud voice at the door.

"There's only one thing worse than raining cats and dogs!" Kathy looked up to see Frank Fielding standing on tiptoe to hang a dripping wet coat in the porch. "Hailing taxis!"

Amanda was on her feet and across the bar before Kathy had had time to reflect on the compliment. Her view was obscured by several pensioners rattling their umbrellas and hanging up their coats, too; then Amanda pushed her way back through them, her face like a squashed tomato.

"How dare Frank Fielding ignore me?" she spat. "Washed-up old has-been! He sets himself up as the Braithwaites' spokesperson, then refuses to answer any of my questions. Anyway,

I'm acting on a tip-off to meet an important American, so ..."

Her vitriol was interrupted by her phone. Kathy, who had spoken to enough credit controllers in her time to recognise the journalist's snappy defences and disingenuous justifications, sipped her drink and tried to identify the flavour on the tip of her tongue. She slipped off her cardigan and glanced accusingly at the fire, which had been set far too high.

At the bar, the man who had dominated Saturday night TV for the majority of Kathy's life flirted with the delighted pensioners. Kathy the snob, who aligned herself with Joy and felt Bianca was common, considered Frank a crass little Weeble; but the woman who sat alone in front of the television each night, the one for whom he had always had a kind word and a harmless joke, secretly thought him quite funny.

She noticed Felicity scoop away the newspapers hastily, but not before a headline caught her eye: CELEBRITIES AND STARS AMONG 600 VICTIMS OF BILL LEWIS STING IN THE UK. Frank had evidently seen the headline too, for he coloured from tangerine to pomegranate. Then, catching Kathy's eye, he made a valiant attempt at a mock bow before retiring to his usual table and settling in behind the newspaper.

Amanda ended her call, and Kathy recognised the sentiments behind her set jaw, too. The woman clearly had money worries. She sipped her drink some more, and the flavour came to her: marzipan. Warmed by the fire, the glow of Italian liquor stealing around her body, Kathy felt gripped by an uncharacteristic display of camaraderie.

"You'll never guess what happened the other day at the Willoughbys'," she said, inching forward. "You must promise not to tell a soul." The absence of any apology after Mrs Willoughby's unjust accusation still stung, and it felt good to be getting it off her chest. She took another sip of her drink.

"I wouldn't dream of it," replied Amanda, with a gimlet eye. "Confidentiality is paramount in my career. Nothing you say will go any further."

"Well, the Willoughbys had a break-in, and they called the police! But guess what? Nothing was stolen, because I'd had the good sense to wrap Mrs Willoughby's trinkets in tissue paper and hide them in the fish kettle while they were away!"

"That was lucky. I bet she was relieved," prompted Amanda.

"No, that was the funny thing – she was furious," replied Kathy indignantly. "She accused me of leaving the door unlocked and letting in the burglars. As if a woman of my experience would do such a thing! And she wasn't even grateful when I revealed that her jewellery was safe. I found out later from Mrs Willoughby's mother that she was seething with Mr Willoughby for breaking the window pane in the back door."

"Why did he do that?" enquired Amanda, discreetly switching her phone to "record".

"Well, according to Myrtle," Kathy continued after taking another sip of her drink, "there was no sign of forced entry, and Mr Willoughby was worried they wouldn't be able to claim on their insurance. Imagine that? A politician breaking the law! I know it happens all the time, what with people at Westminster fiddling with their expenses, buying duck houses and whatnot, but I am surprised all the same." She shook her head in disapproval. "It beggars belief that the Willoughbys could be so cavalier about leaving jewellery on the dressing table, given the recent spate of burglaries in the area. The Braithwaites, bless them, had some expensive antiques stolen recently. Family heirlooms! My heart went out to poor Mrs Braithwaite, so calm and graceful in adversity, so –"

"Yes, yes," said Amanda impatiently, "but what happened at the Willoughbys'? Have you any proof that they tampered with the crime scene?"

"Proof?" Kathy repeated. "Why would I need that? This is all just between you and me, isn't it?" Her voice trailed off as she realised the journalist's attention had been diverted by the arrival of a tall, dark stranger with a scar on his face.

"Well, the police are going to do a stakeout at The White House to catch the criminal!" shouted Kathy, angry at being forced to catch the journalist's attention. Her strident voice prompted Frank to peer from behind his newspaper.

"Thank you so much," gushed Amanda, "it's been fun." With that, she was out of her seat and gone before Kathy could reply. Gathering up her carrier bag of clanking bottles, Kathy followed the journalist, but as she reached the bar, Amanda turned on her heel and made direct eye contact.

"Darling, are you all right about catching the bus after all? Wrap up warm," she said, her voice dripping with concern that her cold eyes belied. Kathy bit her lip. She knew she could not make a scene, so she smiled through gritted teeth.

"Och, no, is that the time? I must be running along," she said smoothly, noting with bitterness that she had missed the 18.17 and would be forced to sit alone for an hour or pay for a taxi. She returned the jug and glasses to the bar and felt grateful to Felicity, who invited her to a party before ordering her a cab home.

Stepping into the cold, damp air, Kathy could hear Amanda Jones' laughter echoing from the bar. The journalist would get her comeuppance one day, of that Kathy was certain. She had a saintly patience when it came to retribution.

TEN

T HE FOLLOWING DAY in Riverside Lane, Luca Tempesta was giving every appearance of enjoying another leisurely afternoon by the river. An ancient fishing rod in one hand and a cold beer in the other, he cast the knotted line nonchalantly and watched in peaceful contemplation as its rusty hook hit the surface of the water, creating tiny whirlpools that sent mayflies scattering.

Sitting astride a green canvas stool, his only thought was of the surveillance team on the upper floors of the Willoughby residence. Tiny beads of sweat on his upper lip were the only indication that Luca was under pressure. Logic told him there was nothing to worry about, that there was no way his troubles could have followed him to a village in England, but his vigilant side, the part that kept him awake at night, warned him to stay at red alert. Luca trained his binoculars on a cormorant conveniently perched on the bow of the Willoughbys' splendid slipper boat. The *Lucky Penny* bobbed on the ebb and flow of the river, and provided Luca with a perfect decoy. He directed his high-definition lens to the top floor of the house, where the two men had cameras poised towards him across the expanse of river. The surveillance was invisible to the naked eye, but to Luca, who was aided by the sophisticated gear he kept stowed in the attic at Kingfisher House, it was as obvious as the Hollywood sign that shone above Los Angeles at night.

He was pleased he had stuck a birdwatcher sticker on his military-issue equipment; he did not want to raise Ivy Midwinter's suspicions further, even though it was unlikely she would snoop again, as he had procured her keys to Kingfisher House from her desk drawer at Village Antiques. It did not help that Riverside Lane was swarming with press; he had been forced to take Buchanan's small boat and alight downstream.

Luca had been wise to befriend the local journalist in the Crown. Amanda Jones had told him that the old woman was spreading rumours questioning his integrity, so his threats in the church had obviously not worked. He would have to turn up the pressure.

He packed up his gear and sauntered into the house, aware that unseen eyes were tracking his every movement. There was nothing else, he decided, but to reconnoitre the Willoughbys. Hugh seemed affable, but Luca had not survived this long through being taken in by subterfuge. He reflected on what Amanda had told him in the pub. "Hugh Willoughby is not the man he claims to be," she had slurred drunkenly.

Inside Kingfisher House, Luca checked his phone cautiously. Yesterday he had received another email from his stalker. He had hoped he might have left them behind in the States, but they had returned, this time making wild accusations. He had forwarded these to Maria, who promised to take care of it.

"You concentrate on the matter in hand," she had urged him. "You don't need this distraction. Keep your head down, make friends and try to blend in with the community." He took a swig of beer. He had already set the wheels in motion with Cecilia Honey-church, who, vulnerable after being abandoned by her boyfriend, seemed a good person to start with. The phone rang and Luca nearly jumped out of his skin, but it was just Maria. He picked up quickly.

"I'm sorry, Luca," Maria said, "but someone's been calling with awkward questions. It may well be this email stalker, but we thought we'd dealt with it – and now the new intern went and told her you're in England ..." Luca's mind whirred as Maria tried to make light of the information she had just imparted. "Don't worry," she said, "England's a big place."

But Luca did worry; his world had just become smaller.

*

Joy Willoughby was up to her elbows in flour, and had a sharp eye on the clock. She was preparing pastry for a *tarte Tatin* when the elegant chimes of the doorbell echoed in the kitchen. She sighed heavily at the inconvenience of Cecilia and her housekeeper both calling in sick. She had been forced to step into the breach and prepare the menu herself for Hugh's dinner party in honour of some luminaries of local industry. She had offered to do so with a smile, but beneath the carefully applied coral lipstick her teeth had been firmly gritted

Joy had been making an effort recently to be more sensitive to Hugh's needs. He was under pressure with a busy work schedule, she told herself; that was why he was sleeping in the spare bedroom. Hugh jokingly put it down to her snoring, but Joy was not fooled. Her husband had been acting strangely, and had taken to working into the night and snapping his laptop closed as she entered his study. When she had brought him bedtime brandy and cocoa the previous evening, she had spotted something that looked frighteningly like a gay dating site. Joy had swallowed down a rising panic. This was not the first time she had suspected her handsome husband of being of the "other persuasion". She had wondered in the early days of their courtship, too. Hugh had followed her around like a lost pup back then, never making a move until, after several months, Joy – with characteristic brusqueness – had demanded to know what he wanted.

"You, Joy, only you," he had declared, before taking her to bed and vanquishing all her worries.

The doorbell chimed again, and Joy removed her starched-white apron and patted her hair. She decided it must be Cecilia, come to make amends for letting her down at the eleventh hour. Not that she would be appeased; Cecilia's excuse of a tummy bug was a barefaced lie. Joy had spotted her making a spectacle of herself with the American, parading around the tennis court in a silly miniskirt, showing her smalls to all and sundry. Even Myrtle, whom Joy found shockingly liberal at times, had commented that Cecilia's behaviour did not reflect well on Clive's standing in the

Village. *You would never catch Penny behaving like that,* Joy had added. She planned to tell Cecilia exactly what she thought and remind her, for the umpteenth time, that she should use the back door at The White House, not swan in through the front as had become her habit.

Opening the door with a flourish, Joy was stunned to discover the American smiling wolfishly and proffering a box of truffles, Joy's favourites, splendidly packaged in a green drum with a big, pink ribbon, just the way she liked them: the exact same ones Clive used to indulge her with. In an ideal world, she would have accepted the gift and then waved him away, but something caught her attention. He had made an effort, she noted, and, standing before her in a smart, navy-blue jumper and polished shoes, newly shaven and with his hair combed back, he looked rather handsome. The scent of Clive's aftershave reminded her of happy times, long before Cecilia, when he would pop by for a fondant fancy and a chat.

"Mr Tempesta, I'm afraid you've caught me at a rather inopportune time – I am preparing a dinner party," said Joy importantly, accepting the gift more keenly than she had intended. Luca smiled, and Joy noticed his eyes were as blue as robin's eggs and crinkled up nicely in the corners. "Anyway, do come in!"

Luca stepped over the threshold and Joy sensed a change in his demeanour. He looked unsettled, furtive even, his eyes darting about as if he was building up the courage to make a move on her. For one tiny, thrilling moment, she wondered if he had come to rape and pillage; she had not had such fantasies for many a year and was surprised to discover the thought not entirely unpleasant.

"We didn't get much chance to talk at the dinner party," Luca said pleasantly, and Joy noticed the laugh lines on the side of his mouth deepen. To her amazement, she found herself offering him tea and scones and felt a thrill of anticipation when he accepted readily. "Do you mind if I use your restroom first?" he asked. "I need to wash my hands."

Waiting for the kettle to boil, Joy felt flushed. She had a million things to do! What was she thinking, inviting this near-stranger into the house? She could hear him racing up the stairs, and regretted not directing him to the downstairs cloakroom, where she had placed fresh flowers and a new deodoriser only that morning. When he returned, Joy noted he was red-faced, and wondered if she had read him wrong. Maybe he was the bashful type after all, embarrassed to be left alone with a woman of the world.

"My fitness levels are not what they should be," said Luca. "You should have seen me in my heyday, before I discovered the Crown's famous fish and chips ... I was more of a man back then." At a loss for what to say, Joy buttered scones heartily while trying not to notice the rippling biceps beneath what she now recognised to be Clive's jumper. She placed the scones on the island between them, along with a pot of Earl Grey.

"Wow, these are amazing," said Luca, taking a huge bite. "Just when I thought I couldn't taste a more delicious cake than Cecilia's, you go and steal the show." Delighted by the put-down of Cecilia's cake-baking skills, which she had always secretly felt to be inferior to her own, Joy regaled Luca with the story of winning first, second and third place in the cake-bake entry at the Village Show, and how she had been handed a rosette by the Home Secretary herself.

Luca listened politely and Joy, who had quite forgotten how good it felt to talk about herself after so many years of being ignored by her children and half-listened to by her husband, waxed lyrical on the merits of living in one of the most esteemed culinary villages in the world and the challenges of running a catering business amongst the gastronomic elite.

"All that, and you've got the decorators in, too," smiled Luca, lifting the Wedgwood cup to his lips and nodding towards the upper floors. Joy stopped in mid-flow, then laughed lightly.

"Oh, no," she said, "they're not decorators, they're the police, come to keep an eye on the shenanigans across the river. There's been a spate of burglaries, you know." It was out before she knew it, and Joy clammed up abruptly; but she was relieved to see that Luca had not batted an eyelid, and was happily wolfing down a third scone.

"Well, I must say, this is all very nice, Mrs Willoughby," he said.

"Joy ... please."

"Joy."

"This reminds me of the days when Clive used to come a-calling."

"Lured in by the cake-baking siren, no doubt," Luca twinkled.

"Mr Tempesta, you are a one."

"Luca ... please."

"Luca. You must pop by again, you've quite taken me out of myself." Joy patted her hair absent-mindedly. The mood was broken by Hugh bursting into the room.

"Frank Fielding is a hypocrite!" he declared, grabbing the television remote and switching on the news channel. "It turns out he's no better than young Rupert!" Joy looked in horror at the footage of Frank shaking hands vigorously with the financier Bill Lewis at a champagne reception while below, on a continuous loop, ran the strap-line: CELEBRITY IN CAHOOTS WITH FRAUDSTER. Joy's heart sank. In the far corner of the screen, barely noticeable to the naked eye, she could see herself enjoying the delights of the free buffet as if she had not a care in the world. Hugh appeared not to notice his wife onscreen, but she did not want to take any chances and quickly switched off the television.

"Hugh Willoughby!" she said tersely, picking up a dishcloth to wipe rogue crumbs from the table, "you of all people should know that a man is innocent until proven guilty beyond all reasonable doubt. It's wrong to cast aspersions on poor Frank's character until we know the truth."

Hugh emitted the sigh of the relentlessly henpecked and smiled at Luca, who, raising his teacup to his lips, added: "Never judge a book by its cover."

Cecilia inhaled the perfumed freshness of the air as she wandered down Riverside Lane a couple of hours later. She had dropped off a wholesome stew for Sam at The Boathouse; the lad needed fattening up, surviving as he was on bread and cheese. He had not been home, so Cecilia had left the Tupperware on the doorstep and lingered awhile. The garden at Kingfisher House had grown at a rampant pace. Wild parsley had shot up along the borders, and the once-manicured lawn was fast becoming a meadow. Cecilia wondered whether or not Clive, a stickler for perfection, knew that Luca had retained neither the gardener nor the cleaner during his absence. She could picture him dead-heading roses at the pinnacle of their beauty, sweeping away their delightful petals and depositing them with relish on the compost heap, and she wondered what he would make of this new wilderness.

She tarried further, luxuriating in the now-fecund garden that teemed with pretty wildflowers, butterflies and honeybees. She was loath to admit it, but she had been hoping to bump into Luca. He had been on her mind constantly since their game of tennis. She felt guilty about letting the Willoughbys down with their dinner party, but had simply not felt able to face Joy's haughty demands after such a wonderful day. Cecilia smiled at the memory.

"You're beautiful," Luca had told her as they shook hands jokingly over the tennis net. "Please have dinner with me."

"I bet you say that to all the girls!"

"I can't help it! It's my Italian ancestry ... It's in my genes."

"Yeah, and that's just where it's staying – in your jeans!"

The funny thing was, Luca was not actually her type. She preferred cerebral English gentlemen with poetry in their souls. The American was a paradox; flirty one moment, intense and serious the next. It was confusing, but not in a bad way – just enough to keep her interested and take her mind off Clive.

Strolling past The Waterfront, Cecilia spotted Frank Fielding opening the boot to an old Nissan Micra. A dry rash glared from his open-necked shirt.

"What's happened to the flash motor?" she joked. Frank tiptoed to kiss her on the cheek.

"Ha ha! Caught in the act!" he laughed. "Can't turn up at the charity in a fancy limousine, can I? It doesn't seem right that I've made a fortune in light entertainment when the good people at the Port Sanctuary have put their lives on the line for this country."

Frank trailed off, and Cecilia was struck at the unlikeliness of such an ordinary little man making it in show business. A high-pitched yapping heralded the arrival of his little white terrier.

"Dubonnet! Where do you think you're going? Come here, my son, we won't have any scallywagging today." Frank buried his nose in the dog's fur before turning to Cecilia. "He's named after the Queen's favourite tipple, you know. She is reputed to enjoy a glass or two while watching the cricket. Speaking of which, I hope you're coming along to support the Village team next month? No excuses!"

Frank glanced at his plain black wristwatch, then carefully unfurled a pair of old spectacles and slipped them onto his nose. "Must be off," he said, dropping Dubonnet through the front door. Returning to his car with a jaunty step, he bid her farewell.

Cecilia watched Frank's rusty little automobile spirit him away, and reflected that, bespectacled, stripped of his gold Rolex, lurid, shiny clothes and the catchphrase-number-plated Range Rover, Frank Fielding had become virtually invisible.

ELEVEN

"**W**HAT WAS IT you told me, babe?" asked Bianca the following day, as she rushed around the kitchen collecting her belongings. Her husband was writing at the table and appeared not to hear. "Frankie," she called loudly, "what were the three 'Ks' I've got to remember when I go out? Keys, cards ... Was it 'car'?"

Frank looked up, irritated at having his concentration broken.

"It's four Ks," he said with a sigh. "Keys, cash, 'cell' and credit cards."

"It's a bit silly, isn't it?" Bianca persisted, hunting around for her phone as Frank continued reading, "because they don't all start with K." Waving her shiny new mobile phone in the air with delight, she added: "It works, though, 'cos I would've left this behind otherwise! But you're not as smart as you think you are, Frank Fielding, 'cos there's one 'K' you seem to have forgotten." Taking her husband's face in her hands, Bianca looked into his eyes and smiled. "Kiss!" she declared triumphantly, before giving him a long, lingering one on the lips and rushing out the door.

"Got to dash," she called. "I'll be late for me class." Frank picked up his coffee and wandered outside to the gymnasium Bianca had insisted he install above the boathouse. He sat heavily at the pec machine and tried feebly to pull down the bar. Through the window, he could see the towpath Bianca had pounded that morning. All around him were the gleaming new machines she shunned in favour of the expensive health club five miles up the road.

For several weeks now, his wife had returned from her daily run, showered, dolled herself up and headed off to the gym in a hurry.

"I just like going, babe," she'd said when he pointed out she had just been for a run. "You know, meet the girls, do a class, have a cap-puccino. You don't mind, do you?" But Frank did mind. He minded because he knew she was lying. He had once checked her kit bag after her return, and the neatly folded Lycra-wear had obviously not been worn. Then there were the receipts screwed up at the bottom of the bag: a coffee here, a paper there – but none of them from where Bianca had claimed to be. The fact she was so hopeless at hiding her deceit only made Frank love her more. And because he loved her, he wanted her to be happy, and he knew the price of that would be to set her free.

He stared at the rotund, Winnie-the-Pooh-shaped character in the mirrored wall opposite; his little legs dangling ridiculously, his fat fingers clutching the sugary latte he found so hard to resist. Frank was no fool. The cheeky chappy who had hit the zeitgeist in the Eighties was becoming a ridiculous has-been. Jolly jumpers, a permanent tan and an irrepressible chirpiness were the key ingredients of brand Frank Fielding, but they did not sit well in the modern age. No wonder Bianca was looking elsewhere. But what could he do? If he moved with the times, changed his look, lost some weight, mellowed his repartee, then "Frank Fielding" would evaporate, and there would be nothing left of the identity he had worked all his life to create. In the early days of their relationship, fame and money had compensated for his lack of youth and good looks, but recently, all that had changed. The work had dried up, and he had still not heard from his agent about his last big hope: a pilot for a prime-time game show he knew he could host blindfolded.

Wandering back into the kitchen, Frank made another coffee and sat back at the table to try and make sense of the accounts Ivy had insisted he read. He did not need to understand them to know he was in trouble. Bianca and Tallulah were financially incontinent, and in the absence of proper work he had allowed himself to be flattered not only into promoting Bill Lewis Investments, but into committing substantial sums in an effort to support his lady loves. The fund had torpedoed, the financial advisor was now under investigation and Frank's reputation was potentially in tatters. The new game show was becoming an absurd dream.

His mouth was dry and his stomach tight. He had always known Bianca would trade him in one day. Twenty years his junior and twice as beautiful as he had ever been, Frank had been unable to keep up with his wife. As his fame had faded, Bianca appeared to have bloomed. He recognised the signs of a new love interest; spurious appointments, extra attention to grooming, guilty displays of spontaneous affection. Goodness knows he had trodden that path often enough himself, and sitting forlornly in his kitchen that morning, Frank feared he would be navigating the muddy end of life's journey alone. He was startled from his thoughts by the phone. The press had been calling all morning, and, assuming it was about the Bill Lewis story, Frank had ignored the calls; but the light was flashing on his personal line, so he picked up.

"Frank Fielding," he said,

"Frank, it's James. I am sorry to bother you, but was everything all right the other day? I tried to call to tell you your burglar alarm had gone off, but you weren't answering your mobile phone. I rang the charity, but got some odd bod who claimed she'd never heard of you!"

Frank replied, without his usual cheeriness: "It was fine. Just the wretched dog setting it off again."

"Are you all right?" the vicar asked. Frank thought about actually answering the question for once, saying what he wanted to say – not what the other person wanted to hear. But he chickened out.

"Yeah, fine, thanks," he replied dully, "just a bit of a headache, that's all."

"Oh, I am sorry," said the Reverend. "Do you think it might be stress? You have had a lot on your plate recently, with all that hoo-ha surrounding Rupert Braithwaite. And now I see your friend Bill Lewis is all over the front pages."

"You're telling me," Frank replied, rolling his eyes, then deflected with: "I feel like a book has landed on my head, but I've only got 'my-shelf' to blame." Frank usually took it for granted that people would laugh at his jokes, but at that moment he was pathetically grateful for the vicar's response.

"Good one! I must remember that for my parishioners," he said, laughing. Then he continued in a more serious voice: "Just one more thing, though. A Pete Walters popped into the church the other day, asking about you. I told him nothing and suggested that he contact you directly. I hope I did the right thing?"

"You did," said Frank, adding: "Sorry, Vicar, the other line is ringing. I have to go."

Frank pressed the button and heard his wife shouting: "Babe ... babe, can you hear me?" He barely could, and he knew from the background noise that she had the roof off the car.

"Are you on the hands-free?" he shouted back.

"Sorry, can't hear you!"

"Pull over," he said. "You'll have an accident." Bianca's driving skills were bad enough without a phone in her hand. "Ring me back when you're parked!"

Five minutes later, she rang again. "You are funny, Frankie," she said. "You're such a stickler for rules. Anyway, I've just arrived, and I wondered if you want to meet for lunch later?"

Frank and Bianca were not in the habit of lunching out on weekdays.

"Sure," he said bravely. "Where shall we go?"

Later that morning, Ivy sat quietly while Frank spoke to his solicitor in the drawing room. She welcomed the distraction. Evil shadows had been stalking her, and her eyes were playing tricks, moving from musical notes to terrifying hallucinations. Last week, she had seen the Devil in church. She had waved him away with the cross of St Christopher, but the experience had frightened her. She blinked back the shapes and patterns that rose up like penance ordered by God, and resolved to visit the optician.

"You're not making much sense, Frank," said Tony, a bear of a man with a wrestler's physique and a chess player's mind. "How's about we go back to the starting gate and take each point separately. You're muddling all the different issues here." Tony Jackson had protected Frank's legal interests since his first television contract. The two of them had been young and inexperienced then, but Tony had spotted Frank's promise and joined the winning team.

"OK," said Frank, pressing his fingers to his temples. "First, there's this whole Bill Lewis fiasco. I suppose you've read the paper?" Tony nodded, and Ivy wondered that the thick gold chain he wore around his neck did not burst with the strain. "Ivy warned me, and I wouldn't listen – and for that, Ivy love, I am eternally sorry. I should've known better than to know better than you."

Ivy lowered her eyes at the compliment, and Frank continued: "Hugh Willoughby tried to give me the heads-up too, but would I listen? Would I, hell! And now I've got the bloody press ringing me, the police are turning my place over and I'm losing money hand over fist."

"Press, we can handle," said Tony, "and it may be a good thing that you're losing money, too – proves you haven't benefited from Lewis's scam. What we need to establish is whether we've got problems with the law." Frank kept scratching at the inside of his elbow, and Ivy wrote in her notepad:

1. *Hydrocortisone cream*

She, too, suffered from eczema, and the fact that Frank's had flared up told her how upset he was. Ivy was only half-listening; she knew it all already. She continued making a list, which read, thus far:

2. *Research other celebrities who have promoted Ponzi schemes*
3. *Return payments from BL or give them to charity*
4. *Check with Frank re: gifts received from BL – return all*

"You'd have to ask Ivy," said Frank, and Tony turned to her.

"Is he contracted to Bill Lewis Investments?" He asked. "Or on a project basis?"

"A project basis," Ivy replied, "paid on results."

"How are the results measured?"

"Spuriously if you ask me," Ivy said, and Frank gave her a shamefaced look. "But the first payment was received thirteen months ago. Since then, there have been seven payments, totalling £63,782. All of them declared to the Revenue." Tony nodded.

"So what've you done, except the television ads I've seen and the odd article?"

Frank thought for a moment. "Bianca and I hosted a 'do' for him here," he replied. "You know, to introduce him to the local nobs."

"Don't suppose they'll thank you much for that," muttered Tony, and Ivy wrote:

5. Check the fine wine gift from BLI after Frank's do
6. Who else invested as a result of Frank's introduction?

"Seems to me like you'll be fine," said Tony. "I need to check a few things, and of course we'll wait and see what comes out of the woodwork, but it looks like an economic bubble – and you weren't involved in the investment, only in the promotion of said investment." He looked to Ivy. "What about damage limitation? I suppose you've considered that?"

Ivy spoke of her plans for the funds Frank had earned through his association with Lewis to go to charity, and a press release to be despatched accordingly.

Frank winced. "My agent will do the press release," he said, worrying at the inside of his wrist with his manicured nails. "It's times like this when I wish I had good PR."

"Don't you instruct them, I will," Ivy said. "I need to decide where best the funds should go, and work out what is due after deductions."

"OK," said Tony decisively. "We have a plan. Frank, you cut off all communication with Bill Lewis, with immediate effect. Do not take his calls, and send his emails and letters to me. I'll send him a 'Dear John', and Ivy will look at channelling the funds into good causes." Everybody nodded their assent and scribbled on their pads. Frank looked pained.

"Next," said Tony with a smile. "What's all this about the police – where do they come into it?" Ivy put down her pencil and listened as Frank began to speak.

"Hang on, Frankie boy," said Tony, interrupting. "You're garbling. Order of events, please."

"I think the first sign was after drinks at the Willoughbys' house the other night," Frank said. "The police arrived and Joy drew the curtains, but not before I'd clocked them taking a load of equipment into the house – looked like surveillance stuff to me. I asked Hugh about it and he tried to fob me off, but he was obviously uncomfortable."

"And your point is?"

"They live right across the river from me," Frank yelped. "Bird's-eye view from there to here! I saw the police again in the morning. They'd been there all night ... There's nothing you can see from there, except for here!" Ivy was itching to tell him to stop scratching, but knew this was not the moment. "And," continued Frank, "the Willoughbys' housekeeper was in the Crown the other night, talking about stakeouts to the local journalist."

"Calm down, Frankie boy," Tony said. "Why would you have a surveillance team on you?"

"I don't know!" Frank was breaking into a sweat. "All this Bill Lewis malarkey, I suppose. Perhaps the cops are looking into the fraud and want to implicate me? Or Lewis's guys are looking to frame me?" He scratched his arms. "Or I s'pose it could be the press. There's been a big to-do since I spoke out on behalf of the Braithwaites." He put his head in his hands and looked down. "Or Bianca," he said dejectedly.

"Bianca? Has she caught you *in flagrante* again?"

"No," said Frank, "it's worse than that. I think it's her playing away from home this time."

"So why would she want *you* observed, if it's her with the dalliance?" asked Tony.

Frank looked distraught. "I suppose because she wants rid of me," he said. "You know, the one-night stands, the middle-age spread – not exactly what she signed up for, is it?"

Tony coughed. "'Middle-age'?" he laughed. "In your dreams!"

"OK, OK," said Frank, not laughing. "But if she's going to go for all she can get, it wouldn't be unusual to run some sort of surveillance first, would it?"

Tony's jaw set hard. "If she's going for all she can get," he said, punching one meaty fist into the other, "I say, 'bring it on, Bianca.'"

Frank shook his head, resigned. "She can have whatever she wants – or at least whatever's left of it," he said. Ivy wrote:

7. Transfer funds to Xenon account

"Plus," said Frank, who was obviously tiring, "I came home from the pub yesterday and my house was full of bleedin' cops!"

Ivy and Tony looked at one another, then at Frank. Ivy knew nothing of this, and she felt a chill.

"What the hell?" asked Tony. "And you wait till *now* to tell me! You should've rung me immediately!"

"I was going to. They were all over the place," he recounted. "But they said the alarm had gone off, and it had automatically rung through to the central station. They said they'd come to check everything was OK."

"How did they get in?" enquired Tony, looking irritated,

"I expect the registered-key-holding company let them in," said Ivy, "and you are connected to the central station, Frank, so it does make sense. But they are supposed to phone me first, and I didn't receive a call."

"Everybody but the cat's bleeding mother was here," Frank said. "That is, except for Bianca, who was off God-knows-bloody-where with her fancy man. And they looked shocked to see me too, I can tell you."

8. Ring alarm company and key holders

"I think all that adds up, Frankie," said Tony, more gently. "I wouldn't worry, my friend. You're getting paranoid."

9. St John's Wort

"Is that all?" asked Tony. Frank looked at the list he had made earlier, and sighed.

"No," he said. "Who the bloody hell is Pete Walters? He's been following me around for weeks now, asking my friends about me, hanging out at the local pub ... but he's not had the balls to ring my doorbell and ask whatever it is he wants to know."

"Probably a journalist," said Tony. Frank shook his head.

"He came into the shop," said Ivy. "I'm sure he isn't a journalist. Unsavoury type. I took his number – told him I'd ring him when I wasn't so busy."

"Can I have it?" asked Tony. Ivy looked to Frank, who nodded, so she recounted the telephone number with no reference to her notebook. Tony laughed.

"You are truly amazing, Ivy Midwinter," he said, and Ivy lowered her eyes. "I'll sort it, Frank. Don't worry about Pete Walters; I've got him covered." He cracked his knuckles. "I hardly dare ask ... but is there anything else?"

Frank shook his head, and Ivy cleared her throat.

"One last thing," she said. "The man living in Clive Buchanan's house is not who he claims to be." And she closed her notepad.

"Intriguing – but not our problem," said Tony, looking at Frank's panic-stricken face. He shook Frank's hand. "Pleasure, as always. But things must be bad, because I've been here an hour and a half and not heard one cheesy joke."

"Sorry," said Frank, smiling at his old friend. "You know what it's like, though: when everything's coming your way, you know you're on the wrong side of the motorway."

Tony groaned. "That's more like our Frank."

*

Bianca arrived at the restaurant first, and ordered champagne. She removed her compact from her *faux*-leopard-skin handbag and checked her ruby-red lipstick. She did not need to take her eyes away from the mirror to know when her husband entered the room. Frank was still a household name, and created a ripple of excitement in public places. She looked up as he approached. He looked terrible.

"Babe," she said, hugging him as though they had been apart for days. "Come on, sit down. You look like you need a drink." She waved to a waiter to fill his glass. "How'd the meeting go?"

Frank shrugged. "You really don't want to know, love," he said. "What're we celebrating?"

"Twenty-two years!" announced Bianca. "'Alf me life!" Frank looked bewildered.

"It's not our wedding anniversary," he said.

"Nah, stupid, that's October, and anyway that'll be sixteen. Twenty-two years since our first kiss," she said delightedly. "I was draping meself over that awful brown corduroy sofa on the set of *Showtime*, when in you walked and swept me off me feet."

Frank laughed. "Off the sofa, actually, but yes – of course I remember," he said, working it out on his chubby fingers. "Yes, it would be … twenty-two years! And of course, you're forty-four. How clever of you."

"Aw, as if I could forget the day me life changed forever," said Bianca.

"Mine too," Frank added, sadly.

"No need to sound so bleedin' 'appy about it!"

"It's been a long haul," said Frank, "but I've loved every minute of it."

"Bloody 'ell, Frankie, what on Earth's got into you?" asked Bianca. "Yer not gonna die or something, are you? How come no joke? Bleedin' 'Enry, yer not gonna leave me? Not after all this time?"

"Leave you?" Frank asked, open-mouthed, "Me, leave *you*?"

"Well, sure as eggs is eggs, I ain't leavin' *you*!" said Bianca. Then, rummaging under the table, she bought out a parcel, "'Ere, look, I've even got you a present!"

Bianca watched as Frank fumbled at the paper, and she wondered if he was well. His eyes were bloodshot, and his eczema looked chronic. She thought perhaps a holiday might have been a more appropriate gift; she had always fancied the Maldives.

Frank's eyes widened in amazement. Bianca was fizzing with excitement.

"Oh, babe, I hope you like it," she said. "I sat for bleedin' *hours* 'avin' it done. You know when I said I was off to the gym? Ta-da! Fooled ya!"

It was a small painting, oil on canvas, showing Bianca's head and shoulders in a traditional pose. She wore a pink, off-the-shoulder gown, and her hair was pinned up. The painting was set in a heavy gilt frame in the shape of a heart.

"I had the frame made specially, 'cos I wanted it heart-shaped. And look," she said, grabbing the painting, "d'ya see what I've got around me neck?"

Frank squinted to look at the depiction of his wife's décolletage. It bore a heart-shaped pendant, on which he could just make out an inscription.

"It says 'FFF'," she said, "Forever Frank Fielding's."

He took both Bianca's hands in his, "It's beautiful," he said, gazing at her across the table. It sounded to Bianca like he was going to cry. "And *you* are beautiful. Thank you, babe. Thank you."

"Listen," Bianca said, "I know I'm not much good to you about all the business malarkey, but whatever it is that's had you walking around with a face as long as a bleedin' 'orse, we'll sort it out. Together. Just don't let the buggers get you down, eh?" Frank squeezed her hands and gave her the first real smile that she had seen from her husband in days.

"As long as I've got you beside me as I slide down the bannisters of life," he said, "I don't care if a few of the splinters face the wrong way."

Bianca laughed. "That's more like my Frankie! Cheers!"

TWELVE

FELICITY THOMAS STRETCHED her long limbs like a cat in the sunshine. She dangled her toes in the river, snatching a few precious moments in the park away from her sons and their maelstrom of adolescent hormones.

Felicity had borne four boys in quick succession, popping them out with minimum effort and snapping back to a size eight, the ease of which she put down to a lifetime of yoga; but while the exercise had toned and balanced her body, it had not stilled her mind. She could not remember when she first realised she was in the wrong life, whether it was before her divorce from Dave or when the midwife cut the umbilical cord on their firstborn, cutting off her exit routes at the same time. She often wondered if she had been switched at birth, which would explain why she had nothing in common with her straitlaced parents. Felicity had been a constant disappointment to them: too irreverent, wild and disrespectful. After being expelled from school for the third time, she had fled the pretty Hampshire town of her birth for the bright lights of London.

Yet contentment still evaded her, like a fleeting shadow. It had been the same when she was married to Dave. "Why can't I ever make you happy, darlin'?" had been his catchphrase, and Felicity's heart had clenched when her youngest son, Chilli, had asked the same question: "Why aren't you happy, Mum?" She did not know the answer; all she knew was that despite spending a lifetime paddling her own canoe upstream, she never seemed able to escape the backwater of her life.

Harley's snoring from a nearby deckchair brought her out of her train of thought.

"At least I've kept my figure," she told herself, standing to smother suntan oil over her slender frame, clad in the skimpiest of yellow bikinis.

"What did you say?" asked Harley, rousing. Felicity watched her old friend sitting under the shade of a majestic willow tree, his cowboy hat set at a jaunty angle. She thought the old rocker was still handsome for all his advancing years, carrying his decades in the music business with the hip insouciance of youth.

"The boys are doing my head in again." She tried to keep the brittleness from her voice, bending down to smooth the pages of the *Daily Mail* and prompting an elderly man on a bench opposite to adjust his glasses for a better view. "Have you seen this report in the paper? It says 'older people feel overlooked by a society, which sees them as a burden and surplus to requirements' ... well, that's how my kids make me feel."

"No point telling them it'll be their turn one day," grinned Harley. "The young think the world exists only for them." Felicity smiled. Harley had always been there to pour a soothing balm on her wounds; he had scooped her into his strong arms when she ran away from home all those years ago, and though often absent from her life, he always seemed to sense when she needed him. Most recently, he had pitched up to save her from financial embarrassment and the humiliation of having to go cap in hand to Dave, paying generously to rent a room in her house and soothing muddy waters with the boys while ensuring their mother kept off the booze and cigarettes.

Then, just when things were settled, he had vanished, and Felicity had been both devastated and riddled with envy at the freedom that allowed him to disappear without a word. His rent payments had continued, but there had been no phone call, postcard or clue as to his whereabouts. She had waited patiently for his return, and six months later he'd swept through the door, plonking himself down in his favourite armchair as though he had never been away. Felicity had not asked, and Harley had not offered an explanation. With typical youthful buoyancy, the boys had taken up where they had left off. If Felicity had questions, she knew to hold them back;

Harley was a kindred spirit, free, feral and unable to live within boundaries. The only difference between them was that he was at peace with the world, while Felicity raged against it. They had been lovers once, many years earlier, when Felicity first left home and was barely legal. At fifteen years her senior, Harley had been more of a father figure, wrapping her in a great cloak of security and protecting her from the hell-raising early years in the music industry, when drugs were rife and rehab was non-existent. It was during this time that he had penned the love song that, despite Felicity's feigned nonchalance, she cherished as much as the man himself.

"I guess I'm feeling my age," she mused. "One moment I'm hip, now suddenly I'm a hip replacement."

"Old age ain't for the faint-hearted," Harley chuckled, "but it's better than the alternative."

"What's that, Harl?"

"Do I need to spell it out?"

"Yeah, well, put like that ..."

"We all end up with the lives we choose."

"But I'm in the wrong one, Harley. This isn't what I chose. I had dreams, plans and ambitions. It's as if I've scaled the wrong mountain – I'm at the top, but I can see a higher peak in the distance that's my true life, and it's out of reach."

"Choose life," said Harley, folding the newspaper and gazing at her kindly. Felicity gave a long sigh.

"You're right, of course, but sometimes I just can't see the woods for the trees. It's a curse that's always followed me."

"I know." Harley smiled gently. "Remember, I've known you for most of it." Felicity wrapped her arms around his gigantic frame, and he whispered in her ear: "You might make it until you're a hundred – that's your lifetime again – so enjoy it, sweetheart. Life is precious."

Felicity changed the subject. She did not want to burden Harley with her insecurities and risk him upping sticks again. Not that he would do that now – he was here to stay, of that she was certain. She had sensed a change in him over the last few months, and their relationship had moved to a higher level. Not sexually – that was over years ago – but to a deeper, more solid love. Harley was emotionally invested in her and the boys, and that was far more valuable than money; it was priceless.

"I'd better crack on, Harl," she said. "I've got tonnes to do ahead of this bleeding accessory party. The things I do to keep the wolf from the door, huh? Even with your contribution, I feel I'm always having to rob Peter to pay Paul, and the worst part of it is that I'm forced to invite the likes of Joy Willoughby into my home because I know she'll dig deep into her purse." Felicity began to gather up her belongings.

"She always looks to me as if she's chewing on wasps. Perhaps a good seeing-to would put a smile on her face?" Harley grinned, and Felicity laughed.

"Wouldn't it be funny to put a vibrator in her goody bag? Can you imagine? That would give the stuck-up old bat something to smile about. Perhaps one for Cecilia, too; she looks as though she could do with some action." Then, inspecting Harley's face, she added: "You stay here, Harl, catch a few rays. You could do with some colour in your cheeks."

Reaching for her sarong and designer sunglasses (an indulgence courtesy of Harley's generous rent contribution), Felicity spied Luca kayaking downstream. Dropping her diaphanous wrap, she adopted a seductive poise and waved. The American almost dropped his paddle, but quickly rallied and steered up close with a smile of blatant approval. Yes, Felicity still had it.

Kathy McConnell was in a state of high excitement as she made her way down Riverside Lane. It was the first time she had been a guest at one of the homes in the Village, and even if it was only Felicity Thomas who had invited her, she was determined to enjoy herself.

She had known immediately what to wear: an elegant peacock-green shift found in a second-hand shop only the previous weekend. She had hoped for something more like Mrs B.'s in dark navy, but this one bore the same three-quarter-length sleeve and the boat neck she had been looking for. She had tried it on at home with flat ballet pumps similar to those Mrs B. had worn, but felt underdressed without heels, so she opted for a high court shoe such as those favoured by Mrs Willoughby. She had woken early on the day of the party and blew her Chestnut Dream hair dry into a bob before setting off for work. She changed into her ensemble in the loo at the cricket club on her way to the party, to which she was the first to arrive.

The door was opened by a bearded, tattooed man wearing a ponytail, with GONNA GETCHA BACK! emblazoned across his massive chest, and Kathy wondered for a moment whether or not she was at the right place.

"Welcome to our girls' night in," he said with a smile. "I'm Harley." Despite his intimidating appearance, the hand he clasped in hers felt strong and reassuring. Kathy had feelings about people – she wondered sometimes if she was ever so slightly psychic – and the energy she got from their handshake told her Harley was a good man. She looked at the yellowing eye bags on his weather-beaten face and wondered if, like Angus, he liked his tipple a little too much. "Am I early?"

"Not at all!" rumbled Harley. "... Well, perhaps a little. Felicity's upstairs getting ready." Five minutes later, Kathy was drying dishes as Harley tackled the washing-up wearing a pair of yellow rubber gloves and an apron.

"I do not know how one woman can make quite so much mess," she said, taking a plate from Harley. "Mind you, women are always the worst; you should see the mess Cecilia makes when she cooks at the Willoughbys'. Though, credit where it's due: she leaves the place spick and span." She added: "As well she should."

Harley laughed, a kind, mellifluous sound that nourished Kathy's tired soul. She did not understand why she had begun to talk about herself, but once she started, she found she could not stop. "... And when we lost the pub, we lost our home as well," she explained, "all thanks to the demon drink. Sometimes I think Angus wants to drink himself into the grave. I try and hide the bottles from him, you understand, but he always finds them. Anyway, we do what we can, don't we? I've been fortunate in my friendship with dear Edmund. He introduced me to his sister Joy, who gave me employment – which is lucky, because Angus doesn't even bother to pick up his social nowadays." Harley listened gravely, and nodded occasionally before passing Kathy more crockery to dry.

"What's the time?" he asked as he handed over the last plate. "Felicity will have my guts for garters if the boys and I aren't out of here by six-thirty."

"*Six-thirty*?" exclaimed Kathy. "I thought it started at six. Oh, well, if I'd been on time, I'd have missed you in that flowery pinney!"

Harley laughed again. "And I'd have done the washing-up alone." His soft whiskers tickled Kathy's hand as he lifted it to his mouth for a kiss. He looked into her eyes and winked. "Be brave, Kathy McConnell."

Rosamund was next to arrive, followed by Bianca, who dragged Felicity into the kitchen and closed the door while her daughter Tallulah marched into the sitting room and switched on the television. Rosamund was left sandwiched in the hall with Kathy, who said: "I do like your hair", and: "What a lovely dress. Such a pretty colour."

Rosamund's upbringing demanded that she make Joy's housekeeper feel comfortable, and Kathy's professionalism dictated a polite and solicitous response, so she could not understand why she invariably left their exchanges feeling unsettled. Kathy was a handsome, Celtic-looking woman with an almost imperceptible habit of projecting her head, tortoise-like, towards the listener. Perhaps, Rosamund wondered as she took a step back, it was her unfortunate tendency to stand too close that bothered her?

"Do you think these earrings are a bit too much, given the colour of the dress?" Kathy asked.

"Not at all," Rosamund replied, edging away as she spoke. Kathy took a step forward to fill the gap and continued to explain her sartorial dilemma.

"Because I had thought a diamond stud, but then it looked a wee bit plain and ..." Three backward steps later and Rosamund was pinned against the table, trying not to sit on Felicity's carefully displayed merchandise.

"Why don't we have a look at these things?" she asked brightly, escaping to pick up a necklace. "This is pretty, isn't it?" Rosamund glanced at her watch as she browsed the trinkets, Kathy following a hair's-breadth behind and agreeing with everything she said. Eventually, to her shame, Rosamund could stand it no longer.

"Knock knock," she called, as she opened the kitchen door to find Bianca and Felicity sitting at the table with a bottle of wine. "May we join you?" she enquired breezily, and pulled up a chair.

Cecilia arrived with Molly, and they were almost toppled over by Dubonnet, who shot under their feet and up the stairs. Molly dived into Cecilia's basket and pulled out a melted crispy cake adorned with Jelly Babies.

"I made you this, Felicity," she announced proudly. Then, turning to Bianca, she added: "Your dog's gone upstairs."

Bianca, who was draped across a chaise longue, roared: "Ta-lu-laaah!" Then, eliciting no response, she said, "Be a dear, Molly, Tally's in the sitting room; pop in and tell 'er to take Dubonnet home?" Tallulah had once babysat for Molly, but she must have done something dreadful because the next day her Dad had been very cross, and they never saw her again. Unable to find Tallulah in the sitting room, she wandered upstairs and opened every door until she found a bedroom. The window was open, the room smelled funny and Molly had never ever seen such a mess. Among the detritus sat a guilty-looking Dubonnet, adorned with blue bows and with something that looked suspiciously like knickers in his mouth. A wardrobe door burst open and out tumbled Tallulah, followed by Felicity's oldest son.

"Oh my God, we thought you were Mum!" she shrieked, hoiking the reluctant child into the room and shutting the door.

Chilli, who was blowing smoke out the window and giggling, asked Molly how old she was.

"Seven and a half," she replied. The teenagers exchanged glances, but Tallulah shook her head.

"No, Chilli," she said. "Don't you dare. She's too young."

"I was younger when I had my first puff," he replied.

"Were you, young man?" demanded a furious Felicity, who had thrown the door wide open. She grabbed Molly's hand and marched her downstairs. A hiatus ensued, during which Bianca and Felicity stormed up and down the stairs, and there was a lot of shouting and door-slamming. A sharp rap from the knocker heralded the arrival of a flushed Joy Willoughby, who bore a potted plant and a look of distraction.

"Sorry I'm late," she declared as Tallulah and Chilli pushed past her through the doorway and charged down the path, "but I have been catching up with Luca, our new neighbour."

"The man staying at Mr Buchanan's house?" enquired Kathy. Joy ignored her, but she continued: "We saw him rowing past The White House on Friday, and earlier this week he was jogging along the towpath in the rain."

Cecilia laughed. "I believe he's on some sort of fitness campaign."

"Yes, well, he'll kill himself if he's not careful," Kathy replied. "Only the other day I read about a man his age, fit as a fiddle by all accounts, just dropped dead on the squash court!"

"I'm sure he'll be fine," said Cecilia. "He's just trying to relax and enjoy his holiday."

Kathy tutted. "Well," she said, "he most certainly looked relaxed in the Crown on Friday night – with the ladies, I mean. You should've seen him with that Amanda Jones. He's stooped and picked up nothing there, if you ask me."

Cecilia was too proud to ask Kathy what she meant or what, exactly, Luca had been doing with the journalist, but she was surprised by how stung she felt. Before she had time to react, Joy, who had helped herself to a glass of wine from the kitchen, came unexpectedly to her defence.

"Nonsense, Kathy, you don't know the first thing about Mr Tempesta," she snapped. "And I hardly think this is the time or the place for tittle-tattle." She grabbed Rosamund by the arm and propelled her away into the lounge.

Bianca poured another drink and looked for Rosamund. While posing for the portrait for Frank, she had availed herself of *Debrett's A–Z of Modern Manners* from the studio bookcase. She had recounted what she'd learned to Frank at lunch, and he had laughed at her.

"You may mock," Bianca replied, exasperated, "but if we're goin' up in the world – which we bleedin' well are, if I have anything to do with it – we need to get things right."

"Exactly," Frank had replied, "and we must, on no account, be turkeys."

"What're you on about?"

"Turkeys. No table manners. Gobble, gobble, gobble!"

"Ha bleedin' ha," replied Bianca. "You'll be laughin' out the other side of yer face when I accidentally go and offend the Queen or something!" Frank had told his wife she was perfect and ought to forget such nonsense, but Bianca could not stop thinking about it: the finishing school stories, the *Debrett's* rules ... they made her feel she walked and talked and entertained "wrong". Bianca did not mind looking up at people, but she certainly did not want them looking down at her. She needed to talk to Rosamund.

Unfortunately, all the etiquette talk that had felt so important in the intimidating surroundings of the Willoughbys' posh lounge began to seem rather funny in Felicity's front room, where Bianca tripped and accidentally tipped her drink onto Joy's handbag.

"I'm afraid," she explained to Joy, whose face had darkened ominously as she clutched a rope of fake pearls in one hand and dabbed at her bag with the other, "that I'm as drunk as a lord. Not drunk as a lady, because ladies don't get drunk ... do they, Tinkerbell?"

"Well, I don't know ..." Joy bristled, looking around for Rosamund, who was saying goodbye to Molly.

"Go on, 'fess up," continued Bianca. "When were you last pissed?"

Joy did not demean herself by answering. She put down the

pearls and, collecting her coat, left behind a smiling Rosamund, to whom Bianca incoherently poured out her woes.

"Don't get me wrong," she said, steadying herself against the doorframe. "I don't want to be boring –" She glanced at the departing Cecilia and raised her eyes, adopting a stage whisper. "– Like 'er. And I don't wanna be a wannabe, like, erm –" And here Bianca jabbed a finger in Kathy's direction. "– But ... I'll tell you what I want, what I really really want ..." She began to sing loudly, but checked herself upon seeing her neighbour's utter confusion. "Sorry," she hiccoughed, "just channelling me inner Spice Girl."

Rosamund laughed politely. "Bianca, you mustn't –"

"But, no, seriously, I do want to be, you know ..." Bianca hiccoughed again. "Ooh, excuse me, I do want to be ... well ... I want to be a bit more of a *lady*. Y'know, like you, Rosamund!" There was a clatter caused by a horrified-looking Kathy, who had tripped over Dubonnet's lead.

"Don't be ridiculous, Bianca dear!" Rosamund said. "You are perfectly lovely as you are."

"That's just what Frankie keeps saying, bless 'im," said Bianca. "But we both know that I'm just the teensiest –" At this point, Bianca's voice went up an octave. "– *weensiest* bit common, and –"

"Common is as common does," said Joy briskly, "and you, Bianca, have had far too much to drink." Rosamund took her coat from Joy and cast Bianca an apologetic look.

"I think we'd better be off," she said. "Sleep well, Bianca dear." Bianca lurched forward to hug her.

"I do love you, Roz," she slurred, nearly knocking her over. Then she turned to Joy and added, "Goodnight, Ma'am." To Felicity, in her stage whisper, she added: "I'm practising for when I meet the Queen." Then she dropped into a drunken curtsy that left her on the floor, giggling. "I am sorry, milady, but at least I didn't turn me back on you!"

Felicity bid farewell to Joy and Rosamund, handing them each a cerise gift bag tied with a purple ribbon and bearing the name of the evening's sponsor around its base.

"Thank you so much," called Rosamund, waving her purchases. "Lovely stuff. Super evening." Felicity gave a languid thumbs-up.

"Goodnight, Felicity," said Joy stiffly. She was irritated by her housekeeper's surprise appearance, piqued at Bianca's behaviour and vexed that she cared at all. The two friends strolled along the path to the sound of birdsong and to Joy's clattering heels. Joy wished she could present a more carefree demeanour, and be more like her friend. The only daughter of an army general and a socially ambitious mother, she had never been feminine or graceful. When her brothers joined the army, Joy was sent to be "finished". A big woman with an equine face and the calves of a prop forward, Joy's lack of grace was more pronounced when she stood beside Rosamund, for whom fifteen years of ballet had ensured a natural elegance no finishing school could ever contrive. Over the years she had learned to hide behind a hard-boiled demeanour. When her brother Piers was killed by a bomb in Northern Ireland, she had reinforced her brusque manner so effectively that in all her sixty-four years, only two people had seen through to the soft centre Joy fought so hard to hide.

"You mustn't mind Bianca," said Rosamund gently, as if reading her mind. "She doesn't have an unkind bone in her body; she's sometimes just a little, well, ill-judged."

"I didn't mind at all. It was actually rather funny," Joy replied gamely. "And I always like a goody bag, don't you?"

Rosamund rummaged in the small pink carrier. "Oh, good, smellies!"

"Well, they'll do for the spare bathroom, at least," Joy commented.

"Oh," said Rosamund excitedly, "A handy torch, too! What colour's yours? Mine's pink!" Joy reflected on how easy her friend was to please, and swallowed back her disappointment at discovering her own bag was torchless.

"Didn't get one," she said briskly.

"Oh, Joy, I'm sorry; I've just spotted your name on this bag, look – the torch was meant for you!"

"No, no. You keep it," replied Joy, in a spirit of goodwill she did not feel. "I can't wait for a decent drink. Did you taste that muck Felicity was serving?"

"Look, Cecilia there's a toy in your goody bag!" cried Molly in delight, rummaging through the gift bag Felicity had presented her as they left the accessories party.

"That's nice," replied Cecilia, absentmindedly spooning heaped tablespoons of organic chocolate into their favourite cocoa mugs. It had been a taxing day, and that always called for whipped cream and chocolate sprinkles.

"It's called a rabbit, but it doesn't look much like one," continued Molly earnestly. "It doesn't hop, but it does wobble a bit. Can I keep it, Cecilia?"

"Of course, darling," mumbled Cecilia, waiting for the milk to boil. She was reflecting on her conversation with Harley at the gathering. She had discovered him quietly smoking his strange herbal cigarettes in the back garden when, stung by Kathy's unkind remark about Luca "putting it about", she had wandered outside looking for Molly. She could not imagine what had transformed the housekeeper from a calm professional to the opinionated, overfriendly and strangely excited woman she had been that evening.

Of course Cecilia found Luca appealing; he was good company, and her battered ego welcomed his cheesy chat-up lines, which made for a pleasant change from Clive's suaveness; but she had no intention of sleeping with him. *Most certainly not*, she thought with righteous indignation. She enjoyed the banter though, responding to his cheeky wit with double-entendres that delighted them both.

"If you push that five-pound note any further into my trouser pocket, I'll have to ask for an engagement ring," she had jested the other day when he shoved the money she had dropped in the park into her back pocket. They laughed, and Cecilia had marvelled at her newfound sauciness. Where had it come from? She had never been like that with Clive.

Yet, for all his fun and flirtatiousness, Cecilia sensed there was a darker side to the American. In unguarded moments, she would notice his expression cloud over, and the humour vanish from his eyes. She had tried to sketch it from memory, but the depth of it was impossible to catch. At first she had put his skittishness down to his separation from his wife, but over the last few days she realised it was more than that; he seemed on edge. Cecilia suspected their visitor was carrying a burden, and she felt compelled to find out what it was.

"Look, the rabbit even lights up! There's a battery included," Molly cried out.

Whipping the cream into stiff mounds, Cecilia reflected on Harley's almost ethereal presence in the glare of the early evening sun. He was not someone she knew well, and she had been tempted to turn tail, but the old rocker had beckoned her over. Something about his warm, engaging smile had made her pull up a seat and join him.

"I was looking for Molly," she had said simply, waving away his offer of an herbal smoke.

"Beautiful kid ... very like her mother, by all accounts," said Harley. Cecilia nodded, and there seemed nothing more to say, so they sat in peaceful silence as Harley blew perfect smoke rings into the air. Unusually for Cecilia, she did not feel the need to break the silence, to fill the gaps with inane conversation. This peace was a revelation to her.

They had sat in quiet reflection for several minutes. Then Cecilia, to her surprise, had blurted out: "I wish I had children." It was out before she knew it – her deepest, darkest secret. It felt strangely liberating.

"Kids are a precious gift, but no one has a God-given right to them," said Harley.

"But I so want one," whispered Cecilia urgently.

"If you don't have children, it won't be a lesser life – just a different one." Harley gazed up at the sky. It was a perfect evening; the heavens were streaked with red and gold, and a flock of screeching parakeets had flown by, perfectly silhouetted against the oncoming night, revealing a brief hint of luminous feathers. The spell was broken by Felicity, tearing into the garden and yelling to Harley to take her kids out.

"Anywhere, just as long as I don't sodding see them for the next few hours," she had screeched. Turning to Cecilia half-apologetically, she added: "Bloody children, cost you a fortune, do your head in." Harley winked, and Cecilia had felt a weight lift from her shoulders.

"Look Cecilia, it's called 'Rampant'," cried Molly. "That's spelled R–A–M–P–A–N–T!" Cecilia finally tuned in to what Molly was saying and promptly dropped her whisk, spinning round to snatch the tool from the little girl's hand.

"It's a funny name," Molly persevered. Cecilia could feel the heat rush to her face. "Rampant Rabbit, Rampant Rabbit … what a cute name!" Molly mused. "Shame it doesn't look like a rabbit … why hasn't it got any fur, Cecilia? Has it been skinned?"

Pulling herself together and forcing a smile, Cecilia placed Felicity's sex toy in a high cupboard, out of reach.

"How kind of Felicity to give us such a thoughtful gift," she gushed. "It will come in awfully handy when we need to plunge the sink."

"Can I take it to school tomorrow?"

"No."

"But it's Show and Tell!"

"Run along, Molly dear. Brush your teeth and put on your nightie. There might be just enough time for a story before Daddy picks you up."

In the quiet of the kitchen, Cecilia flicked through the day's post and spotted Clive's characteristic flowery handwriting and turquoise ink. She had waited anxiously for a missive after he had first left, checking the post every day. Recently, however, she had stopped looking. Perhaps it was the tennis games and walks in the park with Luca, or perhaps she had just begun to enjoy Clive's absence. Either way, she was surprised to note that four days had passed since she'd last thought of him. Placing the letter on the hall desk, Cecilia climbed the stairs to oversee Molly's ablutions. She would read it later, when she had the time.

THIRTEEN

BASIL WHISTLED CHEERFULLY as he sauntered down the driveway with his golf clubs, and Rosamund seized the opportunity to join Joy and Myrtle for an afternoon walk. The blossoms danced in the breeze and the ducks escorted their chicks along the shallows of the river. A pair of crested grebes bobbed with the current, the hen proudly carrying four babies striped like Everton mints on her back. Rosamund and Joy chattered while Myrtle soaked up the pleasure of the early evening sunshine.

"Oh, camas lilies," said Myrtle. "That reminds me ... I caught Kathy picking death camas the other day! Said she had no idea how poisonous they are. The silly woman will be the death of us all!" It was unseasonably hot, and the three women stopped under the shade of the willow to throw sticks for Mungo. The wind was picking up, and the tree swished playfully.

"What a shame," Myrtle cried, "the willow is getting the black scab. Oh dear."

"Will it kill her?" asked Joy with concern.

Myrtle shook her head. "She's been here for nigh on seventy years," she said, patting the bark of the tree companionably. "She'll look a bit less lustrous for a while. It would kill a sapling, but not you – would it, my dear?"

"Myrtle, you are a veritable mine of information," declared Rosamund. The women inspected the tree while Mungo splashed about in the shallows. Swallows flitted from a nearby boathouse.

"It's almost impossible to believe," mused Joy, enjoying a gentle breeze across her face, "they've come all the way from South Africa, crossed the Pyrenees and the Sahara – and they all look as fresh as daisies. How can they be so energetic?"

"We're all of us pleased when we reach our journey's end," Rosamund said softly.

Tucking in her mother's billowing skirt, Joy added: "Speaking of which, shall we?" With that, the three women set off for a well-earned tea at The White House.

Across the river, in a stiflingly hot attic, Luca was impervious to the glories of the day. He was struggling to make sense of an email to which was attached a photograph of Natasha, beautiful and happy, and his heart tightened at the memories it evoked. It was from when they had flown to London from Moscow and joined the throng outside Buckingham Palace, hoping to catch a glimpse of the Changing of the Guard. After the pomp and pageantry, they wandered down to the Embankment and gazed at the ancient waters of the Thames. Luca remembered taking the picture as his wife leaned against the iron railings near Cleopatra's Needle, her hand raised to remove a strand of hair from her eyes. She had been in the first trimester of pregnancy, and her happiness shone as brightly as the sunlit sky.

Luca closed his eyes. He knew the photograph down to the smallest detail. It was the only one he possessed of his then-pregnant wife, the one they had sent to family and friends to announce the happy news before their dreams were shattered by a stillbirth. The view was exactly as he remembered it, only this time, instead of a spontaneous shot from a cheap Instamatic, it had the hallmarks of a Photoshop professional. It was Natasha – the same smile, the same carefree joy – but the city rose up behind her in full, majestic, panoramic glory to reveal the Oxo Tower and the timber frame of Shakespeare's Globe. The Gherkin gleamed like a citadel in a fairytale, and the Shard reached dizzily into the clouds.

Luca had sent the email to Maria, and he paced the room as he waited for her reply. He suspected he had worked out the identity of the sender, but could not be certain. The photograph had disturbed a hornet's nest of painful memories that now swarmed around him, pricking his conscience. It had not been an easy marriage; he had not been the best of husbands, and he was convinced his wife had paid the ultimate price for believing in him. When the phone rang, he picked it up instantly.

"You know the drill," said Maria. "You've got an address. Make contact. Build a relationship, give away a few details of your life and then sit back and see what happens next. Don't let your defences down – it could be a trap." Sweat trickled down his back, and Luca found that he could not breathe. Struggling with the lock, he pushed the window open wide and gulped the sweet air. Across the river, he could just make out the Willoughbys on their lawn. The tinkling of laughter and chinking of china floated on a million dandelion wisps, and were carried off on the breeze. It felt surreal to be considering matters of life and death while, across the water, the English enjoyed afternoon tea.

Luca closed the window; he could not risk Sam snooping among his belongings again. The boy had been in the attic, of that he was certain. There were no visible signs of forced entry, but his papers had been disturbed, and it was easy to tell something was amiss from the way Sam was behaving: jittery, over-polite and unable to make eye contact. Luca was not worried about the cameras and paraphernalia – they could be explained – but the Russian file had been tampered with, and that was a problem.

The serene, green depths of the river beckoned from the window, and Luca felt an urge to strip and dive beneath its tranquil surface. He charged down the stairs, tearing at his clothes, and sped down the garden path. With one flying swoop, he plunged into the river's icy depths, scattering geese and moorhens. A cry from Joy Willoughby caught his attention, and he cut a swathe through the torrents towards her perfectly manicured garden.

At The White House, Hugh felt despondent. He was reluctant to admit it because it was not very manly, but he was suffering from empty-nest syndrome. He knew it was ridiculous; the twins had left home nearly four years earlier, and he and Joy had been glad to see the backs of them. Calm and order had returned, and where once gaggles of teenagers had cluttered the threadbare living room, there was now just Joy and him, living in a haven of peach and cream.

Hugh glared unhappily at the bright, shiny new telephone his wife had bought to replace his battered red-dial one, and reflected on his recent conversation with Amanda Jones. She claimed to have left numerous messages, and while the flashing red light led him to suspect this might be true, he had no idea how to retrieve them. The journalist was demanding a meeting, and Hugh had pencilled her in for a week hence. She had hinted at a big exposé, which he had laughed off; but in his morose mood, he could not help but worry. A scream from the garden prompted him to clamber to the window, where he saw Joy and Rosamund holding their teacups aloft, the tablecloth flapping in the wind and the sunshade lifted from its stand and lying across the table.

"Look, look, Rosamund! He's coming here!" Joy shouted, gesticulating towards the river. Hugh followed her line of vision to where a swimmer was ploughing through the choppy water with the vigour of an Olympian. As he emerged, Hugh held his breath. It was Luca Tempesta. The man looked magnificent, with rippling muscles and a glistening body – even Hugh could appreciate that. He was in much better shape than Hugh had given him credit for, and was displaying a lunchbox that left very little to the imagination. Glancing down at Joy, Hugh saw the woman he had married, feminine and smiling, with a bright-eyed look of amorous anticipation. A twinge of jealousy tightened his chest. Rosamund was giggling, and Myrtle was smiling knowingly.

Luca strode up the garden and, bowing briefly to the ladies, he silently picked up the massive cream-calico parasol that had escaped its moorings in the wind. Clenching every muscle in his body, he lifted the umbrella slowly up to the table. Watching from the window, Hugh – who knew this to be a two-man job – found he was too dumbstruck to call out an offer of help as Luca climbed onto the table in one powerful stride and – wearing nothing but dripping wet shorts – guided the teakwood shaft into the hole. Then, very gently, he lowered it into the metal base below before erecting the parasol's canopy. He paused for a moment and gazed into the distance before stepping down, victorious. There was a round of enthusiastic applause from the ladies, and as Luca swaggered down the path and dived back into the river, Hugh suddenly felt like a voyeur and stepped away from the window quietly.

"Well," said Joy neatly, "that was energising. More tea?"

"Oh, um, I'm not sure," said Rosamund. "I feel somewhat lost for words." She gazed across the water as Luca climbed onto the deck at the end of the garden at Kingfisher House.

"Mmm, tasty," muttered Myrtle under her breath.

Joy looked shocked. "I beg your pardon, Mother?"

Myrtle straightened herself in her chair. "You heard me perfectly well, young lady," she chuckled, helping herself to a sandwich and winking at Rosamund. "I do love a bit of cucumber on a summer afternoon."

"Mother!" said Joy, glancing at her housekeeper, who had witnessed the spectacle and was red with disapproval.

"I might be eighty-nine, but I still recognise an Adonis when one stands on the table above me."

"He did look rather splendid," agreed Joy.

"Perhaps it's all the running he does?" enthused Rosamund.

"I thought perhaps he was admiring my ginger syllabubs," Joy said, girlishly.

"As I was admiring his," Rosamund quipped, and opened her compact to reapply her lipstick.

Kathy was disgusted. Three women, who called themselves ladies, giggling like schoolgirls at an unnecessary display of gallantry and an overt display of manhood. It was simply not appropriate.

"It might be best if I pour, Mrs Willoughby," she said crisply, taking the pot from Joy, who seemed shaky. She offered a top-up to Rosamund.

"Thank you, Kathy," she said with some effort. "Though I have to admit, I do feel rather too hot for tea all of a sudden."

Joy and Myrtle agreed, and there was more fluster, which Kathy thought over the top. She turned away to refresh the teapot and was assaulted by an unseemly cacophony of snorting and squealing as the ladies succumbed to the hysterical laughter they had been struggling so hard to contain.

People can be so disappointing, thought Kathy, as she removed the elderflower cordial from the cupboard.

FOURTEEN

THE FOLLOWING DAY, Sam Buchanan sat in The Boathouse, reading the stolen newspaper cutting with mounting disbelief.

RUSSIAN AGENTS POSING AS SUBURBAN PILLARS OF SOCIETY USED FAKE BRITISH PASSPORTS TO SPY ON THE US, read the headline of the article he had found in a brown manila file stamped "Kuznetsoy". He had also found highly sophisticated spying gear in the attic room that had been sealed off by Luca.

> They lived ordinary, mundane, even boring lives, tending their gardens at the weekend to create a veneer of respectability that enabled them to become highly "Americanised" and carry out secret missions without attracting suspicion. Their technique was summed up by one neighbour, who said, "They can't be spies; look at what they did with the hydrangeas!"

An unwelcome image of Luca pottering among his father's Empress Josephines popped into Sam's head. He pushed it aside and read on.

> They used invisible ink, shortwave radios, stenography and wi-fi in Internet cafés to send coded messages back to Russia. They employed innocent-looking brush encounters to pass messages in public, hid encrypted data in public images and relied on fake identities and false travel documents.

Sam pictured Luca's strange, Seventies-style radio parked on the upper floor of Kingfisher House, and the high-definition lens he had trained from the turret window directly onto Ivy Midwinter's cottage. He could see Luca, bent over his laptop for hours at the pub, and furtive deliverymen unloading unlabelled boxes. He closed his eyes against the flood of incriminating images and tried to think clearly.

He had searched the attic the day before, after Ivy had hinted at dark doings and prompted Sam's already overactive imagination to go into overdrive. Luca had certainly been distracted and jittery of late: maybe confessing his sins via the handy Catholic Church app had opened up a can of worms in the peccadillo department?

An opportunity to investigate had presented itself when Sam spotted a bedroom window open and CCTV showed Luca leaving for his daily kayak. Sam had scrambled up the wisteria, feeling nostalgic for the old days when he had used the same route to return from a night out on the town, his father believing him to be safely tucked up in bed. He jumped into the bedroom, crossed the landing to the bathroom and shimmied up the drainpipe to access the skylight above, pausing to wave cheerfully to the vicar, who had been sipping tea in the conservatory below. It had been a doddle, he reflected, much reassured that if Luca was truly a spy, he might have thought to shut the window.

He was not sure what he had expected to find in the attic, but files on Russian spies and sophisticated espionage equipment had come as a major shock. Ivy had never talked about her past, but Clive had once told him she had worked for the government during the Cold War. Was that why Luca's cameras were aimed at Sunnyside? Was Ivy herself a part of some Russian connection?

"Don't get involved with the American," she had warned portentously. "He has a dark soul, and a darker secret." Sam had laughed. He respected Ivy – she was an asset to his father and to Village Antiques – but to say she was a sandwich short of a picnic was an understatement. He was not laughing now, though; sitting in the safety of The Boathouse, he felt a growing unease as he read the article he had photographed on his phone.

*Anna Charlton, aka Natasha Kuznetsoy, a beautiful woman who ran
her own online real estate business, has been exposed as a Russian
spy. She is being held without bail after prosecutors described her as
a highly trained agent and a practiced deceiver. Her husband is on
the run, but the FBI says the net is closing in.*

Get a grip, Sam told himself. There must be a plausible explanation.
And yet, a niggling doubt lurked at the back of his mind. What did
he really know about the American? Sam kicked back from the
computer screen and gave a small derisory laugh.

"Elvis is alive and well and living with Michael Jackson in Michi-
gan!" he yelled to a silent room. Cecilia was always teasing him
about his conspiracy theories. Luca, a Russian spy? It was risible,
silly, preposterous. And yet he had just returned from Moscow.

He checked his watch; Basil Braithwaite would be arriving soon.
He had invited his neighbour to inspect a box of wartime collectibles
that included an ancient loudspeaker, medals and toys he had
found in the storeroom at Village Antiques. An Internet search
had revealed that they could be rare figurines mass-produced
during World War Two. Sam picked up Hitler and fiddled with his
adjustable right arm, flipping it up into a *Heil Hitler* salute. Yep,
they were certainly Basil's cup of tea. He did not feel comfortable
inviting Basil into The Boathouse; his synaesthesia registered his
name as boiled cabbage, and he did not want his sanctuary pervaded by an aroma of rotting vegetables. The CCTV showed Basil
striding jauntily down the garden path, so Sam hoisted the box
under one arm and stepped out to greet him.

"Lovely weather for it," Basil called pleasantly. The two men shook
hands, and Sam placed the memorabilia on the garden table. Basil
inspected the medals for a long time, then picked up a figurine of
Rudolf Hess and blustered: "By Jove, I can't believe it, Sam, these are
all mine! I thought they'd been stolen. How did you come by them?
I bet that tartar Rupert flogged them to make money. I'll kill him!
How much did the blighter get for them?"

Sam was not offended by Basil's tirade. It did not surprise him that his father had bought Basil's treasure without bothering to quiz Rupert on their provenance. Village Antiques was a one-stop shop for the posh boys at the local independent school to flog their family heirlooms to fund a lavish social life.

"My father risked life and limb in Bomber Command," Basil muttered. "Got shot down twice, but just kept getting back into the cockpit. He was decorated for his bravery with these medals, and his own grandson flogs them to the highest bidder. I'll buy them off you again Sam, I won't see your father out of pocket."

"Don't worry, Mr Braithwaite," Sam said. "It's not about money, it's about heirlooms being returned to their rightful owners." With a small sigh of resignation, Basil selected a figurine of an Aryan boy.

"He looks like Rupert," he observed, smiling mirthlessly and then, placing it carefully on the table, he suddenly barked: "Hands up, Rupert Wellesley Braithwaite! Your time has come!"

The sound of crunching footsteps and jangling keys from the side passageway heralded the arrival of Luca, at which Basil winked and, with a mischievous glint in his eye, picked up the loudhailer and boomed through its dusty microphone: "Come quietly with your hands in the air, Luca Tempesta. You are surrounded. There can be no escape!"

Sam was not sure how it happened. One moment he was sharing a joke with Basil, and in the next it was if they had been teleported into a bizarre kung fu blockbuster. Sam and Basil remained rooted to the spot as Luca flew around the corner, and with one graceful movement transformed into a snake, bending his body backwards then raising his head high as if to strike like a viper. The two men watched in fascination as Luca stretched out his palms, tensing all the muscles in his body to channel energy into his jabbing finger-tips. It took less than ten seconds for him to come to his senses, drop the pose and smile.

"Good God, man!" bellowed Basil, impressed, "Isn't that the Snake? I haven't seen a martial arts manoeuvre like that since *Enter the Dragon*. Bravo!" Luca shoved his hands into his pockets and nodded. "You Hollywood types really do know how to put on a splendid show. You've quite cheered me up," continued Basil with a guffaw, picking up the box of toys and war memorabilia and shoving it under his arm. "Anyway, mustn't monopolise you; the lovely Rosamund awaits." Nodding and chortling to himself, Basil made tracks for home.

"What does 'gone off the boil' mean, Cecilia?" enquired Molly. Cecilia had just put the phone down on Sam and was struggling to make sense of what he had told her. The words "Russia", "spy", "kung fu" and "ninja" swam around her head, and she tried to shake them off before turning her attention to the little girl.

"Nothing, darling; get on with your colouring," she said, absent-mindedly.

"But I just heard you," said Molly indignantly. "You told Sam Luca has gone off the boil. Are you boiling up his head like a can-nibal? You said you'd have Clive's guts for garters. Is that the same punishment?"

Cecilia smiled vaguely and wandered into the kitchen to whip the cream for chocolate truffles. Vexatious situations called for serious comfort food, and Cecilia felt at sixes and sevens. She had not heard from Luca since sending him a saucy text after witnessing his heroism from the Willoughbys' kitchen garden. Sam's rant about conspiracy theories and the Cold War had done nothing to put her mind at rest.

"Well, I haven't heard a word from him," she had said, with studied nonchalance. She hoped Sam would not hear the tremor in her voice; she did not want him to know just how much she had been seeing of the American. Cecilia had not been concerned by Luca's silence at first, but as time passed she had started to worry that she might have overstepped the mark with her lewd text. Their friendship was relaxed and happy, just double entendres and flirtation. Luca's failure to respond had made her worry that she had appeared too available. It had been a long time since Cecilia had flirted, and she was out of practice. She remembered Esther telling her, "Hunter-gatherers get bored after the kill." Cecilia had felt so smug then, cosy in her comfortable relationship with Clive. How she could do with a few wise words from Esther now!

She hoped that she had not given herself away to Sam. It would not do for him to think it was "out with the old and in with the new". She loved Sam's father. *Loved.* The word played on her mind, whirling around her head with a rousing chorus of *spy, FBI, defector.* Yes, she realised with clarity, she had loved Clive – once. But the feeling wasn't there anymore. It was an epiphany, and Cecilia turned her attention to squeezing chocolate fancies from the icing bag into intricate twirls, ruffles and hearts. She was trying to make sense of what Sam had told her.

"Are you telling me that you actually broke in and rummaged through Luca's personal affects?"

"Yes! And there was a file on a famous Russian spy ring, and expensive cameras and a high-resolution telescope pointed towards Ivy's house," he had babbled.

"So what? The man is a private detective, for goodness' sake. Sam, I cannot believe that you –"

"But that's not the best bit," he had interrupted. "Listen to this: Luca isn't really separated from his wife, Natasha – she's in prison! And the FBI is closing in on him. Then he'll be locked up as well."

"Sam, you are being absurd." Cecilia had felt she must stop him before he exploded. "How can you possibly make the leap from a few odds and sods of Cold War interest to international espionage, with Luca as the spymaster? You really do need to get a grip on these conspiracy theories. Get out a bit more. Get a life!" But as Cecilia looked around her, she realised Sam was not the only one who needed to get a life. She sat down heavily, contemplating her own.

Before her friend died, Cecilia and Esther had been collaborating on a book featuring cake recipes from Esther's grandmother, with illustrations by Cecilia. They had even found an agent, but then Esther had taken ill and Cecilia had lost the heart for it all. Without her friend she had begun to believe, as Clive so often pointed out, that she had no talent for drawing. It was no good; she was sure Clive was right about them, but she didn't know anything else, so she continued her drawings in private, keeping them hidden away from judgmental eyes.

"Are these ready to eat yet?" Molly asked, fiddling with the chocolates and waking Cecilia from her thoughts.

"Not yet!" she smiled, and tried to put aside her forgotten dreams.

Indeed, she would have let the dream die entirely, had Luca not stumbled across her art book later that same night, rifling through the dresser for a corkscrew. Cecilia caught him leafing through the pages, marvelling at her careful, precise sketches of village life.

"These are awesome, Cecilia," he said. "I'm no expert, but I defy anyone not to be charmed. You clearly have a talent for composition." Cecilia felt her confidence blossom under the glow of Luca's praise, but still felt the need to put herself down.

"Oh, I don't know, Luca," she laughed. "I'm too old for pipe dreams. I dragged myself out of bed this morning, caught sight of the lines on my face and nearly crawled back in."

"You really epitomise the British art of self-deprecation, don't you?" Luca had said, before gazing at her for a long while, which prompted Cecilia to cover her face in mock horror.

He removed her hands gently. "Why do women like you worry about growing old? You are so beautiful." Every fibre of Cecilia's soul screamed "cheesy chat-up line", but the words had sounded honest, kind and genuine, and so – against her better judgement – Cecilia's heart had thawed a little.

The next day she had spent a few happy hours perusing her sketches. There were several of Molly licking a chocolatey spoon, and Reverend James at the Village *fête* judging the preserves. There was a glamorous sketch of Bianca, all legs and puckered red lips, biting into a cream horn, while Frank got down and dirty at the "Village in Bloom" competition with a bread pudding. There was a good one of Harley at the church summer teas, tucking into shortcake with a grin, and Felicity, all sharp angles and clanking jewellery, picking on a buttered scone, her faced fixed firmly on the horizon. One of Cecilia's favourites was a drawing of Joy Willoughby triumphantly holding aloft the Village Show's First, Second and Third winning rosettes and a magnificent Victoria sponge, while Basil, in a straw boater, admired Rosamund's tasty Battenberg cake and Reverend James gazed to the heavens while indulging in a wispy meringue.

Cecilia tossed aside the drawings of Clive. She had been proud of them once, the way she had captured his quintessential Englishness as he delighted in a strawberry tart; but looking at them now, she thought he looked supercilious and arrogant. She also noticed how Sam had changed since she had sketched him scowling into his death-by-chocolate cake. *He has blossomed, like me, since Clive left*, she thought. Cecilia's favourite drawing by far was a more recent one she had done of Luca, stretched out on the lawn, a splendid Swiss roll perched upon his tummy, his fork aloft, eyes closed in ecstasy.

She ate a truffle and steeled her nerves to call her agent. This would not be the end for Miss Cecilia Honeychurch.

FIFTEEN

LATER THAT WEEK, Rosamund slid silently from her bed and tiptoed out of the room. She released the door handle slowly to avoid a click, then paused and listened, relieved to hear Basil's gentle snoring continue unabated. The thrill of her escape was only slightly moderated by guilt as she boiled the kettle for tea, knowing that without her morning noises or proffering of coffee, her husband would sleep well past eight o' clock – by which time she would be long gone.

Rosamund dressed with care: grey trousers, navy blazer and pumps. It was absurdly important to her that she was modestly attired, even though she imagined that once the introductions had been dispensed with, the clothes would stay on her back for a maximum of ten minutes. With every beat of her heart, she longed to sling a bag over her shoulder and head straight out the door, but she could not bear the thought of Basil's forlorn face when he came down to an empty kitchen and realised that she had gone. She laid out a breakfast tray and made a ham and cheese sandwich, complete with his favourite Mother's Pride, which she left with a note on the kitchen table.

Rosamund had enough emotional intelligence to understand that the food was an apology to her husband. She had been "too tired" once again the night before. Part of her reason for sneaking out at the crack of dawn was to avoid his early-morning glory and a rerun of the previous night's advances. Recently, their marriage had come to feel like a game of chess: Basil would watch his wife and judge when best to make his pass, and she would counter-play, only to have him jump her later. Deflect, advance, deflect, advance. With a limited repertoire of plausible defence techniques,

Rosamund felt perpetually on the back foot. Joy insisted that her friend had disabled Basil by doing everything for him, but she did not know her dreadful secret. The only reason Rosamund spoiled her husband so shamelessly was to compensate for the fact that she was not doing the one thing that he really wanted.

Just as she had begun to resign herself to an old age of avoidance and frustration, Rosamund's saviour had come in the unlikely guise of her new friend Bianca Fielding. Not that she had discussed her sex life with her neighbour, but Bianca had said something on their shopping trip that had caught Rosamund's attention. Trying hard not to look interested, she had taken a dress from a rack and held it up against herself, casually saying, "Sorry, Bianca, you've lost me. Who exactly is this 'Professor'?"

"Ooh, you'd look great in that," Bianca retorted, and Rosamund looked down in dismay to see that she had picked out an animal-print wraparound that really was not her style.

"Oh, no, I'm far too old for this," she deflected, trying to replay the earlier conversation in her mind before adding, vaguely: "But you'd look great in it."

"You're just like me Mam!" protested Bianca. "'Too old for this, too fat for that, yer father wouldn't like the other.'" Rosamund was about to object when Bianca added, with a prurient laugh: "That was, until I sent 'er to see the Prof. Everything changed after that!"

An Internet search, an archived article and a phone call later, and Rosamund was all set. She could barely believe her own daring as she sat on the London train wearing new knickers and a nervous smile.

In the Village, Basil was enjoying breakfast without the constant chatter of the television. *The Daily Telegraph* was propped against his bowl of organic muesli, and he was happily crunching Coco Pops and slurping his coffee. A non-story about the Chancellor of the Exchequer's weight loss momentarily caught his eye. The man looked bloody ill, Basil thought, before reflecting on how lucky he was not to have to worry about gaining weight. He still wore the same-sized trousers as he had on his wedding day.

He had been delighted to discover that the Duchess was spending a day in town, though he was surprised she had not mentioned it. He hoped she would take a little time out to enjoy a gallery and a shopping spree. She deserved spoiling; there was no need for her to be frugal. She should treat herself to something nice, a new scarf or suchlike, he thought.

Basil had never understood women's obsessions with refreshing their wardrobes before their garments had worn out, and he was pleased Rosamund had a more sensible, utilitarian attitude to clothes. Fortunately – for he could not abide shopping – Basil was happy wearing the same attire he had worn for decades. On the odd occasion he found himself in Savile Row, he would splurge on half a dozen new shirts or flannels, but only new versions of his signature look. He favoured a classic style of dressing, and recalled how Rosamund had complimented him on his sartorial elegance when they were courting. Those classic styles had stood the test of time, and Basil thought he still cut a dash at Rotary and on the golf course. He poured more coffee and contemplated a day of uninterrupted warfare with glee.

Dragging an ancient trunk from the corner of his den, Basil carefully removed the British, Dutch, Hanoverian and Prussian militias, and positioned them in the exact spot fought at the Battle of Waterloo. It was a skirmish he had played out for many years, and his enactment of that glorious day in 1815, when the conquering hero defeated Napoleon, still held the power to enthral him. The intricate paintwork on the Duke of Wellington's tin torso reminded Basil of carefree days with Rupert before it all went so horribly wrong. Playing soldiers in the attic of their Chelsea home had been the last time he had truly bonded with his son. He felt a stab of paternal pride that he had even allowed a ten-year-old to play with such expensive antiques. He had also been secretly delighted that Rupert – who bore the illustrious middle name of Wellesley – had never wanted to be Wellington, preferring to lose the battle as Napoleon. Now the boy had become a man, Basil could see his son shared many characteristics with the French leader: arrogance and self-possession, for example, and probably an inclination to despotism and warmongering, too.

Basil was not surprised Rupert had turned out to be a bad 'un; bad blood ran in the Braithwaite family. While Basil's father and grandfather were both decorated war heroes mentioned in despatches, his brother Herbert had turned to the bottle and was now eking out his pension on a Greek island with his third wife, who was twenty years his junior. Who was to say he was wrong, Basil pondered philosophically. He considered how sad it was that, in spite of a fine education, his son's loftiest ambition was to get rich quickly and achieve fame. Basil knew several celebrities. Frank Fielding was one, and though he might not be a big fan of the chap, he did respect the fact that his neighbour had worked hard all his life. For Frank, fame was the byproduct of what he loved doing, not the motivation. To succeed in life, Basil believed, it was necessary to actually be *good* at something – whether that was writing, acting, commanding troops or playing the money markets. His son, as far as he could see, had no discernible talent at all, and if he thought fame and money were the Holy Grail, the keys to happiness, he was in for a shock.

Losing heart for the battle, Basil began hurling Rupert's belongings into plastic bags, remarking to himself that his son's room had the best view in the house and would do splendidly as a new bedroom for him and Rosamund. He would splash out on a king-size bed with a solid-oak-feature headboard, perhaps air-conditioning to cool things down a little. Rosamund accused him of being stuck in his ways; it would be good to surprise her with a few luxurious mod cons – even a mirror on the ceiling might be fun. He could imagine breakfast on the Juliet balcony with his fragrant wife wearing the French negligee he had bought her for Christmas, which she had never worn.

Rosamund was, he mused, quite simply the dearest, sweetest creature on Earth, the love of his life. He had wanted her the moment he had set eyes on her, and married her praying that she would remain the same forever. But bearing a son had created an eternal triangle, with he and Rupert always battling for her affections. Basil would have packed the little tartar off to boarding school, but Rosamund had insisted he remain at home. Then, somehow, the years had flown like migrating birds; seasons had come and gone, and the springtime of his infatuation had deepened into abiding love. The girl he had married so many years ago had, inevitably, changed, thought Basil as he tied a knot in the final bag. She had become perfect.

Rosamund entered the consulting room, and a huge man shook her hand vigorously. She had not expected this: somebody her age, somebody her "type", somebody whom she might meet at a dinner party. The Professor had a mass of wiry, greying hair sat on his head like an angry cloud that protruded from his ears. He pulled a chair out for Rosamund, who perched coyly at its edge with her feet crossed and her handbag on her knee. Back at his desk, the Professor stretched his long legs. Leaning back in his chair, he folded his hands behind his head and smiled.

"Well, what can I do for you?" he enquired. His voice was deep and sonorous.

"I am not really sure," Rosamund stuttered. "I've been having some, erm, symptoms." With an electric flash of enthusiasm, the Professor lunged forward and began to scribble.

"Symptoms?" he enquired, fascinated.

"Yes, well. Nothing awful. Nothing at all, really," said Rosamund, feeling the colour rise up her neck. He continued to write energetically, and Rosamund wondered what he could be jotting down, as she had barely told him a thing.

"Sleeping OK?"

"Oh, yes, like a log,"

"HRT?"

"No."

"Appetite?" His intonations and inflexions reminded Rosamund of a school registrar.

"Good as ever," she replied obediently.

"Any hair loss?"

"Oh, no."

"Feelings of depression?"

"Not at all." She was beginning to relax. Perhaps things were not so bad after all.

"Any weight gain?"

"Well, you know, a bit, but ..." The Professor paused, looked Rosamund up and down, raised his eyebrows and returned to his scribbles.

"Libido?" This was it. He had asked. Rosamund would stay calm and answer this question just as she had the others: no change of tone, no silly jokes.

"Fine," she said, hoping she sounded casual. As soon as the words came out, she kicked herself for missing the moment.

"So how many times would you say you have sex in a month?" A month! A year would have been nearer the ballpark. Rosamund was not going to let herself down again.

"I don't know – a couple?" she lied.

"I'll put 'once'," the Professor said gruffly. "In my experience, any woman of your age who comes here and tells me she is having sex twice a month is having less than half that." Rosamund looked at the Professor with a mixture of shame and despair.

"There are things we can do to help," he said.

"What sort of things?"

"You know, patches, tablets, implants ..." Rosamund tried to adopt a "do go on" expression, but there was no need; the Professor was on a roll. "Low libido is caused by the loss of oestrogen and testosterone. We simply repair the balance! Just a bit of testosterone, and you'll be away."

Rosamund tried to listen, but the Professor had got to his feet, and she was already worrying about the next stage of the appointment: the inevitable internal examination.

"... And tablets are a pain," he continued chattily. "Because you have to remember to take them, so to my mind your best bet by far is an implant."

"How fascinating," said Rosamund, wondering whether or not there would be a nurse present for the examination. "I will certainly think about that and talk to my husband. It does sound as though it is the best solution, though, so ..."

"OK," said the Professor, rubbing his massive hands together to warm them, "hop up on the bed."

Rosamund felt a dead calm as she stepped behind the curtain and began to undress. She kept her top on but carefully removed her grey woollen slacks and pristine white knickers.

"Are you ready, Mrs Braithwaite?"

Rosamund whipped off her pop socks and clambered onto the treatment table in her T-shirt and blazer. How stupid of her, she panicked, she would look silly in a jacket. She wondered if there was time to take it off but quickly reclined on the bed and did her best to adopt a dignified posture when the curtain was opened.

"Yes!" she called a little too loudly, before adding, more quietly, "Thank you."

A nurse drew the curtain back and the Professor approached, wearing latex gloves and holding a grey, cardboard, kidney-shaped dish.

"Goodness," he said with surprise, "you've gone the whole hog! Only needed you to raise your blouse, you know." And before Rosamund had time for embarrassment, the nurse was spraying something cold on her abdomen.

"Just a small prick ..." said the Professor; but Rosamund was not feeling, she was thinking. What was he doing? Was he actually putting in the implant? She was sure that she had not agreed to that! Had she not said that she would talk to Basil about it? "You should begin to feel something in a few days, after which things should be –"

Rosamund's mind was whirring. Excitement, embarrassment and a certain pride were swelling within her, joy at what Basil would make of this uncharacteristic, almost valiant display of courage.

"There you are!" said the Professor, loping over to the washbasin and leaving the nurse to put a dressing over the incision on her stomach. "You may get some bleeding, but hopefully not. Just keep it clean and dry for a few days, and you'll be away. By this time next week, you'll be like a teenage rabbit again!"

As darkness eclipsed nature's magnificence on Riverside Lane, the Villagers closed their curtains on another day. Without the sunshine to showcase its glory, the cherry tree opposite the Braithwaites' pretty stucco home bowed its head in desolation.

Hidden from sight beneath the tree's limbs stood Kathy McConnell, perfectly camouflaged from the occasional passing headlight. Kathy was accustomed to being shut out from the world she planned to join, but was quite comfortable for the moment to be on the outside looking in. She visited often, after work, to bridge the gap between the charm of the Village and the reality of life at home. It relaxed her to watch Mrs B. as she moved about the kitchen, but recently Kathy had felt anger and resentment at such scenes of domestic bliss. She hid it well, never once dropping her mask of dignified, sycophantic professionalism at the Willoughbys' ... but there could be no denying Kathy had not felt like herself of late.

She stood in the shadow, a carrier bag for Angus at her feet and a bottle of whisky in her hand. It had been a testing few weeks. Something was different about Mrs B.; she had not been her usual friendly self at Felicity's soirée, and Kathy tightened her jaw at the memory of Bianca shouting, "I want to be more like you!" As if! That brassy trollop did not deserve to scrub Mrs B.'s lavatory! Only the week before, Kathy had stood on the exact same spot watching in fury as Bianca, Queen of Sheba, stopped her glitzy little car in the middle of the road, screeching, as Mrs B. alighted.

"Honestly Roz, you should've tried it on ..." *Roz*? How dare she shorten her name? It had taken all of Kathy's self-control not to burst out of the undergrowth and punch the presumptuous little guttersnipe in the mouth! Kathy had been forced to inhale the perfume on Mrs B.'s handkerchief to placate her anger.

For once, she had had no problem with Angus's nonsense at home that night. The police had been most understanding, and had not asked too many questions about his injuries as she shed a river of tears while they waited for an ambulance. Some part of her couldn't help but feel her husband had deserved it.

The appearance of Rosamund at the kitchen sink distracted her. Basil was sitting at the table like a despot, doubtless barking instructions at his wife as Kathy had been pained to hear him do so many times before. The invisibility Kathy intentionally fostered at The White House meant she was privy to many conversations between her employer and Mrs B., so she knew the object of her adoration was, like Kathy, living a lie with a man she loathed. How many times had she heard her say, "If it weren't for Basil ..." or "If only I could get rid of Basil ..." and, most tellingly: "If only Basil wasn't around ..." A fox sauntered up the middle of the lane, king of the road. A startled bird took flight, rattling the silence with the beat of its wings. Basil embraced his wife, who, up to her elbows with washing-up, had little defence but to wriggle and squeal. Kathy tasted blood and realised she had bitten her lip. She spat on the ground, trying to block out Basil's hideous laughter as he closed the curtains.

And then she was gone. There would be no more Mrs B. for Kathy that night.

SIXTEEN

I T WAS THE first day of the month of the Blessed Virgin Mary. The sun had been attempting to flutter its lashes and shine through a barrage of showery tears since dawn, and while children skipped around maypoles and Oxford revellers gathered below the Great Tower at Magdalen College to hear the choir sing madrigals, Ivy had spent the morning stocktaking at Village Antiques.

She switched off the computer and, removing a red book from the drawer, was horrified to discover her keys to Kingfisher House were missing. Blinking frantically to clear her vision, she looked again, certain she had left them at the back of the drawer as she always did. And yet either her eyes or her mind were failing, because the keys were no longer there. A cold fear gripped her heart, and Ivy ran her index finger absentmindedly down the money column, trying to quell the panic that commandeered her breath when she was losing control. She needed to keep calm, focus and think things through.

She felt unsettled that she had not yet received instructions from Nigel Bond regarding the American. The Tempesta dossier, with its accounts of the American's association with the Kuznetsoys, had brought back cruel memories for the old man, and he had taken to his bed at the very mention of his nemesis. But Ivy needed his directive. After all these years of carrying out his instructions, the thought of acting on her own volition was almost too frightening to bear. She closed her mind and hummed Bach's *Miserere* to carry her thoughts to a better place, much as she had done in childhood when her father, the deacon, came calling in the dead of night.

Her mind took her back to the convent, and to the nuns singing *miserere mei* and *secundum magnam misericordiam tuam* while, in her hiding place, the young Ivy crossed her fingers and hoped the Lord would have mercy upon her own soul.

Her breathing was easing, and, with an ethereal smile, Ivy turned her face to the watery sunshine that was streaming through the window as she recalled the Palm Sunday nearly fifty years earlier when Peter the Rock had first come into her life. She had been seventeen, and the first job the nuns had given their frightened charge was to awaken Peter from hibernation and bathe him. Seated on the garden steps in the pale morning light, Ivy had washed the sleepy animal's shell with an old toothbrush and a bowl of soapy water. Novice Sister Mary Agatha, a girl only a few months older, had laughed at her nervousness.

"You won't hurt him," she said. "He's tougher than he looks. His name is Peter, and he's a survivor."

"Matthew. Chapter sixteen, verse eighteen," Ivy replied dreamily; then, addressing the tortoise, she added: "And I tell you, you are Peter, and on this rock I will build my Church, and the gates of Hell shall not prevail against it."

And so life had passed. At night, after Compline, when the air was filled with the calming sounds of the senior nuns' psalmody in the old chapel, Ivy would tiptoe to Mary's room clutching her pillow and blanket. She would crawl beneath her wooden bed and lie there, soothed through her nightmares by Mary's steady breathing and the sound of matins, until the dawn prayer signified the hour for Ivy to return to her own bed. Sometimes she would hear Mary weeping, but Ivy's own demons prevented her from reaching out to comfort her friend.

She recalled her companion's gentle wisdom on the night Ivy learned of her father's death. He had left her a surprise inheritance of fifteen thousand pounds, and Ivy had accepted his patrimony despite knowing, in her soul, that the funds must have been embezzled from his parishioners. She had chosen a path that would sentence her to a lifetime of guilt, shame and self-loathing, one that necessitated her departure from the house of God where, for the only time in her life, she had found true peace.

The two girls had whispered late into the night, spilling an ocean of tears until a plan was devised. "Life has treated you cruelly," Mary had whispered. "Go to my father – he's an unfeeling man, driven by an unappeasable craving for power and respect, but he'll know what to do. He'll help you ... but remember, don't make his ways your own."

A week later, Ivy had bid farewell to the convent and to the only person she would ever love, and headed to London with a leaden heart to meet Sister Mary's father.

Her first meeting with Nigel Bond would be etched in Ivy's memory forever. Seated at a walnut desk beneath a portrait of the Queen, his face had been a mask of inscrutability while he listened to her story, taking careful notes with his gold Mont Blanc pen. Ordinary, well spoken, educated and cold, he had an unremarkable face and could be easily lost in a crowd; but when he spoke, his velvety, clipped intonation could never be forgotten. It was a voice that would keep Ivy in Nigel's Svengali-like grasp for almost five decades. Like an alchemist, he magically turned Ivy's inheritance into stocks and shares, then back into cash to purchase a property in the tiny village of his daughter's birth. In return, the civil servant asked only that she undertake small tasks for him, such as delivering packages and receiving messages. Ivy had written to her friend of the new arrangement, and six months later a box had arrived at Sunnyside bearing Peter the Rock, the cross of St Christopher and a letter from Sister Mary that Ivy could not bear to read.

The note from the convent had almost broken her spirit: Sister Mary Agatha had been found hanged in her room. To this day, that last letter from her friend lay unopened and unread.

Ivy inhaled sharply as the telephone shocked her from her thoughts.

"Village Antiques," she said.

"Ivy, it's Tony Jackson. Got a mo?"

"Well, I –"

"I've finally spoken to this Pete Walters character, and after a bit of, well, you know, a bit of persuasion, the geezer admitted he's writing an unofficial biography of Frank."

Ivy's heart slowed a little. "What kind of biography?"

"Well, you know, he claims it's all going to be lovey-dovey and kosher, but he hasn't asked us for input, so I can only assume it's gonna be an assassination."

"How far has he got?"

"Shifty little bugger wouldn't tell me. But I gather he's been on the trail for well over six months, so we've gotta assume he's reaching the end. My question for you, Ivy dear: is there anything I don't know? Any secrets or tawdry revelations? Frank has clammed up."

"I wouldn't know where to begin," said Ivy drily.

"No, seriously, love, if this guy's got anything on Frank, I need to know now, before it goes to publication. My people are onto him, checking his sources, speaking to his publisher, but we can't block his book unless we have grounds to do so – and I suspect those grounds won't become apparent until the damn thing is out." Ivy, who did not like being called "love", was not inclined to make Tony Jackson's life easier and was certain Pete Walters could not have unearthed secrets that not even Frank's lawyer knew; she felt disinclined to enlighten him.

"Nothing at all," she said.

Trying to focus on an omission in the ledger, she turned to the stock list and saw that the missing items were an assortment of war and victory medals to the Duke of Wellington's Regiment. Also absent was a box of lead soldiers, circa 1948, and a brass ship's megaphone. Ivy could picture the missing box, but there was an ominous gap in the "Ms": Manuscripts, Maritime Maps, Metalware … all were all present. But there was nothing under Military Memorabilia. Then she found the hastily scribbled note from Sam: *Items returned to Basil Braithwaite*. She needed to speak to Frank urgently, and as she was unable to complete the stocktaking, she shut the shop early and headed to Riverside Lane. As she walked, Ivy quashed a small worm of discontent. She had never spoken to anyone about Frank's business, and was not about to start now. It was not as though he had given her permission to divulge information.

Finding nobody home at The Waterfront, Ivy glanced at her watch to realise she would be home fifteen minutes earlier than usual; her day had gone alarmingly out of rhythm, and she felt fearful about the missing keys, anxious for Frank and irritated with Sam, who had been wrong to give away his father's stock. Keen to put her time to good use and to return to the security of her routine, Ivy stopped at the Braithwaites' house and rapped the knocker.

She could hear giggling from within, and the sound of somebody thundering down the stairs, then some whispering before Basil's voice called: "Wait a minute! Just finding the key."

"It's here ... Oooh ... Stop it!" exclaimed Rosamund, and Ivy thought she must be interrupting a party. So be it, she thought, crossing her hands in front of her and waiting patiently. It would not take a moment to explain, though why anybody would be carousing on a Wednesday afternoon bemused her. Eventually Basil flung the door wide open and greeted Ivy with a beatific smile.

"Ivy!" he declared, "What can I do for you on this beautiful day?"

In the kitchen, Ivy was surprised to note that Basil was barefoot; moreover, there were no signs of a celebration. She turned down his offer to take her coat, but accepted the chair he held out, on which she sat neatly as she explained the conundrum.

"Sam really should not have given you the goods," she said sternly. "The total value of the medals, the soldiers and the mega-phone is over seven hundred pounds, and I am afraid that he does not have that within his power." Basil had always found Ivy amusing. Her earnestness made him ache to tease her, but he had long ago discovered she was not a woman with a sense of humour. He was glad to clear up the matter of the medals, though; he had felt uncomfortable when Sam handed over the box glibly, waving away Basil's offer of payment with typical teenage embarrassment. He had intended to pop into the shop and see Village Antiques straight, but what with one thing and another – and Rosamund so full of vim and vigour – he had not yet found the time.

"Of course, of course, I suspected so," he said kindly, heading out of the kitchen to fetch his chequebook. "Let me give you a cheque now, mustn't see you out of pocket."

In his wake, Rosamund came into the room, wearing a silk caftan and fluffy mules.

"Hello, Ivy," she said warmly. "Do excuse me being so informal, but we were having a little siesta."

Ivy said nothing and Rosamund, fastening a button as she spoke, continued in slightly hushed tones: "Thank you so much for finding Basil's medals. He is over the moon. I am sure it won't surprise you to hear that he and Rupert have had their problems, and I can only assume that Rupert sold them to hurt his father." Ivy made no effort to acknowledge the confidence Rosamund was imparting. She remained seated upright with her hands folded in her lap, her indifference belied by a slight tightening of the lips and an almost imperceptible straightening of the back. Mungo bounded in, plunging his wet nose into Ivy's crotch, and Basil emerged wearing a hearty smile.

"Here we are," he said, waving a cheque in the air to dry the ink. "I'm not sure who to make it out to, so – oh, hello, Duchess," he said, with a lingering look. "Any chance of a cup of tea?"

Rosamund smiled and said: "I think you can make that for us, don't you, Basil?" She gave him a long kiss on the mouth before joining Ivy at the kitchen table, where she crossed her legs, revealing the slightest glimpse of a red garter. Ivy jumped to her feet as if stung.

"No tea for me," she said, in an unusual staccato, and scurried to the door.

"Off so soon?" asked Basil, following her. "Don't forget this! Who should it be payable to?"

"Make it out to the church," Ivy said. "They need a new organ."

"Perhaps," said Rosamund, with a small, knowing smile over her husband's shoulder, "they might call it the 'Braithwaite Organ'?"

*

Ivy's breath came in short, anxious bursts as she waited in her porch for seven minutes in order to cross the threshold of Sunnyside at the allotted time. Twelve minutes later, she was clutching her St Christopher and sipping tea under the shade of the crab apple tree.

She closed her eyes and recited comforting words from the Book of Psalms, but found no solace. An inner voice mocked her mercilessly until Ivy could bear the taunts no longer; clasping Peter the Rock as fervently as a talisman, she returned to the coolness of the house and shut the door.

SEVENTEEN

AMANDA JONES WORE a soft tweed dress by Burberry and Bottega Veneta bondage sandals. Her hair, swept up in an elegant chignon, was highlighted soft caramel, and her newly whitened teeth dazzled under the restaurant's chandeliers. She had invested in an all-over airbrush tan and splurged on a luxury manicure. She had even gritted her teeth and road-tested a Brazilian bikini wax.

Gazing around the chichi West London brasserie, the journalist felt confident she fitted in well with the mix of urbane professionals and chattering classes. Rupert Braithwaite had booked his usual table, and Amanda, who assumed he would pick up the bill, eagerly anticipated sampling the mouth-watering dishes chalked up on the board.

A small financial outlay to improve her image for the interview was money well spent in Amanda's opinion, although she would need to think long and hard how to justify it to the bank. One could not put a price on boosting self-esteem, but she doubted, somehow, that Julie from NatWest would understand. She did not want to think about how much it had all cost – but she was already drowning in debt, so what was a few grand more? She was not alone, Amanda reassured herself; there were millions like her in Britain. She had recently read a feature that said people all over the world were living with a sense of entitlement they could not afford, spending lavishly on consumer goods because "they were worth it".

Amanda ordered a gin and tonic and reflected on the evening she had spent with the American at the pub once she had ditched the Willoughbys' snooty housekeeper. He had paid for her drinks, which had gone some way to compensating for the three hundred pounds she had squandered on bribing Ivy Midwinter. Luca had laughed out loud when she told him of Ivy's suspicion, cracking open a bottle of champagne and agreeing wholeheartedly that the crone was nuts. Amanda normally fancied younger men, but there was something about Luca that had made her come over. He was a real man, she decided, a world away from the namby-pamby village boys with their floppy haircuts and inherent sense of privilege. His swarthy looks and the rugged scar on his cheek gave him something of a "mafia" air, and he oozed a power and strength that made Amanda feel rather girlish.

He was clearly rolling in it, too, if he could afford to rent the sprawling gaffe of the Village Antiques' proprietor. She indulged herself with a daydream in which Luca became her ticket out of Hicksville. What was wrong with using her womanly charms to secure her financial future? It had to be better than investing in a personal pension plan, and she did not intend to make the same mistake as her parents. When they needed something, they had saved for it, often taking many years to stash away enough money to buy something as ordinary as a sofa. Amanda remembered her mother being in hock to the butcher, and the anxiety of owing him twenty-five pounds had given her shingles. Back then there had been no designer dresses, only hand-me-downs or, if Amanda was lucky, hand-knitted jumpers courtesy of her Gran. The fashionable girls at school had mocked her dowdy image and sensible shoes, but their meanness had only served as a catalyst, propelling her out of the dreary estate into the glossy world of the media.

Amanda had been all bright eyes and killer heels when she arrived in London to take up a job at one of the UK's first celebrity magazines twenty years earlier. She had been little more than a glorified tea lady, but had embraced the role with enthusiasm, moving swiftly through the ranks to reporter. It was thrilling meeting celebrities; she had even interviewed Frank Fielding, who had been a charmer, riding high on his success in *Showtime*. (He had made a pass at her – and much to Amanda's chagrin now, she had been tempted to accept.)

The job had not lasted long. One day, she was summoned to the managing editor's office. He had screamed: "*You* are not the celebrity, Amanda Jones! I have your expenses here: a taxi to Wales, lunch at Le Caprice, flights to Paris. Are you living in Cloud Cuckoo Land? When you said you wanted a word with Princess Diana, we didn't expect you to chase her halfway around Europe! I have an allegation of *stalking* from the Press Complaints Commission! What do you have to say?"

Amanda would never know if he had been about to fire her, because she had gathered up her Filofax, donned her Armani trench coat and exited the room with her head held high. If that poxy magazine wanted to make a fuss over a few minor infringements, then so be it – it was their loss. She would walk into a job at News International tomorrow. Yet for all her dreams and ambitions, the glittering media career had never emerged; a stint on a trade magazine had led to a humdrum role at a PR firm, and Amanda had tried and repeatedly failed to get a job with a national newspaper, finally resorting to a freelance role on the Village rag, producing a weekly "What's On" column of local events and the occasional feature. It paid peanuts, so she supplemented her earnings by writing educational brochures for the local council. Onwards and upwards, she told herself; there was no point in harping on about what might have been.

A kerfuffle at the door heralded the arrival of Rupert Braithwaite, who ambled over in catwalk-cool Ozwald Boateng. He looked mean and brooding, a slick of glossy black hair falling sexily over one eye. Amanda gasped; for all her sophisticated makeover, she felt sixteen again. Rupert resembled her first teenage crush, Shakin' Stevens, the man who still gave her goosebumps on *Top of the Pops* reruns.

"Bloody press," barked Rupert belligerently. "I can't shake them off; they're a bunch of leeches! I'm with Hugh Grant on press reform! Waiter ... *waiter*! Do something about the paparazzi at the door, will you?" The *maître d'* looked baffled, and explained in measured tones that the gentlemen in question were photographing their parents, who were celebrating their golden wedding anniversary.

"Well, tell them not to take photographs over here, then," Rupert said huffily. "I don't want my picture on Facebook without my agent's permission."

"You really do have a lovely smile," Amanda blurted out. "I'm a big admirer of your work."

Rupert looked at her with his dead shark eyes, and Amanda felt a fizz of excitement: she had always liked bad boys. Having dismissed the *maître d'*, Rupert summoned him back and Amanda tried not to swoon as he grilled him on the provenance of the wine, finding his knowledge of the grape strangely arousing.

"Sorry, but I'll have to make this a quickie," Rupert muttered, checking his watch. For one thrilling moment, Amanda thought he had said he fancied a quickie, and she was about to reach for her Louis Vuitton before processing the frustrating fact that Rupert had a second sitting elsewhere. She felt a stab of disappointment and then shrugged it off, determined to enjoy basking in the spotlight of a bona-fide celebrity. She spotted two blondes at the neighbouring table nodding in Rupert's direction, and cast them a superior look.

"How nice to see you again Amanda," said Rupert. "I must say, those sandals do look very foxy." Amanda blushed; then, taking the proverbial bull by the horns, she grilled him on his feelings towards Frank Fielding.

"*That* has-been? Couldn't give a toss," he replied sanguinely, flicking his hair out of his eyes. This would not make scintillating copy. Amanda tried again.

"But you must feel aggrieved – it was *your* fifteen minutes of fame, after all?"

"Fifteen minutes? *Fifteen minutes?*" Rupert barked bombastically. "I think my fame has lasted longer than that! My life has been a social whirl since my book launch: autograph signings, television and radio appearances. I'm in talks with an American film company about a screenplay of *The Sponsored Walk*. I haven't stopped." Rupert paused for a moment; then, staring at Amanda, he demanded: "Where's your notebook? Why aren't you taking all this down for the article?"

Amanda reached inside her handbag and withdrew a voice recorder, struggling to switch it on with her long, Chanel-lacquered nails. Rupert spoke directly into the device: "I'm now so successful, I'm considering signing with another agent, one that specialises in international stars." He proclaimed, with a flourish: "I plan to conquer America."

"Wow." Amanda was impressed, and her mind drifted to an exhilarating world in which she was dining with Rupert in a fashionable Hollywood restaurant. Of course, she would be married to Luca by then, and so forced to spurn Rupert's amorous advances. They would laugh and talk about old times. He would be an A-lister, and she a trophy wife.

"Hel-lo? Anyone at home?" Rupert called, with a sneer.

"Sorry, zoned out for a moment." It was clear to Amanda that there was no chance of a scoop, so she decided to relax and enjoy herself. It was not every day she was invited to lunch by a famous person.

"I love America," Rupert continued into Amanda's voice recorder. "I like the girls there too, especially in New York – they have bags of style, always look as if they've stepped from the pages of *Vogue*."

Amanda leaned forward, allowing a button or two on her tweed dress to pop open. She was pleased she felt every inch a match for the women Rupert admired so much. Still buoyant from his earlier compliment about her sandals (a snip at eight hundred pounds), she crossed and then uncrossed her long legs; the tantalising flash of bare thigh showcased her vertiginous heel to perfection. It was good to be with a man of taste, who appreciated female fashion and the time and effort – not to mention the expense – women put into looking good.

"... Of course, I love it when a woman just crawls out of bed, pulls on her jeans and T-shirt, doesn't put on any makeup on and walks out the door looking drop-dead gorgeous," Rupert continued, "but for any woman over the age of seventeen, that's pretty much impossible. It takes hard work and dedication to pull that look off, something British women are useless at; they're either too lazy or too fat!" Amanda bristled and pulled in her stomach, pleased that the arrival of their *steak au poivre* afforded an opportunity to change the subject.

"I heard your parents were upset when Frank Fielding's comments thrust them back into the media spotlight," she probed. "Surely you have a view on that?"

"Ha ha, I see you're not watching your weight," Rupert said, diverting the subject, and Amanda pushed her chips to one side and shot him a nasty look. On closer inspection, she thought, Rupert's eyes were piggy, and his mouth was nowhere near as full and sensual as Shakin' Stevens'. Rupert prattled on about himself through the remainder of their meal, and Amanda grew bored and drank more wine than was entirely professional. She decided to have one last shot at getting him to badmouth Frank, but instead, found herself hissing:

"Yeah, yeah, good news about your success, but what about your parents? It was not awfully nice that you lied about your father having dementia, was it?" Amanda goaded further: "You must be relieved the story wasn't picked up by the nationals. I hear your parents are remaining tight-lipped to protect your interests, but are forcing you to hand your profits over to charity." She had not intended to pick a fight, but red wine always made her argumentative, and disrespecting British women was a step too far. British women were famed the world over for their quirky cool, she thought: think Kate Moss, Daisy Lowe, Joanna Lumley – the list was endless!

If Rupert heard the question above the chatter of the restaurant, he chose not to acknowledge it, glancing at his watch again and declining coffee as he smiled at the glamorous blondes on the next table. Amanda poured herself another glass and tried a different tack: "I've heard women in America are deadly dull," she said cattily. "All that, 'How are yeeeww, have a nice day' sounds false and vacuous. That's why American men cross the Atlantic in droves to marry British women, who are not obsessed with their careers or their image."

"Not so," Rupert countered, winking at their neighbours, who appeared to be enjoying the show. "American women get their priorities right. They don't think it's beneath them to spend money on their appearance, or to be ambitious. British women sell themselves short – even those who go to top universities and get first-class degrees often end up in mundane jobs. Take you, for example," he added, with a nasty glint in his eye. "You seem reasonably bright and you're OK-looking, yet you have settled for a dead-end job at the *Gazette*. Why's that?"

Amanda felt hot tears prick her eyes, and, fearing her Cheryl Cole eyelashes might fall into her Americano, she shoved the coffee away and wished she had asked for a cappuccino instead. From here on in, she was swapping her caffeine allegiance. She threw back her wine and felt her chignon loosening. Rupert had hit a raw nerve, and all her insecurities reared up. She felt victim to an unprovoked attack and, without a moment's thought, lashed out in return: "My God, you're rude!" she shouted. "The reality is that, for all your poncey education, you have no manners and no talent. You're a nobody – nothing but a jumped-up, bloody *jailbird*!" Tears tumbled down her cheeks.

Rupert's smile was that of a predator. "I think *you* may be on thin ice, calling *me* a nobody, don't you?" he said coldly. Gathering up his car keys and phone, he left the building, his head held royally aloft.

"Plonker!" Amanda screamed at his retreating figure. Then, reaching for the remainder of the Château Pétrus, she poured herself a large glass just as the *maître d'* placed the bill on the table, with a discreet and knowing smile.

Back in the Village, Rupert's parents were finishing warm ciabatta rolls stuffed with mozzarella, salami and rocket, and spread with a tapenade.

"Delicious," declared Basil, chomping through his final mouthful. "No idea what it was, but totally delicious." He picked

162

up his newspaper. "Some sort of fancy designer roll, I suppose, was it?"

"It was just an Italian bread roll," Rosamund replied patiently, but Basil already had his glasses on, and though he responded with a friendly "Mmm", his wife knew he was not listening. She was annoyed by her husband's determined curmudgeonliness whenever she tried anything new, and got up to put the kettle on. Basil patted her bottom as she passed and Rosamund chewed her lip in further irritation.

"Well, it's not like any roll I've ever had, Duchess," he declared from behind the *Telegraph*. "And I bet it cost twice what a basic butty would cost."

Rosamund snorted. "You've never had a basic butty in your life, Basil Braithwaite, so don't go pretending you have ... it's ciabatta. I had something similar in town with Rupert, and I thought –"

Now it was Basil's turn to snort. "That explains it," he laughed. "Nothing wrong with a bit of Mother's Pride and some ham and cheese in my book, but that would be never good enough for our Rupert."

"Well, you obviously liked it," said Rosamund pointedly, picking up his empty plate and turning towards the sink. They were interrupted by a voice calling from the garden.

"Cooee, anybody in?"

"Good God," spluttered Basil, "can a man have no privacy? Don't go, Duchess, we're in the middle of –" But Rosamund was already walking towards the open French doors.

There was a crash, followed by: "Bleedin' 'Enry!" Then a scrabbling noise. Bianca's diamante-tipped nails appeared over the top of Basil and Rosamund's fence, followed by her laughing, perfectly made-up face. "Fell off me perch!"

"Rosamund, kettle's boiled!" Basil called urgently from the kitchen. Rosamund rolled her eyes at Bianca with a smile, and called back: "Don't worry, dear, it turns itself off!" Then she whispered to Bianca: "Sometimes I wish I could just turn him off."

"Tell me about it!" replied Bianca conspiratorially. "I reckon my

Frank's taking them little blue pills. Last night we were at it like bleedin' rabbits!"

Rosamund reddened and busied herself with tucking the potato vine behind the trellis.

"I ran the bath," continued Bianca, oblivious to her neighbour's discomfort. "We're usually done and dusted long before it's filled. Anyway, the whole bleedin' bathroom flooded, and Frank *still* wasn't done!" Rosamund, to whom the correct response usually came easily, was at a loss as to how to respond to the information Bianca had just imparted over the garden fence. Basil inadvertently saved her by barking from the house:

"Rosamund! Where are my golf shoes?"

She smiled. "I'd better go," she said, with the resigned joy of a woman whose husband cannot manage without her. "He is hopeless."

"We've been asked to Ladies' Day at Ascot, and I need you to tell me what to wear!" Bianca called after her cheerfully, switching from sex to fashion with a dexterity that left Rosamund awestruck.

"Oh, lucky you," she replied charmingly. "I would love to."

"Rosamund!" called Basil. She knew him to dislike it when she chatted over the garden fence, "encouraging the Fieldings".

"How about coffee tomorrow?" Rosamund asked, at a volume designed to reach even Basil's selectively deaf ears. "We can talk about it then, Bianca. We might even go shopping together, if you have the time?" Her husband's dismay from inside the house was almost palpable.

"Oh, I'd really like that," said Bianca, and Rosamund walked inside with a giddiness at having discussed sex with her neighbour over the fence as well as the prospect of going shopping with Bianca. Her retired, predictable life still presented the occasional surprise.

Amanda sat on the bus from London and reflected on her disastrous lunch with Rupert Braithwaite. The afternoon had culminated in a humiliating showdown with her editor, who had agreed to foot the eye-watering bill to avoid police involvement after her credit cards were rejected.

"You'll be working for nothing now," he had yelled. Amanda would have liked to tell him to get stuffed, but unlike the Braithwaites of this world, she did not have the luxury of picking and choosing her work. With her return train ticket lost, only shrapnel in her purse and the cash machine stubbornly refusing to hand over money, Amanda had removed her Bottega Venetas and walked barefoot to Victoria Station, where she had purchased a cheap ticket for a coach ride home. It was oppressively hot, and she had been grateful for the seat and the air conditioning.

As the bus pulled off the motorway, she found herself drawing upon reserves of stoicism. She would regroup and renew her efforts to seduce Luca Tempesta, and try again to get an interview with Hugh Willoughby. She could not wait to see the look on Joy's face when she found out that Amanda knew about their tawdry little insurance scam. Bringing them down would feel like vengeance against Rupert Braithwaite, whose parents were the Willoughbys' closest friends. It was personal now.

As the bus drew into the Village, Amanda spotted Ivy Midwinter stepping out of the residential care home, arm in arm with a dapper old man who, in spite of his years, held himself with a proud, military bearing. He looked familiar. Amanda had never seen the old witch make body contact with a living, breathing human before; even when she cut a swathe through village *fêtes* and fundraisers, demanding money for the church, Ivy ensured her sparrow-like body never touched a soul, reeling in horror if elbows clashed or legs brushed, as if Satan was upon her. The woman gave Amanda the cringe. There was something odd about her, something that did not add up. It seemed that she knew everything about everyone in the Village, where all the bodies were buried – but what did anyone know about Ivy?

The face of her even more elderly companion bothered her, too. There was definitely something familiar about him. Had she seen his photograph in the microfiches at Collingwood, where she went to research cold-case stories? Tomorrow, she decided, she would investigate Ivy Midwinter. The bus reached the drab, grey fringes of the Village and Amanda alighted into the litter-strewn street with black, grubby feet and a black, grubby heart.

EIGHTEEN

HE SUMMER SOLSTICE is almost here, reflected Harley, oblivious to the rabble of butterflies dancing above his head. He was enjoying the warmth of the spring day, which soothed his cold bones and eased the pain behind his eyes as he made his way to meet Felicity at the Crown. Harley seldom saw the daylight hours, preferring the enchantment of night, when exotic creatures and fauna came to life in undisturbed darkness. He needed less sleep these days – sometimes his stomach gave him trouble, and he couldn't sleep at all – and had taken to staying up until the darkest hour before dawn, then striding out to enjoy that magical tipping point between night and day. The previous night, an owl had hooted, and a rustling sound had prompted him to turn and stare into the eyes of a roe deer. *A solitary creature like me*, Harley had thought, as he held its gaze. A bat had swooped low and a beetle scuttled by, orienting itself by the Milky Way. Harley reflected on the nightingales he remembered singing in the woods of his childhood. What he would give to hear that sweet sound again, just one more time.

There had been sightings of a gigantic cat prowling the Village. "A black panther!" Frank had proclaimed, having spotted it as he returned home late from his charity work. Only Harley knew the truth: it was a gentle Great Dane, searching for its dead master. He had witnessed more than one altercation between the huge hound and the Fieldings' terrier Dubonnet, whom Harley knew to have the heart of a lion despite his diminutive size. He wondered if the Fieldings knew their small dog slipped out the cat-flap at night to enjoy a secret double life.

In the distance, he could see Felicity leaning against the hostelry wall, hastily stubbing out a cigarette. Harley had phoned ahead to tell her of his wonderful news. Whooping with delight, she rushed to greet him, and he ran, too, as fast as his tired body would allow. He lifted her up and swung her around with a great roar of joy.

Hours later, Felicity poured the last champagne dregs into her glass and waved goodbye to Harley. She watched from the window as he loped off into the sunset. The two friends had spent the afternoon reflecting on his astonishing news, Felicity happily breaking the teetotal campaign she had embraced like a weak rubber band while Harley sipped green tea daintily from an earthenware mug, a gargantuan Cheshire-cat grin on his whiskery face.

"Are you sure it's true, Harl?" she demanded, the words tripping off her tongue in a flurry of excitability. "It's not the boys winding you up, is it? It's not a joke?"

The US's hottest band, Bankrupt Nation, was to sample *I'm in Love with the Vicar's Daughter* on a track for their new album, and Harley stood to make many tens of thousands of pounds. Felicity was reeling from the news. She knew the band – everybody did. Their latest hit was played on a continuous loop on the radio, and blasted from every speaker in her house. Her boys talked about their performance at Glastonbury in hushed tones.

"One hundred per cent true," Harley smiled. "I called my lawyer. Their last album sold more than three million copies in the US, and tens of millions worldwide; she says the next will make a mint, too."

"I don't want to be rude, Harl, but what does a band like Bankrupt Nation want with a corny Seventies ditty like yours? It doesn't make sense."

"It's not the words they want," Harley chuckled, "it's the melody."

"OK, I see," said Felicity, although she was not sure she did. "I can't wait to tell the boys. They'll think we're having a laugh. It's going to make you a fortune!" Harley reached across the table and took her hand.

"Make *us* a fortune," he corrected,

Their position at the end of the bar allowed a view of the room in full, and Felicity sat there alone after her friend had gone. She contemplated another bottle; the night was young, and she felt squiffy and happy. Felicity had not had a real drink in months, having joined "the programme" to please Harley, and she had forgotten how good the kick felt when it hit the bloodstream. She watched Luca arrive for his early-evening pint. *I'm in the mood to celebrate*, she thought, slinging her handbag over her shoulder and preparing to make her advances. The door flew open again and Frank Fielding's voice resonated across the room: "Evening one and all, here I am, fresh from a casting!" Felicity put down her bag.

"Been fishing, have you?" asked one of the pensioners. "You're looking cock-a-hoop."

"Sadly, more hoop than cock," Frank quipped, "but where's the lovely Felicity this evening?" Felicity slunk back in her seat and was grateful to her replacement at the bar for ignoring the question. She loved Frank, but was not in the mood for his jokes and banter. A few moments later Sam walked in, looking fidgety and pale. Over the past few weeks, Felicity had been amused to watch him cosying up to Luca; she was surprised that tonight he walked straight past her with no acknowledgement, ordering a pot of coffee and taking it piously to a table.

Alone and unobserved, Felicity daydreamed about what she and Harley would do with the cash. If it only released her from the indignity of asking Dave for money, it would be tantamount to a king's ransom. Perhaps she could pack the boys off to boarding school, one with a reputation for teaching manners, and hope they did a better job of raising them than she had done. That is what rich people do, she thought dreamily: they chuck money at their problems. Felicity thought she would be rather good at that – but she had so many problems, the money would soon evaporate. Once the boys were off her hands, she and Harley could travel the world. All those places they had talked of visiting: Borobudur at sunrise, stargazing in Chile, the Taj Mahal, the Sydney Opera House.

"Money buys you freedom," Harley had said in parting, and Felicity now wondered if it was true. Would she ever be free of the shackles of parenthood? Harley had managed to sever the ties, but Felicity feared she was held fast by an invisible maternal thread. *Harley knows me, but does he understand me?* she wondered, grazing on a bowl of peanuts to soak up the alcohol. Only one person empathised with the isolation and emptiness that haunted Felicity, and that was Ivy. The two women had forged an unlikely friendship, borne from shared experiences of cold, domineering fathers and childhoods in which they'd been cowed by subjugation to God. Ivy understood. They had never discussed their respective plights, nor ever would, but they were bonded by a mutual, unspoken truth that each struggled to overcome, and fettered by an ecclesiastical brand on their souls. Felicity sought solace in the choir, and Ivy appeased her infinite guilt by raising funds for the church's upkeep. And yet despite their lifelong searches for redemption, both women were blighted by the terrible poverty of loneliness.

"You should get out more," Bianca had insisted. "Being cooped up with that rowdy mob is enough to do anyone's head in." But Bianca's sunny optimism meant she could never understand that *being alone* was a world away from *loneliness*. Felicity savoured solitude, peaceful afternoons spent in the garden away from the noise of the pub and the boys with nothing more than the birds for company. Loneliness was different; it was the dark side of solitude. It was the numbness she felt when her connection with the world was lost. She could be pressed against the wall at a party in full flow, sharing a joke with her sons or making love to a man, and still the black mist would descend, turning her into a stranger on the edge of happiness, an outsider looking in.

Harley had tried to help. "The answer lies in sharing something of yourself," he had told her a few weeks earlier. "Not demanding to be fed, but cooking and sharing your food with others."

She had missed his point and flown off the handle, screaming: "I'm always bloody cooking!" When she had calmed down and thought it through, she felt ashamed and apologised.

Felicity sighed at the memory and decided on another bottle of champagne. She felt relaxed; the alcohol was taking the hard edges off her life, and she felt a rare stab of happiness, a feeling she did not want to relinquish with sobriety. Slipping unnoticed through the side entrance to the bar, she uncorked a bottle of Moët and returned stealthily to her seat in the corner. She felt guilty side-stepping Frank, but she was not in the mood for chitchat, and he was sure to accost her and give chapter and verse on the television show she knew he was desperate to have as the ticket to a Saturday-night comeback. She saw Frank looking around the bar, and ducked behind a beam. On the opposite side of the room, Sam caught her eye and Felicity raised a finger to her lips. He gestured a zip across his mouth and smiled complicitly; then he returned to his laptop, leaving Felicity to her solitude.

Sam was pleased that the Village Antiques wi-fi reached through the wall into the pub, enabling him to update his blog and keep an eye on Luca at the same time. He knew it was madness to continue with his Russian-spy theory – Cecilia had given him a dressing-down on the subject – but something was not quite right, and Sam was on a mission to find out what. He could tell from the way the American was getting stuck into the vodka that he was in for the long haul. Luca did not have his laptop, which Sam thought to be a good sign; nor did he raise an eyelid when Isolda's sugar daddy walked in with cries of "*Dobry vyecher!*" They had rubbed shoulders briefly as Sasha picked up some poncey wine and a couple of glasses, but Sam saw no evidence of documents changing hands. He longed to wander outside into the sunshine and catch Isolda's eye, maybe attempt to chat her up again when her old man was in the loo, but he knew he would be distracted by her endless legs – and he had work to do.

Frank left the pub, and Sam watched Felicity reapply her lip gloss and waft over to Luca in a miasma of perfume and come-hither glances. Placing the champagne ice bucket on the bar next to him, she wrapped her arms around him like a python circling a vole. Sam would recoil from such an invasion of his space, but Luca looked as if he welcomed it, encircling Felicity's waist with a wolfish grin. Sam thought this to be both a good and a bad sign: bad because it was disgusting to witness a middle-aged man paw a woman, and good because, entangled with Felicity, he did not look like someone caught betwixt Russian foreign intelligence and the FBI. He felt glad that Cecilia, who so clearly had a crush on Luca, was not there to witness this overt display of lust. It was disappointing; this was not the behaviour Sam expected from a man he had come to admire, in whom he had confided. Luca was acting like a dog in heat – worse still, he was acting like his father. Just when Sam thought the situation could not get any worse, Luca burst into a cheesy love song, crooning into Felicity's ear: "When the moon hits your eye / like a big pizza pie /that's *amore* ..."

Felicity and the pensioners joined in on the chorus: "Bells will ring ..."

Sam found it painful to watch. He buried his head in his computer and continued to tweet the latest environment statistics.

"Eat, drink and be merry, for tomorrow you may die!" cried Luca.

"Ooh, you look just like Dean Martin," Felicity slurred.

"Perhaps Bankrupt Nation would like me to make a guest appearance at their next concert!" roared Luca to much laughter.

"Here's to Bankrupt Nation!" toasted Felicity. Sam slammed down his computer lid. It was time to save Luca from himself. Invoking bands like Bankrupt Nation at his age was embarrassing; if Sam did not intervene soon, Luca might even sing and "Dad-dance" to one of their songs, which really would be the last straw. He was just about to make his stand when Luca jumped to his feet and gathered Felicity up in his arms, lifting her down from the barstool. The knot at the back of her head loosened and her long, dark hair tumbled down over one eye. *She looks sensational*, thought Sam, before collecting his wits about him. He watched in horror as Luca carried her to the door, as he passed Sam, he doffed an imaginary cap.

"Don't wait up, son!" he laughed as they stepped out into the night.

Sam felt sick to his stomach. Poor Cecilia – she has such dreadful taste in men, he thought, as he gathered up his belongings and headed for home.

NINETEEN

UGH CLOSED THE front door with a sigh. Amanda Jones was misguided and delusional, but she could also be tenacious; every time she made a mistake and it appeared certain she would lose her job, she would rise like a phoenix from the ashes and write something spot-on and spectacular. Hugh had every reason to fear that, should she uncover dirt on his family, she would stamp them into the ground happily on her muddy pathway to career success.

He wandered into the kitchen, deep in thought. It was clear that Kathy had spoken to the media. The undeniable proof of the conversation taped by the journalist was now on his phone. He could handle Amanda. He had done so before. When Joy had picked a fight over the architecture of the new vicarage, for instance, or the time Penny was caught shoplifting and somebody tipped off the *Gazette*.

Joy still knew nothing about that little episode. Hugh could not count the number of times Penny had messed up, following which her father – then, latterly, Tom – had felt it kinder to keep Joy in the dark, protecting her from disappointment and Penny from a roasting. But Hugh was beginning to wonder whether it had been kind or just stupid. Joy was becoming increasingly deluded herself, and Penny more delinquent. Every time Hugh was forced to listen to Joy lauding their daughter, while knowing that, like some bigot, his wife had banished Tom and his husband from their home, he felt a little more distant from Joy and a little less inclined to set her straight.

It occurred to Hugh that it might do both the women in his life good if, instead of pulling strings to rein in Amanda, he threw Joy and Penny to the lions. He could persuade the journalist not to publish this ridiculous non-story about the non-burglary, and give her something juicier in exchange: Penny's teenage drug habit; Joy's homophobic exclusion of her only son; Penny's expulsion from school; Joy's propensity for a secret tipple. Hugh realised, as he considered his wife and his daughter's social downfall, he had a begrudging admiration for Amanda Jones. At least she had made her own way in life – unlike Penny, about whom Joy had such a monumental blind spot it was risible. Not that Hugh would say as much to Joy, of course; that ship had sailed long ago. At what stage in their marriage could he have made a difference, imposing his will on his overbearing wife and his errant daughter? Hugh wondered. Was it that awful day Tom had told her of his sexuality, a secret Hugh had understood for many years? Or when Penny declared herself sick of the sight of her parents, whom she claimed to never want to see again ("Oh, but I need some money and a lift to the airport, Dad!") ... Hugh often had these internal rants, and it was another source of self-contempt that he neither aired nor acted on them.

"Tea, Tinkerbell?" he called as he warmed the pot. Joy, who had been humming quietly as she cleared the croquet lawn, heard her husband from the kitchen and waved her hand. If she could just get the hoops and the "poison" post up, Hugh could mow the lawn before dusk. She stacked the garden furniture and wandered up to the house. It would not be too long before she felt ready to admit to Hugh the extent of their financial downfall. She kicked off her clogs and wondered whether or not it was mild enough to take their tea outside.

"What is it?" she asked, seeing that her husband had his jaw set tight and was grinding his teeth. "What's happened?" Hugh closed the kitchen door before pulling out a chair for Joy and joining her at the kitchen table.

"Nothing for you to worry about," he muttered.

"Well, something's obviously bothering you," she said. "Try me! Who knows, I may surprise you."

"OK," he said. "I've just had a visit from Amanda Jones. It appears she has been speaking to Kathy."

"To Kathy? Surely not! What did she say?"

"That we have made a fraudulent insurance claim. That I falsified evidence by breaking a window. That we have wasted police time."

"We did *not* file a claim," snapped Joy. "At least, we withdrew it."

Hugh's eyes narrowed.

"I think," he said quietly, "you may be missing the point."

"I cannot believe that Kathy would tittle-tattle about our business. She has always been so discreet. So professional. There must be some other explanation."

"And what would you propose, exactly?" Hugh asked coldly.

"The police!" announced Joy. "It would have been them. Most likely that shifty little one who couldn't look you in the eye. I was never comfortable having them in the house, Hugh, but you were so excited by the night-vision goggles and the whole undercover thrill of it all, I didn't want to overrule you."

"Didn't you?" asked Hugh, with a weary smile that Joy found oddly unsettling, "Now that does surprise me! So what do you think happened, exactly?"

Joy began an elaborate story about policemen being the next best thing to criminals, punctuated by anecdotal tales of corruption and media tip-offs. She had apparently suspected the "shifty-eyed one" of snooping around the place, but had not wanted to worry Hugh about it.

"Of course, in hindsight, I should have challenged him – or, even better, spoken to his superior – but I was reticent about being too confrontational, what with you having broken that window and everything. You really did put me in an impossible position with the way you behaved, and ..." Joy observed Hugh over her teacup and stopped talking. He was leaning back in his chair with his arms folded, viewing her as if from afar. "What?" she asked, looking behind her to see what warranted his wry smile. She patted her hair and ran her tongue over her teeth. "Is there something on my face?"

"No, no, you look perfectly lovely," said her husband, but his body was saying what his voice was not. He slipped lower in his chair, arms still firmly folded, eyebrows raised questioningly. "Do go on."

"I don't know," said Joy, pulling at a ragged cuticle. "You've made me completely lose my train of thought ... Oh, yes, it was just that ..." She began to finalise her case with indignation that Hugh should automatically accuse Kathy, a woman who had been unfaltering in her service to them and had, after all, worked for some of the very best families. If only he hadn't bought all this trouble upon them by –

"Enough!" roared Hugh, pushing his chair back and jumping to his feet. His face had paled. "Enough."

"Don't grind your –"

"For once in your life, woman, will you please just *shut up and listen*?" He laid his phone on the table and pressed "play" before walking out of the room and slamming the door behind him. Joy heard the screech of tyres on the gravel as he tore away. Kathy McConnell's muffled voice echoed around the kitchen.

"... There was no sign of a forced entry, and Mr Willoughby was worried that they wouldn't be able to claim on their insurance ..."

Joy had heard enough. She took a final tug at her cuticle, ripping away the flesh as she did so. Blood crept down her finger and she sucked it as she went to the drawer for a plaster, inadvertently initiating a house-that-Jack-built sequence of events. She pulled the heavy drawer too far; it fell from its casing onto Joy's foot. Hopping in pain, she knocked the teapot from the table and slipped on the liquid, catching her eye on the corner of the cabinet before landing painfully on her coccyx. The hand Joy put out to save herself pressed down on the broken porcelain, which sliced into her palm before twisting her wrist painfully out of line. The noise bought Kathy rushing into the kitchen.

"Goodness! Mrs Willoughby! Are you all right?" Joy neither noticed her rapidly swelling eye nor the blood that pumped from the palm of her hand. She tried to sit up, registering an assault of agony so great that the humiliation became irrelevant. She surrendered her body to the floor and listened to Kathy's soothing voice as she fetched a pillow and a large brandy with a straw. "It will help with the pain. Now don't you move," she said gently, wrapping a cloth in ice for Joy's eye, which was rapidly closing. "It will feel a bit sore, but you'd best hold this against your temple while I go and get Mr Willoughby." She pushed aside a strand of Joy's hair that was sticky with blood, "Och, you poor, dear soul, what a state of affairs."

Joy heard Kathy opening doors and calling for her husband, and was determined not to compound her humiliation by crying.

"He must've gone out," Kathy said, returning and flicking through her diary for his number. She began to dial. A buzzing told both women that Hugh had left without his mobile, which vibrated plaintively from beneath the kitchen table. "You poor lass, would you like me to call Mrs Braithwaite?" Joy wiped her eyes and nodded bravely, and Kathy dialled the number she knew by heart.

Rosamund delivered Joy to the Riverside Clinic while Basil, who could not tolerate hospitals, dropped Kathy home before popping in on Myrtle to give her an update. In the car, Kathy chatted politely to Basil, who, although he had found the Willoughbys' house-keeper obsequious in the past, later declared her a "super woman" and "surprisingly attractive, too".

"Not a patch on you, of course, Duchess," he said as he prepared enthusiastically for bed that night, "but very nicely turned out, and a jolly solid sort all around, I would say."

"For goodness' sake, Basil, you make her sound like a horse!"

"Well if she is, she's a hunter to your thoroughbred filly, my dear. She did offer to walk Mungo, though. Said she'll happily pop in and feed him whenever we're away. Could be useful, don't you think? I gave her the back door key just in case."

Rosamund considered expressing her disquiet at this, but it had been a long day and she was exhausted. Besides, she could not articulate her unease to herself, let alone explain it to her husband. Added to which, she knew Kathy was friendly with Joy's brother, and she did not want Basil to get onto the subject of Edmund. He had ranted all the way back from The White House after Rosamund's tentative suggestion she might do some voluntary work at the Port Sanctuary.

"Good God, whyever would you do that?" he had spluttered, before imparting his extremely partial views on "down-and-outs" and "benefit fraudsters".

"Oh stop it, Basil," Rosamund had replied patiently. "You know they're not just dropouts." She was calm in the knowledge that Basil was being inflammatory, and was, in fact, a generous benefactor of the Port Sanctuary. The Pendlegrass family had set up the charity in memory of Joy and Edmund's brother Piers, following his death in service in Northern Ireland.

"I know, Duchess," he had said, continuing the discussion when they arrived home. "Many of them have done wonderful things; nevertheless, some are addicts, alcoholics and vagrants and I don't want my fragrant wife getting her hands dirty there, please. One of them is bound to fall in love with you, and then we'll be in a right bugger's muddle. You'll end up with a ruddy stalker if we're not careful. Leave it to the likes of Frank Fielding to roll up their sleeves ... that place isn't for you. I am happy to increase our standing order, if you would like – I think what those poor sods need is your money, not your time. I, on the other hand ..." he continued, with a glint in his eye.

A small part of Rosamund felt that Basil was right; much as she wanted to help, to do the right thing, she had only once visited the Port Sanctuary. The desperation in the eyes of its visitors had shaken her.

"Perhaps I could see whether they need any help in the office ...?" she countered feebly.

"No!" said Basil, and she wanted to hug him with relief. "You are an angel to want to do it, Duchess, but no. Now, come here and give me a cuddle."

*

178

At The White House, Hugh sat on the bed beside his wife, who was propped against the pillow wearing an apricot bed jacket and holding a cup of cocoa with her good hand. Her eye was bulging and blue, her left wrist was in plaster and her face was pale.

"Poor Tinkerbell," Hugh said tenderly. "I'm sorry I wasn't here to look after you." Joy smiled wanly and said nothing. "It was jolly lucky Rosamund had the foresight to ring Gillian at Westminster, and that she keeps such close tabs on me and had Tom's number."

Still, his wife said nothing. Unaccustomed to her silence, Hugh filled the gaps awkwardly, telling her about his journey from town and how worried he had been when the call came in. He skirted the issue of having been at Tom's house.

Eventually, Joy spoke: "I think it would be better if you sleep in the spare room this evening," she said flatly. "I am black and blue all over, and will only keep you awake." She turned her head away from her husband and closed her eyes.

Hugh wrung his hands, not quite sure how to deal with his uncharacteristically circumspect wife. He sensed this was the calm before the storm. She was bound to be angry and hurt that he had sought sanctuary at Tom and Jake's, and humiliated that Rosamund had tracked him down there. She was not asleep, Hugh knew that much; nor was she going to engage in conversation, though, so he went to the kitchen and poured himself a large whisky.

Upstairs, Joy lay quietly in place, eyes closed. Her mind scrambled to control a tempest of emotions: the pain and humiliation of her accident superseded by jealousy, disgust and disbelief. An angry inner monologue listed Hugh's sins, berating him for knowing Tom's address, having his phone number and visiting him – for keeping secrets from her. But a whisper of conscience interrupted: *He could not tell you. He could not share this with you; you have made it impossible for him to do so.*

Joy tried to steer her mind away from the whirlpool yet to be faced by navigating Tom's catalogue of crimes: drawing his father into his mucky little world, driving a wedge between husband

and wife, tempting his father with his depraved lifestyle. And the whisper returned, asking: *What did you expect? What are you afraid of? Why are you so fearful?*

She tried to appease her conscience by facing it head on. Tom was a homosexual, and Joy did not like it. *Why didn't she like it?* Because it was wrong. Because she did not understand it. Because it was unnatural. *And because it is embarrassing? And because you feel left out? And because you are afraid that the old rumours about Hugh might be true?*

Joy would not, could not, listen. She opened her eyes and turned on the radio. She needed to be in control. She pushed her mental torment away and succumbed to the fatigue seeping up from her toes. A delicious cocktail of painkillers and brandy, along with the subsiding of adrenaline, began to work its magic until the sea of anxiety gradually calmed, allowing the rocks of reason to peep above the surface. She began to breathe more easily, and surrendered to the stillness.With the calm came clarity, and with that, a vision: her beautiful, kind, gentle Tom. His image was so clear that Joy could reach out and feel his warmth, and it was more painful than anything she had ever had to endure. She yielded to the delight of her beloved son, the sight of him, the smell of him, the feel of him, and then she pushed him away. Joy could only bear life without Tom by denying him completely, never thinking of him and never speaking of him. She was a woman for whom weakness was not an option. She was incapable of making herself vulnerable to anybody, even to her husband, who sat downstairs reading the papers alone while his wife looked into the eye of the emotional storm. She knew that it would eventually settle, however, and then – only then – would she feel able to speak.

"Coffee?" Joy asked as Hugh entered the kitchen the following morning. He was surprised to see her already up and smartly dressed, a silk scarf suspending her broken wrist at shoulder height.

"Yes, thank you." Hugh went to kiss her, and felt her stiffen. "You're looking very elegant this morning. How's the wrist?"

"Absolutely fine," she replied, moving away. Her hair was done up in a bouffant and lacquered, and she wore a deep red lipstick.

"All the same, you don't look awfully well," he said. "Are you sure you should be up?" Joy handed Hugh his coffee, then sat at the kitchen table without replying. She leafed tersely through the post, carefully turning her swollen eye away from her husband.

"Though I must say, you're doing frightfully well with one arm." Hugh again received no response. "Listen, Tinkerbell, we must talk about what happened yesterday."

Joy looked up from the post without expression. "I would have thought it was perfectly simple," she said. "I slipped and bumped my head."

"You know I don't mean that," sighed Hugh. Joy put her cup down and looked coldly at her husband.

"Then tell me, Hugh," she said. "What exactly do you mean? Do you mean that we should talk about you storming off without so much as a by-your-leave? Or perhaps about the fact that you chose to go to the place you knew would hurt me the most."

"I didn't –"

"Or maybe you'd like to discuss the fact that, without my knowledge, you have obviously been in touch with – with – you have obviously been in touch all along." Hugh noticed his wife cleverly despatch an escaping tear and looked away. "Which is it, Hugh? Which of these things do you feel we should discuss?"

"I think we should talk about why it has hurt you so much that I went to Tom and Jake's."

"I couldn't care less that you went to 'Tom and Jake's'," she spat. "They disgust me, and, frankly, so do you." She pushed back the table as best she could, one-handed, and got to her feet. "Incidentally, I'm afraid we're going to have to make a few economies. A couple of investments I've made have gone sour." Hugh looked at her sadly. She was so brittle and spiteful, it pained him. "Your fancy car will have to go, for starters."

"Sit down Joy," he said softly, getting to his feet and pulling out her chair. "I'm worried about you."

Joy stood, proud and tall, in the doorway; but it was plain to see that her lipstick had been applied badly, her hair was cemented into an unflattering shape and her right eye, of course, was swollen and closed. Hugh saw that she was mustering a retort, collecting her dignity for that final slap in the face she delivered so well. But instead, she closed both eyes for a few seconds, inhaled deeply and attempted to smooth out her skirt with her one good hand.

"Come on," said Hugh, taking her hand and leading her to the table. "Let me look after you."

The position of the surrendered wife was alien to Joy. She walked to the table and delivered the full extent of their financial disaster almost robotically. Hugh listened, first in shock, then exasperation and finally anger.

"The bloody charlatan," he said. "Lying, devious, cheating little lowlife. I'll see him in prison."

"You won't," said Joy in resignation. "Because he might sail close to the wind, but Lewis is no fool, and he hasn't, as far as I can establish, broken a law in the land."

"Poor Frank," said Hugh distractedly.

"I don't think we need worry about *him*," Joy said. "If it wasn't for Frank Fielding, we wouldn't be in this position. It was he who introduced us in the first place." Joy told Hugh the story of Frank's drinks party, emphasising the attendance of the minor royals but failing to mention that Bill Lewis had sent her a Rolls-Royce or taken her to lunch at The Ivy. Even so, Hugh put his head in his hands and sighed.

"How could you be so gullible?" he asked, and Joy bristled.

"*Gullible*?" she shouted, "Gullible! Says the man who ..." she petered out, but Hugh challenged her.

"Go on, Joy. 'The man who' what?"

She got up from the table and said, quietly: "The man who can't even keep his own son under control. You're just going to have to accept it, Hugh. The gravy train is over. You'll have to make your own money for a change. Face it like a man, for once in your life."

"Something that you, my dear, have been quite intent on doing yourself for the last thirty years," Hugh said in a low voice.

TWENTY

ROSAMUND FELT GUILTY enjoying a day of pampering at the gleaming new spa, while Joy was at her lowest ebb.

"It's a treat from Basil; he does spoil me!" she had exclaimed while taking tea at The White House before registering her friend's sad, swollen face and kicking herself for sounding so indulged and happy. Joy had received the results of a bone-density scan after her surprisingly bad fracture and was struggling with the news that she was osteoporotic. She was to meet her consultant that day to discuss a course of treatment.

Once inside the sumptuous salon, Rosamund was determined to cast aside her concerns and enjoy the day. Joy had suggested she try a post-facial blow-dry, and, emerging from the beauty room with greasy hair, Rosamund felt grateful for her friend's advice. She wore new clothes, sporting slim-fit, geometric-patterned Capri pants and a crisp, white shirt; a new navy swing coat hung neatly on the salon rack. Her hair washed and clean, a junior wrapped a smart black towel round Rosamund's head in a turban, and she was ushered to a row of opulent salon chairs. Catching sight of her reflection in the mirror, Rosamund was amazed to find a radiant face glowing with happiness, her skin bearing a new luminosity and her eyes sparkling.

The junior served tea with dainty lemon biscuits; feeling rather naughty, Rosamund settled down to indulge in the latest celebrity news. A familiar voice sounded across the salon, and from the corner of her eye she was suddenly horrified to see Kathy McConnell stride across the room, a black towel twisted on her head and a junior in hot pursuit. She took the vacant chair beside Rosamund, dismissing the girl with a peremptory, "No, I'll sit here, thank you." A quick comb-through, and the two women were alone.

Rosamund's voice was choked when she said hello. The mirror image that only moments earlier had projected a flattering countenance had darkened, and in the absence of makeup, imprisoned by robes and towels, Rosamund felt horribly exposed. She could clearly remember discussing her spa day plans in front of Kathy at The White House, and felt a creeping realisation that this encounter was no fluke. She forced herself to meet Kathy's eye in the mirror.

"Do you like the new colour?" the stylist asked Kathy,

"Oh, I do," said Kathy delightedly, pointing to Rosamund: "it's the same colour as my friend's, isn't it?" Rosamund swallowed hard. Her good manners dictated a polite response, but her instinct told her to run; she felt surprisingly afraid. She jumped as the manicurist took her hand, but recovered her composure and instructed the beautician to blunt and paint her nails coral pink. The stylist combed through Rosamund's hair and she braced herself against the assault of sharp scissors and sawing emery boards while heat radiated from Kathy's toxic smile in the adjacent chair.

"I think I'll live dangerously and have mine blunted for a change, and coral pink polish too, please," Kathy commanded. Rosamund clutched her magazine, willing the nail varnish to dry and her shaking legs to rally to her command.

"Getting yourself glammed up for tomorrow?" enquired Kathy.

"Tomorrow?" Rosamund felt sweat trickling between her shoulder blades.

"The Village cricket match?" Rosamund had completely forgotten about the so-called "Bashes" and was about to reply, when Kathy continued: "It was so sweet of you to invite me. Should we meet up earlier, or shall I see you there?"

With a sinking heart, Rosamund remembered that Basil had indeed invited the Willoughbys' housekeeper on the night of Joy's fall. "A bit of a thank-you for going above and beyond, don't you think, Duchess?" he had said.

"I think, err, it would be best if we see you there," Rosamund replied vaguely, then, needing to wrest back control of the conversation she continued, briskly: "You are looking after Mrs Willoughby so marvellously, Kathy. You've been at The White House all hours. Angus must be missing you. How is he?"

"Angus is dead," Kathy replied, reaching for her lapsang souchong tea.

"*Dead*?" Rosamund cried out. She quickly determined to stay calm, and added: "I am so sorry. You caught me by surprise. Dead? How awful, how terribly sad." Then, dreading the answer, she added quietly: "Whatever happened?"

Kathy offered Rosamund a biscuit. "Drank himself to death," she said conversationally. "It had to happen someday."

"Oh, dear, I ... How did ...?"

"He lost his keys, and I was fast asleep and didn't hear him knocking, probably flat out with all that chasing after Mrs Willoughby, don't you think?" she asked, looking directly into Rosamund's eyes as if to challenge her. Then, with a shrug, she said: "Anyway, it was a chilly night, one thing led to another and I found him dead on the doorstep the next morning." Kathy signalled to the junior for more tea.

Rosamund was paralysed with sympathy for the poor man. What a ghastly way to die. She remembered Edmund describing Kathy's bungalow: such a tiny place, and a small garden. How could Kathy not have heard his calls? The woman picked up every whisper at The White House. Rosamund longed for Basil's safe embrace. He would know what to do, she thought. He would understand. But would he? After all, he had blithely given the woman their house keys, and at the end of the day, what was there to understand? The coincidence of a hairdressing appointment, a similar hairstyle, a tragic accident ... Kathy chatted companionably, and Rosamund became aware that her robotic smiles and nodding acquiescence were fuelling the woman's delusion of friendship. "... And then you'll never guess who I bumped into on my way to the salon? Frank Fielding! Well ..."

Rosamund thought of her dear friend undergoing tests at the hospital, and, buoyed up by their many years of friendship, dug deep and summoned her inner Joy, drawing herself up in her chair and replying authoritatively: "You must have been mistaken. Mr Fielding is at the charity today; we left Riverside Lane at the same time."

If Kathy noticed the change in Rosamund's tone, she did not show it. The stylists simultaneously dispensed final spritzes of hairspray.

"May I show you ladies the back?" asked a junior, holding two mirrors aloft. Kathy preened and patted, but Rosamund was too busy digging in her bag for money and keys to appreciate the mahogany sheen and perfectly symmetrical cut to the collar.

Kathy patted her own identical chestnut bob and declared: "We look like sisters!"

Rosamund stood abruptly. "I have a lunch appointment, so I'm afraid I can't offer you a lift," she said coolly.

"Don't worry," Kathy replied smoothly, "There's a taxi picking me up in half an hour. See you on Saturday!" she called after the disappearing Rosamund, who marched out of the salon.

"Your sister has left her coat behind, Mrs McConnell," said the junior.

"I'll take it!" Kathy laughed indulgently. "She is lovely, but quite hopeless! I don't think she'd last a day without me watching over her!"

Meanwhile, by the riverbank, Molly Mulholland sprawled on a tartan rug and gazed happily at the expanse of blue sky. Her chocolate-button eyes shone underneath Cecilia's sunglasses, which were propped on her nose. A vanilla-scented breeze wafted around the magnolia tree, and beneath it Molly watched Luca's cigarette smoke swirl around a profusion of pollen spores and dandelion wisps, flitting and drifting in the eternal dance of springtime.

Molly was proud of the mountain of cupcakes piled high on a plate between Cecilia and Luca, though she was disappointed that, unlike her, they had not crammed several into their mouths already. She had made them in a hurry after Luca invited them on a picnic, spooning heaps of sugar into the mixture (but not so many eggs, as she was not overly keen on them). The cockatoo or cock-a-leekie stuff from Cecilia's cupboard was just the ticket for the icing, which was a splendid, vivid blue and bore merry little jelly babies that reminded Molly of the grown-ups whose laughter pinged and ponged between them like a jolly game of table tennis.

She was delighted that Cecilia was so smiley. She had seen her sad too many times since her Mummy had died and Clive had gone, and she looked prettier, Molly thought, when her mouth did not turn down at the corners. A flock of green parakeets flew low, shattering the peace with their high-pitched caws, and Molly leaped from the rug with a howl.

"Look Cecilia! The parrots have just pooed on my dress!"

"Oh dear, so they have!" Molly was annoyed to see Cecilia glance at Luca and suppress her giggles. "It's a sign of luck you know," she said; but, looking at her dirty dress, Molly did not feel much reassured.

Then, behind her, a deep voice remarked: "Parakeets bring a touch of tropical glamour to our gardens, don't you think?" It was Reverend James, enjoying a late-afternoon stroll along the tow-path. He crouched down to Molly's level on the grassy bank before continuing: "All the same, it is very rude of them to use your dress as a lavatory."

"But you're religious, and too important to laugh about poo," Molly replied cautiously. "Would you like a cupcake?"

"Just because I'm religious doesn't mean I can't laugh about poo," the vicar said. "Indeed, I declare laughter to be the highest religious quality." He accepted a cake from Molly's muddy hand. "Wouldn't it be lovely if humankind could agree that, each year, for one hour on an allotted day at a certain time, the whole world would unite in laughter? It would help to dispel the darkness and stupidity on this planet." Molly thought that sounded like a very good idea, and Reverend James continued: "Laughter relaxes you and makes you feel light; it makes life a more beautiful experience."

As he spoke, he tickled her gently, and Molly began giggling uncontrollably, a rumble of thunder from deep within that pumped the blood round her body at a swift speed. She thought that if she were a parakeet, she would fly as high as the sky, into the universe, up to Heaven, and sit on a fluffy, pink cloud and drink tea with Mummy. In the distance, she could hear the peal of an ice-cream van, and when Cecilia nodded her acquiescence, Molly thought her heart would explode with happiness.

"When children laugh, it is a joy," the vicar observed, joining the adults on the rug. "Their whole body is involved; you can even see their toes laughing." Molly ate her ice cream and tuned out as the grown-ups began a complicated conversation about science.

But after a few minutes the vicar was saying: "England is one of the most haunted countries in the world. There are ghost-hunting tours of ancient pubs, hotels and country houses, and television shows with large audiences ..." *Ghosts!* Molly's ears pricked up.

"Reverend James, do you believe in ghosts?" she asked, interrupting him mid-sentence. "My friends say they don't believe in them, but I do! I see Mummy's ghost all the time. She comes to me when I'm having a horrible nightmare, and shoos it away in exactly the same way she did when she was alive." The vicar smiled and patted his knee. Molly climbed on, careful not to muddy his clothes with her sandals.

"Why should we deny the existence of ghosts?" he asked. "We know there are many kinds of creatures living alongside us. Look around you – birds, fish, insects, animals, they all enhance the beauty and variety of life on Earth. If there are ghosts among us too, do they not simply make the world a more interesting place?" Molly looked around and tried to keep up with what the vicar was saying. Cecilia and Luca were not listening. "Wouldn't it be a bit narrow-minded for human beings to deny the existence of life forms different from our own? I never cease to be amazed by the gall of scientists. They declare they have now proved the non-existence of spirits, or the soul, or second sight, or telepathy, when thousands of ordinary people can contradict them from their own experience."

Molly was not sure she understood, but it sounded in the spirit of how she felt. Her ice cream finished, she wandered off to find a bin, then changed her mind when she saw the lady who played the church organ standing still under the tall yellow tree, staring at them in a way that made Molly shiver. She hid the sticky wrapper in her pocket and ran back to Cecilia.

Ivy stood alone, watching the happy group from the shade of the towering laburnum. A sudden gust of wind sent its petrol-yellow pods spiralling about her, but she remained silent and still, her gloved hands clutching the instructions Nigel Bond had given her that morning.

Ivy felt no emotion, observing Clive's girlfriend flirt with the American. She had no feelings for the woman one way or another, and had always known Cecilia Honeychurch to be an unsuitable choice for Clive. Now that she had the true identity of Luca Tempesta, she was certain the caterer would pay a high price for her dalliance. Nigel had tasked Ivy with tracking Tempesta's movements, and she would, as she always had done, obey his command.

She had listened keenly when the new vicar joined the party and began his discourse on ghosts. Ivy saw manifestations all the time: opaque shadows dancing alongside the stars and patterns that disturbed her vision. Sister Mary Agatha was a regular visitor, appearing in the daylight hours, her last, unopened letter in her hand and a beseeching smile on her face. Ivy knew that in order to vanquish her friend she would have to open the missive; but she could not. At night, it was her father, the deacon, who visited, sanctimoniousness etched on his cruel face. But the presence that disturbed Ivy the most was the child. The plain little girl in the red dress, who reached out from the past to invade the present yet remained frustratingly out of reach.

The sun crept behind a cloud and Ivy tightened her cardigan around her shoulders. The deceiver is collecting up his belongings, she thought, observing the conspiratorial smile that passed between Luca and Cecilia as he folded the rug and ruffled the little girl's hair.

Like lambs to the slaughter. The Honeychurch woman would discover soon enough the error of her ways, and there would be consequences. "The Lord giveth and the Lord taketh away," she muttered as she watched Reverend James bid his farewells. "Blessed be the name of the Lord." Ivy lifted herself lightly off the wooden seat and made her way home to Peter the Rock.

Later that evening, at his usual table in the corner of the Restaurant, Nigel Bond held Luca's gaze with cool contemplation. The American was pretending to stare at a point just beyond the window, but Nigel knew he was studying him. The pretty redheaded caterer joined him for dinner, and he noted the American's tight, inscrutable mask lift to portray happy delight.

Nigel recognised the signs of tradecraft; he knew the dark arts of espionage well. This man would lie, deceive, steal and double-cross on behalf of his government. "Bravo, my man, you're good," he thought, as he watched Luca make doe eyes at the woman. Her trusting, animated face reminded Nigel of his daughter, except this one was not fool enough to hide her light beneath a wimple and habit. He dismissed an unbidden memory frostily; he had no time for sentiment, and no time for the Church. He could almost hear that fool Ivy Midwinter praying: honour thy father and thy mother, never kill, commit adultery, steal, bear false witness or covet your neighbour's home and hearth. To hell with that – such basic morality did not apply to the likes of him and Mr Tempesta. Nigel subscribed to the Oliver Cromwell ethos: "... Some men are called to great services, in the doing of which they are excused from the common rule of morality." A waiter delicately dissected the lamb shank, and Nigel continued to stare at Luca, dabbing absently at escaping spittle as he chewed. "What lured you into our dangerous lair, Mr Tempesta?" he wondered, blinking his ancient lizard eyes and savouring a mouthful of finest Burgundy, which was instantly replenished by his obsequious waiter. "Do you work for your country, or against it? In my day, people became spies through political ideology; now they betray their motherland for excitement, money and sex. Which one are you, my friend? And what is your connection to Codename: Kuznetsoy?"

His repast complete, Nigel folded his napkin as a signal to a tall man in a dark overcoat on the opposite pavement, who crossed the street and entered the Restaurant. Still as a heron, beady eyes on his prey, Nigel sat while the tall man signed a docket at the reception, then walked to the table and stood while his charge rose, unaided. He then took his arm without expression or acknowledgement. As he was escorted from the Restaurant, the old man locked his unblinking eyes with Luca's. "Bide your time, Bond," he told himself. "Soon you will know everything."

Cecilia had been keeping busy. It was over between her and Clive now, about that she was left in no doubt; but as that door closed, a new one had opened. Her agent – for she had finally plucked up the courage to call – had still been interested in the cookbook, and she was working hard to finish recipes and sketches for it. Together they had approached an established publishing house, recently taken over by one Nicholas Jowett. After a quick Google search, and judging by his website photograph, Cecilia had decided they would get along splendidly, and they had arranged to meet in London to discuss the manuscript further.

Even so, Cecilia had not forgotten about Luca, nor his conspicuous silence since her saucy text to him. So when he had rung her up out of the blue and invited her to a picnic, she was pleasantly surprised.

The American ended a perfect day with an invitation to dinner at the Restaurant, without Molly in tow this time – just the two of them, he promised. She had dressed with care, smoothing her unruly hair into a sleek chignon and steaming the creases out of a slinky red dress she had never worn (as Clive had declared it "too racy"). She had welcomed Luca's flirtations over a bottle of Rioja. Cecilia was fed up with airy-fairy British men, she told herself, looking seductively into his blue eyes. Over a sublime meal in which Luca appeared to take more pleasure from watching her juggle her seafood than from eating his own, he had taken her hand and aimed his gaze admiringly at her décolletage.

"That's a striking pendant," he said.

"Thank you; it was a gift from my Irish grandmother."

"That explains your red hair, which is as beautiful as a Galway sunset."

"I think you've kissed the Blarney Stone, Mr Tempesta," she laughed. As she did, she found herself momentarily distracted by an elderly man who was staring at them from the corner of the room, whose papery face seemed strangely familiar.

She shook her head, unable to place him, and sipped her wine. Keen to raise the thorny subject of Sam, she changed tack. "There's something more serious I need to speak to you about, though. There's no way of putting a gloss on this, so I'm just going to come right out and say it." Luca inched closer. "Well, Sam has broken into your attic room and found all sorts of state-of-the-art equipment. He is now determined to think you are a spy."

It sounded preposterous, and Cecilia felt silly. Sneaking a peep from behind her long eyelashes, she was relieved to see that Luca was grinning.

"I knew it!"

"So you don't mind?"

"Are you kidding me? It's his house."

"So you're not a spy?"

"Ha! If I was, would I ever admit it?"

"That's true. Well, what's all the equipment?"

"Come with me, I'll show you," he laughed. "I've been looking for ways to get you alone in a dark room for weeks." Half an hour later, Luca unlocked the creaking attic door at Kingfisher House to reveal a row of sleek aluminium lenses trained out of the four turret windows.

"They're telescopes!" he proclaimed. "My dark secret is nothing more mysterious than a geeky obsession with astronomy." He had evangelised about the constellations until Cecilia, uncomfortable with the carnal thoughts she was having in the room above her ex-lover's bedroom, invited him back to her house for coffee. The moment when Luca had finally seduced her had been deliciously embarrassing.

"Where are the coffee cups?" he had called out, as she filled two glasses with generous tots of Armagnac.

"Top cupboard in the kitchen!"

She remembered too late and, spinning on her heels, found Luca delightedly waving the vibrating Rampant Rabbit above his head.

"Wow, you British are more liberated than I have given you credit for," he laughed jubilantly. "Here am I just looking for a china tea service, and look what I find!" Cecilia blushed crimson and grabbed the sex toy as she tried to explain, but the words came out as a jumble.

"So Felicity Thomas gave it to you, right?"

"Yes," said Cecilia giggling uncontrollably.

"Well, this village is getting more exciting by the minute," Luca whispered, gathering her up in his arms.

Cecilia nestled into Luca's embrace.

Afterwards, she stretched out on her wrought-iron bed and offered up a silent prayer of thanks for a wonderful night of passion. She listened to the sweet, haunting song of a nightingale hailing the dawn through her open window, not having heard such warbling since her childhood. The loud, melodious sound stirred long-forgotten feelings of tenderness and magic. Thank heavens for feisty Felicity, she thought, as she drifted in and out of sleep; she has turned out to be a better friend than I could ever have imagined.

The nightingale took flight and Cecilia snuggled down under the covers, listening to the more familiar sounds of the gentle ticking of her bedside clock and water dripping from the faulty bathroom tap. Cecilia didn't know which she was more excited about: the morning, when she and Luca could resume their lovemaking, or her first meeting with Nicholas Jowett at lunchtime.

TWENTY-ONE

THE SKY ABOVE the Village was duck-egg blue, the cricket pitch below, a fresh pea green. A scent of truffle oil drifted on a breeze that tickled the leaves and set the daisies dancing. Basil paced the perimeter of the hallowed turf, sporting a clipboard and a panama hat. He wore cream flannels and a navy blazer adorned with bronze buttons bearing his family crest. A brief gust flurried his pages, prompting him to remove his hat and squint up at the sky. Reassured by the absence of clouds, he continued pacing, stopping intermittently to scribble importantly before resuming his patrol.

At home, Basil's wife dressed with care; the confidence that had bloomed after her visit to the Professor had all but withered since her spa day, but the Bashes was one of the highlights of Rosamund's year, and she was determined that nothing would spoil it. She pulled on her dress and smoothed it over her hips, revelling in the weight of the fabric and the reassuring hoist provided by the clever elasticised lining. She wondered what Joy and Basil would think of this departure from her classic style, and felt a defiant tingle at the reaction she might get. She pressed new black studs into her ears and tried to ignore Kathy McConnell's insidious presence in the shadows of her mind. Rosamund had told nobody about the fears she knew would appear foolish and neurotic in the light of day.

She had nearly confided in Bianca, who had stopped in Riverside Lane to admire Rosamund's new hairdo and invite her on another shopping trip. Her neighbour had taken her hesitation as acquiescence, and before she knew it they were speeding along the dual carriageway, Rosamund clenching her fists tightly as Bianca made a nail appointment on her mobile, sipped Diet Coke and chatted amicably. Her exuberance was contagious, and Rosamund began to experience a giddy delight, pushing aside her worries and surrendering to Bianca's inane chatter.

"I saw Joy!" she announced. "Bleedin' 'ell, she looked dreadful. Hugh been bashing 'er about again?"

Rosamund laughed. "No, she fell. I think her eye looks worse than it is, but her wrist is very painful."

"Aw," said Bianca. "I felt ever so sorry for 'er. Went round later to drop some flowers and a bottle of plonk, but Kathy McCreepy came to the door and looked at me like I was something nasty under 'er shoe."

That was it: Rosamund's moment to pick up on Bianca's comment. "Do you really find her creepy?' she would ask, and Bianca would reply, "God yes, the woman is pure evil." Rosamund would tell her about the hairdressers, about Kathy's parasitic attentions at Felicity's, about her cloying search for approval on every outfit and the way she eavesdropped at The White House, oppressively attending to Rosamund's every need. She would explain how Kathy had conned a house key out of Basil, killed her husband and might quite possibly have designs on –

"You OK?"

Rosamund realised they had come to a halt and were parked, two wheels on the pavement, outside the boutique they had visited on their last shopping trip. "Look! 'Your dress' from last time is in the window! It must be fate!"

Rosamund could not believe she had been persuaded to buy a dress better suited to Bianca Fielding. It was unlike anything she had ever worn before: a wraparound, beige V-neck with a black animal print on a heavy stretch jersey that clung to her curves, making Rosamund feel like an assertive achiever rather than the passive victim she was allowing herself to be. On the morning of the cricket match, she moderated the extremes of the garment to better suit the occasion as well as her age and personality; where Bianca would have worn heavy jewellery and an uplifting bra, Rosamund wore a modest black camisole, and in place of towering heels, she slipped on patent ballet pumps. She scraped back the hair she had spent so much time and money having bobbed and blow-dried and secured it defiantly into a clip.

It was time to leave. Basil's transistor radio warned of a storm, but Rosamund glanced out the window and then dug out a pair of black Jackie O sunglasses. There could be no chance of rain today. She drew her shoulders back, took a deep breath and tried not to look behind her as she double-locked the house and headed up the road to the cricket pitch.

The Willoughbys were also heading to the Bashes. Hugh strode ahead, pushing Myrtle faster than was entirely comfortable and trying not to let his bat – balanced across the handles of the wheel-chair – fall onto her head. Joy followed at a leisurely pace; it felt good to be out on such a beautiful morning. The Bashes were her favourite Village event; she enjoyed the Village in bloom, the summer *fête*, the Christmassy stuff and the open gardens, but those required input, whereas all Joy needed to do on this day was turn up and watch. It was a long-held tradition that the ladies of the Village dress up for the occasion, and Joy wore a flowery chiffon shirtwaister and a large, straw sunhat that fell over her left eye, hiding the remnants of the bruising. Watching her handsome husband marching ahead, elegant in whites and a panama, she felt a pang of regret over her recent behaviour as well as a peep of nostalgia.

"Do you know, this will be our twenty-fourth match together," she called after him. "We haven't missed one since we were married! Add the games you played before you joined up, Hugh – you must have played nearly thirty in all!" But Joy's words were lost to the breeze and Hugh, who was running through the batting order in his head, ploughed on, oblivious to his wife's olive branch.

He did not think of himself as a competitive man, but he did like to win. He hoped the opposition would field fewer students and more pensioners than last year, when the match had been a sham. He and Basil had waited all year to get their own back. Hugh had been a serious cricketer in his youth, representing the county and later the army, before being sent home with the dishonourable discharge that had inadvertently led to his marriage. With nowhere else to go, he had returned to the Village and The White House. He had moved in with his disappointed mother, who, obligingly, died of a heart attack ten days later. He had not played much since then, save for the occasional village match and the odd turnout for Rotary. He had endured a trying week, and to be on the pitch with nothing but the crack of leather on willow, the clatter of bails on stumps and the occasional applause was just what he needed.

Joy spotted Luca, and was pleased they had invited him, even though Basil had been extremely cross when he discovered she had shunned the usual selection of clubhouse sandwiches in favour of the Crown's beer-battered cod and thrice-cooked chips, exquisitely presented in newspaper cones.

"It's a cricket match, not a ruddy cocktail party," Basil had objected, but she had dismissed his harrumphs, pointing out that, as ambassadors for the Village, they had a responsibility to uphold its reputation as one of the gastronomic capitals of the world. She waved at her new friend and looked around to see who else had arrived. Her brother Edmund would be there, of course, ineffectual and insipid as always, and she supposed Rosamund would have insisted upon inviting Rupert, whose presence would highlight the absence of Penny and Tom. She allowed herself a brief memory of her son playing wicket-keeper on Founder's Day, while Penny cartwheeled around the boundary in tennis whites. Tom had been such a fine boy, so fit and strong – not a snivelling bed-wetter like Rupert Braithwaite. Who could have foreseen the way things would work out?

Felicity and Bianca entered through the picket gate, giggling like schoolgirls, both in full-length, colourful dresses and flat sandals. Joy had never seen them look so pretty. Bianca had evidently taken Joy's advice that the dress code was more rowing club than nightclub; her attire today was far better than her tight, Day-Glo ensemble from the previous year. She turned to greet them, but Hugh cut across her.

"Where's Frank?" he barked. "He's batting third. He is coming, isn't he?"

"Don't get yer knickers in a knot, Hughie," laughed Bianca as she squished up against him for a kiss. "'E'll be 'ere. Got new whites especially!" Then Felicity draped her arms around him, and Joy swallowed hard.

"Good," said Hugh. "Well, as long as –" Basil called him away just then, and Joy was relieved to spy Rosamund passing by through the window. Determined that her husband should witness her being sociable and light-hearted, she skipped to the door – only to collide with Kathy. The smile froze on Joy's face. This was very awkward. The two women had not spoken since the previous week, when Joy had given Kathy her notice. There could be no denying that economies had to be made in the wake of the Bill Lewis scam, and Kathy had provided the perfect excuse by gossiping to the journalist. It had been a difficult interview, and although Kathy had behaved with decorum, something in her eyes when she handed over her keys had chilled Joy, who had reached for the sherry the moment she left. And here she was now, at the Bashes, smiling confidently and kissing her employer's cold cheek. Worse still, following in her wake and wearing his trademark gormless smile was her own brother Edmund! Joy stiffened and opened her mouth to speak – surely there could not be something between them?

Then Bianca screeched: "Ros – a – mund Braithwaite! Rock that look!" All eyes turned to where Rosamund stood, smiling, in the doorway.

Felicity watched as Anya, the Kazakh supermodel, sashayed into the clubhouse with all the glamour of a silver-screen siren. A slathering Rupert Braithwaite locked his red Porsche and rushed to keep up with his statuesque companion. Felicity's invisibility complex heightened as she watched Luca appraise the model's lithesome curves, and she turned away. It was galling to be usurped by a beauty half her age and half as lovely as she knew she had once been. Harley insisted there were no beautiful women under the age of thirty, but two decades had passed since he had first uttered those pearls – and the wisdom was starting to lose its lustre.

Luca looked handsome in cricket whites, and Felicity admired his bright blue eyes and the deep grooves down the side of his mouth. He must have laughed a lot, she thought, realising she knew nothing about the man, but that he now knew almost everything about her. She had expected to feel happy after their time together, but opening up her feelings had left her feeling brittle and vulnerable. Osteoporosis of the emotions, she thought, trying to ignore the hot sweat that descended with increasing frequency these days.

Luca looked towards her, and his eyes lit up. Felicity's heart leaped; she raised her hand before realising the smile was not for her, but for Cecilia, who had entered the room behind her. A dark mist of envy settled in, and although Felicity tried to ignore it, her mind turned to insults. *What is she wearing?* She noted Cecilia's long, flowing red hair and plain white cotton dress. Pulling down her neckline to reveal the hint of plunging bra, she sidled up to Luca at the bar, deftly spinning him round out of Cecilia's line of vision.

"I delivered the package for you," she declared winsomely, and was rewarded with a big grin.

"Thanks, Felicity, I knew I could count on you."

"It was no trouble; I was passing through Acton anyway."

"Was anyone in?"

"Oh, I didn't ring the doorbell," Felicity lied. "You asked me not to, remember?" She had his undivided attention now, but did not feel inclined to tell him the door had been answered by a statuesque brunette with a foreign accent who had quizzed her about his location.

"What was the property like?" he asked casually.

"Hmm, you know, the usual Thirties-style suburban semi."

"So I guess I owe you a very large glass of something sparkling. Champagne? Dinner soon?" Felicity did not know what the package had contained, and she had not asked. She vaguely recalled Luca offering an explanation – something about a long-lost niece. It had not sounded very plausible, but the memory was blurred by booze.

"Ooh, champagne, yes please! And dinner would be lovely!" she gushed, casting Cecilia a triumphant look before whispering "*Adieu*" into his ear and sauntering outside with the self-satisfaction of a stalking cat.

Meanwhile, in the pavilion, Bianca greeted Tallulah, who *had* turned up dressed for a nightclub, and smelling of tobacco. Bianca winced, thinking what her father would say, but could not help smiling as their daughter pushed Anya aside and embraced Rupert, winking at her mother mischievously. "Sucker," her expression declared, as he suavely filled two glasses of champagne and passed them over with a flourish. Bianca rolled her eyes at Tallulah, a look that questioned what this beautiful daughter of hers was doing with such a jumped-up little twit, and Tallulah wandered over, raising the glasses triumphantly.

"Like candy from a baby," she laughed, "and I ponced a glass for you too, Mum! Have you seen Rupert's shoes? Dad might be small, but at least he doesn't overcompensate with Cuban heels!"

Bianca laughed. "'E doesn't need to, love; unlike young Mr Braithwaite, yer Dad has a *big* personality!"

"Well, I am going to teach Rupert a lesson he won't forget in a hurry," Tallulah chuckled, but a cacophony of yapping and yelping – followed by an angry boom from Basil – drowned out her words. Knowing the source of the chaos, she shouted: "Come 'ere, you little bleeder!" Then, slipping off her heels, she ran onto the pitch, stooping and weaving amongst the players and commanding Dubonnet to "come awf".

Rosamund wandered in with an empty jug. "Lemonade, please, when you have a moment," she told the barmaid. Then to her son, she said: "Oh, dear, I do think your father might just explode! I had better go and save him!"

"It's not funny!" said Rupert, "That little rat is ruining the game."

Bianca was tempted to tip her drink on his head. Frank might have been forgiving over all the media business after he'd tried to stick up for the Braithwaites, but Bianca still bore Rupert a grudge – and now he dared to insult her dog!

"And by the way, I don't want to be rude, Mother," Rupert continued lazily, "but aren't you a bit long in the tooth for that dress?"

As Rosamund froze, Bianca stepped in angrily to defend her friend. "And *I* don't want to be rude, Rupert," she blurted, "but what're you gonna do for a face when King Kong wants his bum back?" Anya laughed, and Bianca, who had not meant to be funny, was relieved to see her comment had elicited a grateful smile from Rosamund as well.

"Well your father likes it, and that's all that matters to me, Rupert," she said breezily. Taking Anya's arm, she suggested they powder their noses together. "I've got lots of lovely stories I can tell you about Rupert when he was a little boy," she added.

Tallulah whispered into her mother's ear: "Nice repartee, Mummy Dearest. Leave the rest to me." Turning to Rupert she cooed, "Alone at last with the divine Rupert Braithwaite! Let's make up for lost time!"

Cecilia covered her delicate complexion with a wide-brim straw boater, and sprawled on the grass. She was sorry that Sam had used his synaesthesia as an excuse not to attend the cricket match, but she was also secretly relieved. He had called that morning to warn her off: "Don't go, Cecilia, you'll be sorry; Luca is worse than my father. I don't want to see you hurt."

"Don't be ridiculous, Sam," she had replied. "I know it's difficult for you to accept that your Dad and I have split up, but you can't use your disappointment to cast aspersions on Luca's character. You don't even know the man."

"I know he's involved with the Russians, and up to no good," countered Sam. Then he added, accusingly "I saw you all over him at Kingfisher House."

"Sam, Luca was only showing me his telescope."

"I bet he was!" he had yelled, slamming the phone down. Cecilia refused to let his teenage angst spoil such a beautiful day, so she had banished his scowling face from her memory and had not given the matter a moment's thought since. Lulled by the blazing whites and delicious Pimm's, she watched Luca swagger onto the field.

"What are butchers doing here?" he called out, grinning as he pointed to the umpires in their pristine white coats. Cecilia smiled, then gesticulated in mock anger upon noticing he was wearing Clive's expensively crumpled cricket attire and old candy-striped school cap. *He certainly fills it out in all the right places*, she thought – something she would be sure to tell him later.

Making love to Luca had been an awakening, flooding Cecilia with happiness; everything she had touched since had turned to gold. Whether it was magic or pheromones she did not know, but handsome, attentive men seemed to be springing up everywhere. A nattily dressed City worker had caught her eye on the train when she travelled into London to have her first appointment with her publisher; an attractive stranger had sent her a glass of champagne as she revelled in the sunshine on a pavement café; even a wolf-whistle from a workman had elicited a happy response. She would normally have felt tongue-tied stepping into the hallowed offices of Howlett and Snell, but not now. Nicholas was every bit as attractive as his online photograph suggested, and he and Cecilia had hit it off immediately.

"It is going to be so good, Cecilia," he said, casting an appraising eye over her contract. Signed and sealed. She longed to share the news about her recipe book with Luca, and smiled dreamily as Reverend James wandered over from his fielding position.

"I saw you sitting alone under an exultation of mayflies and wanted to check you were all right," he said, waving away the tiny winged insects that flapped riotously above her head.

"I'm well, thank you. In fact, I'm better than that – like the mayflies, I'm triumphant, elated, jubilant even!" A bug made a kamikaze swoop into her drink. "I don't begrudge them their glorious dance; they only have twenty-four hours to mate, after all; but I do wish they'd stay out of my Pimm's!"

Reverend James smiled indulgently. "Elation and jubilance suit you Cecilia; you look wonderful."

"Do you believe in love at first sight, James?"

He crouched beside her, ignoring Basil's apoplectic yells from afar.

"I do. It's a scientific fact that setting eyes on the person of your dreams floods your brain with euphoria-inducing chemicals. The first inkling of love hits twelve different parts of your brain in tandem, and takes a fifth of a second." Basil's angry voice boomed through a loudhailer, and broke their moment of intimacy.

"I wish I could bottle it and keep it forever," Cecilia said.

"I must go. I'm a disappointment to Mr Braithwaite, who expects great things from me because I'm from Jamaica. He doesn't know that I'm only here for the cucumber sandwiches." Reverend James winked.

"I heard that!" shouted Basil, advancing crossly towards them and startling Cecilia, who jumped to her feet.

"My apologies," Reverend James countered smoothly, adopting the stance of a matador facing down a thunderous bull.

"There are team members here who think today is just an excuse for a bit of glorified loafing!" Basil barked.

"Hey, Basil, I'm enjoying catching the rays, but is something going to happen soon?" Luca yelled, sauntering over and winking conspiratorially at Cecilia. "Jeez, cricket is about as exciting as baseball on Valium."

Basil growled. "The glory of cricket is in hitting the winning run or taking the final wicket; it's about strategy and tactics. As the Duke of Wellington once said, 'The Battle of Waterloo was won on the playing fields of Eton.' This country didn't get where it is today without –"

"And Napoleon said that 'an army marches on its stomach,'" interrupted Rosamund, appearing like an angel of mercy with Madeira cake and a jug of iced lemonade. "This will refresh you, darling, but you really must keep your hat on." She set the refreshments down on the lawn, handing her husband a glass while dabbing his brow with a white handkerchief.

Basil smiled beatifically at his wife. "You look ravishing in that dress," he said, clamping his hand onto her bottom and making Rosamund squeal. Turning to Luca and Reverend James, Basil commanded: "As you were!" and marched back onto the pitch.

"Do forgive Basil," said Rosamund, amiably laying a tartan rug down next to Cecilia. "The warm weather tends to bring my husband outside for his battles."

The Village team applauded the victors, and Reverend James presented the ceremonial hammer to the New Town team – an honour normally reserved for Frank Fielding, who had demurred, insisting to everyone's surprise that the vicar was a more appropriate choice to award the Bashes trophy.

"A complete farce!" declared Basil, clapping and smiling as he spoke. "Absolute fiasco! The Fieldings' wretched dog running out on the pitch and peeing all over the field, Luca slathering over the caterer, the vicar chitchatting and missing every catch, Joy Americanising the menu in an absurd effort to transport us to some sort of Hamptons-on-Thames! And why did Ivy have to choose this morning for her wretched organ recital?"

"Oh, darling, how could anyone be put off by the magnificence of the Braithwaite Organ?" Rosamund laughed.

"Quite," replied Reverend James, raising an eyebrow as he came over. "It's only a cricket match, Basil; one needs to put these things into perspective. It's not as if a murder has been committed!"

Rosamund ignored the sight of Kathy clapping on the sidelines, and watched Basil with concern. He took the game so seriously, and would certainly be irritated by Rupert, who had arrived late, forgotten his whites and was now all over the Fielding girl at the bar. Judging from the colour of Basil's lobster-coloured pate, he had caught too much sun, and that would not help his humour.

"Where the hell did Hugh go?" Basil barked, throwing his hands up in despair.

"I was hoping you could tell me," she replied, "it must have been a crisis for them to leave so abruptly. Joy's phone rang, she shrieked and then leaped into the car and headed off at an incredible lick. Left Myrtle here, and everything." Their conversation was interrupted by Kathy, who arrived proffering an elderflower cordial and a pint of cold lager.

"Good God, woman, may you sprout wings!" declared Basil, taking the drink thirstily. "An absolute mind-reader. And your favourite, too, Duchess, eh? How marvellous!"

"A man needs his comforts," replied Kathy soothingly, glancing at Rosamund with an eagle eye.

She smiled weakly and accepted the drink. Then, remembering Joy's brother, she asked Basil: "Is Edmund still here?"

"He certainly is," interjected Kathy. "He wouldn't dream of leaving his mother alone. He's such a kind and generous man. He's been a tower of strength to me since Angus died, there for me in my darkest hour, I don't know how I would have coped without him."

"Oh yes, jolly sorry to hear about Angus's passing, commiserations," mumbled Basil, turning helplessly to his wife, who was lost for words. She wanted desperately to speak to Joy, to be reassured that her dark thoughts over the death of Kathy's husband were nothing more than an overactive imagination, but Joy had rushed off without saying goodbye. She shivered, prompting Basil to wrap an arm around her shoulders. "Come now, Duchess, let's get you into the clubhouse." They headed back to the pavilion together.

"Damned good woman, Kathy," he said. "Lousy timing, losing her job with the Willoughbys when her husband has just died ... It's not like Joy and Hugh to be so heartless. Perhaps we should take her on a couple of days a week. What do you think, Duchess? Give yourself a bit of a treat, eh?"

"No, Basil," said Rosamund sharply; then, tempering her tone, she continued: "She would never have the time, and besides, we're not made of money." Basil stumbled at the pavilion steps. "Are you OK?" Rosamund asked.

"Damned if I know. Suddenly feel dizzy," he said, before straightening up, declaring himself better, tottering forward and announcing: "Actually, no, I feel bloody awful. Must have been that drink."

"Oh, Basil!" said Rosamund. "You've had too much sun. I told you to keep your hat on." Kathy offered the Braithwaites her taxi home – it was the least she could do, she insisted, with a sycophantic smile.

"Edmund can drive me home," she told them. "I shall get delusions of grandeur, though; I feel like lady of the manor in such a grand car! He's even started calling *me* 'Duchess'! Fancy him having the same nickname for me as you, Rosamund!"

Her tinny laughter made Rosamund nauseous. What had started as a perfectly lovely day was descending into a nightmare. She feared for Basil, even beginning to imagine she had seen something suspicious floating in his drink; she was anxious for Joy, too. But above all, Rosamund was afraid for herself. Was she going crazy? Was Kathy's sinister behaviour all just in her imagination?

Assisting Basil into the taxi, Rosamund caught sight of Rupert knocking and waving from a small window at the back of the pavilion. It gave her some small comfort to see him showing concern for his father, especially after Basil had broken the news that he no longer had a bedroom at their house.

"Don't worry, he's OK," she mouthed, "just a bit too much sun!"

Rosamund was halfway home before she thought more about why her son might have been waving so frantically from the ladies' lavatory. Her suspicions were further compounded by the sight of Tallulah and Anya wandering into the Village, laughing hysterically and waving something that looked suspiciously like Rupert's red trousers above their heads.

*

Bianca stood alone on the empty terrace, scanning the horizon for Frank. The game was over, the trophies had been awarded and there was not a soul in sight. The sky darkened, and Bianca shivered. They had planned to join Tallulah for a drink in the pub, but Harley said she had gone, so Bianca slipped away from the clubhouse without saying her farewells.

She could not resist nipping into the ladies' loo before leaving. She knocked at the "empty" cubicle, knowing that Rupert was there, trouserless, squeezed into her daughter's tiny underwear! What a fool; what an egotistical prat the man was, to believe that her lovely Tallulah would be titillated by knicker-swapping sessions with a man like him. He had fallen for her retribution like a tonne of bricks. Her daughter had tipped off the press, moreover, and the paparazzi were on their way. Tomorrow his picture would be in all the tabloids. That would teach him to mess with the Fielding women. This was media-storm payback!

She headed down the footpath, texting Tallulah and hurrying to Frank. They had not spoken all day; Bianca had waited for him at the interval, but he had remained on the pitch, sitting under the shade of an oak tree with Harley. She had considered joining them, but something in the intensity of their exchange made her keep at a distance. His behaviour was at odds with the man she loved, who would normally be buying drinks for everybody at the bar, signing autographs and making toasts. Frank sought the spotlight, not the shadows. He had barely spoken to Edmund Pendlegrass, and though many of the players from New Town had recognised him, it was almost as if he had gone out of his way to avoid them. Bianca prayed he was not sick or something.

TWENTY-TWO

I N TOWN THE following morning, Luca leaned heavily against a
bookshop door, his pulse racing and his breathing shallow. He
had spotted a woman while browsing the blockbusters, half-
noticing a dark ponytail and a blur of navy suit. Then he saw her
slender arm and the golden bracelet – a family heirloom – jangling
on her wrist, and he knew it was her. The shock of seeing his wife
had paralysed him for a few vital moments, and before he could
call out, she had rounded the corner. He hurtled after her, but the
woman had vanished.

As his heartbeat slowed, Luca tried to make sense of the sighting.
In a world of nearly seven billion people, Natasha was sure to have
a doppelgänger somewhere, but her turning up in the place Luca
had travelled halfway around the world to try and forget her could
not be a coincidence.

He shoved his hands in his pockets and struck out along the main
street towards the Village. He knew that the appearance of Natasha's
double and the digitally altered photo turning up in another email
from his stalker the previous week were linked. Somebody was
playing a game of cat-and-mouse. He had thrown down the gauntlet
by sending a "safe phone", courtesy of Felicity, the previous week,
and it appeared that he had been correct in his certainty that this
would prompt his elusive stalker to make contact. His phone jangled
in his trouser pocket and Luca, usually so composed, started. It was
Maria. He sighed audibly as she cut to the chase.

"Final preparations for the trial are underway," she said. "Keep
your head down, your ears peeled and your eyes open, you're
almost home and dry." She paused for a second, and Luca knew
instinctively she was holding back.

"Go on," he prompted.

"I hate to say this, but I think it may be time for you to move on. Some Russian heavies may have gotten your address," she said. "They've been hanging around the beach house asking questions. Micky says they've cosied up to Buchanan, and I'm afraid we can't be sure he hasn't given away details of your safe house." Maria paused; then, attempting to fill the long silence, she added: "I'll try and sort something out. Meantime, sit tight. Four more weeks 'til the trial, then you're a free man."

A steely calm washed over him. Luca stretched out. Breathing deeply, he attempted to loosen the knot of muscle in his neck. *I've come too far to lose everything now*, he thought.

"Any news on the autopsy?" he asked tersely.

"Counting the days. We'll know the truth soon, then hopefully you can lay your ghosts." Luca grunted. He did not mention Natasha's lookalike. It had nothing to do with the case. So he ended the call.

The sound of footfalls sent a wave of apprehension through Luca's body. Squinting into the midday sun, he could just make out the silhouette of a tall man approaching with an outstretched arm. He reached instinctively for his pistol; then, remembering he was unarmed, he braced for combat. To Luca's relief, Harley came into view, the silver skull dangling around his neck and the studs on his leather jacket glittering in the sunshine. He thrust out his hand in friendship.

"Good to see you," he said. The two men walked in silence. After a few minutes, Harley reached into his jacket pocket and offered a roll-up from a crumpled pack.

"Why not?" Luca replied. The cloying scent of mint, cinnamon and lemongrass helped clear his mind, and Luca noted the deep rattle of Harley's breathing and the laboured rise and fall of his ribcage. *A nicotine addict like me*, he thought. For all his height and strength, the big man walked with the grace of a cat. *I am a wily coyote by comparison*. The stultifying air reminded him of the desert back home, where the spring landscape would be a palette of wildflowers stretching like a living carpet across the horizon.

Harley stopped to greet a ballet of swans gliding over the mossy expanse towards them. Luca recalled Cecilia telling him that swans could live for thirty years. They had been in bed at the time, Luca soporific and sated from their lovemaking but feeling a creeping disquiet at having allowed things to go so far.

"If their mate dies, they go through a grieving process, just like humans do," she had said, her liquid brown eyes shining as she spoke. "A pen at the end of Kingfisher House garden lost her cob to a fox. She wouldn't eat; she floated around desolately for a week, then settled down among the bulrushes and breathed her last. It broke my heart." Luca was surprised by a wave of guilt. *I've lied to Cecilia and I've deceived her,* he thought. *She deserves better.*

As if reading his mind, Harley turned. Placing a hand on his shoulder, he said in a voice as strong as liquor and soft as chocolate: "Luca Tempesta, you are not alone. You are among friends." An unexpected invasion of his space normally elicited a right hook from Luca, but something about the big man's gentleness disabled him. The biker thrust a sealed envelope into his hand.

"I have to go away," he said, "and I need you to give this to Felicity."

"Can't you give it to her yourself?" Luca replied brusquely. He did not want to get involved in affairs of the heart.

Harley shook his head.

"Some words just can't be spoken," he said, before grinning and slapping Luca companionably on the back. He accepted the envelope and, folding it once, placed it in his top pocket.

The roar of the traffic had morphed into the sweet song of a blackbird, and Luca became transfixed by a yellow butterfly perched lightly on the biker's leather jacket. Its gossamer wings were tremulous in the breeze, but it held fast before turning towards the sun and taking flight. Harley gave a small salute and lumbered off towards the woods, and Luca headed for Kingfisher House.

Unlocking the front door, he stepped into the musty hallway and ascended the stairs to the attic. He removed the rifle he had bought with Clive's firearms licence and a forged signature: a James Purdey London sidelock. Luca admired its sleek design and the seductive feel of the barrel, then loaded the cartridges and began throwing things into a bag.

On the other side of town, Amanda gawped at Rupert Braithwaite, who glared back from beneath a headline that screamed: EX-CON CAUGHT IN THE ACT! He was stark naked save for a pair of red, frilly knickers and a startled expression. Amanda was glad that she had not ended up seducing such a weedy excuse for a man. She hunted for coins and snatched the tabloid from the vendor's hand, devouring the story as she sipped her coffee and walked blindly along the high street. According to the newspaper, Rupert had refused to reveal the identity of the woman who had lured him into the cricket club's cloakroom to "swap saucy smalls", but an accompanying two-page spread featured the strikingly beautiful supermodel Anya in a why-bother bikini and hinted that it had been a publicity stunt to promote Rupert's book. Below the feature was a banner with the website details of the dementia charity to which all royalties would be donated.

Amanda had been summoned to the *Gazette*'s office by her editor, who was furious that she had missed a scoop "yet again", in their very own backyard. She would normally have felt defensive, but today she had an ace up her sleeve that would put the *Gazette* on the map and assure her a place in the editor's good books for life. She clattered along the pavement in her shiny Valentino shoes, grateful that pawning her Chanel bag had staved off a call to the payday loan company. Passing the New Town church, her thoughts turned to Ivy Midwinter, to whom she felt an uncharacteristic rush of gratitude for inadvertently leading her into uncovering the truth about Nigel Bond. A few discreet enquiries at the residential home and a morning spent perusing the newspaper archives at Collingwood had revealed the old man's extraordinary story.

Bond had been a luminary of the 1960s Civil Service, but the fall of the Iron Curtain and the end of the Cold War had coincided with the revelation of a close relationship between Bond and the treacherous spymaster Jeremy Gosling. Gosling and Bond had met at Cambridge shortly after the war and spent a near-lifetime working together. Bond had claimed to know nothing about his friend passing secrets to the KGB agent Codename: Kuznetsoy, and there had been high dudgeon in the media as he protested his innocence. While nothing was ever proved, Bond had vanished; and although the furore eventually died down, his disappearance led many to assume – in the absence of any determination to prove his innocence – that he was indeed guilty of treason. And Amanda Jones, undercover journalist extraordinaire, had found him! She could not believe her luck, that the man himself had re-emerged in the Village, apparently close to a woman whose web of influence appeared to spin beyond Village boundaries into the world of the security services, politicians and celebrities.

The only person seemingly immune to Ivy Midwinter's spell was Luca Tempesta. Why was that, and why did the old witch hate him so much? Amanda allowed her imagination to work overtime. She had read countless Le Carré novels, so she knew that the protagonists were often ordinary people who blended easily into everyday life while wielding enormous influence behind the scenes.

Since uncovering the truth about Nigel Bond, Amanda had started to track Ivy, following her discreetly around the Village and quickly establishing that she, in turn, was watching Luca – who appeared oblivious to his new shadow, becoming more dishevelled and distracted by the day.

As Amanda's pace quickened and the newspaper's headquarters loomed into sight, an idea began to form. What she needed was a showdown. If she could somehow instigate a meeting between Ivy and Luca, she might learn the truth about them both, and with a bit of luck a feast of lucrative stories would follow.

Clutching the new Lulu Guinness bag she had bought with the money the pawnbroker had coughed up for her vintage Chanel, Amanda strode purposefully into the paper's offices

TWENTY-THREE

FRANK FIELDING STIRRED his coffee and watched, entranced, as tiny whirlpools emanated from the spoon; the faster it spun, the more determined the ripples were to break free from the cup; yet, confounding all probability, the liquid did not spill. He focused on the concentric circles, which beguiled him. The swirling vortex sucked Frank into a fantasy world; down the rabbit hole he went, down, down, away from his storm of troubles.

He had performed *Alice in Wonderland* in a Christmas panto one year. "Would you tell me, please, which way I ought to go from here?" he had asked the White Rabbit at the fork in the road.

"That depends a good deal on where you want to get to," the White Rabbit replied.

Frank had worn a white smock dress with a blue ribbon in his blonde wig. He could not remember which actress had played the Rabbit.

"I don't much care," he/Alice had declared. To which the White Rabbit leaped onto an enormous flowerpot and announced with delight: "Then it doesn't matter which way you go!"

"Babe!" Bianca was shouting. "Babe!" Frank did not answer, and Bianca grabbed the binoculars from his desk and focused them out the window onto the brow of the footbridge. She was right. "Frank Fielding!" she yelled again.

"Oh, dear! I know I'm in trouble when you call me that," said Frank, coming to his senses. "What is it?"

"It's Joy," she replied, grabbing her husband's arm and pulling him to the window. "I think she's gonna jump!"

The phone rang.

"Fielding residence!" announced Bianca distractedly. Frank

214

went back to stirring the coffee that would swallow him up, Joy completely forgotten. He had taken many gambles in his life and until now, like the tablecloth underneath his cup, he had escaped unblemished. Lately, though, the risks had spiralled out of control, and were threatening to destroy his perfect existence. Now he remembered! The White Rabbit had been played by a Page Three girl, Georgina Lox! She had propositioned him after the show. They all had, in those days. Poor Bianca had nearly caught them in the act.

"Ford squad?" Bianca asked, still looking anxiously out the window. "Is this to do with advertising or something? You should speak to Frank's agent. He doesn't deal with advertisers direct. I'll get you ... you what? *Fraud*? The fraud squad?"

Frank stopped stirring, and the muddy liquid, which now had its own momentum, splashed over the rim of the cup, drenching the white Egyptian cotton tablecloth.

"Babe," Bianca called. "It's for you!"

Joy had a thundering headache, and had been sick during the night. She attributed her malaise neither to the trials of the last few days, nor to the alcohol consumed alongside her painkillers. It was, she declared after lunch with her hapless husband, caused by the weather. Hugh, ever the attentive spouse, had danced around offering tea and sympathy, but, unable to stand his fussing a moment longer, Joy had stormed out of The White House, slamming the door behind her.

It was not just the weather that beleaguered her. It seemed her mind was changing so fast even she could not keep up with it. Little wonder, she reflected, that she had a migraine. She teetered down the drive, ruing her silly choice of shoes, and breathed deeply. The air felt stagnant, and she struggled to fill her lungs.

The nub of Joy's discontent was that she had, the previous night, finally met her son-in-law. An urgent phone call to the cricket club, a mad dash into town and four anxious hours in a hospital waiting room had forced her to confront the unfaceable. Tom was gay. He had a husband. And – something for which she had been utterly unprepared – the man was delightful.

Another surprise had been that Jake's parents, who were already waiting anxiously at Tom's bedside, were as charming as their son. Hugh, it seemed, knew them well, having enjoyed countless Sunday lunches and celebrations together with them over the years. Jake's parents had been kind and solicitous, asking questions about Joy's "endless charity work", "back-breaking commitments at Sugar & Spice" and "vital work in the community". Hugh had, apparently, smoothed the choppy waters of her absence with a multitude of fictitious excuses. Indeed, the man Joy had made it her life's work to control had placed her on a pedestal and protected her from the judgement of these good people. She felt almost contrite; but, unfamiliar with the emotion, she dismissed it and continued her walk, pondering the events of the last twelve hours. Tom had been riding pillion on Jake's scooter when they had hit a pothole. It was a blessed relief that he had escaped only with a broken arm, and Jake only with a few cuts and bruises.

Joy's court shoes started to pinch, and her wrist throbbed. Two magpies squawked accusingly from a nearby tree. Catching her foot in a tangle of bindweed, she yanked it out angrily to free herself and limped onto the footbridge. A broken wrist, a broken bank, quite possibly a broken marriage and now a broken heel. She paused to take stock at the bridge's summit, put down her bag and removed her shoes, trying to stem the sulphurous surge from her stomach. *If I can just lean against these railings for a while,* she thought, *the sickness will pass and then I will go ... where?* Where could she go? She could not face returning home to Hugh, and Rosamund seemed so wrapped up in Basil these days. Sweat prickled her skin, and her stomach bubbled and heaved.

Hugh is lucky, she thought belligerently. He has a son to turn to in a crisis; I have nobody – not even Penny, now that she is living on the other side of the world. The small, inner voice whispered its blame, and Joy choked back the tears. Watching the river flow by on its purposeful journey, she felt stultified and paralysed by regret. Tears escaped down her cheeks, splashing into the water below, joining the fast-flowing eddy towards the ocean.

The storm was brewing now, and gigantic black clouds sped across the sky. Joy knew that she had failed Tom and spoiled Penny. She had treated Hugh abominably, too. In fact, she had let down her entire family by being a stubborn fool. Why could she not be more like Rosamund? She did everything for Basil and had devoted her life to Rupert – even though the blighter did not deserve it. Rosamund Braithwaite, her sweet, kind, loyal friend. Little wonder her husband called her his "duchess" and worshipped the ground she walked on.

Joy thought again of Tom. He had grown so handsome and tall. The mirror image of his father. She let out a wail, and blubbered noisily into her handkerchief.

"Stop!" a voice shouted, and Joy half-turned to see a barefoot Bianca barrelling towards her. With every step, the small bridge vibrated, and Joy's head throbbed "Don't do it!"

On top of her overwhelming feelings of defeat, Joy was now faced with the humiliation of Bianca Fielding witnessing her darkest hour. She put her face in her hands and tried to stem the nausea that was threatening to erupt.

"It isn't worth it!" Bianca panted, catching up to her. "Why would you throw your life away? Think of Hugh, an' the twins! What about Myrtle? An' Rosamund?" Bianca leaned against the railings, clasping a rigid Joy to her, and continued her platitudes. "Wot's 'appened? Believe you me, it can't be that bad. Why don't you come back to mine for a cuppa, and we can talk about it?"

Joy kept her head resolutely in her hands and said not a word. She felt tired and bruised, but she was not broken – and she certainly had no intention of jumping into the river! She did quickly realise that the idea of somebody to mollycoddle her, even if it was only Bianca Fielding, appealed. Of all the people Joy might have expected to bestow kindness, Bianca would have been the last person – and yet here she was, rubbing her back and telling her how valued she was, how important, how loved. And to Joy's surprise, where she would normally have felt irritation she felt soothed. Instead of contempt, she felt gratitude, and her self-pity ebbed away slowly as she soaked up Bianca's kind words like a dry sponge.

"I know I tease," Bianca jabbered, "but it's obvious that Hugh adores you. Believe you me, I know men, an' I can tell by the way 'e looks at you."

Joy allowed herself to be conducted back over the bridge, Bianca chatting soothingly all the while about her own experiences of despair – her Mum leaving home and her Dad, the hard-boiled East End boxer with a soft centre for his beautiful daughter, who scraped a living in the street markets and whom Bianca had nursed into the arms of Hell when he succumbed to lung cancer. "'E used to say 'whatever doesn't kill you makes you stronger'," she said cheerfully, "an' course, it did kill him in the end." The rain had started to pelt down, so they rushed for cover to The Waterfront.

"Come on in!" Bianca cried as she unlocked her front door and Joy, who had only been half-listening, was jarred back to reality. She quashed her instinct to turn tail, but her body ached and the thought of a soft armchair and a tot of brandy diluted her disquiet at allowing herself to be befriended by Bianca Fielding.

"Let me just tell Frank I'm home. Frank!"

"Oh dear," thought Joy, "oh dear," as her knees crumpled and she slid down the doorframe and onto the floor in a faint.

Frank, who was deep in thought in his office, could not hear his wife calling, and so was unaware of their visitor. He had watched through his binoculars as Bianca rescued their neighbour, then seized the opportunity to leave a message for Tony Jackson, scratching at his eczema as he waited for the lawyer to return his call. A ping from his computer caused him to take a sharp intake of breath; it was the long-awaited reply from the director of the new Saturday night entertainment series. His heartbeat quickened as he hovered the cursor over the message link, pausing to savour the moment of the announcement that could predicate his career comeback and put an end to his money worries.

He clicked.

The words "not quite right", "wrong market" and "axed" leaped out at him; before Frank could absorb their full implication, the phone rang and he snatched it up.

"Frank Fielding," he barked, staring at the screen. "Tony? Is that you?"

"No, my name is Desmond Wilson. I'm from *The Sunday Record*," said a voice.

Frank cut across him: "I am not –"

"Just listen," said the caller. "I am only ringing as a courtesy to tell you we'll be running a splash on 'The Secret Life of Frank Fielding' next weekend. Unless you'd like to give us your version, that is?"

Frank dropped the phone as if it were a scalding rock. The email that had crushed his dreams paled into insignificance compared to Britain's best-selling Sunday newspaper vilifying him across its centre pages. It was almost too much to bear. He needed to talk to Bianca, to tell her the truth. He opened the study door, and his wife's ringing laughter pealed down the hallway.

"It's like me Nan said, just add a pinch of sugar to everything you say to yer man, and take a pinch of salt with everything 'e says to you," she giggled.

Frank froze at the realisation that Joy Willoughby was in his home. He did not know whether it was cowardice or a timely excuse, but suddenly all he could think of was getting away.

"... And so long as you're never as busy, as tired or as important as 'e is, you'll be OK. Oh, and always have sex with 'im before a business trip!" Bianca noticed her husband and said, smiling, "Speak of angels." Frank stood before her, visibly clammy and hot, his temples pulsating. "You're not ill as well? 'Ere, have some Alka Seltzer – you poor thing, you look 'alf dead!"

Frank gazed with infinite sadness at his irrepressible, optimistic wife. "I've gotta go, love," he said gruffly.

"Where're you off to then, babe?"

"I just ... I just need to get away. Be by myself ... I just ..."

Bianca rose from her chair in slow motion. Joy, who had sipped three cups of sweet tea, swallowed two strong analgesics and was now tucking into the sherry, was starting to feel much restored.

"Babe?" said Bianca tentatively, as though she had not quite understood Frank's words. Then she shouted, "Babe!" as she ran down the corridor towards the garage. "Frank! Frank Fielding! Where the 'ell are you goin'? Frank!"

An engine fired, and Bianca cried out. Joy was starting to feel a distinct discomfort at having made herself vulnerable to her neighbours – what on Earth had she been thinking, sitting in this woman's house, sharing confidences and listening to her fatuous marital advice?

"Frank, come back!!" her hostess wailed from the street. Feeling a little more like herself, Joy threw back the dregs of her sherry, straightened her skirt and picked up her bag. *That silly woman should have minded her own business instead of forcing me into this awkward situation*, she thought, hobbling out the front door and feeling strangely better.

TWENTY-FOUR

DAYS AND NIGHTS limped by as Bianca kept a vigil at The Waterfront. She stared blindly through the kitchen window, where dawn seeped through the vicious clouds that promised another grey day of relentless rain.

Cradling her tea, she wandered down to the river. "Tea is for mugs," Frank had told her every morning for the last twenty-two years as he sipped his coffee, and each time, without fail, Bianca had laughed. She was not laughing now. Frank was not at home. He had been gone for nearly a week, and she had no idea where he was.

Swallows swooped in and out of the boathouse in silence, as if to respect the mood of sadness, and Bianca sat, small and barefoot, on the wooden pontoon and pulled Frank's hoodie around her. She was shivering, but not cold; empty, but not hungry. The world had changed for her, and she simply could not make sense of it.

Drizzle settled onto her upturned face, and she closed her eyes. She needed to cry, but tears would not come, only words: *Where are you? How could you? Why don't you?* She felt she was missing something; if she only concentrated enough, tuned in properly, listened carefully, she would feel Frank's presence, and he would comfort her. But she could not hear or feel her husband's love, and she tipped the cold tea into the river and hurled the empty mug at the boathouse wall before marching into the house and slamming the door behind her.

Bianca had endured this lonely existence for days. The mornings were the worst: the realisation that another wretched twenty-four hours had passed, another sleepless night got through, and still – no word. She carried her phones everywhere, her heart soaring every time they rang, only to be knocked down as another well-meaning neighbour launched into a soliloquy of sympathy.

Tallulah was in America, and oblivious to events at home. News had travelled along Riverside Lane and her neighbours had closed ranks, sparing Bianca the indignity of media intrusion and her daughter the agony of learning about her father's disappearance in the newspapers.

Ivy Midwinter had called around, claiming not to know Frank's whereabouts, but Bianca saw through her vagueness and knew she was lying. She had begged, then commanded the old bat to disclose her husband's location, but Ivy had stood firm, blinking in that weird way that was her habit, soaking up Bianca's screams and claiming ignorance, a martyred expression on her self-righteous face. Bianca had wanted to slap her, but instead had snatched away the house keys and fired her.

Tony Jackson telephoned every day, barking as though Bianca were in some way complicit in Frank's disappearance. Bianca felt like a racehorse on a tight rein; she needed to run. Damn him if he wanted her, and she was not at home – he deserved to suffer a little! Wearing dark glasses and a baseball cap to protect her privacy, she raced along Riverside Lane and over the footbridge. Running gave Bianca mental clarity, and the whirlpool of hysterical what-ifs marshalled themselves into a comprehensible order. She listed them in her mind. Frank had driven off of his own volition, so he had not been kidnapped. He had left his phone, so she could not ring him. He had taken the Nissan instead of their flashy car, so was unlikely to be recognised. She had imagined him sickening or something on the day he had vanished, but perhaps he had been stressed, or frightened. He had taken a call that morning. Who had it been from? If only she could remember. She had searched through his emails, desperate for clues, so she knew about his game-show host rejection – but that alone could not explain his disappearance. There had been nothing to suggest a secret affair, which did not surprise her. Back in the days when Frank had dallied, Bianca had always known but never let on, and she felt certain he had stopped playing away long ago. She turned onto the towpath and, glancing across the water, caught sight of Ivy's neat little garden, the splendid wisteria adorning Sam's boathouse and then her own empty lawn stretching forlornly down to the waterfront. Panic washed over her; Frank might be ringing, unable to reach her at the one moment she was not there. The willow trees formed an honour guard, and Bianca ran beneath them. In the dimly lit, leafy tunnel she became aware of a noise, one she did not recognise; then she realised that it was coming from her, an agonising wail of desperation. She sprinted for home and the tears finally came, coursing down her cheeks, salty on her swollen lips.

A gunshot away from The Waterfront, Bianca spotted a stranger at the gate. Jogging the final furlong, she remembered who Frank's call had been from: the fraud squad! Could he have been arrested? Surely not. She stopped a couple of yards away to collect her thoughts, hands on her knees so the visitor would not recognise her, but her mental clarity dissipated. With a feeling of dread, Bianca approached the stranger and waited for the words she felt certain would fall from his lips and crush her.

A few hours later, Bianca sat at the kitchen table, papers strewn about her. She still wore her running kit, now crusty with dried sweat. A manuscript lay in front of her. On her face she wore an expression of pure shock. In her hand she held the phone, which she had been staring at for almost an hour. She was frozen with disbelief, trying and failing to recall the chain of events that had led to this moment, struggling to understand the words she had just read.

Like a premonition of doom, a cloud had covered the sun as she had approached the dishevelled man standing at her front gate earlier that morning.

"I need to talk to you," he had said, moving to block her entry.

"You've gotta be kiddin'! Get out the way or I'll scream! My 'usband's coming along in a minute, 'e'll –"

"No, he's not," the stranger replied quietly. "Your husband has disappeared, and you don't know where he is." He looked at her pleadingly. "Please, I am not going to hurt you. I know that Frank has disappeared, and I may know where he is. Just give me a moment."

Bianca stared in disbelief as the stranger reached into a battered briefcase and extracted a fat, brown envelope. If he meant her harm, she decided, he would not be outside her house at midday, standing under a security camera.

"What is it?" she asked, taking a step back. "Who are you, and why would you know where my Frank is?"

The stranger smiled sadly. "Oh, you'd be surprised what I know about Frank. But listen, you don't want to talk about this on the street."

The words "fraud squad" still fresh in her mind, Bianca wondered if he was a henchman connected to that Bill Lewis palaver. And yet, oddly, there was something about the man that she trusted.

"Well, I ain't askin' you in," she declared almost apologetically, and the stranger nodded. "Just tell me where Frank is."

"Not now." He held out the envelope. "Read this. Then, if you want to talk, call me. My number's in there."

He had a gentle voice, but he sounded tired. He turned to walk away, head bowed, shoulders slumped, and Bianca called out, not wanting their exchange to end.

"Listen – Pete, did you say your name is? – are you OK?" She felt for her pockets, but had nothing, "I'll get you a card. Frank's agent. Tell 'im we met. I'd like to help you, but now's really not a good time for me."

"I've spoken to him," Pete said, resigned. "Before Frank did a bunk. Tony Jackson, too, and Ivy Midwinter. None of them would listen."

"Well I've never 'eard of you," Bianca replied. "What did you say yer name is? Pete ...?"

"Walters. Pete Walters." He nodded towards the envelope, "Just read it. Then ring me."

"Why are you doing this?" Bianca asked, more gently now. "What d'you want? Money?"

"No," he said, staring at her dully. "I need my life back. And I wanted to warn you."

"Warn me of what?" Bianca's heart had turned to ice.

"I dedicated a year to researching and writing this biography on Frank." He pointed to the package. "It's no hatchet job, either. But now, thanks to your husband and his Rottweiler, Tony Jackson, my publishers have dumped it and I've lost my job, my reputation and any chance of future work. My wife's kicked me out, my home is being repossessed and I'm living in my car."

"What the 'ell's my Frank got to do with all that?"

"Ask him."

"Believe you me, I will," she said. "When I find the bugger! Listen, I'm sorry for what's 'appened to you, but I don't believe my Frank's got anything to do with it. 'Ee's a good man."

"That's as maybe," said Pete, "but he's not the man you think he is. You think you know him, but believe me – you don't. That's why I came. You seem like a nice lady, and you should know that because of the injunction slapped on my book, I've been forced to sell a sensationalised version to *The Sunday Record*. They'll be running it next weekend."

"Oh, bleedin' 'Enry! What does it say?"

"I'm sorry, Bianca. Read it," he urged. "At least forewarned is forearmed."

"'Ang on a minute. Two ticks." Bianca dashed into the house, returning with her hand outstretched. "'Ere," she held out a fifty-pound note. "Take this."

Pete shook his head. "I don't want your money, just read the manuscript."

"Oh, for Gawd's sake, take the money, will you? You look like you could do with a bath and a good meal."

Pete laughed and nodded. "OK. Thank you. And for 'Gawd's sake', you take the package and read it."

The memory of Pete Walters' dejected face and stooped shoulders as he turned to walk away still haunted Bianca. Sighing heavily, she stuffed the manuscript back into the brown paper envelope and sealed it shut. Picking up Walters' card, she dialled his number.

"Pete?" she said in a flat voice. "It's Bianca Fielding. I think you'd better get over here."

"Get us a cup of tea, will you, pet? I've been on my feet all day." Frank filled the kettle and chuckled as he reached into the cupboard.

"You know, tea is for –"

"Mugs, I know," Sandra groaned. "And *you* know tea is for two, so why don't you get us both a pot and sit down with me. I got us some nice biscuits from the 'damaged' selection at work. Nothing wrong with them at all, as far as I can see. Cranberry and orange. Delicious."

Frank joined Sandra in the sitting room, carefully setting down the tea tray before kneeling by the gout stool and taking her swollen feet in his hands.

"Ooh. that feels nice. They've come up like balloons again," she said.

"I don't know why you insist on going in. You know what the doctor said about your blood pressure; you shouldn't be on your feet all day. You don't need to go, you know. We can more than manage."

"And *you* know there's more to life than money. Going in to work's what keeps me sane, what with, well ... you know. It's what I do, where my friends are." Frank nodded and began to pour the tea. "Besides, judging from what you said last night, I'm not sure we *can* manage." Frank began to protest, but Sandra waved away his objections, passing him a broken biscuit before dipping her own in her tea and sighing. "Anyway, you know I don't love you for your money. I know I shouldn't, what with everything that's going on and all that, but it is lovely to have you here, Frank."

Frank took another biscuit and smiled. "You say that, but obviously not lovely enough to marry me."

Sandra laughed. "The old jokes are the best, eh?"

She reached for the remote control and settled into her chair. Before long, she was asleep. Frank ignored the television and pushed away unwelcome thoughts, settling to watch the rise and fall of Sandra's breathing. Sandra Evans was a few years younger than he was, yet she wore the years heavily – and he had begun to fear for her health. They had endured a scare a few years earlier, and although she had lost weight and given up smoking, her blood pressure was still elevated and she struggled to breathe after relatively little exertion.

Watching her in repose, Frank reflected that Sandra had not only inherited her mother's no-nonsense attitude and work ethic, but her looks as well. Age was not kind to the Evans women, and there was now no sign of the beauty Sandra had once been, though to him she would always be the same sweet chorister who had stolen his heart on *Showtime* all those decades ago.

Frank had first proposed to Sandra on 14 February 1975. He remembered the day as if it were only yesterday. He had parked his Bentley Continental on the yellow lines outside the hairdresser where Sandra worked, and, clutching a bunch of red roses, got down on one knee and declared his love. She had laughed and turned him down, and he had vowed to ask her again twelve months later. After her third refusal, Frank began to take up with other women, but Sandra still had the power to enthral him. He had bought her a semi in the suburbs in the fourth year, yet still she had refused his proposal. Forty years had passed since then; Frank had enjoyed countless lovers and two wives, while Sandra had remained resolutely single. And every Valentine's Day, as sure as night follows day, Frank would turn up on Sandra's doorstep with an armful of red roses, get down on bended knee and ask her to marry him.

As his first love snored gently in her armchair, Frank cogitated on what had been, what should have been and what must now be. What had started as a small white lie had mushroomed into a lifetime of deceit, and the veil of secrecy on his double life was about to be ripped away. He scratched at the eczema that had proliferated from his wrists to his elbows, and for the hundredth time reflected on the injustice of it all: those he loved most in the world would be devastated by the newspaper's exposé. He had been such a fool. And yet, he had only been doing what he thought was right and good and true; taking care of the people he loved.

Early the following morning, wrapped in a violet candlewick dressing gown, Sandra prepared coffee for Frank as he lay snuggled under the eiderdown, absorbed in a *Reader's Digest*. Hearing a noise outside, she collected the empty milk bottles and opened the door – but instead of the milkman, Sandra was greeted by a tall stranger.

She tried to slam the door shut, but it was too late; his foot was in the jamb, and he said: "My name is Pete Walters and I need to speak to Frank. I have a message for him from Bianca."

Ever the pragmatist, Sandra opened the door wide and, indicating he should remove his muddy shoes, she said: "You're the biographer. Well, you'd better come in, love." She guided him into their small, neat living room and climbed the stairs to Frank.

"The time has come, pet," she said, entering the bedroom. Frank looked up at her over his half-moon glasses. "We always knew it would."

TWENTY-FIVE

B ASIL REACHED FOR the teapot, his laughter reverberating around the kitchen. Kathy leaned across and took it instead, smiling indulgently.

"Oh no," she said. "I'm far too old-fashioned to let a gentleman pour my tea. Allow me to be Mother."

Basil chuckled as Kathy added milk and carefully selected two sugar cubes with Rosamund's silver tongs. He raised his hand to object. "Rosamund's got me on a strict diet. She says –" But Kathy simply tutted and waved away his objections.

"Nonsense," she said, looking directly at him as she stirred in the sugar. "Like I always say to Edmund, a bit of what you fancy and all that. You've been poorly, after all! We need to build up your strength!"

"I'll say," Basil agreed, and noisily slurped his drink.

"Speaking of which," said Kathy, reaching into her basket, "a get-well gift."

"How very kind!" Basil accepted the cake tin with delight, lifted the lid and inhaled the smell of fresh-baked goods. Kathy smiled her slow smile, and not for the first time Basil thought what a fine-looking woman she was. "Nothing quite like homemade shortbread, and made by a bona-fide Scot, too! I am honoured."

"Och, Mr Braithwaite," said Kathy, lowering her russet lashes and exaggerating her accent. "You can be sure that the honour's all mine."

"*Basil*," he said sternly, "for goodness' sake, call me 'Basil'. From which part of Scotland the Brave do you hail, good lady? The misty Highlands?"

"I was born in the Trossachs, just north of Edinburgh and a wee bit south of Stirling," Kathy replied, and Basil sighed.

"Linlithgow," he said happily. "I know it well! Battle of Bannock-burn! I took Rosamund there on our honeymoon. Beautiful place. We toured the British Isles, visiting all the major battlefields. Splendid, quite splendid. Of course, there are quite a few in Scotland – Glen Shiel, Culloden, Inverlochy." Basil jumped up at the sound of a key in the door, but Kathy was ahead of him, walking across the kitchen and kissing his astonished wife on the cheek when she entered.

"There you are, Duchess!" Basil declared. "I was just telling Kathy here about our honeymoon."

Basil bid his visitor farewell and, whistling, sauntered into the kitchen where Rosamund was unpacking the groceries.

"What was she doing here?" she asked.

"Came to return my jumper – apparently I'd left it at the cricket, though I clearly remember putting it in your basket! Must be going gaga in my old age. She brought me some shortbread, as well! Wasn't that sweet?" Rosamund slammed a cupboard door and said nothing. "Are you alright, Duchess? You look a bit peaky. Don't say you're going down with this wretched tummy bug, too?"

"No, I'm fine Basil. It's just ... Well ... It's nothing," she said, before blurting: "How long was she here?"

Basil blustered a bit before replying, "I don't know – fifteen, maybe twenty minutes."

Rosamund laid her hands on the kitchen counter. Fear, anger and embarrassment fought for first articulation.

"I don't want her here, Basil." The words came out more shrilly than she intended.

"Whatever do you mean? I've asked her to walk Mungo for us when we're up in town tomorrow."

"Well, you can un-ask her," Rosamund snapped, aware she sounded unreasonable. "Tell her we don't need her to walk our dog, and we don't need her ruddy cakes, either!" She pulled open the bin and picked up Kathy's tin, flinging the shortbread away.

She stifled a sob just as a realisation dawned on her bewildered husband.

"Good God, Rosamund!" he said, smiling with delight. "I do believe you're jealous! You really shouldn't –"

"No, Basil," said Rosamund, quietly. "I am not jealous ... I am ..." But as she spoke, Rosamund realised that admitting she was scared would lead to accusations of hysteria, whereas being seen as possessive and proprietary would be ego-boosting and puff her husband up effectively. She turned to face him, and took both his hands in hers.

"You're right," she said, smiling up at him shyly, "I admit it, Basil. I am jealous. You're an attractive man, and Kathy isn't blind. I've seen her type before, they ..." As Rosamund talked, Basil's smile grew wider; he grew a little taller, his chest a little fuller. He pulled in his belly and he squared back his shoulders. "... And so call me old-fashioned, but I just don't want her near my man."

Basil poured Rosamund a sherry by way of mollification, and tried hard to temper his pleasure as he sat opposite her and looked into her eyes with a grave face.

"If she's upsetting you, Duchess, then she must go!" he declared, and Rosamund enjoyed a small, secret thrill of triumph. "She will be cast out, banished, never again to darken our doors. I remember once, when I was stepping out with ..." Rosamund could feel a bit of a speech coming on, and settled down happily with her sherry.

Later that day, Basil took Mungo for a walk in the rain, and Rosamund finished putting the groceries away. He passed Felicity and Luca under the cover of a large umbrella, deep in conversation; but, distracted by the conversation he had just had with his wife, gave only a cursory nod. In all their years together, he had never seen her like that. Of course, he would do what she asked and expunge the Willoughbys' former housekeeper from their lives, and now that she pointed it out he fancied that perhaps the Scot did have a bit of a glad eye for him, what with the shortbread and everything; but it was unlike Rosamund to be insecure. Perhaps all the worry about Joy, and the scales falling from her eyes with regard to Rupert, had been too much for her? What she needed, he reflected, was a good holiday. He would take her away somewhere nice, get some Mediterranean sunshine on those heavenly limbs of hers.

Kathy stood at the delicatessen counter of the Royal Farm Shop, pointing imperiously to the items on display.

"... And two slices of game pie," she commanded the shop assistant. "That piece of *pâté de foie gras*, and a pound of your best ham." Her thoughts turned to Basil Braithwaite as the assistant prepared her order. His barbaric tales of dragging his delicate young bride on a tour of Scottish battlefields, gloating, no doubt, over sites where her countrymen were slain at the hands of the Sassenachs. The man was a monster.

"No, no! *Thinly* sliced, I said," she chided the assistant. Basil had shaken off the ill effects of the laburnum far quicker than Joy Willoughby had. The foolish man had even talked to her about it, saying he was pleased she had not caught the "bug". She had been so sympathetic as she'd handed over the laxative shortbread, and he had been so foolishly, so pathetically touched. That should send him running back to the loo! She chortled spitefully, delighted to have provided poor Mrs B. with a little respite from those unbearable spousal maulings. She shuddered at the thought. Basil was a monster, but then so were all men. Kathy had yet to meet a man who would not succumb to her wiles and eventually bow to her will. Poor, dear, simple souls, she mused, crushing a money spider that scuttled across her handbag as she brandished Edmund's platinum credit card at the cashier. She did not believe for a moment that they brought good luck; the black widow, on the other hand, she decided, as she summoned another assistant to pack her perishables, was definitely more her cup of tea.

Hugh was absorbed in an uncomfortable game of mental ping-pong as he strolled over the footbridge to join Basil for a drink that evening. He felt happy that Joy was restored to her splendid, redoubtable self – thanks, it seemed (and this he did not even pretend to understand), to an inexplicable hiatus at the Fieldings' house a few days earlier. But he was worried by the osteoporosis diagnosis, and had yet to comprehend what that might mean for the future. It was a great relief to him that Joy had finally met Tom's in-laws, and he chuckled at the memory of how he had kept back the news of their substantial family wealth until she had declared them "utterly charming" on the way home. And yet, though Hugh's smile was ready and bright as he wandered through the churchyard, waving cheerily to Reverend James, behind the confident politician's façade, his heart was heavy. Tom had just confided that he and Jake planned to move overseas.

"Not sure where we're going yet, Dad. Barcelona, Paris, maybe even New York," he had declared airily. "Jake's skills are so portable, and with his languages he could work pretty much anywhere – and I'm happy to tag along. Maybe I'll write a book or something!"

While Hugh was delighted his son and the man he adored were embarking on an exciting new chapter of their lives, his feelings were tinged with a deep, secret envy. He had laughed bravely and said: "And we golden oldies are supposed to feel sorry for the gilded generation."

"Come on, Dad, you Baby Boomers are the luckiest lot that ever lived. You didn't even have to pay for uni – we'll be saddled with debt forever. *And* we'll have to pick up the tab for your lot's self-indulgence and inability to plan the country's future!"

Reluctant to engage in a political debate, Hugh had shrugged his shoulders and harrumphed, but he could not help feeling out of touch and left behind by his carefree son. Oh, to be young and free from responsibility, he thought. How he coveted Tom's liberty to be true to himself, to live the life he wanted. The younger generation did not know how lucky they were. Cheap flights, the Bank of Mum and Dad, freedom to marry whom they wished … they were truly citizens of a world that was their absolute oyster, and they did not even know enough to appreciate it! He thrust his hands into his pockets and felt deep regret that Tom would no longer be in town for him to visit at whim. He wondered if Penny would ever return home. Dispelling thoughts of a future without them, he crossed the road to the pub. A sweat had begun to form on Hugh's brow, and he could feel the moisture of another storm in the air. A few rays of sunlight forced their way through the bruised sky, and Hugh paused for a moment to look up and accept a kiss from them. He closed his eyes and enjoyed the pungent aroma of freshly scythed hedgerow. Somewhere close by, a woodpecker chiselled a tree, piping in a clear, high voice while a fracas amongst the geese scattered the swans that drifted away, their willowy heads held high with disdain. Very slowly, he allowed his childish indulgence to pass. He was a man of the world, married to a wonderful woman without whom he could never have circumvented the conflicts of his life with such success. He took a deep breath and opened the door to the Crown.

At the bar, Basil greeted him with characteristic bonhomie and an outstretched hand. Felicity had two pints waiting, and, longing to get to a dissection of England's recent cricket performance, Hugh hastily performed the nicety of enquiring into Rosamund's health.

"Splendid, splendid," Basil beamed. "And Joy?"

"Never better."

"Good-oh! Tom fully recovered?"

"Oh, yes, on tremendous form. Rupert OK?"

Basil rolled his eyes. "Making a fortune for the dementia charities with that book of his, apparently. Somehow that boy always seems to come up smelling of roses," he said, sipping his beer. Hugh nodded.

"Well, that's all good, then," he said, leaning back in his chair and stretching his long legs out before him. "What did you make of England's fiasco at the weekend?"

It was a familiar conversation, almost rote, practised over many years of friendship. The two had settled down to a companionable hour discussing the captain's recent performance when a scream of despair froze Basil in mid-sentence.

"Dead?" Felicity wailed from the bar. "But I only saw him this afternoon!" Clutching her phone to her breast, she bolted out the door.

"Who's dead?" shouted Basil.

The pub fell silent, as regulars, including Cecilia, Sam and the usual gaggle of pensioners, contemplated the alarming news. But nobody seemed to know.

A feeling of dread stole through Hugh's body, bringing with it a primitive need to return to the security blanket of his hearth and home and to the comforting embrace of his wife. The world at once felt cold and empty. Hugh acknowledged to himself that, deep in his heart, he was not an adventurous man after all. Family, friends, respectability, security and routine were the qualities he held dear. It was time to start appreciating what he had, and stop hankering after what might have been.

TWENTY-SIX

THE FOLLOWING MORNING, Molly lay on her tummy and watched fat raindrops splash down the windowpane. She longed to play outside, but fearing she might be struck by lightning, she contented herself with making up stories while trying to ignore the growl of thunder. She could hear snatches of Cecilia's quiet telephone conversation in the hall.

"Just bang on the door and make sure he's OK," she whispered urgently; then, sounding like a teacher, she continued: "Yes, Sam, I *know* he won't answer if he's dead! Just pull yourself together and go and check."

Molly thought Cecilia looked like she might cry. She determined to be very grown-up, stay quiet and not add to her godmother's stress with questions. She bit her lip and stared hard at the raindrops, drumming her feet against the cream carpet. It was a topsy-turvy day, like when Mummy had died; everybody was behaving strangely, and Molly did not like it. Daddy had told her that nice, smiley Mr Fielding had vanished into thin air, and Molly imagined him doing a conjuring trick like at the circus. That would explain why Cecilia said he had hurt his wife unforgivably; thank goodness she had that cute dog to cuddle. Perhaps Mr Fielding had sawed her in two? In the circus, she would reappear in a lovely princess gown, and everybody would clap.

Mrs Fielding would make a lovely princess, Molly thought, drawing tiaras and coronets in the condensation on the window as she embellished her fairytale. Mrs Braithwaite could be the fairy godmother – she was pretty and twinkly – and Mrs Willoughby's housekeeper would have to be the ugly sister, because even though she tried to look like Mrs Braithwaite, wearing the same clothes and lipstick, she did not look nearly as nice. Molly could not decide who Mrs Willoughby would be in her story; first, she thought the wicked witch; but since she got her black eye and broken wrist, Molly had begun to feel sorry for her, and Mrs Willoughby had actually smiled at her when she took over her get-well-jelly-tot cake. Perhaps she should be the good witch instead?

"I am not hysterical," Cecilia shouted. "I am worried." Molly heard her slam the phone down and march up the stairs. She had argued a lot with Sam recently. Molly had heard him say that Luca was "living a lie". She did not like lies; they got you in trouble and ended in tears. Luca seemed too nice to be a liar, but as Daddy always said, 'you never can tell', and she felt sad for Cecilia, who liked the American man and would be disappointed if he turned out to be a fibber. And on top of all this, someone was dead and the grown-ups did not seem to know who it was! Most probably the person had been struck by lightning like the cartoon characters whose skeletons lit up inside, Molly decided.

Nobody seemed to know what to do. Cecilia was sending Sam to knock on doors, everyone seemed to be looking for Felicity and her sons and nobody knew where Mr or Mrs Fielding were. Molly had suggested somebody telephone the hospital but that was the trouble with being seven and a half: no one ever listened.

She hoped the dead person was not someone she liked. If it absolutely had to be someone, Molly hoped it was the old lady who played the church organ and followed Luca around in the shadows. According to Sam, she had just been sacked by the beautiful princess Bianca; Molly was not absolutely sure what that meant, but it sounded like she had been banished from the kingdom, which was good – although who would play the organ in church? It was wrong to spy on Luca, though, and Molly reckoned she, of all people in the Village, was the best person to "pop their clogs", as funny Mr Fielding liked to say. She hoped he would return home soon.

*

Across the Atlantic, Clive Buchanan had chosen the worst possible moment to make a video call to his son in The Boathouse. Sam was soaked to the skin after hammering the door of Kingfisher House in the driving rain, hoping to find Luca alive and well inside. He had peered through the letterbox and even climbed the wisteria again, ducking between sheets of lightning to gawp through the attic window, but the place was deserted. Before that, he had sprinted to Felicity's house, hollering for Harley and the boys from the garden – but no one was home. He was now towelling his hair furiously and pondering his next step while his father jabbered on about Frank Fielding.

"I knew it! He's a greedy man – nothing's ever enough!" said Clive excitably. "I bet he's got a bit on the side, a young sexpot, no doubt. He spent half his life at the New Town estate; I bumped into him countless times when I was doing house clearances, and always thought he looked shifty." He continued loftily: "If Bianca asks, I shall consider it my duty to tell her the truth." Sam tuned out as his father's mutterings became faint, white noise: "... Dark horse ... Leopards never change their spots ..."

Sam's only concern was for Luca's safety. Had the American's dangerous past finally caught up with him? Had he been murdered by Russian intelligence, or resisted arrest and been shot by the FBI? His imagination soared. Perhaps there had been a shootout at Kingfisher House? He could see no signs of disturbance from the window, but law enforcement had pretty sophisticated weaponry these days ...

Sam decided it was best not to tell Cecilia about his mounting concern for Luca. He had watched him the day before, pacing the garden like a man possessed, unkempt and jittery, the weight of the world on his shoulders. He longed to share his fears about the American with his father, who was soliloquising about his future plans. A jumble of phrases swam around the fog of Sam's anxiety: "... It's a wrap ... Hawaiian-themed restaurant ... make an honest woman of her ... resurrect the film studio and make a horror movie ..." It was only when the monologue became more animated that

Clive's message cut through: "Mafia ... unsavoury characters, loitering outside ..."

"Come again, Dad?" he interrupted. Clive leaned into the camera and repeated himself, adding: "I don't mind saying son: Luca Tempesta has turned out to be a bit a mystery. I've had endless phone calls from a young woman demanding his address, as well as dodgy characters turning up at his front door. I've done a bit of digging, and it turns out nobody has ever heard of him in the film industry! My film contact came clean and admitted he was only a 'sort of friend of a friend', and when pushed he said he couldn't remember exactly how he'd come by his details."

"Oh, Dad!" cried Sam. "I told you to be more careful ... you have no idea what you have done, you –"

"Spare me the lecture, Son," said Clive, cheerfully. "It's all worked out fine. I'll be home next week. Look on the bright side: at least the house is still standing."

"Tell me about the 'unsavoury characters'." Sam glanced nervously out of the window, half-expecting his father's house to explode before his eyes. "What did they want?"

"They seemed perfectly nice, once we got to chatting," Clive replied blithely. "They were jolly interested in my plans."

"You didn't give them your address, did you?"

His father snorted with derision. "Don't be ridiculous. Do you think I'm that much of a fool –" Clive stopped mid-sentence just then, and squirmed uncomfortably. "Well ... I might have let slip the name of the Village. I told them about the Restaurant, you see. They hadn't heard of it, which didn't surprise me much, as they clearly weren't foodies – doubt they could even spell 'gastronomy' – but they were very interested in my Hawaiian theme and my plans for resurrecting the old film studios. I gave them some information. Think I threw them off the scent, though, by signing 'James Bond' on the back of my business card!"

Clive sniggered, and Sam's heartbeat quickened. *That means Luca's nemeses are already in the Village*, he thought, peering through the rain at his father's beloved home standing fortress-like against the storm. Was that a shadow from the boughs of the cedar he saw? Or was there a movement in the upstairs window?

"Listen, Son ..." Sam turned his attention back to his father, who leaned into the screen and said, gently: "Don't look so worried. I'll be home next week. I know you've missed your old Dad, and I can't wait to get back." He chortled, adding: "You and Cecilia must be desperate for my return; I bet the Village has been a morgue since I left."

It was Sam's moment to tell Clive the truth, but he did not know what to say or how to begin, so he simply replied: "Yeah, you could say that." He flicked the switch on the computer monitor and watched despairingly as Clive's handsome face faded to grey.

A few doors down, Ivy was reading the missive that had been pushed through her letterbox that morning. Her hands trembled, and bile rose up in her throat. She fingered the pages of an old Bible. "Be strong and courageous," the Book of Joshua told her. "Do not be afraid; do not be discouraged, for the LORD your God will be with you wherever you go." But Ivy could not feel His presence, and she was afraid.

She had been shaken to discover the handwritten envelope on her doormat at dawn, six o'clock not being the designated hour for postal delivery. The communiqué had tormented her from the kitchen table all day, ruining her precious routine and vanquishing her already meagre appetite. So by the time the clock struck four, the appointed time for reading post, Ivy was already in a state of high anxiety.

Grappling with the letter opener, she had sliced her index finger in a desperate bid to open the envelope; then, hampered by the shapes and patterns that muddled her vision, she had been forced to use a magnifying glass to decipher the blood-splattered scrawl.

You and I have more in common than you might think. Meet me at the church before you lock up at 6pm. I shall give three sharp knocks on the door.

Luca Tempesta

The American's words whipped up around her like a hurricane, forcing Ivy to cower and wrap her arms around her body in defence. These were dark days. Only a fool would not fear them. She and Nigel Bond had found out the truth about Luca Tempesta, and now he had summoned her – and she knew she must go.

She pulled on her Pac-a-Mac and stepped out into the storm. It was not visiting time at the care home, but Ivy needed to see her mentor in order to have a clear vision and be shown the path ahead. She could not, would not act without Nigel Bond's permission.

"Forgive us our sins," she pleaded as the strange shapes danced and the hailstones raged, battering her tiny frame and flagellating her conscience, "as we forgive those who sin against us."

To her great distress, when she arrived at the care home, Ivy's entry to Nigel's apartment was barred by two nurses. "You can't go in, love, he's with the consultant," one said firmly. "Remember, he's undergoing cognitive functioning tests today."

Back on the pavement, the rain fell in torrents. Ivy began to shake uncontrollably. The thought of acting without permission made her retch. Maybe God would show her the way?

"Forgive us our trespasses," she begged as she scuttled back along the high street and through the churchyard, not noticing Amanda Jones until she stepped from the shadows near the lychgate.

"Ah, Miss Midwinter, just the person! I have some information that might interest you." Ivy, startled, waved her away, scurrying as fast as her sparrow legs would allow for the safety of home. She could hear Amanda chasing her, and emitted an involuntary anguished cry.

"OK, OK, keep your hair on!" the journalist called, and her footfalls died out. Home at last, Ivy felt she was standing on the brink of madness, and threw herself down on the cold, hard flagstones of the kitchen, surrendering herself to the mercy of the Lord.

"Yea, though I walk through the valley of the shadow of death, I will fear no evil, for Thou art with me; Thy rod and Thy staff, they comfort me ..." she muttered. But still, she could not feel Him.

Several minutes later, Ivy shook her head as if awakening from a dream and lifted herself from the floor. The room was silent, save for the relentless ticking of the clock and Peter the Rock lumbering somewhere nearby. She felt the presence of Sister Mary and reached out a hand, but there was nobody there. At the bureau, she ignored her friend's unopened letter, omnipresent against her photograph, and instead removed the Tempesta file and a set of ancient keys.

"Lead us not into temptation," she whispered, carefully placing the document into a plastic bag so it would not be destroyed by the rain. Then, still wearing the same damp raincoat, keys jangling at her side, Ivy made her way to the church, propelled by an acceptance of the inevitable and possessed by a new, icy calm.

The church was silent; the slight rasp of Ivy's breathing as she knelt to pray was the only sound to be heard.

"Dear Lord," she said, "give me the strength to face my fears." There was a rumble of thunder, and the church clock struck six. Then there came three sharp raps. "Deliver us from evil," Ivy intoned, and rose to open the door to Luca. He towered before her, his heavy black overcoat dripping with rain.

TWENTY-SEVEN

I T WAS A difficult encounter, and one he had hoped to avoid, but the old woman had summoned him to the church. Unable to risk his cover being blown, he had been forced to silence her. She had been prepared as he stepped from the driving rain into the church vestibule.

"I know all about you, Mr Tempesta," she spat, her large pupils shining like bullets as he wiped away the raindrops that streamed down his face like tears. "You and your friends make it your business to destroy people with your lies. You cheat, deceive and ruin."

He followed in silence, keen to hear how much she knew as she walked ahead of him to the nave. "Your friends ruined Nigel Bond's life," Ivy hissed, kneeling at the altar step and closing her eyes. "Their actions destroyed him in a way the death of his only child, my friend Sister Mary Agatha, could not. Have you no shame, Mr Tempesta?"

As she joined her hands in prayer, Luca placed his own hand upon her shoulder in an attempt to make her look at him. Ivy recoiled and grasped at her neck chain. "Don't touch me!" she shrieked, pulling away and curling into a ball at the foot of the altar. A movement near the door indicated that they were not alone, but the old woman brandished her St Christopher like a talisman against evil and continued hysterically, rocking to and fro: "You and your compatriots are demons! You are devils incarnate, and I shall expose your wrongdoings to the world!"

Luca felt a fleeting shame at fanning the flames of her madness, but he was left with no choice. "You will do no such thing, Miss Midwinter," he whispered, taking a firm hold of her arms and forcing her to look into his eyes. "Because you know nothing about me, and I know everything about you." The touch of his hand seemed to bring her to her senses, her mask of wrath slipping to reveal the vulnerable, frail old woman beneath.

"Eternal Father, I offer Thee the Most Precious Blood of Thy Divine Son ..." she gabbled, and Luca shook her a little to make her listen.

"Your work for the British secret service is small currency compared to your early years, isn't it Miss Midwinter?" The cruel words shot straight to the heart of his target, but were inaudible to the listening shadows. "I know everything about your life in Scotland."

Ivy pulled away, crying out as her skeletal frame hit the hard floor. She remained there, supine and shaking.

"... For the holy souls in Purgatory, for sinners everywhere, for sinners in the universal Church ..."

Her prayers could not protect her from Luca's pitiless attack. "I know of your violation at the hands of your father, and of the illegitimate child you bore him," he continued. "I know your baby was spirited away, and that you failed your friend in her suicidal despair. And I know that your life has been financed by money your father embezzled from his parishioners. So please, don't talk to me about 'demons', Ivy, because I am well acquainted with every one of yours. If you so much as whisper my name, they will come back to haunt you – and I will reveal everything to your precious friends."

A glimmer of light followed by the sound of angry voices from the vestibule prompted Luca to straighten up and step out of the shadows. A familiar silhouette rose sharply against a backdrop of powerful torchlight. Appearing to recognise the figure, Ivy called out: "Sister Mary, is that you?"

She rose from floor and looked around blindly for the saviour whose presence she had sensed. "I will read your letter, my love," she whispered. "Come, Mary, don't hide away, step into the light!" But Ivy's salvation turned away from her.

"You had an eavesdropper in the vestibule – the journalist," the newcomer said angrily to Luca. "I managed to despatch her. Now, *you* disappear. I'll take over from here." She crouched over Ivy's tiny frame, and the old woman smiled serenely as her nemesis slipped away into the night.

A dead calm followed the storm, and the next day Luca watched from the cover of a mighty oak as the funeral proceeded along the winding path towards the church. The only person to notice him in his dappled hideout was Cecilia, who, tearstained and lovely in a yellow dress, half-turned and caught his eye before being spirited away on a tide of mourners. He drew heavily on his cigarette, extinguished it underfoot and saluted the coffin as it disappeared through the ancient doors. *The Devil walks in straight lines*, he thought, cutting through the cemetery and trampling primroses and forget-me-nots underfoot.

"Dearly beloved," Reverend James' resonant voice sounded gently around the crowded church, "we are gathered together to celebrate an extraordinary life. A father, a friend, a hero and a healer, Harry Davidson – or Harley, as he became known – was an extraordinary man." The silence was interrupted only by the occasional sob. "Harley had pancreatic cancer, and he knew he was dying; but like Jesus in the storm, he faced his death with great calm, understanding that his Heavenly Father would be with him, watching over him on this, his last journey." Some of the congregation, whom Reverend James knew to be Harley's biker friends, smiled sadly.

"Harley and I often read the Bible together," he said to murmurs of surprise from those gathered. "And some verses from Thessalonians inspired him to leave us a list he called 'Harley's Revelations', to help us understand that his time on Earth had been full and varied and happy – so we may celebrate his remarkable life rather than grieve his passing. And we shall start with the most sensational." The vicar then declared, dramatically: "Did you know that our big, gentle friend once had afternoon tea with Mrs Thatcher?"

Delighted laughter rang out from the congregation, and

Reverend James breathed a sigh of relief; he had been anxious about his sermon, but it had got off to a good start. "And more importantly," he continued, "Harley had eleven children and five grandchildren, all of whom are here with us today." The mourners looked around them, seeking out Harley's family, seated together at the front.

The click of a latch echoed around the church, and Reverend James glanced up briefly to see a red-faced Frank Fielding tiptoe in and take a place at the back. The villagers pretended not to notice.

"I wrote this sermon yesterday," said the vicar from the pulpit. "I sat in the vicarage kitchen, the weather raging, and I thought of those who have departed this Earth, who are already beyond the tempest – and how, today, we come together to celebrate Harley's journey to that peaceful place." He waited a moment for his metaphor to settle, glancing over to the new organ where Ivy sat, blinking and tense. She had not been herself of late, and the vicar prayed that she would not falter on this important day.

Below Ivy, the west transept of the church had been set aside for the villagers. At the far end, Joy bowed her head to pray. The eyes that twinkled from the pulpit brought to her mind Harley's wink at the Fieldings' dinner party; she recalled the discomfort it had invoked. Yet somehow, that knowing glint in his eye had made her feel feminine, like the woman she was afraid to be. Hugh squeezed her hand, and a sentimental tear was released down her cheek.

"The next of Harley's revelations relates to the following hymn," said Reverend James. "Long ago, straight out of school, Harry Davidson was a 'greaser' in the Merchant Navy, and I believe there are a few of his fellow seamen with us today. So please, stand for the 'Sailors' Hymn', and join together in *For Those in Peril on the Sea*."

Hugh leaped to his feet. "Eternal Father, strong to save," he roared.

From the pew behind him, Cecilia leaned over and offered Joy a handkerchief. She was surprised to see her indomitable employer weeping for a man with whom she was barely on nodding acquaintance, but then again, Harley had touched many people's lives – her own included. She remembered the gentle wisdom he had imparted on the day she had told him of her secret yearning for a child. Cecilia was not sure whether it had been the relief of confession or the kindness in his voice, but a burden had lifted from her that day, and she had immediately understood that her desire for offspring issued from a fear of loneliness. Gazing at Molly now, her quizzical face trying to make sense of the hymn, Cecilia realised she would never be lonely, because she had Esther's child to love. She also had Sam. And a wonderful new man. *My cup runneth over*, she thought dreamily, and gave a quiet prayer of thanks.

Beside her, Sam drew comfort from Cecilia's closeness. He breathed in the fragrance of her name, which, despite the morbid surroundings, filled his senses with the wonder of a summer day. That scent had guided him through his teenage years and would, he was now certain, persist into adulthood, irrespective of his father. He glanced at the sombre faces of Harley's eight sons and felt sadness at their loss of a good, kind father, though he was a man they hardly knew. He felt overwhelmed with a fondness for his own old man, and relief that he was returning home to the Village.

Two rows down, Basil appeared determined to drown out Hugh Willoughby.

"Whose arm hath bound ..." he rumbled. Rosamund sang prettily beside him, smiling inwardly at the ridiculous stiff upper lips of two men she knew had been shaken at the death of a villager younger than they, singing out their sadness to give him "a good send-off". Since the news, Rosamund had sensed a slight change in her husband – less of the Coco Pops and more of the muesli, perhaps one less glass of Rioja at night. "Tiny steps," she thought, glancing at Bianca, who sat in front of them alone and distraught.

Reverend James continued his address: "Harley returned from the sea and applied to do marine biology, but, the course being full, he undertook a degree in botany instead, then proceeded to a Master's Degree and then a PhD in the subject. Perhaps this explains the extraordinary oneness and love for nature that he carries to the grave, his body committed to the ground, entwined in its ivy shroud – earth to earth, ashes to ashes, dust to dust."

There was a sob near the front and a commotion at the back; then Frank walked, head bowed, down the aisle to where his wife sat weeping. He slid into the pew and laid a tentative arm around her. He could hear the intake of breath behind him. Would she reject or rejoice in his show of solidarity? Frank himself did not know.

"From rock and tempest, fire, and foe, protect them wheresoe'er they go," intoned Reverend James, and Bianca laid her head on her husband's shoulder and took his hand in hers. Frank looked up at the vast granite statue of Jesus and the Virgin Mary, and closed his eyes.

"Thank you, Lord," whispered the lifelong atheist. "Thank you."

"You may know that, like many seamen before him, Harley's first tattoo, lest he incur her wrath, was 'Mum,'" Reverend James told the congregation. "Few of you will know, however, of the time when, somewhat worse for wear, his friends took him to a tattooist who did not speak English and – or so they claim – misunderstood his request for 'Harry' on one cheek and 'Davidson' on the other. And so a legend was born, and I believe that Harry, or 'Harley' as he then became, could barely sit for a month!"

There was muted amusement from the congregation, but one laugh – a little too loud – rose above the crowd and caught Bianca's attention. She glanced over her husband's shoulder to see Kathy McConnell, her head crowned with a black, feathery fascinator, clinging to the arm of Joy's brother Edmund.

"Bleedin' 'Ell, look what the cat dragged in!" she whispered to Frank, as though nothing had happened between them. Shaking her head in disbelief, she searched her handbag for some cream, which she quietly applied to her husband's eczema-ridden wrists.

"It is easy for us to see the storm as our sea of troubles," said Reverend James.

"Yer tellin' me," Bianca whispered. "You should've seen me

yesterday. A tempest in a bleedin' teapot." Frank squeezed her harder.

Felicity sat in front of Bianca, still as a statue, dry-eyed and hollow. Harley had been her patient sun, ever-present, strong and healing.

"Some of you will know that Harley was an insomniac. Not many will know that he was a night owl at our local charity, the Port Sanctuary, where he sat through the midnight hours listening to the woes and worries of despairing and disenfranchised ex-military personnel, supporting them in their darkest moments before he returned home through the woods and crawled, exhausted, into his bed at dawn."

How had she not known that? Felicity wondered. How had she lived with Harley, known him all those years, and never known about the grandchildren, the Navy, the PhD or even the local charity? Her throat constricted and her breath shortened, and as her panic rose, so did her need to escape, to be free.

"We have weathered the storm, and today we bask in the restorative rays of the sun, in the love and warmth of our Lord," said Reverend James, and Felicity shivered. "Death takes us beyond the tempest of our existence; it frees us from the storm of our daily lives for a calmer place. So let us join together for our last hymn: 'The strife is o'er, the battle done; the victory of life is won; the song of triumph has begun. Alleluia!'"

That evening, Luca leaned against the iron railings at Cleopatra's Needle and watched a London barge chug slowly upstream. A screech of gulls drowned out the rush-hour traffic, along with the sound of his heart banging noisily against his chest. Catching his breath, he remembered standing in the exact same spot with his pregnant wife all those years ago, and how giddy they had felt with the dream of a new beginning.

He sensed her presence before she stepped into view and watched, as if through a lens, as the "camera" panned towards her beautiful face and London's dramatic skyline rose up behind her in glorious cinematic colour. Luca recognised her instantly. She was the woman who had sent his pulse racing in the New Town supermarket. The same brown hair, tied into a ponytail; the same golden bracelet, jangling against her arm. He regretted not finding the necessary words before they met. But what was the point? His stalker knew the truth anyway.

She was close now, so close he could smell the heady fragrance of jasmine and sandalwood on her skin. He stood perfectly still, his hands bunched neatly together.

"You came," she said, her manner tentative, her face closed.

He held her unblinking stare. "You found me."

"You haven't made it easy for me, Luca. But now that I have found you, please don't think about running; I have all your exits covered."

The ghost of a smile swept across her face, and Luca's heart ached at the familiarity of her luminous skin and sharp-angled body. Trying to keep his emotions in check, he stared down at the ancient Thames and its beach of infinite shingle. Above them a candescent sun had turned her hair into a halo of flaming gold.

"Come," she instructed. "We have a lot to talk about."

He wanted to cry, but there were no tears. Luca knew it was game over.

TWENTY-EIGHT

S PRING WAS FLOURISHING into early summer, the delights of which shone down on Rosamund as she made her way to the Willoughbys' that Friday morning. She and Joy were off to Monkey Island to choose the menu for Joy's Sunday afternoon shindig in honour of Luca, who was returning to America after his holiday in the Village.

Rosamund knew from Basil that the extent of their friends' financial collapse was not as drastic as Joy had believed, thanks to secret investments Hugh had not declared "for fear," according to Basil, "that Joy give it all to that wastrel Penny. We men weren't born yesterday you know, Duchess." She thought of the countless times she had quietly bailed out Rupert and felt ashamed. If she had not indulged him, might her son have grown up honest and honourable like his father?

Crossing the footbridge, Rosamund spotted Bianca and Tallulah chatting and laughing in their garden. She batted away a pang of regret at never having had a daughter, and was surprised by an almost maternal pride in her new friend. Bianca was, after all, twenty years her junior; she had endured a lot these past few weeks, and comported herself with the dignity of a true lady after Frank vanished. Rosamund smiled as she recalled her typically glib response to this praise: "Oh, I'm like a teabag, I am – you never know how strong I am till you put me in hot water!"

"Well, I admire you," Rosamund had countered. "Not many would have been so magnanimous."

Bianca's naïve response had charmed Rosamund: "Yeah, bu-ut ... if I get bitter and jealous, isn't that like drinking poison an' hopin' it'll kill Sandra?"

Rosamund thought, again with shame, of her own reaction to the unwelcome attentions of Kathy – whom she had, after all, gone to some trouble to charm in the first place.

"You are very wise, Bianca Fielding," she laughed. "I could learn a lot from you. But I still think you're brave."

It had been Bianca's turn to laugh. "Not *that* brave – 'ave you 'eard how old she is? 'Ave you seen 'er?"

"No."

"Ha! Well," said Bianca, scrolling through her phone, "take a gander at this!" Rosamund had been surprised when Bianca presented a photo of a lady who looked not unlike her old headmistress.

"I know 'e's an old fool," Bianca had reasoned, "but even I can't be jealous of that! Me Dad was a bit of a one, and Mam always said, 'Bianca, you 'ave to find a way to love yer man without trustin' 'im.' Well, I always knew I couldn't trust Frank; 'e just loves women too much! And e's too soft, poor lamb. Anyway, all real men 'ave a drop of philandering in their veins, don't they? The trick is getting' 'em to come 'ome afterwards. Surely Basil has played away at some time, 'asn't 'e?"

Rosamund, who never discussed her marriage, had surprised herself with her candid response. "The closest we ever came to blows was over Rupert," she replied. "I always sided with him over poor Basil, but when he went to prison I realised what a blind fool I'd been. I should have stuck by my man like you have, Bianca. You are an example to us all."

Bianca had squeezed Rosamund's hand. "Oh, Roz, I do feel sorry for you, it must be awful 'avin' such a prat for a son!"

How life had changed these past three months, Rosamund reflected; she would not have found Bianca's comment about her wayward son amusing until recently. She slipped off her shoes to wander across the Willoughbys' lush croquet lawn, enjoying the feeling of spring grass between her toes.

Thinking about it, the catalyst to change had been Clive Buchanan's departure and the arrival of Luca in the Village; it had caused a butterfly effect, and even Joy had been tickled by the flutter of its wings. Rosamund suspected that when he returned, Clive might sense a change of allegiance in his former admirer, who was being uncharacteristically girly about the party preparations and had a new spring in her step. Hugh seemed in fine fettle too, and he and Joy were delighted with their new Tuesday night Rock Choir, to which they cycled together on shiny new bicycles (a gift from Tom and Jake). Rosamund was far too discreet to ask, but she could not help suspecting that her old friend might just have heeded her whispered advice and paid a visit to the Professor.

While his wife was helping to prepare the send-off for the charming American with a penchant for kung fu, Basil was getting their garden in shape for the upcoming Village in Bloom competition. He had planned a military-inspired garden, but Ivy had told him, in no uncertain terms, that this year's theme would be wildflowers – in honour of Harley's love of nature – and that Basil must adhere to it. Rosamund had suggested they employ a landscape gardener, but he could not see the point in throwing money away when any fool could hack things back a bit. True, he did not know a daisy from a delphinium, and his wife often accused him of massacring the borders, but as far as Basil was concerned, if it was green and leafy then a good chop would improve it. He strimmed away happily; the house-swap agency had made an appointment to visit on Monday, so he needed to get their plot ship-shape for them too, and then – Basil gave a little skip as he dwelled on the prospect – he and the Duchess were to take a sabbatical in the City of Love.

He revved the strimmer and set about the honeysuckle as he dreamed of pavement cafés, walks along the Seine and starlight over the Eiffel Tower. He was assailed by the sweet fragrance of decapitated flowers as they flew in every direction, and by the time he came to his senses, even Basil could see he had neutered the poor plant in its prime. He had only intended to trim the odd trailing strand. He looked at the naked, woody skeleton clinging to the pergola and went off to get the leaf blower. Perhaps Rosamund was right – it might have been better to get somebody who knew what they were doing.

Blasting away all evidence of his slaughter, Basil's mind turned to Kathy McConnell. He had never seen Rosamund take against somebody as she had the Willoughbys' former housekeeper. He even wondered whether her jealousy had been the inspiration for their forthcoming summer of love. He indulged in a little chuckle when Hugh told him Kathy had hooked up with Edmund Pendlegrass; no wonder the man had a bit more colour in his cheeks of late! He wondered how long they had kept that little secret. Basil loved Joy, but she could be somewhat turgid, and although Rosamund had made him promise not to, he longed to tease her about Kathy's promotion from fired housekeeper to sister-in-law. Basil could not see the problem; his wife had been scandalised at first, but he suspected she was relieved that the happy couple were apparently moving to Scotland, where Kathy would be far away from the temptations of the Basil Braithwaite love machine.

Joy waited until the promise of dusk and slipped out of the house. She wore a tweed skirt, a shabby polo neck jumper and a stout pair of gardening shoes. She searched in the garage for a basket in which to transport the bedding plants she had bought for the church garden, and a moment of whimsy struck when she noticed her shiny new bike – with its perfectly proportioned basket. She clambered on and headed along the towpath, the white lobelia quivering before her.

Alighting to push the bicycle over the footbridge, Joy paused to marvel at two young punters propelling themselves against the current with surprising speed. She watched the punts grow smaller as they cut through the water like hot knives. How had Bill Lewis covered his tracks, she wondered? To whom should she speak to establish the whys and wherefores of his decade of duplicity? Perhaps she would look into it, she thought, as she mounted the bike and began to turn the pedals; it would do her good to focus on something other than hearth and home. The bicycle gathered momentum, and an idea began to form in Joy's mind. It was important, she reflected, to be a good female role model for the daughter she had not heard from for several weeks, but whom she felt certain would be home soon. Hurtling down the descent, she stuck out her stout legs and let out a squeal of anticipation, pedals spinning and skirt flying up in the wind. As she deftly ducked a bramble, she suddenly knew exactly what she would do. She would form a pressure group to establish what had happened. She would lobby the government for recompense, expose Lewis as a charlatan and a crook, and ensure that such financial impropriety never happened again.

TWENTY-NINE

S AM WAS BESIDE himself with concern, and had been for days.

"Try not to worry, Sam," Cecilia had reassured him after Luca vanished. "At least we know he's not dead; he's probably taking a trip." But Sam *had* worried. At best, he decided, the FBI had carted Luca away, and at worst, the hoodlums – acting on a tip-off from his own father – had murdered him. The skin around Sam's nails was raw and bitten to the quick after so many days on a knife-edge.

Then, one quiet afternoon some days after Harley's funeral, Sam heard the American's familiar laughter ringing out from behind Reverend James' garden hedge. He approached with caution, leaning his ear into the box hedging to be sure. The chatter was unmistakable: Luca was back. After days spent fretting over his disappearance, it felt like a slap in the face to find him this way. It was the last straw: Sam took a running jump and climbed over the garden wall. Luca and the vicar appeared unsurprised when his beet-red face appeared through the wisteria.

"Hello, Sam," his neighbour said pleasantly, lifting a china teapot and giving it a shake. "Darjeeling? Do join us."

Luca waved a red napkin and pointed to a mountain of jelly-tot cakes stacked up between them. So even Molly knows he's back, Sam fumed, charging over to the tea party with the bluster of a stampeding bull.

"So, don't you mind about me," he said irately, pulling up a chair. "I've only been beside myself with worry for five days, that's all. Hardly slept a wink, waiting for you to come home, and here you are" – Sam paused and swallowed hard – "drinking tea!"

"Who are you, my father?" Luca quipped, raising an eyebrow, Sam shot him an acid look.

"So you think it's a joke?" he demanded. "The question is not who am I, but who are *you*? It's time you came clean about the Kuznetsoy trial, and the fact you're some sort of Russian spy." He paused for dramatic effect. "I've got the police on speed dial," he warned, holding his phone aloft. "Just one button and they'll be here in a flash."

Luca released an exasperated breath and flung his hands in the air in surrender. "Jeez, not you as well?" he exclaimed. "Here I am, trying to hide out in England and keep the darned Kuznetsoy trial a secret, and it turns out the world and his dog knows about it." He laughed drily. Then, noting Sam's angry expression, added: "That's Shakespeare, right?"

"No!" snapped Sam, helping himself to cake. His concern for Luca had put him off food for days, but he now found himself gripped by a mad sugar craving, and he was rather partial to Molly's cakes. The vicar smiled benevolently and placed his china teacup on the table.

"It must be galling, Luca, to realise that so many of us know about your involvement in this trial," he said calmly. "It is a case of Chinese Whispers, I'm afraid: Ivy telling Sam, Sam telling Cecilia, Cecilia telling Molly and Molly telling me. That's why I thought it best to invite you for tea and try to put an end to the gossip." He chuckled and refreshed Luca's cup. "The English are famously oblique. They are disinclined to say what they mean or mean what they say, and they avoid confrontation at all cost, preferring to tittle-tattle with each other rather than tell us what they think."

"Well, I did mull over the trial with a few friends," Sam squirmed, before adding pointedly: "We all agreed you seem pretty laid back, considering the FBI is after you."

Sam was unable to interpret the American's searching look, as if Luca was making up his mind about something. Then, as a yellow sun dipped behind the alders and ashes, he finally came clean.

"I'm not a Russian secret agent," he said very seriously. "Far from it. The secret I've been trying to hide, apparently without success, is that I'm the lead witness in an important Russian spy trial. It was me who uncovered the spy ring you read about in the newspaper, and my evidence will bring down Anna Charlton, *aka* Natasha Kuznetsoy." Sam, who had his mouth stuffed with cake, almost choked.

"But Natasha's your wife!" he cried, spluttering crumbs all over the table, "Cecilia told me."

Luca smiled sadly. "My wife – my ex-wife – is dead. The name is pure coincidence."

"So I was right! You are involved in something mega!"

"Massive," Luca nodded. "I couldn't confide in you, because I didn't want to involve you. There has been some pretty heavy stuff surrounding this trial, and I couldn't afford to risk my identity becoming known."

Luca proceeded to tell his rapt audience of the events leading up to the capture of Kuznetsoy, the Russian spy who had been masquerading as Anna Charlton, and how, after Clive had revealed his location, he had been forced to abandon Kingfisher House and seek refuge elsewhere. Sam listened to his tales of shootouts and derring-do in awe.

When it grew chilly, the two men bid Reverend James goodbye and headed home. As they strolled along Riverside Lane, Luca slung an arm around Sam's shoulder, and the teenager felt happy for the first time in days.

They headed back to The Boathouse and had beers on Sam's balcony, staring silently into the black river, the pungent smell of ancient sediment rising up to greet them.

"So why are you discussing the trial now?" Sam asked, "What's changed?"

"Well, I'm only telling a select few," replied Luca. "Now that Charlton's husband has been arrested, it's believed my life is no longer in danger. As for the rest of the villagers, well, you can spill the beans after I've gone!"

Luca watched Sam closely. He had only scratched the surface

in recounting his story, not wanting to frighten him; far better, he reckoned, that Sam thought of it all as a thrilling adventure. He had purposefully not mentioned Natasha's violent death in a fireball on the freeway, just days after Luca had gone to her for advice. She had cast her net wide, using her Russian contacts to gather information, and three days later she was dead. The autopsy results had come just before Luca disappeared, proving his suspicions of murder to be unfounded. Her death was apparently a freak accident. No one was to blame. Luca had telephoned Natasha's mentor in Moscow to share the news.

"Time to lay her ghost to rest, Luca," the academic had advised sagely. He had to admit it was a relief.

Orion burst through the night sky and stars glittered across the heavens like dewdrops on a spider web. Luca thought back to the last day he had seen his wife; he had not only wanted help with the trial, he had hoped for reconciliation. Despite having been divorced for almost ten years and both parties having had numerous affairs, no one had ever lit up his life like Natasha, or even come close. He pondered briefly how life might have been had they been blessed with a son like Sam, and then relegated the thought to the back of his mind. Meeting Cecilia had gone some way to helping him block out the pain of his wife's death and remain focused on the trial, but he knew that he had to face the agony of his loss one day.

"So let me get this straight," Sam deliberated as Luca kicked off his shoes and reclined in his deck chair. "You almost killed Ivy Midwinter?"

"Yeah, almost," he replied cheerfully, reaching for his beer. "The old broad got into such lather, I thought she was going to have a heart attack. Luckily, Felicity was in the church and took charge of things. She also caught that journalist from the *Gazette* taping our conversation. Apparently she suspected Ivy and me of some sort of dark collaboration, so she tricked us into meeting in the hope that we would reveal our secret, and she would get some scintillating copy!"

Sam, who was trying to keep up with Luca's version of events, was not quite so amused.

"But what was Ivy's connection to all this in the first place?" he asked, slurping his beer. "How did she know about the Kuznetsoy trial? And why did she get her knickers in a twist over it?"

Luca smiled. "That was a different trial from a different time, unconnected save for the coincidence of the 'Kuznetsoy' name – which is as common as 'Smith' in Russia," said Luca. "You jumped to conclusions over a Christian name, and Ivy jumped to conclusions over a surname, and so a tangled web was weaved." He recounted the extraordinary story of the old spymaster Nigel Bond and his Svengali-like influence over Ivy; but he did not reveal the secret of her tragic teenage years, and her child born of her abusive father. Those stories were not Luca's to share; indeed, had he known Ivy was so unstable, tyrannised by illness, guilt and the wild fantasies of an old man gripped in the twilight of his past, he might not have been so cruel.

"But she did have something on you, Luca," Sam reasoned. "She suspected you from the start. How did she know you had flown in from Russia?"

Luca flicked his cigarette packet. "Man, I admit that baffled me for a long time," he said. "Then I remembered her clocking my cigarette packet in the shop when I picked up the Kingfisher House keys. Java Gold – a Russian brand! It's always the little things that give you away in the end. Guess I wouldn't have made a great spy after all."

Luca's phone buzzed. He checked his message and smiled; it was from the person who, during his brief time in hiding, he had come to nickname "Stalker" affectionately.

Yesterday is gone. Tomorrow has not yet come. We have only today, let it begin. Her words reached out to him in the darkness.

THIRTY

F ELICITY SAVOURED THE silence of the empty house. The boys were with their father, and she wondered briefly how long his new marriage would survive with four kids to break up the happy party. Same problem, different wife, she thought, as she flung another item of clothing into the pannier.

Harley's ghost was everywhere, from his books piled high in the living room to the contours of his heavy frame still outlined on the cushion of his favourite armchair. She could swear she had spotted him that morning tinkering at the piano, his straw hat set at a jaunty angle, and as she had tossed and turned in her bed the night before, his gravelly voice had called to her from the garden.

The last item Felicity packed was Harley's love letter, the one Luca had given her the day he died in the woodland amidst his cherished wildlife. She did not like to think of him dying, cold and alone, in the coppice – but it had been his wish, so she tried to take comfort from the thought of her big man gazing up at the vastness of infinite space as he exhaled his last breath. *He is with the stars now*, she thought sadly.

Harley had bequeathed to Felicity the royalties from the special song he had penned for her, and his lawyer said she would be rich – very rich. In her desperate need to flee, Felicity had handed the travel agent the list of exotic destinations she and Harley had drawn up together one rainy afternoon by the fireplace. It had all been nothing more than a castle in the sky back then, something to dream about on a cold, depressing day, and she could hardly believe their fantasy would now become reality. But at what cost? Would the journey be the same without Harley? Felicity had felt compelled to give it a go, knowing in her heart this was what he would have wanted.

The thought of Harley's letter brought to mind the tragic note she and Ivy had read together the night before his funeral. Felicity had been mired in grief, seeking solace in the church vestry, when her peace was interrupted by whispers and footsteps. Peering over the transept, she had spotted Amanda Jones fiddling with a tape recorder. She had marched downstairs and given the journalist a what-for.

It had been upsetting to then find Ivy, broken and cowering in the nave, and Felicity had been furious with Luca for frightening her friend so badly. She had sent him away and lifted Ivy gently from the floor, leading her outside into the rain to where Amanda sat in her car typing frantically into her phone.

"Take us to Riverside Lane," Felicity had commanded, bundling a sobbing and soaked Ivy into the back and climbing in beside her. Amanda had tried to apologise, offering some cock-and-bull story about bringing Luca and Ivy together for an almighty showdown, but Felicity had not let her off the hook.

"Are you nuts?" she had demanded, clutching the shaking Ivy.

"Mary ... Mary," her old friend kept calling, and Felicity had stroked her back and shouted at Amanda.

"Why on Earth would you think Ivy and Luca were in any way connected?"

"I dunno," the journalist replied, pulling up outside Sunnyside. "Just a hunch, I guess. But I still want to know about her connection with the spymaster Nigel Bond."

"Nigel! Nigel, yes, we must consult Nigel," Ivy had cried. Turning to Felicity, she whispered: "You broke his heart, you know, and you broke mine – why did you kill yourself?"

"Look what you've bloody gone and done now!" Felicity berated Amanda, who, frightened by Ivy's raving, despatched her passengers with unseemly haste.

"Must I take my own life for us to have one last farewell?" Ivy had cried in despair.

Inside the austere little cottage, Felicity had poured them each a brandy, which had comforted her friend. Eventually, Ivy's weeping subsided. As if awakening from an anaesthetic, she slowly became aware of her surroundings and was much astonished to discover Felicity holding her hand.

"How did you get in?" she asked in a small, bewildered voice.

"Don't worry about that now, Ivy, just relax and take it easy. You've had some sort of breakdown."

"Well that explains the dream," she said, sipping the amber liquid. "God visited me and told me to face up to my demons, or I would be answerable to the Devil."

Felicity gulped back her drink and decided there could be no benefit in disillusioning her friend; better, perhaps, that she dismiss the experience as hysteria than be haunted by the stark reality of her encounter with Luca. Looking down at Ivy, Felicity understood that although she longed for her bed, the cool, cotton sheets and the luxury of crying alone, her strange friend needed her; Felicity took strength from providing another soul with the comfort that still eluded her.

"On the bureau you will find a letter. Please hand it to me, Felicity." Ivy pointed to an oak cabinet in the corner of the gloomy room. The letter was yellow with age, and Felicity watched as Ivy opened it with trembling hands. She read every word slowly, reverently. A radiant smile lit up her face as she looked up.

"I have lived for decades believing that I failed my dearest friend in her suicidal despair," she whispered, in tears. "But I did not. Sister Mary loved me, but she was beholden to voices in her head I could never have drowned out. They told her to die, to kill herself, to free her soul from the burdens of this mortal world."

Not knowing what to say, Felicity had taken Ivy into her arms and consoled her.

"Don't you see, Felicity," she had whispered, "Mary has released me, freed me from my burden. There was nothing I could ever have done to save her. Oh, how I wish I had had the courage to open that letter all those years ago."

The two women had rocked backwards and forwards, Felicity taking comfort from her friend's gaunt embrace, Ivy sobbing out relief from a lifetime of guilt. They clung to each other for a long while, weeping for their regrets and mistakes, and for that which was gone and could never come again.

Her packing complete, Felicity fastened the panniers. The night of the storm had been cathartic. The squall had whipped up a frenzy outside the window, and washed clean the two women's fear and remorse. Felicity no longer needed to worry about her friend, who had banished the memory of her encounter with Luca – the Devil, no doubt – from her memory and emerged renewed. Frank Fielding had promised to take good care of her, and Felicity knew she would be in safe hands.

She hauled her luggage downstairs and cast her eye around the living room one last time. Outside the Georgian windows she saw Harley seated amidst the curly hazel, smoking a herbal cigarette. He raised his hand in greeting and mouthed: "Choose life." With that he was gone, and so was Felicity, roaring down Riverside Lane on his Norton Commando, the wind in her hair and the open road stretching ahead.

THIRTY-ONE

THE SKY WAS cornflower blue, and a charm of goldfinches was raiding Ivy's bird table when Frank parked his Range Rover outside Sunnyside the following morning. He was resplendent in a harlequin-chequered jumper, Brylcreemed and perma-tanned to perfection.

"Knock, knock!" he called as he let himself in. "Ready?"

Ivy remained motionless at the kitchen table, her handbag on her knee, her straight spine eschewing the comforts of the chair back. She said nothing, so, glancing at his gold Rolex, Frank continued: "Come on, let's get this over with. The early bird, and all that."

Ivy followed obediently, and he opened the passenger door and bowed with a flourish as she climbed into his car's kidskin embrace.

"Belt up," he said, and gently humming to himself, he slipped the transmission into "drive" and they glided silently out of Riverside Lane. "It's the longest day today, nearly time to do something with that tortoise of yours, isn't it?"

"He sleeps outside between the equinox and solstice," Ivy replied woodenly.

Frank laughed. "That's right. And if memory serves me correctly, you barely get a wink of sleep for fear of losing him!"

Ivy did not laugh, and Frank felt awkward. He was not comfortable around personal problems he could not fix, so he chatted fatuously until, to his relief, he saw Reverend James waiting as they pulled into the clinic car park. He jumped down and shook his neighbour's hand.

"Thank you so much," he said quietly. "I'm not sure what I would have done without your help."

"It's nothing," said the vicar. Then, lowering his voice, he asked: "How is she this morning?"

"I don't know. Quiet, chastened ... terrified, I imagine." Reverend James nodded.

"Jonathan is expecting you," he said. "He's an excellent doctor, and will see her straight away."

Frank shook his hand, and under a hail of thank-yous he opened the passenger door and called out in a hearty voice: "Come on then, Ivy – it's showtime!"

Ivy was back at her desk at Village Antiques by lunchtime. Frank had tried to persuade her to go home and lie down, but she would have none of it. She had things to do.

Pouring tea from her flask, she offered a prayer of thanks, but instead of being carried through the ether by angels, her words stayed with her – and Ivy understood that God was no longer listening. Had He ever listened, she wondered? Had He really been there in the dark days, when her father visited her bedroom at night, or when she and Sister Mary Agatha so desperately sought His guidance and strength? Ivy had spent her adult life believing that He watched over her, judged her and punished her. She had believed the hallucinations that had threatened her sanity to be her penance; yet, now that she was relieved of that madness by a simple, scientific diagnosis, God appeared to have evaporated from her soul.

Charles Bonnet Syndrome. It had taken less than an hour for the doctor to make the diagnosis that restored Ivy to a clarity she had feared she would never have again. "It's an ophthalmological condition, not a neurological one," he had explained. "The eyes playing tricks. Sometimes shapes and patterns, sometimes more elaborate, always static and often frightening for the patient." Ivy had sat mute, tears of relief streaming from her deceiving eyes. The doctor had turned to Frank and explained: "The main problem with CBS is that sufferers are often too afraid to tell anybody about the disturbances and hallucinations they experience."

"Afraid they'll be carted off to the loony bin, I suppose," Frank had chipped in cheerfully.

The doctor glanced at Ivy and continued: "It is not uncommon to fear the onset of madness, which, of course, brings more serious consequences."

Frank nodded gravely, and Ivy spoke at last. "The musical notes, the shapes and patterns, the people from my past ... the Devil?"

"All just tricks of the eyes," the doctor nodded.

"And I'm not going blind?"

"No. You have cataracts, which are obfuscating your vision, but they are not yet advanced enough for surgery, though we will need to change your eyeglass prescription," he said. "Unfortunately, there is no cure for CBS –"

But Ivy batted away the details, and jumped from her chair declaring: "But I *am* cured! Praise the Lord!"

She collected her handbag and looked expectantly at Frank, who said: "Looks like we're off! Thanks, Doc." He promised to book Ivy's regular follow-ups, along with a trip to the optician, shook the doctor's hand and chased after Ivy, who had already left the building.Her veil of madness lifted, Ivy knew Nigel would not find such simple deliverance. His redemption had come in the form of an Alzheimer's diagnosis, which might eventually free him from his anger and remorse at his daughter's suicide and the shame of his ignoble withdrawal from the world he had dominated for so long. Ivy had suffered for decades at the hands of Nigel's overwhelming guilt, and felt tied to him by Sister Mary's unopened letter. Now she knew the truth at last, and her friend had freed her from that cruel master.

She kissed her St Christopher, filled her pen with ink and began a letter to her former subjugator. She would not be visiting Nigel Bond again.

THIRTY-TWO

I T WAS A Saturday morning, and Cecilia peeped out her bedroom window and watched admiringly as Luca unhooked the garden gate and sauntered down the driveway. He reminded her of the tough guys in the Spaghetti Westerns Clive admired so much, and she felt excited as he rang the doorbell. Pausing for a moment to watch unobserved, Cecilia decided that for all his swaggering masculinity, Luca had the kindest eyes of any man she knew.

She opened the door with a flourish and saw immediately that he could not meet her eye.

"Come! Death-by-chocolate and your favourite Italian coffee await," she reassured him, grabbing his arm and guiding him into the kitchen. She ladled coffee into the percolator, waiting patiently for him to speak as she mulled over the extraordinary email he had sent to her in the early hours of the morning.

She had struggled with the bedside lamp and tried to make sense of his words. At first, she had thought it was Sam's tomfoolery, but as she devoured its contents she had finally understood the truth. Luca had signed off with a terse admission that he was too shamefaced to tell her all this in person, and she had replied immediately, summoning him to her cottage mid-morning to "clear the air". So here they were now, silently spooning cake into their mouths, the room heavy with unspoken words.

"I'm so sorry, Cecilia, " Luca said eventually.

"What in Heaven's name are you sorry about?" Cecilia replied lightly, placing a tray on the table between them.

"I'm sorry. My behaviour's been pretty shabby, and you deserved better."

"Oh, for goodness' sake!" she cried, "How many times do I have to tell you, Luca, there is absolutely nothing to apologise for. I knew

exactly what I was getting myself into; I am a woman of the world."
She paused to refill his coffee cup. "Of course, I didn't believe your
flimsy story that you were in England on holiday, nor did I know
the full extent of your shenanigans – although Sam did try to warn
me, but my instincts always told me you were a good guy."

Her outpouring broke the ice. Luca looked up tentatively from
the cup he was nursing and gave her a smile, the one that made his
eyes crinkle in the corners and her heart soar. She reached over and
touched him lightly on the fingertips.

"I should be thanking you," she continued. "You awakened passion
in me. I have been sleepwalking through life for years, imagining I
was happy when I was not. You encouraged me to submit my book
and reach for my dreams. It was only after our night together that I
realised I had been missing out!"

"And I guess you did the same for me," Luca replied, returning her
grin. "You've been good for me, too."

"Well, now that we've got all that over and done with, tell me
about the trial!" Cecilia teased, leaning forward and propping her
face in her hands. "Go on! I'm all ears!"

She listened, transfixed, as Luca recounted the tale of his capture of Anna Charlton, trying to commit to her memory every last
thrilling detail. It would make a gripping novel, and she made a
mental note to suggest it to Nicholas Jowett on Sunday. The sun's
rays lit up the kitchen, and Cecilia saw that Luca's face was no
longer animated. It was an expression she had seen countless times
before, and it told her he was holding back.

"Go on, Luca," she urged. "Out with it."

Once he started, it appeared that he could not stop. His face
was impassive as he told Cecilia of Natasha's untimely death, his
fear that she had been murdered and the eventual confirmation
that she had not been. When he finally looked up, she could see
that his fathomless eyes were heavy with unshed tears. She did not
know what to say, but she understood that what Luca needed at
that moment was a shoulder to cry on – so she reached over and
embraced him. She was not surprised by his revelation; thinking

about it now, feeling the strength of his hard body against her, she knew that he had carried his melancholy around him like a cloak of sadness. After minutes that felt like hours, she asked: "What will you do after the trial?"

"Start again," Luca replied, releasing her. "And you?"

"The same – a fresh start."

"I want you to be happy, Cecilia." She could see from the blaze in his bright blue eyes that he meant it. She toyed with a tendril of her auburn hair and felt the heat of his gaze, enjoying a sliver of satisfaction that she still held it in her power to beguile him.

"I will be happy, Luca," she declared, rising from the chair with the empty cups and opening the dishwasher. "I've met someone special, and I think this time he's for keeps. I think I might've found love at last!"

"I'm pleased. You deserve it, " Luca replied, though a look of slight regret crossed his face. Then, reaching into his jacket pocket, he removed his phone and started scrolling through his messages. "I've found love, too! Would you like to see a picture?"

"I would!" Leaning forward to look, Cecilia felt a small leap of envy at the sight of a beautiful, young woman with lustrous dark hair against the backdrop of the London skyline.

"Who is she?" she asked, trying to keep the sting out of her voice.

"That's Emily, my stalker," grinned Luca. "Or should I say, my daughter."

Reverend James was seated at the end of the garden, his toes skimming the water as hundreds of mayflies emerged to foxtrot on the surface in their ancient mating dance. A pair of bullfinches flew low, their rosy red breasts brightening the sky as a scud of wispy clouds raced by.

Across the river, preparations were underway for the Willoughbys' "Farewell to Luca" party, and a little downstream the American was kayaking with a young woman the vicar now understood to be his daughter, Emily. He felt touched that Luca had confided in him, and remembered the wonder in his eyes as he had chronicled the extraordinary sequence of events that had led to the discovery he was a father.

"... So while sleeping with my wife's sister before we married wasn't my finest hour," he concluded, "good does occasionally come from bad."

"How did Emily find out the truth about you and her mother?" Reverend James had enquired.

"After my wife died, her sister felt able to tell Emily the secret of her paternity. She confessed to our one-night stand and how she'd kept it secret from the family, at first out of guilt for betraying her sister, and later to protect her from pain in the knowledge that Natasha was unable to carry a child to full term." Luca had paused, blinking as if to properly recall the memory. "I wonder if she suspected all along. Natasha kept me away from her family. She claimed they didn't like me, and thought she could do better – and they weren't wrong!"

"It must've been difficult for Emily to understand why it was kept from her for so long," Reverend James prompted, and Luca had nodded gravely.

"Yeah," he replied. "She was angry at first. Bitter at so many wasted years. But I think she gets it now. We were all young and reckless. She seems to respect her mother's decision, but it hasn't been easy for her."

Reverend James had been awestruck as Luca continued the rest of his story, thinking it ironic that Clive Buchanan had travelled to Hollywood to make a film when a blockbuster story was unfolding in his own garden.

Luca's daughter had tried to contact him, but because of the security surrounding the trial, his staff had been cagey until they carried out their own investigations. Then somebody at Luca's beach house had simply told her that Luca was in England.

"She must have worked out I was sceptical, and emailed me a recreation of a family photo, replacing Natasha with herself to prove their likeness," Luca explained. "I thought it was a ruse by the enemy to draw me out, so I asked Felicity to deliver a safe phone to make contact. Of course, what I didn't know was that she gave her my address. "Anyway, we eventually met, and she is the mirror image of her mother. Undeniable proof right in front of my eyes."

"Three things cannot be long hidden," quoted Reverend James. "The sun, the moon and the truth."

Plunging his toes into the cold water, he reflected on the boundless beauty of springtime and prayed in thanks to God for His happy conclusion to such a troubled matter.

THIRTY-THREE

I T WAS SATURDAY night, and the Village buzzed with the vibe and excitement of London's West End. Frank stepped from a sleek, black limousine into a blare of paparazzi flashbulbs, smiling and waving as he sauntered down the red carpet into the Restaurant. Amanda Jones, his new PR agent, greeted him at the door and ushered him inside while bellowing into her mobile and wagging her manicured talons at a deliveryman. It was the launch of Frank's new biography *Showtime: The Secret Life of Frank Fielding*, and he thought that he might just die of happiness.

Pete Walters arrived, virtually unrecognisable from the unkempt, nervy character who had turned up at Sandra's door only two weeks earlier. Frank clasped in friendship the hand that had borne him Bianca's letter.

Babe, Pete won't tell me where you are but he says you're safe and he can get this message to you. Now I know you're OK, I need to get away for a bit so I'm off to visit Tally. I've read Pete's manuscript so I think I know what you've done but you can't hide away forever so why not come home and face the music?

B X

PS: Pete's a good bloke. Whatever it is you and Tony did to ruin his life, undo it or you'll have me to answer to!

Frank had panicked, but Sandra had been the voice of reason: "What do you mean, you don't know what to do? It's simple: you must do as your wife asks. Go home, and be there for her when she gets back."

"But this is my home ..."

"No buts, Frank," Sandra said firmly. "The Waterfront is your home, and we both know that. Bianca is your wife, and you love her. She is your future, and I am your past. Go and sort out the rest of your life; then, if Bianca allows it, come back and tell me what you're going to do with it – I shan't be going anywhere." And she had begun collecting his belongings, folding them neatly into a holdall.

"We've never packed before, love," he protested, "just leave it and I'll –"

"This time it's different, and we both know it," Sandra replied. "We've had a good run, pet, but we always knew it would end." A part of Frank had died that day, as Sandra walked ahead of him and opened the door.

"But how –"

"I said no buts ... I shall be fine. Now, off you go." The cardigan she pulled around her heavy frame could not hide the telltale flush that rose up her neck, and there was an unbearable tightness behind her brave smile. "Go on," she said, shooing him out. Her hand trembled as she passed Frank his bag, and words failed him as he accepted it. He could not bear the loss in Sandra's eyes, or for her to see the desolation in his, and so he climbed into his little car and fled without looking back.

Inside the Restaurant now, trussed up in a tortured lilac silk suit and an emerald green tie as journalists and television anchors jostled for a comment, Frank turned to Pete and said chirpily: "It's showtime!"

It had been easy to fulfil one of Bianca's wishes. Frank had contacted Pete as soon as he returned home. The newspaper had agreed to postpone the exposé in exchange for serialisation rights on the authorised biography, and the two men had spent the next two weeks around the kitchen table thrashing out the revised version while Frank waited for his wife to come home.

Those had been the loneliest days of Frank's life. Sandra had forbidden him from visiting, and he had heard nothing from Bianca. He dared not leave the house for fear of the welcome he might receive from the villagers and friends he had deceived, not only with his duplicity but by bringing the charlatan Bill Lewis into their lives. That was, until Amanda Jones had arrived, terrified and bedraggled one night, banging on his door.

"Quick! You must come! Ivy Midwinter's going to kill herself!" she had cried. Frank had snatched up his car keys, and Amanda had jumped into the car beside him, babbling about threats and demons and strange women. Letting himself in at Sunnyside, he had burst into the kitchen like a shot from a blunderbuss, only to find his old friend safely entwined with Felicity Thomas, a bottle of brandy and a yellowing letter lying open on the table before them.

Ivy had turned and looked at him coldly: "Oh, you're back."

Felicity, paler and thinner than ever, had stared with dead eyes. "Where have you been, Frank?" she asked. "Harley's dead. We're burying him tomorrow."

Frank had muttered something about the storm and checking on Ivy, then turned tail and left. He had been dreadfully shaken by the reception; his old friend, in her hour of despair, had not needed him; his wife's best friend had lost the love of her life and Bianca was not even around to comfort her, because Frank had driven her away. Oblivious to the undercurrents and unaware of his recent capers, Amanda had suggested a drink and Frank, who was desperate for company, had invited her home – but once the brandy bottle was open and the glasses out, he understood that Amanda's was not the company he sought, and had watched her work her way down the bottle until he could bear it no longer.

"Let me run you home," he had said.

"I used to be desperate to interview you, but I've moved on," Amanda declared as they pulled out of Riverside Lane. "I've found much better stories about your friends."

"Good," said Frank distractedly, "I'm sure they're far more interesting."

"They certainly are. I know all about Hugh Willoughby tampering with crime scenes. And I know Basil Braithwaite doesn't have dementia, and his son is a lying little con artist." Frank's radar began to sizzle, and he tuned into Amanda's drunken rant. "I even know that Luca Tempesta is up to no good, but I've not managed to nail that one yet. But believe me, I will!" Frank tried to speak, but Amanda had not finished. "I also know where the spymaster Nigel Bond is hiding! Who'd have guessed there was a Cold War collaborator in the Village? And that Ivy is complicit in covering up his whereabouts!"

Even though he only comprehended half of Amanda's litany, Frank had understood that the journalist was about to cause considerable trouble. It was risible that the only story of any real substance was sitting right beside her in the car, and yet she was oblivious to it. But while Frank's secrets had to be told, those of his friends and neighbours were private; they had not, as he had, sold their souls to the media, and if he could protect them from Amanda's tawdry revelations, perhaps it might compensate for the trouble he had caused them.

Amanda's silence had been negotiated in a cold, wet lay-by outside the new town chip shop. It had been expensive, but Frank felt it to be worth the price. Tony Jackson would bash out the terms of the deal and Frank, content that the ghosts and skeletons of his friends would remain firmly inside their closets, had returned home to brush down his funeral suit.

The following day, he had slipped into the back of the church to pay his respects to Harley, intending to creep away before the service finished – but witnessing Bianca, distraught and alone, he had felt compelled to comfort her. They had gone straight home after the service, and Frank could still not believe that it had taken less than ten minutes to clear the air after so many years of deception.

His wife only had two questions.

"'Ow old is she?" she had asked, and then: "D'you 'ave sex and stuff?"

Hearing the answers, she paused for a long moment before declaring: "Then I don't see what all the bleedin' fuss is about. Come 'ere!" All Frank had wanted at that moment was to gather her up in his arms, but he knew they had to talk.

"But I don't wanna 'ear," she had objected. "I love you. That's all that matters, innit?"

He had walked her to the kitchen table, sat her down and forced her to listen to the saga of his forty-year relationship with Sandra.

"Now," he said when he had finished, "look me in the eye and tell me you love me." And to Frank's complete and utter delight, she did.

He still could not believe how easy it had been, how easily Bianca had accepted Sandra into the family fold. Amanda, however, had not proved quite so easy.

"PR?" Bianca had screeched. "You've gotta be jokin'! That woman called me a 'talentless gold digger'!"

"But babe, that was over twenty years –"

"I know when it bleedin' well was. Don't you lecture me, Frank Fielding! I swore I would never forgive 'er, an' I never will."

Bianca had eventually seen reason. Frank knew she would give Amanda a rough ride, which perhaps was not such a bad thing. It would be good to keep the woman on her toes.

There was a commotion on the pavement outside, and Frank peered out the window and rejoiced at the sight of Bianca and Tallulah stepping from a blacked-out limousine into the gathering media throng. Flashbulbs exploded as Amanda marshalled the photographers and FRANK'S FABULOUS FIELDING FEMALES (as a recent tabloid had described them) posed and smiled for the camera. A sentimental tear of pride made its way down Frank's cheek, and he blew his nose noisily on a monogrammed handkerchief while Bianca glowered at Amanda.

Clever PR spin and a large dose of Fielding humour had captured the public's imagination; copies of Frank's book were predicted to sell briskly, with critics hailing it as the "read of the summer". The Fielding family had been gracing the sofas of all the primetime chat shows, as well.

All's well that ends well, thought Frank as he entered the fray. So preoccupied was he with the happy resolution to his troubles that he almost missed the unexpected guest who had slipped, silent and unseen, into the Restaurant.

"You came!" he cried out, and Sandra smiled happily,

"I wouldn't miss this for the world, pet," she whispered as they embraced.

"I do love you."

"I know you do," Sandra laughed, turning him around and sending him into the crowd. "Now go and do what you do best; I'm not going anywhere ... It's showtime!"

THIRTY-FOUR

"QUAIL EGG, VICAR?" asked Joy.

"Thank you," said Reverend James, cheerfully availing himself of the warm hollandaise and then patting his ample stomach. "Praise the Lord that cassocks are so forgiving of my middle-age gut! May I have another?"

"Let me take that," interjected Jake, relieving his mother-in-law of the silver platter. "You must look after that wrist, or it will never get better. These canapés really are exquisite, by the way; did you make them?"

"I did," crowed Joy. Tom and Reverend James smiled as Joy and Jake worked the room together, Joy's voice singing out above the crowd.

"Quail egg? ... Have you met Tom's husband Jake? Quail egg? ... They live in Knightsbridge, you know ... Quail egg?" Exquisitely elegant in a duck-egg blue linen suit, Jake glided in Joy's wake, laughing at her jokes and flirting dutifully.

Hugh watched happily from the alcove where he, Basil and Edmund were discussing cricket. He had been delighted when his wife told him that Luca's party was to be held at the Monkey Island Hotel, where they had married. He had spent many happy hours exploring the shores with his father, then brought his own son back to the smooth waters and camped under the old skiff's canvas cover while bats and night swallows fluttered through the lacework of willows along the river's edge. They had swum around the island at dusk and dangled off the bridge like the eponymous monkeys. No such shenanigans nowadays, he thought, accepting lobster-toasted brioche and tuna sashimi from an nattily attired waiter. "We don't want Luca thinking we are ignorant and parochial," Joy had insisted. "After all, the Village is to London what the Hamptons are to New York." And so, with a lot of strings pulled by Jake, it had been arranged that Luca's farewell party would be held at one of the world's most romantic hotels, and Hugh had been happy to return to the magical island oasis of his youth.

Joy came padding across the lawn, smiling happily. She wore a floaty, watermelon-coloured dress, flat sandals and matching toenail polish, the entire ensemble purchased on a shopping spree with Jake after which she had gone, flushed and excited, to join him and Tom at their favourite Pimlico brasserie for lunch. That was the day she had told them about BLAG.

"I do *not* like being taken for a ride," she had announced. "We need to stand up to such people." And so the Bill Lewis Action Group was born, and to Hugh's amazement, Joy had gone cap in hand to Bianca Fielding and asked her to front the group.

"She is far more media-savvy than I am," Joy had reasoned. "I can be the brains, and Bianca can be the beauty."

Hugh felt suffused with love at the memory of what had happened next.

"To me you will always be the beauty," he had said, tentatively taking her in his arms where, to his delight and surprise, his wife had been receptive to his further advances.

"I suppose the housekeeper will allow you to come down for Lord's, will she?" Basil asked, interrupting Hugh's thoughts. Edmund nodded happily.

"Oh, yes," he replied. "She says she'll come along, too!"

Basil choked on his champagne, declaring: "Steady on. Best not get too carried away, eh? Cricket's a bit boring for the ladies, don't you think, Hugh?"

Molly interrupted, holding aloft a plate of cheese straws generously decorated with hundreds-and-thousands.

"I made them myself," she announced. "They're an experiment. I'm thinking of including the recipe in my cookbook." The men declared Molly's experiment a success; she carefully ticked several columns in her yellow notebook, and moved on to where Kathy was telling Ivy about her plans to relocate with Edmund, who walked over to join her.

"I have found Edmund and me such a wonderful abode on the east coast, just half an hour north of Aberdeen," she proclaimed.

"Cheese mores?" enquired Molly, bearing the plate. The two women waved her away.

"But surely, with Edmund's health problems, that cold weather will be the death of him?" said Ivy.

Kathy smiled, squeezed Edmund's hand and clucked: "Och no, I'll fix you some of my nourishing mushroom soup, picked fresh from the woodland, and fatten you up with some real Scottish shortbread. It'll be the making of you, Edmund, dear."

"You know best, Duchess," Edmund simpered. Then, turning to Ivy, he said: "There's something I want to ask you. We'll be needing somebody to run the Port Sanctuary when I'm gone. I don't suppose you'd consider taking over, would you?"

"Oh, no," replied a startled Ivy. "My hands are full running Clive's shop and Frank's affairs. I haven't a moment to spare. I only came today because –"

A howl of laughter announced the arrival of Bianca, who was holding court by the entrance dressed in tight Pucci-style flares and a vest top that left little to the imagination. Joy set off to nudge the Fieldings away from the door – and the vicar – before her guests of honour arrived.

"Oh, it's all go," Bianca told a transfixed Reverend James,. "My Frankie's gonna take over from Harley as a night owl at the Port Sanctuary. An' me and Roz Braithwaite are setting up a dress shop called 'Brass with Class'. Of course, Roz is off to gay Paree, and I'm gonna be far too busy to run it, but it'll be a nice little job for our Tallulah, and give me and Frank lots of excuses to visit the Braithwaites in Paris!" As she made her way across the crowded room, Joy could not deny that Bianca really did draw the eye. She would make an excellent ambassador for BLAG if she would just behave and stick to the script.

"Everybody wants my Frank now," she declared, waving her

champagne flute in the air. "The director of *Gone to Pot* is beggin' 'im to 'ost his show, but they've burned their bleedin' bridges 'cos there's talk of a film being made out of Frank's biography ..."

Through the glass door, Joy could see her VIPs traversing the fairytale footbridge onto the island; but her progress across the room was hampered first by Molly touting cheese mores, then by Basil, grumbling about the prospect of the Fieldings visiting him and Rosamund in Paris.

Joy watched helplessly as Tom welcomed the new arrivals and waved to Jake, indicating that his parents had arrived.

"Joy," called Myrtle from her wheelchair.

"Not now, Mother," Joy said, pushing forward and elbowing past a group of pensioners Luca had apparently befriended at the pub.

"Yoo-hoo! Yoo-hoo!" she shrilled above the crowd, but her newly arrived guests could neither see nor hear her, and she could only watch in horror as social disaster unfolded before her eyes.

"Bianca, have you met Phyllida and Frederick?" Tom enquired politely.

"Oh, no, pleased to meet you, I'm sure," replied Bianca, squashing up against Jake's astonished father to allow the waiter space to pass. Unfortunately, she had not reckoned on him choosing that moment to accept a champagne glass, which he promptly tipped into Bianca's splendidly bejewelled décolletage.

"Bleedin' 'Enry," she yelped, throwing her head back in laughter. "It's gone all down me boobage!" Joy eventually reached the door, glowing with the effort at having cut through the crowd on such a balmy day.

"Bianca, Frank," she said stiffly, "I see you've met Lord and Lady Pengleton-Black." As an astonished Bianca dropped an involuntary, almost imperceptible curtsy, Joy took her son's in-laws by the hand and led them triumphantly into the throng.

Amanda was thrilled to be invited to the plush new hotel. As Frank Fielding's PR, it was important she look the part, so she had splashed the cash at Harvey Nichols, where a stylist had kitted her out in sharp tailoring, striking the sartorial divide between glamorous and professional. Julie at NatWest had something to say about it, of course, but when Frank's cheque cleared, Amanda closed the account and told her to "shove it where the sun don't shine". She was on a roll.

She watched as Frank worked the room with Bianca. She was grateful he had stumped up to buy her silence. What he had not known then – and Amanda had no intention of enlightening him – was that she had never had a chance of dishing the dirt on his neighbours. At the first whiff of trouble, the villagers had done what they always did: join forces to shut the portcullis and lift up the drawbridge. She had found it impossible to corroborate her stories, and without evidence she doubted they would even make the local rag.

Helping herself to champagne, Amanda was content to be an outsider looking in. She cast an expansive eye around the room and understood that, for all their wealth and success, the Village patricians were no different from her. *They were all just human beings trying to make the best for themselves*, she thought, glancing at Kathy McConnell cosying up to a cornered-looking Rosamund Braithwaite, who in turn was clinging to her husband's hand for dear life. *We all struggle with the same feelings, needs and desires; we are all vulnerable to temptation, loneliness, fear, depression and pride.* Frank caught her eye and flashed a cheeky-chappie grin; raising his glass, he mouthed: "Showtime".

Amanda lifted her drink in return, and smiled. She was thrilled that Frank's book was set to trump Rupert Braithwaite's *The Sponsored Walk*, which had fallen off the bestseller list. For all the money he had raised for charity, Rupert was not a generous man, and that was the difference between him and Frank, she decided, quaffing the fizz and reaching for another glass. Frank had a heart of pure gold, which was why he had emerged from the Bill Lewis scandal and the revelation of his double life intact, and Amanda Jones – publicist to the stars – planned to cling tightly to his coattails.

She would ask Luca Tempesta for his business card and "do lunch" when they were over the pond, Amanda determined, picking up the Chanel handbag she had reclaimed from the pawn shop and sashaying over to the corner of the room where the American stood with a brunette half his age.

Spotting the approaching journalist, Luca neatly sidestepped her and introduced his daughter to Sam, who was tongue-tied and trying to disguise the fact he had been sniffing her hair. He needed to warn the boy not to do that in Los Angeles, Luca thought, or he would land himself in a whole lot of trouble.

"So your flight is booked," he grinned, ruffling Sam's hair. "You know you're welcome to stay with me anytime."

"Are you crazy?" laughed Sam. "You think I'm going to hang out at your gaffe with gangsters and mafiosi turning up on the doorstep? Dad's done the honourable thing and checked me into the Hilton. Just as well, as we have a lot of talking to do." He gave Cecilia a meaningful look; she was wrapped tightly in the loving embrace of her new publisher, Nicholas Jowett. Luca was pleased that Clive had invited his son to join him for the final week of his movie odyssey.

"Yeah, Dad feels guilty because he suspected Ivy had lost the plot even before he left for LA," said Sam. "Apparently she went off on one about vengeance and inflicting pain, but typical Dad, only hears what he wants to hear." Sam's voice trailed off, and he stared at his feet; but when he looked up, his face was beaming. "This should be a bit of quality bonding time."

"So you're blowing me off to hang out with the movie elite, huh?"

"Hardly," laughed Sam. "The old man's not earned a jot from his foray into the movie business, but he's had a good time, and at least he hasn't lost money. He's confident he will recoup his losses when the film comes out." Sam's expression indicated that he was not so sure himself. "He's got big plans when he gets home: a Hawaiian/Asian fusion restaurant ... don't ask! More interestingly, he wants to buy the old studio and resurrect the Village's horror-film industry. Ivy's already researching the tax breaks available for filming in the UK. You wait, Hollywood will soon be flocking to the Village!"

"All power to you, son, reach for the stars," he enthused, knowing his phoney business-mantra speak worked a treat on the boy, and happy to indulge it.

Luca could see that Emily was disarmed by the teenager. His daughter had told him she had chosen to study medicine in London because she loved English eccentricity. "The Americans and the English are poles apart, 'divided by a common language'. I love that," she had said, smiling with the exact same eyes as Natasha.

"Like us?" Luca replied lightly. He was trying to keep his emotions in check. There was so much he had yet to learn about his daughter. He could not believe this beautiful, bright young woman was his own flesh and blood. It was nothing short of a miracle. After so much unhappiness and tragedy, it was as if God had offered him an olive branch – and he was going to grab it, hold it close and enjoy every moment.

"We're like chalk and cheese, aren't we?" Emily grinned.

"I prefer yin and yang," said Luca, as he clapped his arm around her shoulders.

By the bar, Cecilia was leaning against the manly chest of Nicholas, who, erudite and charming, held court with Lord and Lady Pengleton-Black. She was pleased to see Luca looking so happy and relaxed. His eyes met hers, and they shared a moment of intimacy that brought butterflies to her stomach. Cecilia would never forget Luca Tempesta. He had changed her life in every sense; his arrival had been the starting point for her journey of self-discovery.

"Penny for your thoughts?" interrupted Reverend James, tapping her gently on the shoulder. A flurry of introductions ensued, after which Cecilia replied: "I was actually thinking about the journey of life, and how we are all looking for love and acceptance."

"Yes, the ultimate goal of our journey is happiness," the vicar replied. "The best advice is to be clear about your destination before you set off, or you will go round and round, and always return to the same point – and that will cause you a lot of trouble."

Molly, who was seated under the table indulging in a secret stash of meringues, was not sure what Reverend James was talking about, but felt certain that Cecilia knew her destination – it was honeymooning on a beautiful island paradise with a palm tree with Uncle Nick, who was tall and smiley and awfully good at Lego. The only person to spot Molly in her clandestine hideout was Myrtle Pendlegrass, who smiled kindly as Tom steered her wheelchair onto the terrace.

"Here you are, Granny!" Tom fussed, tucking a soft blanket around her legs. "A lovely glass of lemonade. I'll pop back again shortly to make sure you're comfortable." Myrtle smiled up at her grandson. She appreciated the fine young man he had become, though she was disappointed that he had not thought to refresh her glass with a gin and tonic or a tot of whisky. It was a little late in the day for them to be worrying about her turning to drink.

She adjusted her hearing aid to drown out the chatter from the party. Her daughter had softened since the ding-dong with Hugh, and Myrtle was delighted to see Tom back in the fold. All she needed now was for Penny to return home – but the girl was flighty, and Myrtle hoped Joy would manage her expectations in that regard. She was pleased that Edmund had finally found a lady to love; Kathy seemed a good, capable woman, though she did worry the Scottish weather might be detrimental to her son's health.

Then she closed her eyes and imagined the ancient Thames flowing ceaselessly. A river has a life just the same as any living being, she reflected, envisaging the raindrops falling from the skies, trickling into creeks and brooks then branching into tributaries, tumbling down gorges, cascading over waterfalls, meandering through valleys and cities, until the river reaches the estuary and then the ocean beyond.

Myrtle felt a great peace lap over her like waves. *We're all of us pleased when we reach our journey's end*, she thought, and she slipped into a deep, beautiful sleep.